Dominican Crossroads

Christina
Cecelia
Davidson

Dominican Crossroads

H. C. C. ASTWOOD and the
Moral Politics of Race-Making
in the Age of Emancipation

Duke University Press   *Durham and London*   2024

Printed in the United States of America on acid-free paper ∞
Project Editor: Livia Tenzer
Designed by Courtney Leigh Richardson
Typeset in Merlo and Real Head Pro by Westchester Publishing Services

Library of Congress Cataloging-in-Publication Data
Names: Davidson, Christina C., author.
Title: Dominican crossroads : H. C. C. Astwood and the moral politics of
race-making in the age of emancipation / Christina Cecelia Davidson.
Description: Durham : Duke University Press, 2024. | Includes bibliographical
references and index.
Identifiers: LCCN 2023057427 (print)
LCCN 2023057428 (ebook)
ISBN 9781478030942 (paperback)
ISBN 9781478026693 (hardcover)
ISBN 9781478059929 (ebook)
Subjects: LCSH: Astwood, H. C. C. (Henry Charles Clifford), 1844–1908. |
Consuls—Dominican Republic—Biography. | Diplomats—United States—Biography.
| Racism—Political aspects—United States—History—19th century. | Dominican
Republic—Foreign relations—United States. | United States—Foreign relations—
Dominican Republic. | BISAC: SOCIAL SCIENCE / Ethnic Studies / American / African
American & Black Studies | HISTORY / United States / 19th Century
Classification: LCC F1938.4.A88 D38 2024 (print) | LCC F1938.4.A88 (ebook) |
DDC 305.868/7293073—dc23/eng/20240701
LC record available at https://lccn.loc.gov/2023057427
LC ebook record available at https://lccn.loc.gov/2023057428

Cover art: Plano de la ciudad de Santo Domingo, Compañía United Lithograph, 1882.
Sketch of H. C. C. Astwood, *Colored American*, April 28, 1900.

Contents

    Social Morality, and the Making of a Liberal Nation   159

6   Leasing Columbus: Holy Relics, Public Ridicule,
    and the Reconstruction of Two Americas   195

7   "The Cheekiest Man on Earth": H. C. C. Astwood
    and the Politics of White Moral Exclusivity   228

    Conclusion   261

    Notes   271
    Bibliography   317
    Index   337

Note on Terminology

Historians face the complicated task of choosing terms to describe individuals and groups of the past. I recognize that racial, national, class, and gender terms change in meaning across space and time, and the terms I use here do not necessarily reflect how individuals and groups identified themselves in the past. Given the challenge of writing across geographies, cultures, languages, and time, I employ the following identity terms for the sake of clarity.

American: An individual born or naturalized in the United States.

African American/US Black/Black (American): A person or people group of African descent born or naturalized in the United States whose skin color, other physical traits, enslaved condition, poor class status, and/or family history prohibited their social advancement and passing into white society.

Afro-Creole: A person of African and French descent in Louisiana whose ancestors were generally free people of color (*gens de couleur*) who maintained a middle-ground status between whites and enslaved Blacks.

Negro: A nineteenth-century term used to refer to Black people. This term is employed in italics on occasion to emphasize the predominant US racist mindset.

white American/Anglo-American/Euro-American/Anglo-US: A person or people group whose light skin color, Western European physical and cultural traits, and absence of known African heritage qualified them as racially white in the United States.

British Caribbean: This term may refer to England's Caribbean empire or a British subject residing in the empire.

Black: An individual of predominantly African descent whose dark skin color, other physical traits, enslaved condition, and/or poor class status formed barriers to their social advancement in the British Caribbean.

colored/colored class: A mixed-race person or people group whose ancestors were free people of color and who formed a middle racial class between Blacks and whites.

white: A person or people group whose light skin color, Western European physical and cultural traits, and absence of known African heritage qualified them as racially white in the British Caribbean.

Dominican: An individual born or naturalized in the Dominican Republic.

African American descendant/Afro-American Dominican: A Dominican who descended from African American emigrants who arrived on the island in the early nineteenth century.

Afro-Dominican/Black (Dominican): A Dominican person or people group of predominantly African descent whose dark skin color, other physical traits, and/or poor class status formed barriers to their individual or collective social advancement.

Dominican elite/lettered class: A Dominican person or people group whose relatively high social class, literacy, and access to education enabled them to participate in national debates through the written word.

Euro-Dominican: A Dominican person or people group of predominantly European descent whose light skin color and other physical traits enabled their social advancement.

Haitian: An individual born or naturalized in Haiti. The author recognizes the diversity of skin color, class, and ethnicity within Haiti, and reminds readers of this throughout the text. Additional terms for Haitians, however, are not employed in this book.

mixed race: An individual of notably mixed racial heritage. Used for people of mixed descent (generally African and European) across locales.

FIGURE P.1. View of the colonial fort (the Homage) and military school from the Ozama River, Santo Domingo, Dominican Republic, ca. 1900. Photo: Detroit Publishing Co. Library of Congress, https://www.loc.gov/item/2016808510/.

Preface

In April 1888, an American businessman from Massachusetts traveled to Santo Domingo for the first time. Arriving aboard a passenger ship, American and European tourists entered the city by day since, as seasoned ship captains knew, it was hazardous to navigate the shallow Ozama River and the port's large sandbank at night.[1] A late afternoon or evening arrival meant another overnight stay aboard. Then, with the sun rising in the east, weary passengers could take in the town's south side, a view that consistently inspired foreigners setting eyes upon the oldest European settlement in the Americas. Situated on a hill above the mouth of the Ozama River and surrounded by a rock wall, the skyline of Spanish colonial buildings overlooked the turquoise Caribbean Sea. Traveling north up the river, visitors especially noticed the looming Spanish watchtower, the Homage (figure P.1). "The first impression you get of Santo Domingo is of this magnificent old castle, frowning down on sea and shore, dominating the whole scene, as well as your own thoughts," reminisced one nineteenth-century voyager.[2] The Dominican city, it seemed, gazed back.

Due to the sandbank, large watercrafts could not deliver their passenger or freight cargo without aid. Thus, along with other passengers, the traveler waited as a small tugboat guided the ship inland. This method not only ensured a safe approach but also drew out the drama of the American's advance. His anticipation was likely palpable. Since the 1830s, US intellectuals like William Hickling Prescott had fashioned colonial Latin

American cities and pre-Columbian Indigenous relics as part of the United States' cultural heritage.[3] This identification with Latin America's past filled Anglo-American visitors with a dual sense of awe and ownership as they approached Santo Domingo's gates. Like Mexico and Peru, the Dominican Republic existed as yet another Spanish colonial space where white Americans could identify with European conquest.[4] Undoubtedly, though, the island nation intrigued foreign visitors all the more for reasons of its own. Unlike the former colonial viceroyalties of New Spain and Peru, Santo Domingo, in the Anglo-American mindset, was a Black man's republic, and it laid claim to a relic that Americans valued even more highly than Aztec and Inca artifacts: the mortal remains of the hemisphere's so-called discoverer.

Having eagerly disembarked, the American traveler now came to the gates of the capital. Perhaps, in this quintessential moment of first contact, apprehension overshadowed the thrill of setting feet to ground. What exactly would he find inside? "We have all heard tales of Haiti. . . . The Black Republic, they say, is gradually relapsing into barbarism," explained American tourist Susan de Forest Day in her 1898 travelogue. "But here, side by side with Haiti, is another Black Republic."[5] If Haiti was known to be "uncivilized" according to the racist and fantastical fictions of pseudo-historians Sir Spenser St. John and James Anthony Froude, what could be said of the Dominican Republic?[6] No matter how much Anglo-American tourists identified with Spanish conquistadors, they did not quite know what to make of the Latin American nation that shared the island of Hispaniola with Haiti and had once formed part of the hemisphere's first independent Black state. And, in a moment of drastic social change across the hemisphere, neither did anyone else.

Various people—Dominicans, white and Black Americans, Europeans, and Latin American Creoles—had carefully drawn designs for the country's modernization despite their trepidations. The American traveler, however, was likely blissfully unaware of the diversity of plans, contracts, treatises, and treaties that drove the city (and hopefully the nation) toward an elusive progress. He thought not of such nuance as he blithely traversed the city gates and began a slow trudge up a steep incline.

At once, the senses activated. The heat radiating off the dirt road and stone buildings distracted from the cacophonous noise of the wharf's market where Black men and women sold their wares. The faint sound of a rehearsal in a convent-turned-theater bewildered, while a whiff of an old Spanish church used as a butcher's shop overwhelmed the smell of the ocean flowing steadily on the breeze.[7] Foreign eyes surely darted from one novel scene to the next, unsure of what to take in first: the busy storefronts and verandas? The people of various skin tones clothed in the latest European fashions? The Spanish colonial architecture, tragically romantic in the foreign mind's eye, captivated and divided the attention: two-story homes painted blue, pink, and white; a row of "balconied piazzas supported on pillars of [solid stone]"; a defunct sundial; a dilapidated palace once owned by Christopher Columbus's son.[8] These edifices gestured to a time long ago. Ruins, such as the wrecked Franciscan convent destroyed by the British pirate Sir Francis Drake, tethered the city to its colonial past and provoked a sense of nostalgia in the present.[9] Catholic priests still presided over the seventeen ecclesiastical edifices in the city, including the first basilica of the New World.[10]

And, all of a sudden, there he was standing before it. Within a few short city blocks, the traveler had come at last to the central plaza where the ancient basilica hulked. The colonial square boasted a new artistic feature. A bronze sculpture of Christopher Columbus, unveiled only a year earlier, depicted the admiral pointing north toward the United States, a symbol of industry and Western modernity (figure P.2).[11] At the base, a diminutive image of the Taíno princess Anacaona inscribed the voyager's name on the monument, eulogizing him with honorifics. The American likely paused to view this metal symbol of conquest that augured good fortune just ahead for the nation. The statue was a curious depiction of the relationship between the victor and the vanquished. It portrayed a compliant, even appreciative, female Indigenous sovereign, despite the fact that Spain had subjugated the Taínos, who died from disease, and then repopulated the island with enslaved Africans. The half-naked Anacaona perched at her attacker's feet wrote not of the horrors her people survived, only to pass to the next life completely undone.[12] Instead she praised her assailant, who stood in all his glory for Spain, supposedly the most fiendish of empires.

Yes, according to the "Black legend" myth that pervaded the American traveler's history books, Spaniards had been the most brutal colonizers, crueler than any other European enslavers—especially the masters of the old US South.[13] This myth, despite its name, had little to do with the Africans who tilled the land across the Americas. Rather, it was an invention of British upstarts who believed that Catholic Spaniards had done a shoddy job of the colonizing business.[14] The British were better suited for the task because they had better religion, they thought. Protestant Anglo-Americans inherited this idea. Thus, while identifying most with

FIGURE P.2. Columbus Statue in Plaza Colón, Santo Domingo, Dominican Republic. Photo: F. L. Vasquez, *Official and Exclusive Photographs of the First Forts, Town, Churches, &c. Built by Columbus* (New York: F. L. Vasquez, 1893), 2. Library of Congress, https://www.loc.gov/item/93515058/.

the Genovese explorer, the American businessman, in a split second, may have felt pity for the Amerindian princess who symbolized Spain's ruthless conquest.[15] *If only his ancestors had arrived first in the Americas...* This pity transferred to the present. In the racist US mindset, the fact that mixed-race people—descendants of Spaniards, Africans, and Indigenous peoples—now governed more than half the hemisphere was a lamentable reality that proved Spain's misrule.[16] That *Negro* Dominicans safeguarded the admiral's remains further vexed Anglo-US sensibilities. Such sacred relics, many Americans believed, would certainly be safer in Euro-American hands. That is, if the reports were true.

A quick jaunt across the square brought the American to his prize and promised to settle any doubts. Behind the cathedral doors now, he stepped into a cool, damp nave. Lit candles signaled pious devotion to God, Jesus, Mary, and the saints. Intricate stone arches rose to the heavens. Ornate metal crosses abounded. The American had entered a holy place much unlike the dusty streets outside. Here was the seat of European colonial power. And, after a brief ceremony, behold now the bones of Columbus!

This was a truly religious experience, it seemed. But, now came the moment of truth: Did the pilgrim truly believe?

This question cannot be answered. So we must turn to others. How did the traveler get here? Who (or what) exactly led the American down this path? There are myriad answers, no doubt, but let us consider a simple one first.

From his home near the Ozama River, the first Black US consul to Santo Domingo, Henry Charles Clifford (H. C. C.) Astwood (1844–1908; figure P.3), could observe the foreign ships come in and count the passengers as they stepped onshore. He may have been perched at home or in the nearby customhouse that day in April 1888, watching, calculating, and waiting as the US businessman disembarked. It is possible that Astwood first approached the traveler who had a name, but who at once was one and many. Although no historical record attests to this meeting, we might envision the two of them standing there before the sacred bones. Perhaps this was the moment when the infamous idea to lease the same was birthed in the mind of the visiting enthusiast. Although we cannot know for sure,

FIGURE P.3. Sketch of H. C. C. Astwood, from the *Colored American*, April 28, 1900.

it might have happened this way because such tours had their procedures. To view Columbus's remains back in 1888, American pilgrims in Santo Domingo needed to follow policy, and the first step in the process was to meet with US Consul Astwood. It was he who led the way (at least this time).

Did the American tourist take note of the man who brought him to the doors of the basilica and directed him toward Columbus's human remains? Probably not. Why would he? H. C. C. Astwood existed to serve the businessman's interests and therefore did not play a central role in this traveler's narrative. Thus, upon first meeting Astwood, the visitor, like other white Americans, may have noted that this Black man was a "gentleman of unusual intelligence" and then paid him no further mind.[17] Historians have done likewise. Nevertheless, we might choose to reconsider. What is gained by turning an eye from the tourist to his guide?

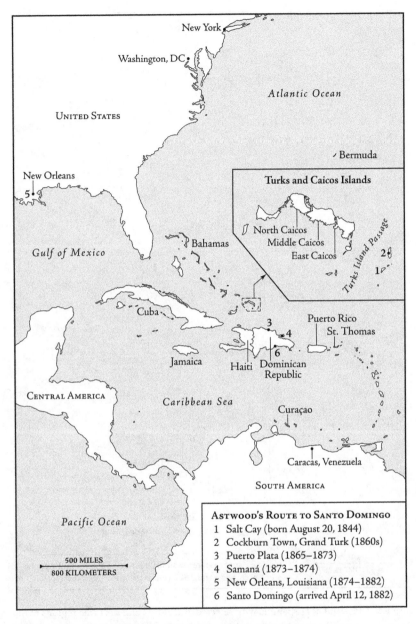

MAP P.1. Astwood's US-Caribbean sphere. Map by Kate Blackmer.

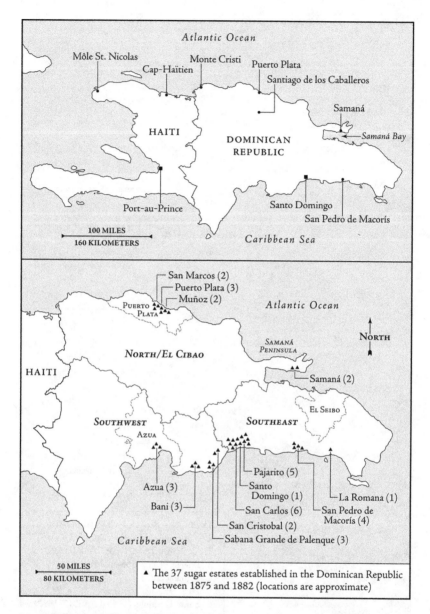

Atlantic Ocean

Môle St. Nicolas
Cap-Haïtien
Monte Cristi
Puerto Plata
Santiago de los Caballeros
Samaná
Samaná Bay

HAITI

DOMINICAN REPUBLIC

Port-au-Prince
Santo Domingo
San Pedro de Macorís

100 MILES
160 KILOMETERS

Caribbean Sea

San Marcos (2)
Puerto Plata (3)
Muñoz (2)

PUERTO PLATA

Atlantic Ocean

NORTH/EL CIBAO

SAMANÁ PENINSULA

NORTH

HAITI

Samaná (2)

EL SEIBO

SOUTHWEST

AZUA

SOUTHEAST

Pajarito (5)
Azua (3)
Santo Domingo (1)
La Romana (1)
Bani (3)
San Carlos (6)
San Pedro de Macorís (4)
San Cristobal (2)
Sabana Grande de Palenque (3)

Caribbean Sea

50 MILES
80 KILOMETERS

▲ The 37 sugar estates established in the Dominican Republic between 1875 and 1882 (locations are approximate)

MAP P.2. The island of Hispaniola with selected cities (*top*), and the three regions of the Dominican Republic showing selected provinces and sugar estates (*bottom*). Map by Kate Blackmer.

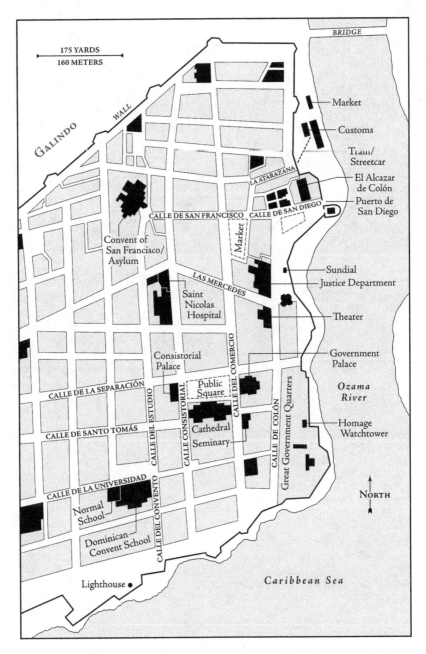

MAP P.3. Partial view of Santo Domingo in 1882, showing selected locations. Map by Kate Blackmer. Source: "Plano de la ciudad de Santo Domingo," Compañía United Lithograph, 1882, Harvard Map Collection, Harvard University.

Acknowledgments

My engagement with Dominican history began in 2007 when I spent seven months of undergraduate study abroad in Santo Domingo. Back then, I had no idea that my experiences would inspire an academic career. I write these acknowledgments as an extension of my appreciation for the scholars, friends, and family who have guided me in this journey.

Relationships with AME leaders in the United States and the Dominican Republic have shaped my historical perspective over the years. For this reason, I would like to first recognize my Evanston, Illinois, and Dominican church families. Thank you for your constant support as I pursued higher education and academic research. There are also a few church folk whom I must mention by name. In the Dominican Republic, I am especially grateful to the Rodríguez family of Santo Domingo, La Romana, and Samaná; the Valera family in San Pedro de Macorís; the Jimenez Jones family in the capital; and María Green of Samaná. All hosted me in their homes at one time or another between 2011 and 2019. Many other Dominican AME Church members have welcomed me into their homes and lives, and I am deeply grateful for their friendship. I am also grateful to AME bishops Carolyn Tyler-Guidry, Sarah Frances Taylor Davis (1948–2013), John White, Anne Henning Byfield, and their spouses for allowing me to attend Dominican annual conferences and for sharing their perspectives with me. John Thomas III, current editor of the *Christian Recorder*, has been a close friend and constant source of insight on church matters since 2008.

My AME connections have also led to friendships in the Iglesia Evangélica Dominicana (IED) and the Asambleas de Dios. I am thankful for the support of IED leaders Miguel Angel Cancú, Samuel Grano de Oro, Betonia Figueroa, José Peguero, Odalís Rosario, and Ardell and Gordy Graner. Within the Asambleas de Dios, I extend special thanks to Juan Abel Encarnación and Benjamín Silva.

I am grateful to the many scholars on the island who have assisted me in various ways. Pablo Mella was my professor back in 2007 and has since encouraged my research. Martha Ellen Davis met with me in 2011 to discuss my research interests and has answered questions ever since. The Fundación Global Democracia y Desarrollo hosted my 2014–15 Fulbright-Hays year abroad and facilitated my research in Santo Domingo. Thanks to Marcos Villamán and Bienvenido Alvarez, who served as mentors that year, and to Raymundo González, who helped me navigate the Archivo General de la Nación (AGN). I am also profoundly grateful to the archivists and staff at AGN for their assistance in locating vital records in 2014–15 and 2018. Thanks to Alanna Lockward (1961–2019), Quisqueya Lora Hugi, and Beba Finke for their intellectual engagement with my research, and for traveling with me to Puerto Plata in 2018. The Academia Dominicana de la Historia welcomed Alanna Lockward and me in 2018 to present our respective research, and Susana Sánchez hosted my presentation at the Universidad Nacional Evangélica in 2018. Frank Moya Pons also pointed me to vital secondary sources in 2019. My scholarship is also indebted to the research of Dominican historians past and present—especially George Lockward, Alfonso Lockward, Alanna Lockward, Mu-Kien A. Sang, and Jaime de Jesús Domínguez—who have written extensively about topics covered in this book.

In the United States, my formal intellectual formation took place at Yale and Duke universities. I am grateful to the Mellon Mayes Undergraduate Fellowship and mentors at Yale who helped guide my research in 2007–9, particularly Lillian Guerra, Stephen Pitti, and Saveena Dhall. At Duke University, I am thankful to my advisors Laurent Dubois, John D. French, Andrienne Lentz-Smith, Michealine Crichlow, and Brendan Jamal Thornton (UNC–Chapel Hill). I am also grateful to the Duke history department, which supported my applications for fellowships and postgraduation year of teaching. Duke library staff Carson Halloway, Kelley Lawton, Liz Milewicz, and Will Shaw provided crucial research support. Fellow graduate students Ashley Elrod, Rochelle Rojas, and Ashley Young were always willing to read grant applications, and students Annie Delmedico, Juan Jimenez Lizardi, and Mina Ezikpe helped with document organization and interview transcriptions. Thank you all.

While my research on the AME Church in the Dominican Republic prepared me to write *Dominican Crossroads*, this book emerged as a separate project based on research conducted between 2018 and 2022. During this period, I was also privileged to receive two postdoctoral fellowships at Harvard University and Washington University in St. Louis. Prior to starting at Harvard, I returned to the AGN and Washington, DC. Regarding the latter, I am especially appreciative of David A. Langbart's advice on US foreign service records and the staff of Howard University's Moorland-Spingarn Research Center.

Harvard's Charles Warren Center postdoctoral fellowship enabled me to publish articles and write early drafts of chapters 1, 6, and 7 of the present book. I am grateful for the support of Walter Johnson, Arthur Patton-Hock, Monnikue McCall, and my faculty mentor Mayra Rivera. Faculty fellow Saje Matthieu and postdoctoral fellows Tej Nagaraja, Juliet Nebolon, Tina Shull, Courtney Sato, and Hannah Waits read and gave feedback on early iterations of the aforementioned chapters. Graduate student Massiel Torres aided me in the collection of consular and diplomatic records, and students in my Creole Spirits and African American and Latin American Intersections courses provided comments on chapter 6 and another chapter that I have since excised from the book. Alejandro de la Fuente, Tamar Herzog, and participants in the Latin American History seminar offered extensive comments on the same excised chapter, as did Cyrus Veesar and commentators Samuel Martínez, Richard Turits, and Neici Zeller at the 2019 Global Dominicanidades conference led by Lorgia García-Peña, Elizabeth Manley, and Sharina Maillo-Pozo. I am also grateful to Lorgia García-Peña, Vincent Brown, Marla Fredrickson, and Todne Thomas for their mentorship and scholarly advice. Walter Johnson, Vincent Brown, and invited commentators Juliet Hooker, James Campbell, Jana Lipman, and Naomi Paik provided invaluable feedback during my 2019 Warren Center book manuscript review.

Washington University's John C. Danforth Center on Religion and Politics served as a fruitful intellectual home during the COVID-19 pandemic and allotted me time to complete the manuscript. I am grateful to the center's faculty and staff for their mentorship, feedback, and flexibility during two very challenging years. In particular, Leigh Schmidt read and offered feedback on chapters 5, 6, and 7. Lerone Martin and Marie Griffith provided invaluable professional advice regarding publication and other matters. I am also grateful for intellectual discussions I had with Laurie Maffley-Kipp and Mark Valeri, and for Leigh Schmidt's and Fannie Bialek's leadership of the postdoctoral program. Postdoctoral fellows Candace Lukasik, Alexia Williams, and Andrew Walker-Cornetta were constant sources of support during the pandemic. I am also thankful to the regular participants in the center's biweekly seminar. Undergraduate student Gracie Hoagland helped to organize documents for chapters 1 and 2. Sheri Peña and Debra Kannard helped with all things administrative, especially coordinating my 2022 book manuscript review. Regarding the same, I am extremely grateful to Judith Weisenfeld for her close read of my manuscript and insightful feedback.

Dominican Crossroads could not have been written without the critique and advice of friends who came together during the pandemic. I am immensely thankful to Anne Eller, Sophie Mariñez, and Wendy Muñiz for feedback on chapters 1, 3, and 7, and to Wendy for providing digital copies of the *Boletín Eclesiástico*. I am also indebted to Tina Shull, Courtney Sato, and Hannah Waits, who read drafts of chapters 1 through 4 and 7. In 2020–21, Wendy Muñiz, Massiel Torres, and I formed a reading group that provided invaluable background for chapter 5. Regarding the same chapter, I am also grateful to conversations I had with Wendy Muñiz, Andrew Walker, Maria Cecilia Ulrickson, and April Mayes during our panel at the 2022 Cultural Studies Association conference. Saje Matthieu's continued mentorship during these years and beyond have been invaluable to me; Saje, you are a constant source of inspiration, and I am beyond grateful for our friendship.

A vibrant community of scholars of African diasporic religion, African American history, and Dominican history have contributed to the development of this book through seminars and conferences. I am grateful to participants in the Crossroads Project's Black Religious Studies Working Group, who provided feedback on an early draft of this book's introduction. A 2018 C. L. R. James grant from the African American Intellectual Historical Society (AAIHS) funded archival research in the Dominican Republic that year. I am also thankful for the AAIHS's intellectual community, especially feedback by panel discussant Lara Putnam at the 2019 AAIHS conference. Lara has provided invaluable mentorship over the years. Jesse Hoffnung-Garskoff also gave essential research advice for this project at the 2019 AAIHS conference and the 2019 Latin American Studies Association (LASA) conference, and during a 2020 phone call. Members of the Haiti-DR section of LASA have been a source of constant support. I am especially grateful for conversations with Silvio Torres-Saillant, April Mayes, Anne Eller, Elizabeth Manley, Raj Chetty, Ginetta Candelario, Lorgia García-Peña, Sophie Mariñez, Wendy Muñiz, Médar Serrata, and Jennifer Baez. A 2017 CUNY-Dominican Studies Institute Archive and Library Research Award funded early historiographical research for this book. I am grateful to Ramona Hernández and Sarah Aponte for their support. Sophia Monegro provided research support that summer and has since been a stimulating conversation partner. Fellow scholars Lauren Hammond, Brandon R. Byrd, Ryan Mann-Hamilton, Dennis R. Hidalgo, April Mayes, Richard Turits, Robin Derby, and Cyrus Veesar have also provided advice at conferences such as the Dominican Studies Association and through one-on-one conversations. A special thanks goes to Gisela Fosado and Alejandra Mejia at Duke University Press and the anonymous reviewers whose comments made this book so much better.

My deep dive into the histories of the Turks and Caicos Islands and New Orleans for chapters 1 and 2 began during the COVID-19 pandemic. I am grateful to Neil Kennedy, who helped me navigate the historiography of the Turks Islands, and oriented me to research on Bermudan, Bahamian, and Turks and Caicos history. I am also appreciative of Neil Kennedy and Bermudan archivist Karla N. Ingemann for providing research advice, electronic versions of slave registries, and Bermudan population registries compiled by C. F. E. Hollis Hallet. Toni Butz offered crucial information over email on the Lightbournes and Astwoods of Bermuda. Emma Cass of the British Library digitization studio provided images of the Turks and Caicos Islands' *Royal Standard and Gazette* during the pandemic. Librarian Amanda Rudd at Washington University in St. Louis arranged for my private use of the library's microfilm machine to view Wesleyan Church files. In a similar vein, I am thankful for the assistance of Phillip Cunningham and the Amistad Center staff, who rescheduled my visit to the center three times during the pandemic. Jari C. Honora at the Historic New Orleans Collection generously advised on the Grand United Order of the Odd Fellows and the Ternoir family tree. Through AME Church relations, I connected with pastors Jay Augustine, Otto Dunkin, and Demetrius Philips, and church members Alvin Jackson and Rogerwene Washington. I am grateful for their sharing of resources and their insight on New Orleans's Historic St. James AME Church.

During my research, I was fortunate to make contact with a few of H. C. C. Astwood's relatives and descendants. I am grateful for conversations with Wendy Soto, Arturo Trinidad, and Corliss Strickland-Alston, who each shared their oral histories, digital newspaper clippings, and family photographs on distinct occasions.

My own family has been a source of constant support throughout the research and writing process. To my parents and sister—Neil, Clarice, and Catherine Davidson—thank you for encouraging me to pursue my dreams. To Tom and Adey Wassink, I am grateful for our many conversations about religion, race, and writing. Thank you to Kevin and Marya Outterson for opening your home to my family and for making it possible for me to get so much writing done during the pandemic. I am especially grateful to Tom Wassink and Caiti Outterson for reading chapters and offering feedback. And to my partner, Joshua Wassink, thank you for believing in me and this project, which would not exist without your constant support. This book is dedicated to you.

Introduction

At the turn of the twentieth century, Americans heralded Henry Charles Clifford (H. C. C.) Astwood as "one of the most prominent colored men in the country."[1] From the outside looking in, the skilled politician represented opportunity for both Black and white Americans. His trajectory as a poor African-descendant migrant from the British Caribbean to Reconstruction-era New Orleans to the US consulship in Santo Domingo in 1882 demonstrated his ingenuity and personal achievement. In the United States, Astwood quickly became a race leader, a position secured through his ties to the Republican Party and religious duties as a minister of the African Methodist Episcopal (AME) Church, the first independent Black Protestant denomination in the United States. White Americans also took notice of the Black statesman, hoping that his personal connections, political shrewdness, and linguistic abilities would literally pay dividends. With an Afro-Creole wife and multiple children at his side during his consular years, the clergyman-politician epitomized US Black masculine respectability, Protestant work ethic, and social mobility. No wonder then that the smattering of American history books that mention Astwood place him among the era's most celebrated Black elite.[2] In an ironic twist of fate, US scholarship has forgotten that H. C. C. Astwood was a controversial international figure whom Dominicans best remember for his involvement in a scheme to lease Christopher Columbus's mortal remains.[3]

The silences around Astwood's life and political trajectory are curious, and yet purposeful. Astwood built his career by remaining in the shadows of powerful men with the means to advance his position. His exploits in the Dominican Republic, notorious at the time they occurred, faded to obscurity in subsequent years. Astwood had an explanation for each accusation; he excelled at spinning facts in his favor. He did so with the help of powerful politicians and business associates and in spite of his adversaries' efforts to ruin his professional opportunities. When the rumors exposed a baser side of US diplomacy, international business, and African American international politics, Astwood's friends—US and Dominican government officials, prominent American capitalists, and influential African Americans—eagerly pushed aside the controversies and red tape (at least at first). Today, Astwood remains an enigma on the sidelines of US history because of a concerted effort to shield the public from the dealings of a duplicitous middleman whose extraordinary life defied borders of all kinds: national, cultural, racial, and moral.

Using Astwood's early life and polemical career in Santo Domingo as a guide, *Dominican Crossroads* examines the intersection of moral discourse and racial capitalism in the Americas at the end of the nineteenth century. By doing so, this book centers the Dominican Republic in ongoing conversations regarding the intersections of religion, race, and US empire during a period of hemispheric transition.[4] It argues that as the last pillars of plantation slavery crumbled in the Americas, the city of Santo Domingo became a metaphorical crossroads in a hemispheric debate over Black men's capacity for citizenship and political authority.[5] This debate occurred at the level of moral discourse. For various elite people in Santo Domingo—Dominicans, white and Black Americans, Europeans, and Latin American Creoles—claims to morality based in Christian (Protestant and Catholic) worldviews were a currency of power that gave individuals interpretive authority. A handful of ruling men wielded this currency in order to assert immediate power over the Dominican nation and instill their distinct visions of race within a transnational sphere that included the United States, Haiti, Latin America, and Europe.

By analyzing this moralized contest for power, *Dominican Crossroads* especially shows how Astwood, a man of African descent, participated in the era's moral politics of race-making—defined here as the purposeful deconstruction and reconstruction of racist moral logic—in order to command political authority. As demonstrated throughout the text, the moral politics of race-making was more than realpolitik. Instead, it was a component part of racial capitalism, a theoretical framework first advanced by Cedric J. Robinson and further developed by other scholars to explain the mutual constitution of racial ideology and modern world capitalism.[6] Scholars of racial capitalism have recognized the moral dimensions of racial discourse as part of human antirelationality, a necessary part of capitalism.[7] However, such work has paid less attention to the ways that racial theory and Western Christian theology also developed in tandem. Rather than viewing racist moral discourse as soft power in service of hard power, this book takes seriously the equally significant mutual constitution of race and Western Christianity.[8] As discussed throughout the chapters, the moral discourse examined herein abided by a strict dichotomy between good and evil based in Christian theology. Such theology, in its hegemonic white supremacist form, not only justified the capitalist exploitation of nonwhite people but also sanctified their violent suppression. Astwood's ability to deconstruct and reconstruct racist moral logic at will depended upon this belief system. Thus, *Dominican Crossroads* fundamentally considers the moral politics of race-making as religious race-making, a component part of racial capitalism.

As a politician and preacher, Astwood engaged in the moral politics of race-making to claim power over US-Dominican international relations and Protestant religion in the Dominican capital. His actions ostensibly combated the era's greatest myth—that is, the myth of white supremacy. And yet Astwood's methods were unconventional. As a middleman, Astwood constantly manipulated Western conceptions of good and evil. His actions not only reveal the constructed nature of this dichotomy but also demonstrate that the transnational fight for Black political authority in the Americas was intrinsically a battle over interpretive authority. Always claiming the moral upper hand, Astwood aimed to construct and control narratives of the past and present. By doing so, he, like other people in governance and high society, hoped to enact his own racialized visions of the Dominican Republic's future.

The Dominican Crossroads and the Middleman as Trickster/*Tíguere*

During the late nineteenth century, it seemed that all eyes were on the island of Hispaniola, where enslaved Africans had defeated their French oppressors and created the first independent Black republic in 1804. Much had changed since then—and not just on the island. After the Haitian Revolution (1791–1804), Hispaniola was divided into its western Haitian and eastern colonial Spanish parts. But, in 1822, following a short year of independence, the eastern Spanish side of the island unified with independent Haiti. For twenty-two years, the whole island triumphed under Black rule, defying the basic tenets of white supremacy. Then, in 1844, Spanish Creoles in the east declared independence from the Black state. The Dominican Republic was born. Next came the turbulent decades of the 1850s to the 1870s on the island and everywhere else. Eventually, war erupted across the hemisphere, in the United States, the Dominican Republic, the broader Caribbean, and the republics of South America. The slave system was falling. The Spanish Empire found itself under renewed attack in its last colonial holdouts, Cuba and Puerto Rico. The question of Black social equality percolated from one society to the next. This question pulsed beneath the shallow surface of all politics in the US-Caribbean sphere—from labor protests in the British Caribbean, to cross-border disputes over Dominican annexation, to the travails of US Reconstruction, to Cuba's Ten Years' War (1868–78). Meanwhile, there remained one constant: whites across the hemisphere continued to villainize Haiti because its independence persistently proved Black humanity and signaled the possibility of social equality. The Dominican Republic, however, represented a question mark. What would become of this independent nation of majority mixed Spanish and African descent?

Everyone who inhabited the capital of Santo Domingo at the end of the nineteenth century had an opinion about the country's future, as both outsiders and nationals sought to convert it into a modern Western nation. White foreigners and most Euro-Dominicans believed that such a conversion depended upon an absolute rejection of the nation's historical ties to Haiti and the Dominican nation's own racial Blackness.[9] This dominant viewpoint, however, was not hegemonic during this crucial moment after war when the Dominican lettered class sought to invent a national character.[10] As elsewhere in Latin America, the lettered class's musing on the future of their nation existed on a spectrum that did not always evince overt anti-Blackness.[11] And, whereas some Caribbean Creoles from Venezuela, Cuba, Puerto Rico, Curaçao, and St. Thomas aligned with the Europhile Dominican elite and articulated conservative racist views about the nation they came to inhabit, other interested parties forged alliances with Dominicans and Haitians during the island's decolonial struggles.[12] Afro-Dominicans, as well as Black labor migrants residing on Hispaniola's northern coast and in the growing sugar industry ports of the island's south, also had a stake in the nation's anticolonial, potentially racially democratic project—a vision articulated, and seemingly embodied, by a few Dominican generals and politicians visibly of African descent.[13] Taking pride in the existence of these Black officials, African Americans in the United States sought to "racially uplift" the Dominican nation along with Haiti.[14] Thus, while some outsiders considered the Dominican Republic to be a racial borderland suspended between Black Haiti and white United States, this symbolic borderland was simultaneously a cosmopolitan crossroads where various stakeholders sought to enact their racialized visions of modern progress.[15]

The Dominican Republic of the late nineteenth century also marked a temporal crossroads as slavery fell throughout the hemisphere, and the United States came to figure prominently in Dominican history. From a US historical view, the rise of US empire in the Dominican Republic and the greater Caribbean coincided with the fall of Reconstruction and the dawn of Jim Crow. The juncture between Reconstruction and the Jim Crow era generated a racist moral discourse that directly affected US-Dominican diplomatic relations. Most notably, in the 1880s and 1890s, the US government considered the Dominican Republic to be a Black nation akin to Haiti and Liberia and in desperate need of social and moral reform. It therefore showed little respect to the island republic, which white Americans exploited economically. It also appointed Black foreign service agents to the country, a policy that reflected both white Americans' racist outlook and African Americans' efforts to secure dwindling federal posts.

By following the early life and political career of one such Black US agent, this book recounts how H. C. C. Astwood navigated the Dominican crossroads. As stated above, Astwood's methods were unconventional. His very existence as US consul challenged the myth of white supremacy. Yet his engagement in the moral politics of race-making not only reinforced said myth but also disrupted notions of cross-border racial solidarity. This fact drew critique. The nineteenth century's most famous US Black activist, Frederick Douglass, and his son Charles R. Douglass, for example, believed Astwood to be an "unmitigated trickster" and perhaps even "a villain of the deepest dye."[16] These accusations were not idle insults. Rather, they referenced the African American folklore figures of the "trickster" and "badman," which both featured heavily in late nineteenth-century African American folktales.[17] While the trickster figure came to symbolized subversive behavior during slavery and later Jim Crow, the badman represented an outlaw whose sadism was "a source of unrelieved violence in the black community."[18] At times, Astwood displayed characteristics of both figures. In fact, the Douglasses intimated on multiple occasions that Astwood used trickery to escape being classified as a badman. Accordingly, this book examines Astwood's trickery as a component part of the moral politics of race-making at the Dominican crossroads. This association is fitting since, in Afro-diasporic religion and folklore, the trickster is the master of the crossroads.[19]

Considering the parallels between Astwood and the Afro-diasporic trickster figure, *Dominican Crossroads* not only analyzes the historical grievances against Astwood within his contemporary US context but also considers the Dominican Republic's version of the trickster, the *tíguere*. In the Dominican Republic, the word *tíguere* traditionally referred to a person "who rises from poverty to a position of wealth and power, often through illicit means."[20] This term is especially relevant in Astwood's case because it emerged in the late nineteenth century as a derogatory term for Afro-descendant men who lived in the barrios outside the capital and who surpassed their class status.[21] Placing Astwood within the *tíguere dominicano* framework both highlights the parallels between African American and Dominican folk hero narratives and emphasizes the similarities between white Americans' and Euro-Dominicans' anxieties over Black political authority in their respective countries.

Even more significantly, I argue that the *tíguere* figure may serve as an analytical framework for understanding both Dominican Blackness and US Black internationalism. First, the *tíguere* serves as an apt metaphor for what US academics and mainstream media have labeled "Dominican self-hatred, negrophobia, and anti-Haitianism."[22] This US stereotype has denied Dominicans the spectrum of racial sentiment and *vaivén* (ebb and flow) of Black expression that existed across Latin America where Blackness is "a moving target."[23] The pervasive US stereotype that Dominicans deny their own Blackness, as Raj Chetty and Amaury Rodríguez have written, "can only lead to the conclusion that Dominicans are not invested in forging ties with their international brothers and sisters in the region, nor even in the US."[24] However, thinking through the *tíguere* figure as metaphor for Dominican Blackness demonstrates the ways in which *tigueraje* (trickery) factored into Black individuals' struggles for survival even while such trickery sometimes counteracted collective Black liberation. As with Karl Jacoby's scholarship on William Ellis, another nineteenth-century African American social climber who, like Astwood, straddled Latin American and US racial systems, the *tíguere* metaphor suggests that periodic subterfuge was sometimes necessary in an individual's fight against white supremacy.[25] Thus, whereas critics have rendered the trickster a "symbol of the corruption of humankind . . . [and] an obstacle to regional [Caribbean] enlightenment and progress," Astwood's *tigueraje* prompts us to step away from making strict moral judgments about the correct (i.e., US hegemonic) way to embody Blackness and fight global white supremacy.[26]

Similarly, this book considers Astwood's *tigueraje* as a prism through which to reevaluate nineteenth-century US Black internationalism. Scholars have used the term *Black internationalism* to describe the myriad ways that African Americans have joined over time in a global fight against white supremacy both inside and outside the United States' geographic borders. While scholarship on US Black internationalism has concentrated on the twentieth century, which lends itself to more unequivocal versions of antiracist Black solidarity, a few works have used this framework to understand African Americans' ambivalent engagement with Hispaniola in the nineteenth century.[27] Lorgia García-Peña, for example, has argued that a hegemonic form of Blackness originated in the late nineteenth-century United States as African Americans joined the US empire–building project in Latin America, especially in the Dominican Republic and Haiti.[28] In order to justify their alignment with US empire, African Americans saw themselves as superior to Afro-Latin people whom they hoped to uplift through Protestant conversion, US education, and industry.

Like other African Americans of his era, Astwood assumed this biased attitude. However, he also revered the Afro-Dominican president Ulises Heureaux and shifted his anti-Catholic, anti-Dominican rhetoric depending on his audience. Thus, Astwood's political *tigueraje* demonstrates that, like the *vaivén* of Dominican Blackness, US Black internationalism also existed in flux. While the US stereotype of Dominican racial identity has reified Dominican Blackness as "negrophobia" and would likely judge Astwood's moral politics of race-making similarly, the *tíguere* framework adopted here critiques such judgments as overly proscriptive. Bringing an Afro-Dominican analytical framework to US Black internationalism means viewing Astwood's moral politics of race-making as an expression of Black internationalism that contrasted the racial solidarity expressed with Haiti by Black diplomats such as Ebenezer Don Carlos Bassett and Frederick Douglass.[29] This perspective allows for the multiplicity of Black expression that existed in the nineteenth century.[30] Accordingly, it redirects scholarly attention to the fundamental question of narrative construction in order to understand how such multiplicity came to be.

By analyzing Astwood's moral politics of race-making as a form of political *tigueraje*, *Dominican Crossroads* reveals the ways that individuals gained power over narrative through moral discourse. Accordingly, this book is not a conventional biography. Astwood's name appears scattered across newspaper articles, lawsuits, government documents, and personal letters produced in the United States, the Dominican Republic, and the British Caribbean. Yet, rather than providing a full picture of Astwood's life, these documents attest most acutely to the ways that power operated in the world he inhabited. Astwood's early life and tenure in Santo Domingo demonstrate that his political outlook and actions were not reflective of his individual choices alone. His periodic subterfuge existed as one of various reactions to his era's primary question: Did Black men have the capacity to become equal citizens in the hemisphere's racial capitalist societies? Astwood believed the affirmative, and he did whatever it took to evidence this truth in his own life and prove a world full of naysayers wrong. Consequently, although Astwood serves as an invaluable guide, *Dominican Crossroads* is most fundamentally a history that examines the moral politics of race-making in Santo Domingo—a transitional place and time— during a moment when US empire in Latin America and the Caribbean loomed large.

The United States' Racial Gaze upon the Dominican Republic in the Nineteenth Century

The history of US relations with the island of Hispaniola is well known in broad strokes. At the hour of Dominican independence in 1844, the United States refused to diplomatically recognize the new nation, a position that reflected its policy toward Haiti. While Black people across the hemisphere praised the Haitian Revolution and Haitian independence, the United States and other foreign powers shunned the sovereign Black republic.[31] On this point, the United States' stance proved unyielding because the island's free Black population threatened American slavery. Consequently, Washington maintained its foreign policy of nonrecognition even after Haiti agreed to indemnify France 150 million francs in 1825 for its lost colony in exchange for official recognition. Nearly two decades later, the US government similarly withheld recognition from the Dominican Republic.[32] The United States still maintained this position in the 1850s when European nations established official diplomatic and commercial relations with the two nations. By then, the US debate over slavery was so fraught that any perceived challenge to the "peculiar institution" could ignite interpersonal violence. Only during and after the US Civil War (1861–65), a battle waged over slavery, did the United States finally grant diplomatic recognition to Haiti (and Liberia) in 1862 and the Dominican Republic in 1866. The United States' recognition of Haitian and Dominican sovereignty ostensibly signaled a new era of diplomatic and commercial relations in which the United States was willing to negotiate on equal terms with nonwhite nations. The truth, however, was much more opprobrious. Between 1869 and 1871, the United States considered annexing the Dominican Republic with the hope of someday also gaining Haiti and then the rest of the Caribbean.

Meanwhile, on the island's eastern side, Euro-Dominicans knew that their geographic and historical ties to Haiti and their large Black population made their territory a joint target of the Western world's scorn. Consequently, their lobbying efforts to unencumber the Dominican nation from the era's racist politics of nonrecognition began at the moment of separation from Haiti in 1844. To curry favor for Dominican independence, Dominican agents in Washington claimed that whites governed the eastern side of the island where, as they alleged, the general populace was racially and culturally distinct from Haitians (despite Haitians' own class and color diversity).[33] Thus, Dominican elites portrayed the east as a land full of whites and mulattos in danger of "pure Black" Haitian invasion.[34] This portrayal continued into midcentury and served as a principal reason why Dominican elites sought annexation to a European power or the United States. Such efforts found success when, by invitation, Spain recolonized the Dominican Republic in 1861.

US commercial agents, filibusters, and lobbyists who wished to control the whole island and reenslave its Black population prior to 1865 bought into Dominican elites' convenient version of events, and they subsequently implored Congress to defend Dominicans in a "race war" against Haiti with a show of military force.[35] This initial cooperation between Dominican government officials and US speculators established a pattern. Whenever white US opportunists attempted to lobby for US domination of Dominican territory—whether through white settler colonialism (1840s–50s), annexation (1865–71), or purchase (1850s–90s)—they argued that Dominicans were racially whiter than Haitians.[36] Dominicans were whites, mulattos, or Latins—not *Negro* Blacks like Haitians or African Americans. Nevertheless, despite various iterations of this argument used throughout the nineteenth century (and into the twentieth), the strategy generally did not work. The association of eastern Hispaniola with Haiti and racial Blackness proved to be too strong in the popular Euro-American mindset.[37] This association did not shift substantially until after the US invasion and occupation of the Dominican Republic in 1916.

In retrospect, the prominence of Haiti in US foreign policy toward the Dominican Republic is unsurprising. Indeed, only three factors fundamentally distinguished US-Dominican international relations from US-Haitian relations in the nineteenth century. First, whereas Haitian officials resented American commercial agents stationed in Haiti prior to the date of official diplomatic recognition, US agents overall received a hearty welcome from Dominican presidents and politicians anxious for foreign investment. Dominican elites' approbation of US agents formed part of their lobbying effort to transform the international community's racist image of their country. Second, while Black US ministers served in Port-au-Prince beginning in 1869, the United States sent only white commercial agents and consuls to Santo Domingo until Astwood's appointment in 1882. This difference is likely due to the two annexation efforts. During and after Spanish annexation (1861–65) and in the early 1870s when the United States negotiated its own annexation of the republic, the United States used white men to represent its interests. This practice endured in the capital throughout the 1870s, despite Charles R. Douglass's token assignment to the Puerto Plata consulship in 1875.

The third difference was a critical issue for Astwood—and likely weighed heavily upon Dominican officials too in the 1880s and 1890s. Unlike Haiti, which since 1862 had hosted a US diplomatic legation in Port-au-Prince, the Dominican Republic did not receive a similar honor independent of Haiti until 1904.[38] The reason for this discrepancy is simple. After the possibility of US annexation died, the United States lost diplomatic interest in the country, although white consuls continued to intercede between the Dominican government and US investors.[39] By the late 1870s, the US consulship in Santo Domingo became a neglected, thankless role at the margins of the US State Department's weak, underfunded international apparatus. Thus, even as Astwood's appointment in 1882 marked a shift in the racial makeup of US consuls in Santo Domingo, it simultaneously reflected the marginal status of the post and Americans' continued association of the Dominican Republic with Haiti.[40] In other words, the Dominican Republic was both Black and of lesser importance than Haiti. This US viewpoint held through to the end of the nineteenth century despite all arguments, for better or worse, to the contrary. And, like the decade of the 1880s, it remains an understudied aspect of US-Dominican relations.[41] Astwood's consular years (1882–89) reveal this racialized outlook and the diplomatic dynamics that resulted.

Nevertheless, the appointment of Black US officers to Santo Domingo also reflected an achievement for African Americans. Like white Americans, African Americans sometimes grouped the two nations of Hispaniola together or subsumed them both under the banner of Haiti or "San Domingo."[42] Consequently, during US Reconstruction, when white Americans argued that political turmoil and war on the island proved that Black people were incapable of self-government, African Americans recognized that their own fate was tied to the whole island and its continued struggle for sovereignty.

US Black Internationalism and Dominican Protestantism in Retrospective View

The Dominican Republic's potential as a racial democracy made the country a crucible of US Black internationalism in the late nineteenth century. While Haiti remained paramount in African American thought, the Dominican Republic represented an alternative to America's racial divide. By the late 1870s, some African Americans even came to believe that the Spanish-speaking, mixed-race people of Hispaniola served as a better model for race relations in the United States than Haiti.[43] Whereas the Haitian Constitution prohibited white landownership, Dominicans of all colors reportedly worked together in government, and liberal principles seemed to reign as the country opened itself to foreign capital and saw its first "colored president," Gregorio Luperón, rise to power in 1879.[44] Soon thereafter, another Afro-Dominican, Ulises Heureaux, assumed the presidency and maintained power for the rest of the century. Thus, as in the days of the US annexation debate, throughout the years of Astwood's consular tenure, "Santo Domingo seized the [American] imagination . . . because it offered an opportunity both to advance and to vindicate a radical vision of racial belonging."[45] After the failure of Reconstruction, the Dominican Republic remained a beacon of hope for a functional racial democracy; if a racial democracy could not yet exist in the United States, then at least it existed somewhere. Such imaginations about the Dominican Republic drove increased US Black engagement with the country in the 1870s and 1880s as Black orators and newspapers featured stories from the island, and the AME Church saw the country as an open missionary field. Due to such attention, a few African Americans even immigrated to eastern Hispaniola.

This flurry of activity at the end of the nineteenth century formed part of a longer history of African American engagement with the island dating back to the Haitian Revolution and the founding of Haiti in 1804. As stated previously, Black people in the United States and elsewhere across the hemisphere saw Haiti as a symbol of freedom. Accordingly, in the decades after 1804, thousands of Africans and their descendants fled the US mainland and surrounding Caribbean islands for Haiti's shores. In the United States, the largest such emigration movement occurred during the unification period when between 1824 and 1826, upward of thirteen thousand African Americans responded to an invitation from Haitian president Jean Pierre Boyer to join the republic.[46] Known by scholars as the Haitian emigration movement, the mass migration represented a significant moment of Afro-diasporic solidarity. The Haitian government granted African American immigrants citizenship and land upon their arrival, and African Americans hoped to join Haitians in building the hemisphere's first Black state. Although most historical scholarship of the movement emphasizes the fact that many recruits soon returned to the United States, historian Brandon R. Byrd has argued that biased white US newspapers exaggerated the number of returnees.[47] Believing that God guided their path to the Black "Promised Land," many thousands stayed.[48]

As in the 1880s, the AME Church played a critical role in the Haitian emigration movement of the 1820s. The AME Church originated from the Free African Society, which, under the leadership of the formerly enslaved preacher Richard Allen (1760–1831), broke from the white-led St. George Methodist Episcopal church in Philadelphia in 1787.[49] The Free African Society became the first AME congregation, later known as Mother Bethel AME Church, and inspired various other free Black Methodists to form independent congregations of their own. In 1816 these congregations incorporated as the AME Church and elected Allen as the first bishop. Thus, like Haiti, the AME Church became a symbol of Black self-determination for African Americans.[50] It also served as a central site for Black social life and political organizing in the US North. It is no wonder then that the Haitian agent Jonathas Granville presented Boyer's immigration proposal first to the Mother Bethel congregation.[51] Unlike the contemporaneous American Colonization Society's efforts to send free Blacks to West Africa, the Haitian plan enabled African Americans to maintain control over the process as the Bethel congregation negotiated the terms of migration with Granville. Consequently, many Bethelites, including Allen's son, were among the first recruits.[52] Allen also appointed ordained AME preachers as missionaries who left for Haiti along with other migrants. Within the first decade of their arrival, such immigrants established AME congregations across the island, maintaining contact with Allen and other US-based AME leaders whenever possible.[53] The AME Church's critical involvement in the migration remained in the immigrants' corporate memory for generations.

However, because slavery continued in the United States and surrounding islands, African American immigrants in Haiti could not maintain formal connection to the AME Church throughout most of the nineteenth century. In response to this loss, immigrant communities in Port-au-Prince and elsewhere sought connection to another Methodist body: the Wesleyan Methodist Church. Unlike the AME Church, this British denomination was a white institution that originated in the Church of England's Methodist movement, led by Methodism's founder, John Wesley (1703–91). After Wesley's death, the Wesleyan Methodist Church became an independent British denomination with overseas missions in Africa, Asia, and the Americas. The first Wesleyan missionaries to Haiti arrived in 1817, but it was not until after African Americans landed in large numbers that the Wesleyans permanently established missions on the island.[54] Although some African Americans protested Wesleyan affiliation on racial grounds, immigrants in Port-au-Prince and along the northern coast ultimately invited the British missionaries to lead their congregations because they wished to remain within a formal religious body.[55] The Wesleyans' presence in Puerto Plata and Samaná, which later became Dominican territory, especially impacted local culture as the missionaries established schools that served African American children as well as Haitians, Dominicans, and British Caribbean migrants. These ports, in turn, became nodes in the Wesleyans' Caribbean network, socially connecting African American immigrants to the British Caribbean in a way that eluded the AME Church for most of the century and forming the basis for an endemic Dominican Protestant identity.

Ultimately, for African American immigrants, their religion more than their skin color or even their continued use of the English language distinguished them from the island's Catholic peasantry. This distinction especially sustained African American communities on the eastern side of the island through the trials of the 1840s–70s, when the Dominican Republic separated from Haiti but it was still not clear if the new Dominican nation would endure. Spanish annexation represented the greatest challenge for such immigrants during this period. Prior to 1861, the independent Dominican government followed Haiti's lead, granting the immigrants and their children Dominican citizenship and protecting their religious freedom. Spain, however, appointed a new Catholic archbishop who targeted these Protestants, shutting down their churches and schools. This persecution explains why many immigrants supported the Dominican War of Restoration (1863–65), which reinstated Dominican independence.[56] It also ironically helps explain why annexation to the United States, a Protestant nation, seemed appealing to some immigrants in the early 1870s.[57]

The US annexation debate represented a new moment of African American engagement with the island. For US-based African Americans, time had not erased the memory of family members and friends who boarded ships for the island in the 1820s. Thinking of those who left and the annexation debate, many African Americans assumed Dominican annexation and other coeval events to be "clearly parts of one drama" working for the "glory of God."[58] They were encouraged in this thought when US President Ulysses S. Grant appointed Frederick Douglass to the US Commission of Inquiry in a tour of the Dominican Republic to assess Dominicans' willingness for annexation. Once on the island, Douglass met African American immigrants and their children in Samaná who endorsed the annexation.[59] Douglass then brought news of these experiences back to African Americans in the United States through publications and speeches delivered in Black churches. Listening to Douglass and reading US newspapers, African Methodists especially believed their denomination to be uniquely poised and divinely appointed to spread to the Dominican Republic.[60] After the US Civil War, AME missionaries had flooded the US South, gaining the denomination over 200,000 members.[61] Due to this success and contemporaneous white Americans' efforts to evangelize foreign nations in the 1870s, AME leaders thought it their duty to evangelize Black people across the world.[62] Such leaders viewed African American immigrants on the island not just as kin but also as settler colonists who would pave the way for AME expansion. Yet immigrants and their children were Dominican citizens who had adapted to their local society in ways that allowed them to slip in and out of various modes of belonging.[63]

Astwood met such Afro-American Dominicans and their descendants at two distinct moments in his life. First, as a British Caribbean migrant, he joined the Wesleyan missions in Puerto Plata and Samaná in the late 1860s. Later, as US consul in 1882, he met African American immigrants' children in the Dominican capital. The AME Church subsequently appointed him its official missionary to Santo Domingo in 1883. By then, the stories of mass emigration from the United States were family lore. Details embedded in first-person accounts of US racial oppression had mostly passed away along with the elders, replaced with more immediate concerns of maintaining the community's Protestant church. Given that Wesleyans had never established missions in the city of Santo Domingo, Afro-American Dominicans in the capital had struggled for sixty years to support their religious endeavors independently. Yet, even as this immigrant community practiced an independent form of Methodism in the Spanish-Catholic land, their Protestant church had become part of the social fabric of the capital. Ignoring this nuance, AME leaders in the United States charged Astwood with advocating on behalf of Black Dominicans and "civilizing" them through American religion. This vision, however, failed to account for significant cultural, linguistic, political, and historical distinctions between US-based African Americans and the island's peoples. It also did not consider the fact that Dominican society was already replete with its own civilizing moral discourses.

Dominican Liberalism, Social Morality, and the Catholic Church

Naturally, the Europhile men of letters who constituted the Dominican Republic's political and intellectual elite resented the racial prism through which Black and white Americans continued to view their country at the end of the century. Dominican intellectuals, the majority of whom were white or light-skinned mixed-race men, saw themselves as possessing high-class European culture, and they too had thought long and hard about their country's needs. Their pressing questions reflected both concerns over the island's African heritage and the Dominican Republic's struggle for national sovereignty: How could the Dominican Republic modernize when the majority of its population was of African descent? Did dark-skinned people have the capacity to become equal citizens in Western societies? And how could the nation progress despite the United States' and other foreign powers' constant interference? Dominicans' answers to these questions were never monolithic. Indeed, their ideas ranged across a conservative-liberal spectrum that, on the one hand, had precipitated Spanish annexation in 1861 and, on the other hand, had led to war and the restoration of independence in 1865. However, the ideologues who gained the most influence during the 1880s "were of one mind regarding the philosophical tenets of their labor: they were Liberals, rational men, positivists."[64] As such, they believed that modernization depended upon the transformation of the populace, and they cast the ideal Dominican citizen as manly, bucolic, hardworking, patriotic, and possessing Spanish culture, high moral integrity, and a skin color that appeared "more white than black."[65] Their vision of society betrayed their anxieties over the country's racial Blackness and their own adherence to white supremacist notions of human civilization and morality.

Dominican liberals, however, purposefully avoided using overtly racial language. Instead, like the Cuban thinker José Martí, they espoused a racially inclusive, anti-imperialist, color-blind nationalism. For dark-skinned Dominicans and Black migrant populations from the United States and the surrounding Caribbean, the social transformations that occurred after the War of Restoration lent credibility to this more inclusive form of national identity. By the 1880s, a new generation of African-descendant military officers counted among the country's national heroes, and both Gregorio Luperón and Ulises Heureaux had served as the country's president. Between 1879 and 1884, these exalted generals paved the way for more social changes. Luperón, for example, endorsed the educational reforms of his friend Eugenio María de Hostos, the Puerto Rican intellectual who became the director of the republic's first secular normal school in 1879. Although the school served mostly Euro-Dominican elites, a handful of young mixed-race men and a few Protestants joined the ranks of scholars who matriculated and adopted Hostos's positivistic view of society.

For his part, Heureaux was also a liberal positivist, but his version of this ideology manifested mostly in his economic policies: friendliness toward foreign capital and defense of private property. This disposition, which advantaged Americans and other foreigners over Dominicans, became even more pronounced after 1887 when he consolidated power and imposed a dictatorship.[66] Still, during his first administration (1882–84), Heureaux maintained the liberal reforms of his predecessors (Luperón and Fernando A. de Meriño), including freedom of the press. He also supported the Protestant community in Santo Domingo in the reconstruction of their church; he did so even though he and other members of the liberal nationalist party (known as *azules*) remained closely aligned with the Catholic Church.[67] This nuance helps explain why some dark-skinned Dominicans as well as descendants of African Americans in the capital possessed a sense of their own inclusion in the nation's body politic even though the daily concerns of the peasant class remained marginal to the inner workings of the government, the Europhile elites' goals, and the aims of local and foreign investors friendly with Heureaux.

For Afro-American Dominicans in the capital, the social and educational reforms led by Eugenio María de Hostos were especially beneficial. Hostos, a liberal positivist, espoused a secular moral ideology known as *moral social* (social morality) that considered the pursuit of science and modern progress to be a moral imperative. His call for the secularization of education and moral thought challenged Catholic orthodoxy, and indeed Hostos criticized Catholic dogmatism as antithetical to modern progress. At the same time, he cast a more favorable light upon Protestantism in his written work.[68] Thus, the philosophy of *moral social* benefited Protestants as Hostos's ideas became popular among a group of educated Dominicans known as *normalistas*. This group advanced liberal democratic principles, including the idea that freedom of conscience and freedom of religion were Dominican national ideals. While such ideas did not lead to widespread Protestant conversion in Santo Domingo, they did enable the capital's small African Methodist community to grow modestly. Even more significantly on a symbolic level, Black Protestants gained public visibility and inclusion in the Dominican nation. Within Hostos's line of thought, African American descendants were Protestant Dominicans whose social ties to known *normalistas* influenced one of the era's most radical visions of Dominican national belonging.[69]

Nevertheless, despite the fact that secular positivist ideology carved out space for Dominican Protestantism at the turn of the century, Catholicism endured as the state religion, and the Catholic Church remained hegemonic. Indeed, in the post-1865 period, the Catholic Church gained even more cultural influence over Dominican society as Catholic clergy, Dominican intellectuals, and government officials worked to construct a Hispanophile nationalism that relied heavily on Catholic religious symbolism. While such Dominicans harbored anticolonial feelings against Spain, they still identified with the old colonial Spanish conquistadors, which produced a "peculiarly anti-Spanish Hispanophilia."[70] The apotheosis of Christopher Columbus especially provided a foundational basis for such identification. These sentiments intensified all the more after the discovery of Christopher Columbus's human remains in the Basilica Cathedral of Santa María la Menor, the oldest cathedral in the Americas, in 1877. The discovery set off an international dispute with Spain over which country possessed the explorer's true bones.[71] Spanish-Catholic nationalism abounded in other ways as well. During this period, Dominican intellectuals produced the nation's first works of history, sociology, and fiction, which emphasized the country's links to the Catholic Church and colonial Spain.[72] They also laid claim to Spanish colonial ruins as an unofficial archive and searched for other national relics such as the cadaver of Juan Pablo Duarte, the nation's most celebrated founding father.[73] Located in Venezuela, Duarte's remains were disinterred and shipped to Santo Domingo for reburial in the basilica in 1884. Three years later in 1887, Heureaux authorized the erection of a monument to Columbus in the plaza fronting the cathedral to celebrate the 1877 discovery. These symbolic acts fused Catholicism with Dominican culture, but association between church and state did not stop there.

The Catholic Church's influence in Dominican society was also political. Not only did the state grant special privileges to the Church, but throughout Dominican history Catholic priests had served in the government. This tradition reached a climax in 1880–82, when Father Fernando Arturo de Meriño served as president of the republic. Meriño, like Heureaux and Luperón, was a member of the liberal Partido Azul. Unlike these Afro-Dominican generals from Puerto Plata, however, Meriño was of European descent and hailed from the traditionally more conservative capital. Although he remained quiet on the issue at first, he ultimately rejected the secular reforms to education and the ideology of *moral social* that took place under the first Azul administrations (including his own). Meriño believed that the Catholic Church, not positivist reformers like Hostos, should exclusively set the terms for morality within Dominican society.[74] After his presidency, Meriño became the country's first Dominican-born archbishop in 1885, and thereafter worked to nationalize the priesthood and strengthen the already strong bond between the Catholic Church and the Dominican state. In the following years, the Catholic Church's alliance with Heureaux's dictatorship grew all the more as Hostos and his followers, outspoken critics of Heureaux, became new targets of the regime, and Heureaux used displays of Catholic devotion to fortify his power. By the end of the 1880s, it became clear that the radical visions of secular social morality and expansive Dominican national belonging embodied in both *normalista* ideology and the city's Protestant church were under threat. Such ideas ran up against Spanish-Catholic nationalism, Catholic religious orthodoxy, and ultimately Ulises Heureaux.

As US consul, Astwood counted Heureaux among his close friends, and indeed the pair were partners of sorts. Not only did they know each other prior to Astwood's appointment, but they had similar life trajectories. Once impoverished men of color, they both came into positions of authority in the 1870s and 1880s. They were both known for their thirst for political power. And, when necessary, they both resorted to stratagems to force their way. As the following chapters show, Astwood, like Heureaux, unabashedly wielded racialized moral discourse to command political authority in Santo Domingo. He did so in spite of the many local forces—including Catholic authorities, *normalistas*, and even Protestants—who challenged him.

The Road Map

Following Astwood's early life and consular career, *Dominican Crossroads* bridges the fields of Latin American and Caribbean history, African American history, Afro-diasporic religion, and US diplomatic history. It provides the first study of Astwood's life, the first in-depth analysis of Black Protestantism in the Dominican Republic, and the first critical examination of US-Dominican relations during the 1880s.

Part I, "Beginnings," examines the multiple freedom struggles that occurred in the Caribbean and the United States in the second half of the nineteenth century. Centering Astwood's birthland, the Turks Islands, chapter 1 links the British Caribbean's transition from slavery to free labor and the question of Black civic capacity to the Dominican War of Restoration, the US Civil War, the Morant Bay Rebellion, and other contemporaneous events. It shows how Turks islanders assisted Dominicans in their war against Spain. It also demonstrates how white Turks islanders' ideas about the Dominican Republic and Haiti shifted after the events at Morant Bay. Last, the chapter reveals the historical, economic, social, and familial ties that Black and mixed-race Turks islanders—especially the Astwood family—held to Hispaniola's northern coast. Chapter 2 then considers the transnational organizing and social networking that connected the era's various freedom struggles. Following Henry Astwood's trajectory from the Turks Islands to Puerto Plata to Samaná and finally to New Orleans, it demonstrates how people of color in each locale united and adapted their strategies in their struggles for liberty. Most significantly, this chapter not only highlights Astwood's upward mobility and path to the consulship but also reveals the various ways in which Black Protestantism in the Dominican Republic and the US South formed part of the era's transnational political organizing for freedom in various forms.

Part II, "Black Political Authority," argues that the decade that encapsulated Astwood's tenure in Santo Domingo (1882–92) represented a significant moment in US-Dominican relations when US constructions of Dominican Blackness and morality discourse took center stage. Chapter 3 considers Astwood's aspirations for the Dominican Republic within the context of the United States' racial imaginary of Haiti/Hispaniola, and it documents his struggle to assert his political authority. As consul, Astwood faced discrimination against his color and the United States' racist disregard for the Dominican Republic. This chapter shows that due to these dynamics, US-Dominican relations depended upon both official and unofficial diplomacy bifurcated along racial lines. This form of segregated statecraft reveals the dialectic relationship between the building of US empire and the defense of Black political authority. Instead of accepting the subordinate status of his post, Astwood strategically manipulated racist US stereotypes about the island through discursive performances of righteous indignation on behalf of US capitalists. Such performances enabled him to gain legitimacy and assert his authority among three competing groups: US State Department officials, American capitalists, and Dominican government officials.

Chapter 4 presents a case in point of this process by analyzing the events surrounding the Dominican government's accidental killing of the American citizen John J. Platt in 1885. It additionally argues that racial moral discourse drove the dialectic between US empire and Black political authority. Whereas the US government in Washington preferred to ignore the killing, Astwood declared it a case of murder and insisted that both the Dominican Republic and the United States engage in diplomatic negotiations under his watch in order to avert international scandal. Through an analysis of the racist and gendered language in the case, this chapter grapples with Astwood's Blackness and the persistent racist stereotype of Black misrule that white Americans and Europeans applied to the island and its leaders. Ultimately, the chapter probes Dominican elites' reproductions of this stereotype through moral discourse, particularly as fear grew over Heureaux's rising authoritarian rule. Thus, chapter 4 exposes the contours of transnational moral discourse regarding Black political authority within the diplomatic sphere and uses a close reading of Astwood's consular dispatches to construct a new vision of US-Dominican international relations as a struggle for the power to determine right and wrong.

Part III, "Social Morality," turns to the cultural sphere to analyze racialized moral ideology in Santo Domingo. Chapter 5 decenters Astwood in an analysis of two Black institutions that he led in Santo Domingo: the AME Church and the Grand United Order of the Odd Fellows (GUOOF). Focusing on the historical and ideological ties between these organizations and

Dominican liberals, the chapter shows that these links grew stronger in the post-1865 period as radical liberal positivists promoted ideas that benefited non-Catholic Dominicans, namely the separation of Church and state, the freedom of thought, and the freedom of religion. Tracing the intersecting histories of the AME Church, the GUOOF, and Dominican liberalism through the eyes of African American immigrants' descendants, chapter 5 shows how the founding of these institutions in Santo Domingo reflected radical visions of Dominican national belonging. It also argues for a redefinition and a wider application of Hostos's term *moral social*. Social morality, as chapter 5 asserts, was an expansive liberal public discourse that often served as a proxy for racial discourse and at times made various non-Catholic creeds—white US capitalism, African American Protestantism, and Latin American positivism—seem compatible with each other as well as with local expressions of Dominican Catholicism. These convergences, however, also had their fault lines.

Juxtaposing the liberal convergences explored in chapter 5, chapter 6 takes up the dominant narrative of Spanish-Catholic nationalism through a close study of Astwood's most infamous scheme: his attempt to facilitate the lease of Christopher Columbus's exhumed remains to a US businessman in 1888. The transatlantic debate with Spain over which nation possessed the true bones not only cast doubt on Dominican officials' integrity but also challenged the Dominican Republic's symbolic claim on Columbus, a figure of Western modernity and whiteness. In 1888, Astwood argued that by leasing the remains and exhibiting them in the United States, the Dominican Republic would gain ground in its dispute with Spain. This proposal, however, violated Western notions of social morality, specifically the divide between the sacred and the secular. What began as a private scheme between a few power brokers soon became an international scandal. A fervent cross-border effort to shame the "immoral" Black US consul quickly ensued as white Americans and Creole Latin Americans found common ground in saving the quasi-religious figure of Western civilization (and themselves) from disgrace. Chapter 6 demonstrates how both US and Dominican reactions to the event reinscribed symbolic racial and national borders through racialized moral discourse. Racial and gendered ridicule, as this chapter argues, ultimately reasserted the hegemonic racist capitalist system, which depended upon the strict divide between white and Black, American and Dominican, the sacred and the profane.

The book's last chapter shows how, through the moral politics of race-making, individuals attempted to construct and control narratives of the past and present. Analyzing the aftermath of the Columbus bones debate, which led to Astwood's dismissal, chapter 7 exposes the contours of moralized race-making as a competition for authority over fact and fiction. Despite public embarrassment, Astwood refused to surrender his post, and then, once finally discharged, he immediately began to lobby for his reinstatement. Behind the scenes, prominent American businessmen and AME clergy debated Astwood's fitness for office. This debate reflected a larger transnational dispute over Black men's capacity for citizenship and political authority. Various individuals, including US postmaster general John Wanamaker, got involved. On each side, the Christian dichotomy between good and evil became a moving target as various elite white Americans and African Americans lobbied to see their candidate of choice in the consular office in Santo Domingo. Moving beyond Astwood's case, the chapter also explores the diplomatic appointments of Frederick Douglass (US minister to Haiti) and John S. Durham (Astwood's successor). Letters of recommendation in each case demonstrate how power over historical narrative was based in moral claims. It also demonstrates how such power, which white men claimed as an exclusive right, was always contested. In this way, both white and Black Americans attempted to control the past and thereby direct the future.

Last, the conclusion considers events that took place in the Dominican Republic, the United States, and the broader hemisphere in the wake of Astwood's consular ousting in 1888–89 and final departure from Santo Domingo in 1892. Describing the Santo Domingo Improvement Company's advent in the Dominican Republic and the Chicago World's Fair in 1893, among other events, it demonstrates how white supremacist concepts of morality consolidated a new US world order in the 1890s. Consequently, it foreshadows the US Supreme Court's decision in *Plessy v. Ferguson* (1896), the Spanish American War (1898), and the subsequent US occupations of Haiti (1915) and the Dominican Republic (1916).

Dominican Crossroads explores how H. C. C. Astwood and his contemporaries strategically engaged moral discourse to navigate racial borders, control international policy, negotiate the politics of US empire, and direct the course of history. It, moreover, traces how Black male politicians' ability to play this discursive game shifted over time. The narrative may seem familiar and yet somewhat alien to experts on Caribbean, Latin American, US, and African American history. The histories of African American consuls and Black Protestant clergy, for example, do not often feature in studies of the Dominican Republic, just as the Dominican Republic does not often take center stage in hemispheric visions of the Americas. The chapters of this book, however, present a vision of Santo Domingo within a racialized geopolitical context at the end of the nineteenth century. In this world, moral discourse became the vernacular of choice in a transnational debate over Black social equality, Black civic capacity, and Black political authority. By focusing on the moral politics of race-making as a component part of racial capitalism, *Dominican Crossroads* foregrounds the dangers and uncertainties that people of African descent confronted during this turbulent era and their remarkable ingenuity, including subterfuge, when facing impossible odds in Santo Domingo and in the broader Americas.

PART I

Beginnings

1

A SHADOWY PAST

Henry Astwood and the Transition from Slavery to Freedom

The times were dangerous and uncertain at the hour of Henry Astwood's birth as Atlantic world slavery came under threat. The slave system's fall commenced at the beginning of the nineteenth century on the former French colony of Saint-Domingue, where enslaved Africans emerged victorious in a revolutionary war that established the independent Black Republic of Haiti in 1804. The anticolonial Haitian state abolished slavery, striking terror in the minds of whites from Europe to the Americas. Haiti proved whites' greatest fears—that fundamental beliefs in white supremacy and Black inhumanity were somehow questionable, perhaps even myths created to veil Western society's heinous deeds. For white power to persist, such notions had to be censured. So European nations and the United States refused to officially recognize the Black republic.

Yet the cry for freedom could not be contained. In 1822, the eastern side of Hispaniola came under Haitian governance, and slavery was abolished across the island.[1] Then emancipation spread incrementally to Latin American and British territories over the next forty years.[2] By the time the hemisphere faced the multiple social upheavals of the 1860s—civil and revolutionary wars, European annexations, and anticolonial movements—slavery's doom was clear.[3] So too was the seismic nature of the shift. The 1860s brought abolition across most of the Americas, signaled the final decline of the Spanish Empire, and raised the possibility of Black social equality.[4]

But new barriers to Black advancement quickly emerged as the debate over slavery transformed into scrutiny of the civil capacity of Black people. Whites no longer ruled over enslaved Blacks, but were formerly enslaved people to become whites' social equals? For most whites, the answer was a resounding no. Both white religion and racial science denied Black humanity and portrayed African descendants as unqualified for equal citizenship and incapable of self-rule.[5] How then were Black men to govern with and over whites?

Thus, everywhere the fight for Black equality met anti-Black protest and violence as white reactionary forces across the Atlantic world sought to stem the tide of progressive change. The ruling class found countless ways to force the formerly enslaved population to work in the same conditions they had under slavery. Redistribution of land and wealth was nonexistent. For most of the century, filibuster intrigue jeopardized Haitian sovereignty, and freebooters put Black people on Hispaniola at risk of reenslavement. In the United States, white vigilantes murdered Black people with impunity. Throughout the hemisphere, life was uncertain for people of African descent, whether enslaved or free. Basic necessities like water, food, and housing almost always required Blacks' integration into a capitalist system that fundamentally protected white power. Freedom earned or won was never quite freedom guaranteed.

In the midst of the changing tide of race relations at midcentury—the impending fall of slave regimes throughout the hemisphere, the tentative signs of Black social and political inclusion in the Caribbean and the United States, and the violent reactionary backlash—a boy named Henry Charles Clifford Astwood was born on August 20, 1844, on Salt Cay, a part of the British Turks and Caicos Islands located due north of Hispaniola.[6] Keeping the broader context of mid-nineteenth-century hemispheric transformations in mind, this chapter uses fragments of genealogical records, missionary letters, and the Turks and Caicos Islands' newspaper, the *Royal Standard* and *Gazette* (referred to hereafter as the *Standard*), to reconstruct Astwood's shadowy biography and recount the turbulent times in which he lived. By doing so, it presents the context from which Astwood emerged. Henry's early life was characterized by the legacy of Caribbean slavery. He was born a decade after British emancipation in 1834. His mother was a woman of color. His father was a member of the white master-merchant class. His existence was wrought in the racial and sexual violence of the era. Consequently, this recounting of his early life begins by describing the colonial slave context in which his progenitors lived.

The remaining sections zoom in on the 1860s, when Henry witnessed various regional social upheavals firsthand. Surviving these years was not an easy task. Henry's early life afforded him little material wealth and even less political influence. His upbringing, however, did expose him to the era's racial politics at micro- and macroscales, the moral logics of Black and white Protestants, and the daily operations of interisland maritime trade. It is within this context that Henry forged initial ties to Dominican society and became acquainted with a few of the nation's leaders with whom he would later reunite. It is also within this context that Henry not only formed a deep knowledge of international commerce but also came to understand exactly how to navigate a world in which his own chances for wealth, prestige, and political authority were extremely slim.

The Astwoods of the Turks Islands: Salt Traders, Slave Masters, and the Specter of Haiti

Henry lived his childhood and young adulthood years on the Turks and Caicos Islands, a group of about fifty islets and cays located on the southeast end of the Bahamian archipelago. A lesser-known site of the British Empire, the Turks and Caicos are best known for two things. First, three of its islands are speculated to be the site of Columbus's first landfall in the Americas.[7] Considering Astwood's later encounter with the explorer's remains, it is tragically ironic that his life would begin there some 350 years after the *Niña*, *Pinta*, and *Santa María* first touched ground. Second, and also ironically, on these miniscule islands where the combination of sun, trade winds, and low annual rainfall led to the quick evaporation of ocean water along the edges of shallow lagoons, a massive trade in salt emerged.[8]

The development of the salt trade on the Turks and Caicos was slow and initially unintentional. At first, colonial powers paid little attention to the natural saline deposits on the lagoons, distracted as they were by the gold and silver to be had on Hispaniola and then later on the North and South American continents. However, as empires grew elsewhere, attitudes toward these small islands changed. British privateers from Bermuda began to rake salt on two of the nine Turks Islands, Grand Turk and Salt Cay, sometime in the mid-seventeenth century.[9] These Bermudian saltmen collected the deposits on a seasonal basis, raking salt in the spring and returning to Bermuda before hurricane season. Later, they set up shop, bringing enslaved Africans to the islands and developing a common-use system for the distribution of raking rights.[10] By 1750, the Turks Islands sent over 100,000 bushels of salt to Bermuda.[11] That is when colonial competitors began to pay attention, and soon the Spanish and French began to raid the territory. After one French raid in 1764, the British Crown officially claimed the Turks and Caicos as its own and placed the new acquisition under the jurisdiction of the Bahamas' colonial government.[12]

With formal colonial recognition came the regulation and expansion of the salt trade, but Bahamian oversight also caused a great deal of consternation between new Bahamian arrivals and old Bermudan rakers, who competed for control over the salt lagoons. For example, when Andrew Symmer, the first Bahamian king's agent to the Turks Islands, arrived in 1766, he passed a series of laws that forbade nonresidents from salt raking and tightened control over slave labor.[13] These regulations angered Bermudans who depended upon seasonal raking and resented the new limits. At the same time, though, not all of Symmer's changes worked against the Bermudan salt proprietors. The regulations increased Bermudans' permanent settlement on the islands. Symmer also established free trade—much to his superiors' consternation.[14] The empire's efforts to curb free trade on the Turks Islands failed miserably. By 1770, the saltmen were trading with the French, Spanish, and Dutch, along with other British Caribbean possessions and the eastern seaboard of British North America. They even secretly carried on illicit trade with the United States during and after the American Revolution. Symmer's brother, for example, ran ships from Philadelphia to Hispaniola's northern coast and back again, stopping at the Turks Islands to load salt each way.[15] By the start of the nineteenth century, the sea channel between the Turks and Caicos Islands, a deep trench known as Turks Island Passage, became a significant route in Atlantic world trade.

The first Astwoods to settle on the Turks Islands came from Bermuda sometime in the early nineteenth century, although not much is known about the family. The Astwood name does not appear in the earliest church records, and the Bermudan slave registers of 1821, 1827, and 1834 leave few clues regarding the Astwoods of Grand Turk and Salt Cay.[16]

However, a unique letter book from Turks Islands resident and salt proprietor John Lightbourn might provide some clues. It contains multiple missives written between 1806 and 1812 to Lightbourn from his nephew, the Bermudan lawyer William Astwood.[17] It is possible that the Astwoods of Grand Turk and Salt Cay descended from William Astwood (who died on Grand Turk on April 1, 1818), his son William Amelius Astwood, or one of their mixed-race bondspeople who raked salt under the watchful eye of Uncle Lightbourn.[18]

At the very least, the letter book betrays the quotidian violence that pervaded colonial slave societies and permeated the Astwoods' cryptic family history. Since William did not reside permanently on the Turks Islands, he sent his human chattel to his uncle. Their correspondence was laden with references to specific individuals: Ben, Deborah, Been, Toney, Sary, and others. In one instance, William shipped "[his] mulatto man Jim" to Salt Cay for being too "assuming" and begged his uncle to sell him as soon as possible.[19] In another case, William promised to purchase a man for John and send him posthaste to the salt beds; he ultimately bargained to pay £86 for a boy named Tom.[20] It is impossible to know precisely what happened to Jim, Tom, and other enslaved people that William and John owned, but, like sugar, the Atlantic world's other "white gold" took its toll on the bodies of the enslaved.

In short, labor in the salt fields for captives like Jim and Tom was torture. In her 1831 narrative, the enslaved Bermudan Mary Prince recounted how enslaved people waded in the Turks Islands' saline lagoons from dawn to dusk, causing painful boils on their legs that sometimes reached down to the bone due to overexposure to salt and sun.[21] At night, enslaved rakers barely slept because of the pain. The islands' white population, however, ignored these agonies. Prince detailed how the boils on her feet inhibited her from moving quickly, and the punishment she received for not working faster. "Mr. D—has often stripped me naked, hung me up by the wrists, and beat me with the cow-skin, with his own hand, till my body was raw with gashes," she related.[22] Such torture was commonplace, as were the other run-of-the-mill techniques that Prince related. With easy access to salt, the punishment of tossing the crystals on enslaved people's raw, bloody bodies was routine.[23] A man named Ben underwent severe beatings for "stealing" rice.[24] The master's son Dickey beat another elderly woman to death.[25] "In telling my own sorrows, I cannot pass by those of my fellow slaves," Prince reasoned, "for when I think of my own griefs, I remember theirs."[26] Enslaved people on the Turks Islands were connected to bondspeople across the Caribbean in other ways as well. The salt they raked and loaded on northbound merchant ships arrived in New England, Nova Scotia, and Newfoundland, where fishermen used it to preserve their catch. The same fish eventually returned to the Antilles to feed the enslaved.[27]

William Astwood's bondspeople, like other captives on Turks Islands, developed few strategies to resist their dehumanization. Unlike larger Caribbean islands where escaped slaves formed independent societies in center-isle jungles, the Turks Islands' small size and sea-level sandy geography prevented this form of *marronage*. So, when possible, fugitives stole barges and directed them to other islands. Principally, they fled south to Haiti. In 1823, for example, many of John Lightbourn's bondspeople (and presumably William Astwood's too) broke out of their barracks and, in small lighters, traversed the treacherous one-hundred-mile sea passage to the Black Republic.[28] That same year, Black captives on the nearby South Caicos stole the schooner *Polly*, which they likewise directed toward Haiti's northern coast.[29] Slave owners complained bitterly to the British and Haitian governments about the fugitives, and (per usual) the British Navy sent a warship to pressure Haiti to expatriate the escapees. But, since Britain refused to grant official diplomatic recognition to Haiti, Haitian president Jean-Pierre Boyer had little incentive to comply with the British islanders' demands.[30] Thus, like the thousands of free and enslaved African Americans who concurrently fled the United States for Haiti's shores in the early 1820s, hundreds of former Black captives from the Turks Islands made the Black Republic their new home.

However, not everyone could escape, and many enslaved Turks islanders found other ways to resist the slave system in seemingly insignificant, everyday actions. Mary Prince, for example, suggested resistance in a spiritual form. After returning to Bermuda, she learned that the people she had left behind on Salt Cay had cut boughs and leaves to erect a prayer house.[31] The master class twice pulled it down. Undoubtedly, the whites feared that the Blacks' prayer meetings would lead to rebellion.[32] Black religion had inspired a failed uprising in Charleston, South Carolina, in 1822, led by African Methodist preacher Denmark Vesey. Other religiously inspired revolts on the North American mainland and Jamaica alarmed British masters the same year Prince's narrative was published.[33] And, of course, whites on the Turks and Caicos felt constantly threatened by the island where Vodou spiritual power had initiated and sustained the Haitian Revolution.[34] Mary knew of Black spiritual power too—or at least she believed that Providence had acted on the side of the enslaved when she recounted how God sent a flood to destroy the white islanders' homes and overflow the salt ponds. "I do think this was for their wickedness; for the Buckra men there are very wicked," Prince attested.[35] In Prince's worldview, Black spirituality could occasion physical freedom as well as trigger supernatural retribution.

A minority of Christians among the "Bukra" (whites) believed similarly to Prince, and feared God's judgment upon the world for the sin of slavery. Together with Black Protestant preachers and laypeople, these white Christians launched the abolitionist movement at the end of the eighteenth century. The abolitionists believed that they waged a battle not only against an entrenched economic system but also against demonic forces. This belief formed the basis for their worldly activism, which eventually yielded the slave trade's end in Britain in 1807 and in the United States in 1808.[36] Yet, even as the abolitionists gained ground, the Turks and Caicos Islands likely became a key site for illicit trade in human cargo between Bermuda and the southern United States.[37] For these religious activists, the fight for full freedom in British Caribbean territories would continue until the Slave Emancipation Act was passed in 1833.

Still, when British abolition finally did occur, emancipation brought little relief to formerly enslaved people. Leading up to August 1, 1834 (when the Slave Emancipation Act took force), anxious Black captives on the Turks Islands took action. Many people absconded to Haiti. Others created disturbances—public displays of insubordination and the like.[38] The master class acted quickly to curb the flight and quench the fight. The government enlisted the islands' clergy, who, according to H. E. Sadler, informed the people that "they should expect no sudden and dramatic changes."[39] Troops were sent to counter "petty disorders," and the salt proprietor Henshall Stubbs used his own boat for coast guard duty between April 1832 and March 1834.[40] By August 1834, it was clear that nothing had truly shifted for the islands' Black population as Britain's notorious four-year apprenticeship period began. As apprentices, Black Turks islanders lived in the same slave quarters as they had before emancipation, and, in exchange for food, land use, and clothing, they worked the lagoons for the same individuals who had been their former masters.[41] If they refused these conditions, they were severely punished.[42] The apprenticeship system lasted until 1838. Yet, even while Black people were then technically free by law and some of them could finally receive shares in the salt lagoons as compensation for their labor, the same economic structures and racial hierarchy remained in place. Few Blacks were able to pool their shares to become salt proprietors, and buying land was impossibly out of reach for most.[43] These conditions persisted when Henry Astwood entered the world six years later in 1844.

The timing of Henry Astwood's birth might be described variably as fortuitous and inauspicious for a British subject of mixed African and European descent. On the one hand, Astwood was fortunate that he never experienced the brutality of slavery or apprenticeship himself. Moreover, mere days after his birth, salt proprietors on the Turks Islands petitioned the queen for a second time in two months for separation from the Bahamas.[44] The formation of the Turks and Caicos Islands as an independent colony occurred four years later on December 25, 1848, and was feasible only because of an economic boom from which the white side of Henry Astwood's family likely benefited.[45] The 1840s, however, still harbored great danger for a mixed-race person like Henry Astwood. Naturally, not everyone benefited from the Bahamian separation and the concurrent economic surplus. The Turks and Caicos Islands' new constitution restricted the franchise to the literate, which meant that only the leading white class and a few mixed-race individuals could vote.[46] The rest of the population remained dependent upon these landowners whose own wealth fluctuated with the yield and price of salt, which were sometimes very low indeed. In 1852, for example, half of the island's population was "reduced to circumstances of great want" due to a combination of factors—the poor salt yield, the lack of available wage labor, the scarcity and high prices of food, and the whooping cough—and many people felt the pain of starvation.[47]

Henry, though, may have been insulated from the worst of these contextual hardships due to his parentage. Among the 676 people living on the Turks Islands in 1845, about six hundred of them, men and women, labored in the salt ponds.[48] Henry's father, Adolphus James Astwood, however, was counted among the thirty-six white males who were salt proprietors. He and other white Astwoods of the era were never as rich or influential as the most prominent landowning families, but white male Astwoods served as merchants, clergy, and judicial magistrates on the Turks Islands, and their names appeared frequently in the islands' weekly newspaper, the *Standard*, throughout the 1860s.[49] Henry Astwood's mother, Elizabeth Batson, was most likely a free Black or mixed-race woman, perhaps a servant to the Astwoods or another white family. Her race meant that she and Adolphus never formalized their relationship. Even so, it was openly known in Turks Islands society that Elizabeth was Adolphus's sexual partner. She bore

Adolphus at least eight children (possibly nine) between 1837 and 1854, and together the pair stood before the altar as the Anglican rector baptized each of them.[50] Four other women each bore Adolphus one son, bringing Henry's siblings to a total of eleven.[51] Anglican records that welcomed this new generation of mixed-race children into the church's spiritual body obscured the systems of sexual coercion and racial exclusion that now render any further information on the family's genealogy impossible to trace. Still, the complicated intimacies of kinship produced a few social anomalies in this postemancipation period.[52] Openly recognized by his father, Henry Astwood was one such case.

Unfortunately, not much more is known about Henry's childhood. According to his own account, Henry received education in the colony's mixed public schools.[53] He then worked in the revenue service for the colonial government as a young man. He also joined his half-brother George in managing the commercial house George A. Astwood and Bros. on Grand Turk. These roles seldom took Henry to other ports, although he once traveled with his father and one of his sisters to St. Thomas.[54] Indeed, it seems that Henry's early life on Salt Cay and Grand Turk was spent in service of Adolphus's and George's mercantile pursuits.

Still, maritime trade was instructive. While laboring in the shadows of his family's business, Henry learned about the events unfolding around him. And between the ages of seventeen and twenty-one, Henry especially learned about the simultaneous wars occurring in the two nations that would soon have a profound impact on his young life.

Currents of Change and Exchange: From the Turks Islands to Puerto Plata

In April 1861, war broke out in the United States. A year later, people living on the tiny Caribbean salt islands hundreds of miles away were suffering. The American war had cut the islanders off from their principal buyers in the US South. On Grand Turk and Salt Cay, money and food were in short supply. Worse still, the islands' government had recently demanded that rentals on the ponds be paid by a certain date.[55] Rumors of resistance mounted in response, but no collective protest materialized. Salt-raking lessees, most of whom were Black, sacrificed everything to make the payment. A few succeeded, but many others lost their rights to the ponds. Heartbroken and hungry, people began to leave the Turks Islands for Hispaniola, where they hoped to find food and labor. They could only pray.[56]

Most emigrants from Grand Turk and Salt Cay went first to Puerto Plata, a town located on Hispaniola's northern coast. This port had long served as a haven to Turks islanders, although it differed so much from their own home. The low-lying Grand Turk had but one peak, seventy feet above sea level. A traveler to this islet could spot its glistening pink salt piles, still moist with water, and its white sand beaches speckled with flamingoes while yet miles out to sea.[57] The natural beauty of the place, like elsewhere in the Caribbean, belied horrors old and new. Yet, unlike other Antillean ports, Grand Turk did not boast a diversified export economy and visitors rarely invested in the place. By contrast, travelers to Puerto Plata, the most important Dominican port, saw the mountain of Isabella de Torre "with its head in the clouds" upon their approach.[58] Nestled between this extinct volcano and the cyan waters of the Atlantic, Puerto Plata and its population of over four thousand inhabitants seemed like "a pearl in a green velvet casket" to late nineteenth-century travelers.[59] And, indeed, in many ways it was.

Puerto Plata had always been a gem of sorts. For decades prior to 1862, the town had possessed a vibrant export economy that was a center of commerce for the Gulf of Mexico. This status, as historian Anne Eller has written, earned it the nickname "la Novia del Atlántico" (the Bride of the Atlantic).[60] Puerto Plata's bustling economy tied eastern Hispaniola's richest region, the Cibao valley, and its cash crop tobacco to trading ports throughout the greater Caribbean, Latin America, and Europe. Such trade brought riches and foreigners to the town. Merchants from Europe and the Americas docked in the port, their vivacious discourse interchanging fluently between Spanish, English, German, Dutch, and French. The city had also previously been a principal landing site for Black people fleeing slavery, and hundreds of immigrants from the United States and surrounding islands had settled there during the era of Haitian unification (1822–44). Among these were the descendants of the Florida plantation owner Zephaniah Kingsley, who emancipated his progeny and settled them on 35,000 acres of land just outside the city in the 1830s.[61] A few years later, these Black Anglophone communities attracted British Wesleyan preachers from the Turks Islands, who founded a church and school in Puerto Plata, linking the town to a missionary circuit that followed the trade routes.[62]

Considering this record—Puerto Plata's steady economy and historical exchange with the salt islands—this town might have seemed like a haven to poor Black Turks islanders suffering the effects of the US Civil War in 1862. But it was not. In fact, British subjects traveling to Puerto Plata that year had reason to feel anxious about their sojourn. Spain had annexed the Dominican Republic in 1861. At the behest of the Dominican president, Pedro Santana, the annexation had occurred only a month before the outbreak of war in the United States and had adversely affected the city's denizens—especially the communities of Anglophone Blacks already living there. The tension between locals and Spaniards was palpable.

Most people in Puerto Plata had not desired the annexation. Anticipating the city's resistance to the takeover, Spain had sent nearly one thousand troops to the port after already securing the rest of the republic's territory.[63] As the Spanish flag rose above the town on March 26, 1861, a sense of dread befell the local people and provoked small acts of resistance: the hiding of the Dominican flag, the raising of Haitian colors, the stares and tears of defiance.[64] "It was a melancholy spectacle on Tuesday last to witness the natives weeping and bemoaning the injustice of their chiefs who have thus clandestinely cheated them of their country and liberty for which they have fought for these 17 years past," reported James Darrell, the Wesleyan minister stationed in the city.[65]

Dominicans and Black denizens from elsewhere—Haitians, US immigrants, Turks islanders, and other Afro-Caribbeans—who had settled in the town understood that they were to be classified as second-rate imperial subjects as Spanish racial prejudices manifested in small and large ways. Dominicans later recounted the cruelty of the Spanish soldiers who spoke disparagingly of Black people, demoted Dominican officers of color, attempted to disarm the population, blocked freedom of movement, encroached on peasants' lands, and met opposition with violence.[66] Moreover, the new Spanish archbishop, Bienvenido Monzón, perceived Puerto Plata's Wesleyan church as a den of heresy, and Darrell ultimately fled the island.[67] These injustices and the enduring slave system in nearby Cuba and Puerto Rico menaced the city's African descendant population with the possibility of enslavement under Spain.[68] Soon the menace would provoke unrest. "So far no resistance has been made by the natives," Darrell wrote in 1861, "but it is heard by many that the profound silence that exists forebodes a coming storm."[69]

Across the channel on the Turks Islands, the locals had also mourned the Spanish annexation. Yet, as the US Civil War dragged on and the salt trade crashed, some Turks islanders had no choice but to search for work in Puerto Plata, even with the Spaniards in charge. "Unless the Divine Being interpose, many of our people must starve," concluded the Wesleyan minister Francis Moon in 1862.[70] A year later, things were more or less the same. "The members at Salt Cay continue to suffer in consequence of the [salt] failure," Moon reported again.[71] The prayers for divine intervention as well as the exodus continued.

Like other families living in the Turks Islands, the Astwoods also found themselves in dire straits in the early 1860s, although not everything was lost. They had watched others pack and leave the island, but it is unlikely that the Astwoods were forced to migrate themselves at this point, since Adolphus owned his salt pond territory outright. Cash was scarce, forcing small proprietors like Adolphus to use credit, and all landholders worried about overextending themselves as the situation grew worse by the day. Nevertheless, port arrival notices in the *Standard* suggest that Adolphus and George were able to mitigate complete ruin by carrying on trade with St. Thomas and possibly Cap-Haïtien in the early 1860s.[72] There were less material matters for which to be grateful, too. It was celebrated, for one, that freedom had been declared for enslaved people in the US South. Some Turks islanders theorized that this move signaled the US federals' weakness, but for certain members of Adolphus's mixed-race family (like young Henry) Lincoln's Emancipation Proclamation undoubtedly qualified as joyous news. Concurrently, the Wesleyan society that Henry joined at some point during his early years seemed to be doing well despite the hardships. The congregation on Grand Turk had grown "increasingly large" by March 1863, and it was reported that the parishioners prayed for "a copious out-pouring of the spirit from on high" as they waited upon specie and provisions from anywhere.[73]

Change came suddenly to the Turks Islands in 1863, and not in the way hoped for or expected. The same month that the Wesleyans celebrated their revival, news of skirmishes in the Dominican interior reached Grand Turk.[74] Much unlike the US Civil War—which had devastated the salt islands' economy but still occurred far away—the Dominican-Spanish war was dreadfully proximate, and its effects upon the Turks Islands were almost immediate. Turks islanders watched gloomily as Puerto Plata experienced the worst of the fighting.[75] After the scuffles in the interior, Spain placed the northern port under martial law and shut down the Wesleyan church there. The Protestants of the city—Turks islanders, African Americans, and other Black immigrants—protested to the US and British governments, but it did not matter.[76] A few months later in August 1863, hundreds of Spanish troops arrived at the port; they met upward of a thousand Black and mixed-race insurgents ready to repel them.[77] Over the next months the fighting intensified, and many people (British subjects and others) fled for Grand Turk. By mid-September, 165 Dominican refugees were living on Grand Turk, and vessels were preparing to return to Puerto Plata to pick up more people.[78] The total refugee population ballooned to approximately 667 a few weeks later.[79]

The people alighting from packed boats with no more than a suitcase in hand brought news of horror. "Puerto Plata is in ashes," Francis Moon related in October, days after the Spanish garrison pillaged and torched the town.[80] The troops had plundered the Wesleyan mission house there too, destroying Spanish Bibles and hymnbooks and burning the premises; the losses amounted to £2,000. Even worse, refugees told how Spanish soldiers had indiscriminately shot Black men in the streets. One British subject was assassinated in front of the Wesleyan church, and another, Mr. Cooper, was killed as he struggled to save his home from the flames.[81] The Spaniards captured and jailed two other British subjects, and nothing could be done to ensure their release.[82] Stationed a boat ride away, Moon condemned Spain's actions as "disgraceful in the extreme."[83]

Over the next two years, Turks islanders supported Dominicans in whatever ways they could. Materially, they rallied to care for the hundreds of indigent refugees with the little that they had (or did not have). They also smuggled ammunition and provisions to the insurgents.[84] And when the Spanish Navy intercepted their schooners—which occurred more than once—Turks islanders suffered alongside Dominicans in prison; at least one man from Grand Turk died from disease contracted in Santo Domingo's bastille.[85] Back on the salt cays, the people also voiced moral support for the revolution. The public, by and large, hoped for and predicted a Dominican victory, although many people surmised that it would come only after a bloodbath.[86] Meanwhile, the *Standard*, which reported weekly on the conflict, reprinted a correspondent's censure of the "brutal and uncivilized species of warfare adopted by the Spaniards, that of setting fire to all dwellings in their way, and making prisoners of all female inmates and children—*for the purpose of sale, as is alleged, in Cuba*."[87] Whereas British officials in London apparently felt unclear about which side, Dominicans or Spaniards, wreaked more havoc on Hispaniola, Turks islanders had no qualms about pointing the finger at Spain. Rumor spread among Dominicans and Turks islanders alike that Spain wanted to enslave all the Blacks.[88]

The *Standard* was also quick to defend Dominicans against the Spanish press. As the editor, Joseph Hutchings, accused, Spanish newspapers in Cuba and Santo Domingo generally depicted the insurgents as "a horde of unchained and infatuated savages, committing on every occasion the horrors which signalized the slave insurrection in French Santo Domingo."[89] The purpose of such gross distortion was straightforward. By using racist stereotypes of Haitians to describe Dominicans, Spain discounted Dominicans' grievances and angled for the international community's sympathies. They easily convinced many. The *New York Herald*, for one, eagerly reprinted the disinformation. Turks islanders, however, did not take the bait. "[Dominicans] have a right to fair dealing," Hutchings argued. "The cause in which they are engaged is interesting to humanity; it is a struggle for independence and liberty," he continued. "They deserve the sympathy of the world."[90] The *Standard*'s position reflected both Britain's imperial competition with Spain and the Turks Islands' frequent intercourse with Puerto Plata. Thus, while the *Standard* was not devoid of racist animus toward the island (especially regarding Haiti), in these years the editor joined the general population in the hope that the Bride of the Atlantic would one day be restored.[91] A few years later, this show of support remained in the collective memory: "No people ever felt more interested in the affairs of another country than did the inhabitants of this little colony for their neighbors during the time they were under the Spanish yoke."[92]

Undoubtedly, the Astwoods harbored the same feelings toward the Dominican-Spanish war as other Turks islanders, and thus they likely rejoiced when the predictions that Spain would lose materialized in 1864 and early 1865. Indeed, for many Turks islanders, it was incredible that the Spaniards had lasted this long. From the start, the Dominicans were motivated. Graffiti on Puerto Plata's burned buildings warned of reenslavement.[93] Desperate to defend their freedom, Dominicans resorted to guerrilla tactics. Spaniards unfamiliar with the tropical terrain fell by the thousands to Dominican guns and machetes.[94] "The Spanish will find that instead of vanquishing the Dominicans they will only acquire a cemetery," the *Standard* had warned early in 1864.[95] Moreover, as the paper reasoned, even if Spain were to succeed, the European nation would gain nothing from an island that ran a $1,684,585 annual deficit on Spain's account before the revolution and whose most lucrative port was now destroyed.[96] "It is nothing but foolhardiness on the part of Spain to be losing so many thousand lives and about a million of dollars a month in such a fruitless war merely for military pride. . . . This is all nonsense," the editor concluded.[97] As anticipated, by July 1864, Spain was losing—and badly. The Spanish troops that had occupied the northern port of Monte Cristi were dying of disease and exposure, and Spain's blockade had failed.[98] In September, Dominicans were never more "sanguine of their success than at present."[99] In October, it was whispered that "there [was] a probability of the cessation of hostilities."[100] Spain wanted out of the war, provided it could leave "with the maintenance of her honour in the eyes of European nations."[101] By the new year, the *Standard* was reporting on negotiations between the two countries.[102] And, in March 1865, victory was complete: "The patriotism exhibited during the last three years by the Dominicans has been gloriously rewarded and their independence successfully restored."[103] All Turks islanders celebrated.

Soon, though, the triumphs of early 1865 were overshadowed by anxiety over race relations in Henry Astwood's immediate regional sphere. Indeed, the Dominican War of Restoration (as it later became known) was only the first in a series of international events that year that provoked impassioned debate over Black people's freedom and capacity for equal rights in the region at large. The US Civil War's end in April 1865 came next, heightening angst in both the US South and North over the incorporation of free Black people into the Union.

From afar, Turks Islanders tracked the proceedings in the United States as they had with the Dominican war. The *Standard*, however, generally avoided editorializing on US political and social affairs. Salt proprietors expected that the end of the American war would make the demand for salt "very brisk" and found no need to offend would-be trading partners in the US South who, as the *Standard*'s readers learned, were "not conscious of having been in the wrong."[104] Instead, the newspaper republished articles from the United States that showed their hand.[105] For example, in "The Black Man's Own Testimony," the editor reprinted a selection from a New Orleans Black newspaper in which it was argued that "the colored man and the white man cannot live together. . . . This country is not our home."[106] The counterargument found no space in the *Standard*. Another article lambasted Black freemen who refused to work on steamboats even when offered higher wages. "It was not the wages they found fault with; they felt they were free, and because free, wanted to have a good time in spending the money they had earned."[107] The reprinting of such articles in the *Standard* revealed white Turks islanders' own anxieties over Black freedom and invoked old arguments made during the 1830s apprenticeship era: Blacks were naturally lazy, it was believed, and thus had to be taught the value of laboring for whites.[108]

Comparisons to the 1830s surfaced all the more in the aftermath of two more events that further increased racial tensions in the British Caribbean: the Black insurrection (or war) at Morant Bay, Jamaica, and the sinking of the British warship *Bulldog* by Haitian revolutionaries off the coast of Cap-Haïtien in October 1865. In making sense of the first event, the *Standard* reprinted "The Rebellions Contrasted" by Reverend James Watson, who compared the Morant Bay uprising to the 1831 slave revolt in western Jamaica known as the Baptist War.[109] Both acts of rebellion, Watson underscored, were due to "bad religion." The enslaved insurgents of 1831 had followed Black preachers, "fugitives from the discipline of the Churches" whom Watson accused of "deluding others with a religion of ignorance, obeahism, myalism, and fanaticism."[110] Similarly, in 1865, Watson explained, Morant Bay's Native Baptist preacher Paul Bogle had led an armed rebellion against British authorities. As historians have argued, Native Baptists' faith, a syncretic mix of Christian and African beliefs, lent "moral authority to an alternative world-view" that "gave a strong millennial undercurrent to their vision of political entitlement and social justice."[111] This religious worldview understood whites' oppression of Blacks as evil and armed resistance to such tyranny as righteous and just. Whites like Watson, however, perceived Black objections to social repression as "imaginary grievances" and "wickedness."[112] Watson furthermore praised the "heroic energy" and "unflinching courage" of the British militia, which by "the blessing of Almighty God," as he put it, subdued the Morant Bay rebels.[113] He additionally lauded the British authorities who massacred 439 Blacks and flogged 600 more in the aftermath of the uprising.[114]

The same authorities linked their sense of Black "evil" to Haiti, an emblem of Black freedom. There was widespread fear among whites that the Morant Bay protesters had conspired with Haitians in an attempt to create a "second Haiti."[115] This fear of Haiti was compounded when news of the *Bulldog* incident spread from Le Cap to the British Caribbean and England.[116] The affair took place in the context of the revolutionary war against Haitian president Fabre Nicolas Geffrard's government, which was friendly to British and other foreign interests. The revolutionary forces under General Sylvain Salnave controlled Cap-Haïtien and enforced a blockade. When Captain Charles Wake of the HMS *Bulldog* put his ship between the revolutionists' warcraft, the *Voldrogue*, and the object of its pursuit, the *Voldrogue* rammed into the *Bulldog*. This altercation ended with the revolutionists searching the British consulate at Le Cap for political opponents and ordering the assassination of Wake should he land there. In response, Wake decided to attack the *Voldrogue*, but his tactic backfired when the *Bulldog* got caught on a coral reef, and Wake ultimately had to abandon his ship, blowing it up in the process.

Like Watson, British officials interpreted this event in moral terms. In their view, Salnave's forces were "insolent" and "criminal" because they had challenged British colonial power and thus deserved to be punished.[117] Accordingly, the British Navy bombarded Le Cap while Geffrard attacked the revolutionary forces by land. The supposed immorality of Haitians who defied British power (even on Haitian territory) reflected a white supremacist outlook in which all Black people were considered subject to white policing.[118] Across the region, whites associated the *Bulldog* affair with the Morant Bay War and all other struggles for Black rights, and they mobilized the symbol of independent Haiti to "[warn] against black political agency."[119]

These concurrent events proved to whites that Black people could not be trusted with freedom and self-rule. Many white Turks islanders no doubt agreed. In December 1865, the *Standard* celebrated that "law and order" had been restored on Jamaica; the paper said very little about the ship down at Le Cap.[120]

It is within this context—one in which Black freedom, Black rebellion, and Black religion came under intense scrutiny in the British Caribbean—that some Turks islanders thought twice about their relationship with the now-independent Dominican nation led by armed, mixed-race men. And evidently it is also within this context that Henry Astwood's ties to the Dominican Republic strengthened as he and his family came into close connection with the same leading Dominican revolutionaries. These social ties were important because they drew Henry and his family into inter-island conversations over the Dominican Republic's future. Such discussions also necessarily signaled the era's broader debates and anxieties over Black freedom and Black civic capacity.

Dominican Connections: The Astwood Family between Grand Turk and Puerto Plata

One day in 1865, Henry braved the sea route to Puerto Plata. The voyage across the channel took less than two days if the weather was fair, but it was nonetheless known to be "of such difficult navigation" that wrecks were common in it.[121] Any anxiety or seasickness that Henry might have felt during the trip, however, is unknown. One may imagine, though, that as his schooner proceeded carefully through the choppy waters, Henry might have ruminated over the even more tempestuous times.

Henry was well informed on current affairs. From the *Standard*, he would have known all about the events taking place in Jamaica, Haiti, and the United States. He would have learned too that the Dominican Republic was undergoing problems of its own. Soon after the Spanish troops exited the country, old hierarchies ousted the War of Restoration's radical visionaries from power and installed Buenaventura Báez as president.[122] Báez, who had served as president before the annexation, had spent the war in Spain, where he was dubbed a field marshal in the Spanish army.[123] He never fought in the war. Still, Báez returned to Santo Domingo and assumed the presidency in the fall of 1865, while the most liberal leaders of the Restoration protested his rule, rebelled, and then eventually retreated. Henry traveled to Puerto Plata in the midst of this political disruption.

Once in Puerto Plata, Henry would have been privy to the city's liberal bent. The ideas circulating there included some of the country's most radical calls for national renewal. The new Dominican Constitution of November 1865, for example, instated birthright citizenship.[124] And, back in March, the Dominican Constitutional Congress had reinstituted "the liberty of conscience and tolerance of religion."[125] The townspeople now hoped that the Wesleyan missionaries would come back and rebuild their chapel and school. "Shops and dwelling houses" were already rising from the ashes in September 1865, and there were plans for more buildings on the way.[126] The port's denizens wanted their city and its trade back—and quickly. One dark spot loomed large, though. Many people in Puerto Plata believed Báez to be a traitor unfit to govern the independent republic. They wanted General Gregorio Luperón, the city's foremost Restoration leader, to be president. Or, if they could not have Luperón, they believed that at least one of his allies should rule instead of a Spanish sympathizer. This viewpoint reflected the sentiment of the city's merchant class to which Luperón and, incidentally, Henry Astwood's family held ties.

These mercantile relations hint at the connection between the Astwood family and Luperón. Although no direct correspondence from either side remains, certain coeval events made the alliance certain. First, Henry Astwood's very presence in Puerto Plata in 1865 suggests that he met the general at that time. As the son of a merchant and a customhouse worker, Henry was connected to the merchant class and "lower national petty bourgeoisie" whose interests Luperón represented.[127] Henry also likely already spoke Spanish at this point in his life, which meant that he could easily converse with Luperón whenever their paths crossed.[128] He may have even met the general's family and friends, including Ulises Heureaux, Luperón's military protégé (whose biography is further discussed in subsequent chapters).

Second, if not through their mercantile relations, Henry and Luperón would have met through their Protestant church connections. In fact, due to Henry's social position and language ability, he may have been the same person Francis Moon sent from the Turks Islands in 1865 to "see the Authorities & secure possession of the Missions lands."[129] The same man carried back to Moon a petition that evidenced the social intersections between Henry, Luperón, Heureaux, and other prominent *puertoplateños*. Written to the "Secretary and Committee of the Wesleyan Missionary Society," the letter entreated this body to reactivate its missionary work in the city. The petitioners listed three reasons for this request: (1) Puerto Plata was a center of commerce in the Gulf of Mexico and therefore qualified as "a most desirable position to be occupied and cultivated by Christian philanthropy"; (2) the public recognized the former missionary schools as "productive of great good," and Dominicans who studied in them were "heartily thankful for such a boon from enlightened Protestant liberality"; and (3) the merchant class and many Catholics had expressed their desire to "aid in reopening the mission and to assist in rebuilding the Mission premises."[130] As Moon explained, all classes, "natives and foreigners," supported the petition.[131] The signatories filled two pages with their names and went on to a third. Henry Astwood's signature appeared on the first page. Luperón's and Heureaux's followed on the second, where various other prominent figures also signed (figures 1.1 and 1.2).[132] Both war heroes, Luperón and Heureaux, were among the Dominicans who benefited from the city's missionary schools, and Heureaux held familial ties to the Wesleyans.[133] Thus, as Henry interacted with Luperón and other *puertoplateños* via his merchant networks, he also connected with them through the Protestant church, which the general public viewed as instrumental in the nation's future prosperity.

Hopes for the Wesleyans' return, however, went unfulfilled at this time. In a broader Caribbean context in which white British subjects excoriated the relationship between Black religion and Black revolt, the rebuilding of the Wesleyan mission at Puerto Plata—a majority Black congregation in an unsettled country next to stigmatized Haiti—was suspect. The secretaries of the Wesleyan Missionary Society never complied with the town's requests, and the Turks Islands' *Standard* reported very little about the progress of the Wesleyans' Dominican missionary churches.

Suspicions of Afro-Dominicans rose again in January 1866 when Luperón visited Grand Turk, where he likely met with Henry Astwood's family. At that time, white Turks islanders were still coming to terms with

FIGURE 1.1. First page of signatories to the petition to the secretary and committee of the Wesleyan Missionary Society, February 12, 1866. H. C. C. Astwood's name is tenth from the bottom in the first column.

the Morant Bay uprising. They now bristled at news of a Dominican civil war and lamented the whole island's supposed proclivity for revolution. Countering this response, one Turks islander took it upon himself to mollify those who would protest Luperón's presence. Under the pseudonym Ciudadano (Citizen), this sympathizer—who was perhaps a member of the Astwood family or Luperón himself—explained the circumstances in a letter to the *Standard*'s editor.[134] Luperón was "one of the most valiant and successful leaders" of the late revolution, Ciudadano asserted. Yet this general had been supplanted by Báez, who had abandoned the country

FIGURE 1.2. Second page of signatories to the petition to the secretary and committee of the Wesleyan Missionary Society, February 12, 1866. Ulises Heureaux's name appears at the top of the second column. Gregorio Luperón's name is third in the same column.

during the War of Restoration. Thus, understandably, some people in the Cibao had revolted. Luperón, though, had left the Dominican Republic for the Turks Islands because he preferred "expatriation to the alternative of plunging his country into a revolution."[135] In other words, white Turks islanders had no reason to fear the arrival of Luperón and his troops on their shores. To clarify, Ciudadano emphasized that he himself had "no wish to vindicate the Cibao move" but instead wrote "to counteract any wrong impressions made by designing persons respecting [Luperón's] presence in this colony."[136] Clearly, as a man visibly of African descent and a general,

Luperón would have to tread carefully on the neighboring salt islands where whites felt anxious around any leading Black man wielding political power, whether with a Bible or a gun.

Despite growing local suspicion of the Dominican Republic on Grand Turk, the Astwood family continued to deepen their ties to Luperón and the Dominican nation. Henry's 1866 marriage provides another key example. On March 21 of that year, Henry exchanged vows with Margaret Julia Francisco, a Dominican woman from Puerto Plata.[137] Margaret likely was a relative of Julián Francisco, a military captain who had fought with Luperón in the War of Restoration.[138] In the Turks Islands, though, she was identified as the granddaughter of Madame Francisco, a woman of European features and also of Dominican descent.[139] The young couple wed in Madame Francisco's house on Grand Turk Island in the presence of their relatives and friends. Henry's cousin John T. Astwood, the son of the prominent William T. Astwood, served as witness alongside Margaret's relative Charles Francisco. Various friends surrounded them on their wedding day. Luperón may have attended the ceremony, since he was in town at the time and probably already connected to the family.[140] The wedding guests additionally included one Elizabeth Jane Pardo, likely accompanied by her shopkeeper husband Federico Pardo and seven-year-old daughter Theresa.[141] Federico was from the Danish Caribbean (possibly St. Thomas), but owned property in Puerto Plata.[142]

The links between the newlyweds and the Dominican Republic strengthened all the more when, a month after their wedding, Henry received goods from Puerto Plata on the schooner *Dreadnot*.[143] That same day, the *Dreadnot* cleared Grand Turk for Puerto Plata with 113 bushels of salt. Henry and Margaret sailed with the saline load, while General Luperón and his entourage traveled back to their home in the *Elizabeth*.[144] A few years later, the newlyweds would welcome their first child, Mildred Julia Astwood, born in the Dominican Republic, into their expanding interisland world.

Henry's father, Adolphus, also became closely affiliated with Luperón and the Dominican government in these years. A few weeks after Henry and Margaret departed Cockburn Town for Puerto Plata, a notice appeared in the *Standard* listing Adolphus as the "Commercial Agent of the Dominican Republic" on Grand Turk.[145] This role made Adolphus the primary spokesperson on Grand Turk for Luperón, who, after returning home, became the governor of Puerto Plata. Adolphus's labor in this capacity, however, was unsanctioned by the British government. Indeed, as one anonymous editorialist complained, "Under the title of 'Commercial Agent' a gentleman exercises his functions in the Turks Islands for the ports of the Dominican Republic; he certifies invoices, grants passports and visas, and all this without having obtained up to the moment, the exequatur of Her Majesty the Queen."[146] The official-unofficial nature of Adolphus's role, however, points to both the Dominican government's urgent need for such work and the fact that Luperón trusted Adolphus to deal fairly (or at least in the Dominican Republic's favor) in interisland trade.

It also suggests the broader anxieties at play over race. In 1866, the Dominican government needed income. The mandate that Adolphus upheld required all persons shipping cargo from the Turks Islands to first gain an invoice of verification and passport from Adolphus.[147] By imposing these regulations via their agent on Grand Turk, Luperón and other officials in Puerto Plata aimed to curtail smuggling and thereby increase customs revenue. Shipmasters who did not comply with the law would be treated as smugglers, and their crafts would be confiscated, Adolphus warned the public.[148] Although not stated explicitly, these terms were also a way to protect Black Dominican denizens from kidnappers who sought to enrich themselves through the clandestine slave trade. People living on Hispaniola's northern coast were hyperaware of such danger. In the prior decade, freebooters had staked out in the Turks Islands with designs to conquer Puerto Plata and reenslave its people.[149] And even after the War of Restoration had ended in 1865, a Spanish warship had captured a Turks Islands crew who were never heard of again.[150] Adolphus's work thus provided extra security for both the Dominican government and the African-descendant people (like Henry, Margaret, and even Luperón and his men) traveling between the two locales.

Unsurprisingly, though, the increased regulation did not sit well with some Turks islanders. The editorialist, for one, interpreted the unsanctioned consulship as a part of a slew of crimes Dominicans had allegedly perpetrated against foreigners in Puerto Plata ever since the end of the War of Restoration. Dominicans who declared "we have beaten the whites" needed to learn respect, the writer intimated: "They overlook the past that if they did whip the whites, they were but Spaniards."[151] This telling statement reflected the prevalent racist and anti-Catholic notion among Anglo-Saxon Britons (and later Americans too) that their version of colonialism was somehow better—more robust in defining race relations and therefore more principled—than Spain's.

Joseph Hutchings, the *Standard*'s editor, concurred. Although Hutchings admitted that at first he had found the editorialist's statements to be "overdrawn," upon second thought he was thoroughly convinced.[152] To the *Standard*, the battles between the various Dominican generals (Báez, Luperón, and others) had turned tiresome. Furthermore, the editorialist delineated other problems: the ambitions of lowly Dominican soldiers who wanted places in government; the generals' need to pay their troops and the consequent overprinting of paper money; the inflation of Dominican currency; and the ill treatment of foreigners and consuls. Calling upon "law and order" as in the case of Morant Bay, Hutchings now expressed a wish for the Dominican "mob" to be "put down" and peace restored throughout the republic so that "Trade and Commerce—the hand-maidens of civilization—[could resume] their proper and legitimate sphere."[153] These words sent a clear message. The problem with the Dominican Republic in 1866, as white Turks islanders saw it, was that the country had turned into a "revolutionary republic" like Haiti. And, instead of bowing to foreign capital, it imposed trade regulations that white British subjects judged worse than Haitian policy.[154] What the republic needed, in this view, was a strong authoritarian leader or, better yet, a strong colonial force. The British could not do it, but perhaps the Americans would step in. In any case, the point was this: for many white Turks islanders, the broader currents of social change in 1865 demanded a skeptical approach to any future reciprocal exchange with Dominican leaders and the whole island's majority African-descendant population.

Nevertheless, for the newlyweds and the uncertified consul, the cranky gripes of naysayers probably mattered little in the spring of 1866. Indeed, this moment was a time of hope centered on Dominican territory. Henry and his father had made friends with the Dominican Republic's leading men. Adolphus controlled all exports from the Turks Islands to Puerto Plata as the Dominican commercial agent, a role that surely had its kickbacks. And, if all went well, Margaret could count on future financial and political stability in a land that was her original home. In September that same year, Luperón's liberal forces triumphed over Báez, and Luperón's ally General José María Cabral became president.[155] Luperón subsequently returned home to family and friends in Puerto Plata. Henry and Margaret may have joined others in the welcome party. The atmosphere all around seemed optimistic. It was, once again, merely the calm before the storm.

Conclusion

Henry Astwood grew up in a context that was hostile for Black and mixed-race people. He was born into a time when slavery, albeit abolished in the British Caribbean, still existed in Cuba, Puerto Rico, the United States, and Brazil. On his birth island of Salt Cay, Black people continued to endure the agonizing pain of labor in the salt ponds. Very few salt rakers escaped poverty, and, faced with starvation, many of them fled to Hispaniola. Such migration, while precipitated by economic necessity at midcentury, also formed part of Black people's historic quest for Black freedom and sovereignty. It was to Haiti, after all, that escaped bondspeople sailed in the decades after 1804.

The pattern of Turks islanders' immigration to Hispaniola intensified again in the 1860s when the quest for Black freedom and self-determination came under renewed attack in the British Caribbean and elsewhere. As race wars erupted in the United States, the Dominican Republic, and Jamaica, and civil war continued in Haiti, whites across the region questioned the civic capacity of Black people and warned against Black political authority. Turks islanders were hyperaware of these events, dependent as they were on US and interisland trade. And while there were some triumphs for African descendants such as abolition in the United States and Dominican independence, the conclusion that white British subjects drew about these events by and large did not bode well for Black Turks islanders. To whites, the multiple race wars and the sustained political instability in Haiti and the Dominican Republic proved what they had believed all along: Black people were unfit for equal social rights, let alone self-rule.

Henry knew what the white people around him thought about his color. However, it might also be said that he never accepted the labels and limitations that white society placed upon him. In time, he would come to use his background to his advantage.

The hostile Caribbean milieu from which Henry emerged was instructive. Due to multiple silences in the historical record, it is impossible to determine exactly what Henry thought about the various regional wars and social upheavals of the 1860s. Later in life, Henry spoke little of these political developments, and he kept all details of his early life closely guarded. Yet these events undoubtedly affected his political outlook and later opportunities. Most obviously, Astwood's presence in the Turks Islands and Puerto Plata during critical political moments made him acutely aware of the Dominican Republic's place in regional geopolitics as well as its national state of affairs. He additionally knew much about how such politics affected Dominican macroeconomics, interisland trade, and customs revenue. It was also in Puerto Plata that Astwood interacted with various Dominican leaders, including Gregorio Luperón and Ulises Heureaux, for the first time. It was here as well that he socialized with various Anglophone Dominican denizens, including African American immigrants. And, as discussed in chapter 2, it is through these relationships that Henry not only first joined the Wesleyan church and other religious and civic organizations but also came to learn how to navigate the various racial and political regimes that shaped his world.

2

A RECONSTRUCTED LIFE

Becoming H. C. C. Astwood in the US-Caribbean Sphere

The sun rose on September 30, 1866, like any other day that year in the Turks and Caicos Islands. With the colony prospering, hopes ran high for the future. Recent months had brought a large production of salt and a surplus in the government's treasury.[1] But by afternoon, a sudden wind picked up, pushing dark clouds toward shore. Sheets of rain descended. Gales shot shingles, water tanks, and loose branches into the air, dropping them only to hoist them again. Whole houses and government buildings blew over like sticks, adding to the debris. The Wesleyan minister and his family on Grand Turk took shelter in the corner of the mission house while water gushed everywhere else. Meanwhile, sixty families found refuge in the Wesleyan chapel on Salt Cay, but others were less fortunate.[2] In the breadth of one night, lives and livelihoods were destroyed. The people were left in shock. "From the greatest prosperity we change to the deep-est adversity," the *Standard* lamented.[3] Of the 4,331 inhabitants on the is-lands, 21 people were killed and 236 injured. On Grand Turk, 362 of the 546 houses were leveled, and all 153 water tanks were impaired.[4] On Salt Cay, 98 of 181 houses and all 66 water tanks were down. The estimated property damage to the Turks and Caicos totaled £74,589 (£7,346,451 in 2021). No family escaped the tribulation. Even the oldest inhabitants of the island could not remember a more severe storm than the hurricane of 1866.[5]

Left destitute after the storm, Turks islanders once again fled to Puerto Plata. Despite hope for a new life in the Dominican Republic, however, their settlement in the town took place within the context of renewed political turmoil on the island and elsewhere. In the Spanish Caribbean, people took up arms to protect themselves against colonial rule. While a second annexation scheme—this time to the United States—portended more bloodshed in the Dominican Republic, Cuba and Puerto Rico re-belled against Spain. Haiti too was soon engulfed in war. Turks islanders witnessed as liberal-minded Dominicans, Haitians, Cubans, and Puerto Ricans forged alliances, joining forces against US annexation and to sup-port Haitian, Cuban, and Puerto Rican revolutionaries. Meanwhile in the United States, Radical Reconstruction initiated a short-lived American ex-periment in racial democracy that saw the election of hundreds of Black men to state and federal office as the nation sought to unify North and South. For this advancement, Black families paid a hefty price in lives lost during the subsequent scourge of white "redemption." Still, US Blacks ad-vocated for equal treatment under federal and state laws. Afro-descendants throughout the hemisphere also championed abolition in remaining slave territories as they self-organized and claimed political belonging within Europhile societies.[6]

Within this tempestuous context, where natural disasters and wide-spread resistance to colonial and racial oppression pushed people across borders, Henry Astwood dreamed of a brighter future for himself. Whereas only a decade before his birth, Henry's enslaved progenitors would have faced death if their hopes for freedom were betrayed, by the late 1860s Henry could pursue fresh opportunities: marriage to a light-skinned Black woman, migration to new lands, involvement in progressive racial politics, ordination in a Black church, attainment of prestige and wealth. These possibilities drew closer for an enterprising mixed-race man like Henry as they became realities for a few other people of color in his US-Caribbean sphere.[7]

After the 1866 storm, Henry migrated between four Caribbean ports: Grand Turk, Puerto Plata, Samaná, and New Orleans. In each place, he not only learned about the era's tumultuous political context but also witnessed how people of color forged multiethnic networks of political, commercial, and religious varieties in order to survive and because they believed in the possibility of change. Henry observed such activism not as a disinterested bystander but as an active participant and quick study at local and regional racial power structures. Knowledge gained at each locale applied to the next, so that by the time Henry reached New Orleans, he was able to swiftly cultivate ties with powerful heads of political groups, churches, fraternal societies, and newspapers. Across locales, he did whatever it took to lift himself up, even at the cost of his family and friends. Henry's life trajectory demonstrates his unyielding ambition as he navigated varying political and racial regimes, never sticking to just one racial or ethnic identity. It also reveals the set of debates, ideologies, and institutions—such as US expansionism, *antillanismo*, Freemasonry, US Republican Party politics, and Protestant churches—that characterized his world and that would later impact his consulship in Santo Domingo.

In the Midst of the Storm: Survival and Resistance in the Turks Islands and Puerto Plata

The months immediately following the 1866 hurricane brought some relief to the Turks Islands as initial acts of solidarity met the trauma head-on. The government opened a soup kitchen for the destitute, and a Relief Committee assessed the damage.[8] Meanwhile, carpenters and other day workers set about reconstructing buildings.[9] Within weeks, vessels brought food, clothing, and money from abroad. Gregorio Luperón and other authorities at Puerto Plata sent flour and fruit via Adolphus Astwood (Henry's father) on Grand Turk, who then turned them over to the Relief Committee for immediate distribution to the poor.[10] The Dominican port authority at Puerto Plata also suspended tonnage dues for vessels from the Turks Islands to lessen the burden on merchants. Then, in November, packages of clothing and food arrived from St. Thomas and £500 worth of supplies were brought in from Barbados.[11] Any goods not of immediate use were sold at auction to buy building materials. News of the disaster did not reach England until November, too late for public institutions to respond in 1866, but private individuals sent "liberal" contributions and pledged more donations.[12] By December, news of the hurricane was published in every British colony, and it was hoped that more aid would arrive quickly.

Too soon, though, unity gave way to competition, animosity, and more grief. By the new year, a sense of desperation set in. People were dying from disease and exposure; there was no shelter, clothing, or food for those in despair.[13] Salt proprietors were also in a bad way, as the hurricane had proved a great social equalizer. Merchants' boats were lost or damaged. Salt bags, supplies, warehouses, and docks were destroyed. "Those who are engaged in the shipping business have either lost their houses or they are so much injured that they consider it their first duty to secure a shelter for themselves and families," the *Standard* reported.[14] However, while the hurricane was no respecter of persons, relief was not equally distributed. By January 1867, the government no longer offered assistance to poverty-stricken islanders.[15] The *Standard* accused some impoverished individuals of bartering their soup kitchen tickets and clothes for booze and admonished the dealers in spirits "not [to] encourage such a gross perversion of the charity which has been granted to these unfortunate people."[16] Such accusations betrayed white elites' stereotypes of Black people and overall distaste for government handouts. Yet suspicions ran high of the Relief Committee and government authorities too. Wesleyan ministers complained that the committee had unjustly rejected the denomination's application for aid.[17] Adolphus wrote to set the record straight regarding the Dominican relief funds; he had remitted £63.15 to the committee, of which only £35 was later publicly reported.[18] Next, a fire scare brought public scorn upon officials who did not act quickly enough to quash the flames.[19] The same came under renewed attack in February and March as water supplies on the islands ran impossibly low; nearly every tank in the island was dry due to the hurricane.[20] The people were frantic and angry. In an act of defiant desperation, someone at last broke into the new iron building where the Relief Committee met; stole the tribunal's day book, cash book, and ledger; and scattered all the other papers and vouchers across the room. The population was so fed up with the poor distribution of relief that no one turned the person in—not even for a £250 reward.[21] For Black and mixed-race islanders such as Henry, it was clear that white elites had exploited public funds to secure their private holdings, leaving the Black underclass to fend for themselves.

As a family caught between racial castes, the Astwoods experienced both sides of the mounting drama, and, like other Turks islanders, they did all they could to stem their own losses. In 1866, however, circumstances were so much worse than any difficulty they had encountered before. Not only had racial and class tensions reached a zenith, but the Astwoods had also suffered combined losses that left them in ruins. At Cockburn Town, Adolphus's damages summed to £200, and included one house, one water tank, three outhouses, 3,000 bushels of salt, and clothing.[22] On Salt Cay, the family lost their home, one outhouse, one tank, one boat, one abutment, and 25,000 bushels of salt.[23] The Salt Cay losses amounted to £300. As a small salt proprietor, there was no way for Adolphus to sustain this blow.

Attempts to generate income proved futile. By February 1867, Henry had returned to Grand Turk to help. He set up shop as a tailor in the house of one Madame Glass located behind the *Standard*'s office, and ran an ad for the next few weeks.[24] Yet by May that year he was charged with debt, and by 1868 he had returned to Puerto Plata, where another ad for tailoring appeared.[25] Adolphus, too, attempted to generate income and salvage his business. He maintained his role as commercial agent of the Dominican Republic through at least midyear.[26] He also continued trade with Puerto Plata in April and October, despite increased danger that year due to political unrest in the Dominican Republic.[27] By November 1867, though, Adolphus was caught up in legal battles, and by February 1868 he was no longer the Dominican agent.[28] Worse still for the Astwoods, a large portion of Adolphus's property was soon confiscated by the courts for outstanding debts.[29] Adjacent to the *Standard*'s advertisement on February 29, 1868, for the new Dominican representative, John C. Bremer Jr., appeared the notice of sale for A. J. Astwood's multiple homes and titles to lots in the salt pond Gray's Salina. For the Astwoods of Turks Islands, this signaled the beginning of the end.

While the Astwoods and other Turks islanders struggled to make ends meet, their friends on Hispaniola faced turmoil of another kind. In Haiti, the struggle between generals Geffrard and Salnave continued. Turks islanders witnessed as several Haitians, including General Salnave, sought asylum on Grand Turk in February 1867 even though the island had nothing to offer after the hurricane.[30] The exiles returned the following month to Cap-Haïtien after their forces made Geffrard abdicate, and in June that year Salnave was elected president.[31] Things were quiet for a few months, but Salnave soon imposed a dictatorship, and by 1868 civil war ensued.[32]

Meanwhile, whispers of a Dominican war surfaced in Grand Turk in September 1867. General Buenaventura Báez was said to be organizing forces against President José María Cabral while in exile at Curaçao.[33] Rumors spread quickly. In November, it was alleged that Cabral had sold the Samaná Peninsula to the United States.[34] Báez's party, popular among impoverished Dominicans, benefited from this news and the additional accusation that Cabral had abused Haitian refugees.[35] It was also rumored that Cabral would start a war with Haiti to distract the masses from the coming conflict with Báez. No one thought that Cabral would succeed in this campaign; there was at least one Dominican party in the interior that still wished to reunite with the Black republic.[36] Then, as expected, Báez's forces mobilized and the fighting began. Soon, Santiago was in ruins, and people in Puerto Plata were once again heading for the Turks Islands.[37] This time, though, the Turks Islands government refused to take any "destitute" foreigners.[38] Luperón, who protested the "inhumane" measure, was excluded from this category.[39] The now ex-governor of Puerto Plata arrived on Grand Turk in December 1867—just as the Astwoods' world came crashing down.[40]

Over the next three years, 1868–70, two opposing forces emerged within Henry's Caribbean sphere. First, Turks islanders avidly followed news regarding the United States' attempts to acquire Dominican territory. In May 1868, Báez regained government control and established a dictatorship. He then sought to sell or lease Samaná to the United States, even though his political party had criticized Cabral for doing the same thing.[41] A year later, it seemed that a lease would go through, and the *Standard* repeated the widespread belief that after Samaná, the United States would soon annex all of Hispaniola "as a matter of course."[42] The year 1870 brought even more news: a US warship headed from Puerto Plata to Cap-Haïtien in January warned Haitians that the Dominican Republic was now under US protection, and any aggression from Haiti would be cause for retaliation.[43] Soon after this, it was said that the US Congress would consider Báez's petition to annex the whole republic.[44] By April 1870, Turks islanders felt "some little curiosity, not unmixed with anxiety" as they waited along with Dominicans for the US Congress's answer to the annexation bid.[45]

Turks islanders also kept close tabs on the counterforce: a regional anticolonial movement known as *antillanismo* that sought cross-island cooperation in defense of Dominican and Haitian sovereignty and Cuban and Puerto Rican independence. Proponents of this movement advocated for a confederation of these islands.[46] Luperón, a chief advocate of *antillanismo* and the Antillean Confederation, believed that the Dominican struggle against US annexation was part of a broader regional effort against European and American colonialism.[47] He and his allies also rallied behind Cuban revolutionaries as Cubans launched an attack against Spain's colonial government just a few months after Báez's inauguration in 1868.[48] Puerto Rican freedom fighters, such as Emeterio Betances, joined the Dominican and Cuban efforts in hopes that freeing these lands would mean the same for Puerto Rico.[49] Meanwhile, Haitians fought with Dominicans against Báez, and Luperón and Cabral supported the Haitian general Jean-Nicolas Nissage Saget and other liberals in their battle against Salnave.[50] In the end, all sides were against the United States entering the Caribbean. In 1869, for example, the Dominican generals Luperón, Cabral, and Pedro Antonio Pimentel met with Saget and Betances in St. Thomas, where they signed a contract to fight the proposed US annexation.[51] All the while, Turks islanders kept track of Luperón via the *Standard* as he and other Dominican generals moved in and out of Grand Turk, one of the various Caribbean ports where they sought asylum and regrouped.[52]

Sentiments about the Dominican Republic varied on Grand Turk. Undoubtedly, some Turks islanders hoped that Luperón would prevail in his fight against Báez. As a measure of the governing class's opinion, however, the *Standard* leaned in favor of Báez and US annexation, although it ostensibly claimed neutrality. The reason was simple: many white Turks islanders believed that Báez and the annexation would bring political stability, which was good for business.[53] Thus, although the *Standard* confessed bewilderment at Dominicans' alleged eagerness for US annexation, the paper ultimately supported the cause.[54] Accordingly, the paper regarded the July 1869 appearance of Luperón's warship *Telegraph* off the coast of Puerto Plata as ominous.[55] And, with respect to the Antillean Confederation, the *Standard* implied that such a conglomerate could be imagined only if under US or European control. "Shall St. Domingo lead the van in adding the three Antilles to the United States, or shall it take position as the nucleus of a free trade confederation under European patronage?" asked the *New York Herald* regarding the Dominican Republic, Haiti, and Cuba.[56] The *Standard* ran the reprint without comment.

At the same time that these oppositional forces circulated in Henry's environs, the Astwood family's financial crisis intensified. The Turks Islands' economic state had not improved in the years after the hurricane, and in November 1869, Adolphus attended a public meeting hosted by the colony's elected council to assess the situation. Both exports and imports pointed to distress: the salt crop had fallen short two years in a row, and provisions remained in short supply.[57] Grand Turk was dependent upon ships from the United States, as the trade with Haiti and the Dominican Republic was sporadic due to ongoing conflicts. Of greatest concern to officials, the colony's coffers showed a deficit. The meeting's purpose was to consult with constituents regarding the best measures for raising revenue to make up the 1869 losses and the anticipated deficit in 1870. Adolphus and the other attendees unanimously voted against raising taxes, fearing the kind of unrest rocking the colony's neighbors. "Neither a property tax nor a further increase of the import duties would be quietly submitted to," warned the council.[58] Instead, Adolphus and others voted that the council should seek a loan from a private bank or the Crown fund.[59]

Such a loan, however, would not save Adolphus's business assets. In July 1870, he lost the rights to a half lot of pond in the Red Salinas on Grand Turk due to debt.[60] Then, unexpectedly, he lost his son George to death.[61] Later in life, Henry remembered the grief surrounding George's death as the impetus for the family's departure from Grand Turk.[62] Financial ruin, however, compounded the loss and served as a second compelling push factor. So broke were the Astwoods that at the point of George's death, the family could not even afford to publish a proper notice in the *Standard*. Then, in October and November 1870, liquidation ads ran for the family's remaining property, which included a house on Salt Cay and all the furniture, silver plateware, and books therein.[63] All persons with demands against Adolphus or his firm were advised to make their claims on or before November 2 as the family declared its intention to move to Puerto Plata.[64]

The Astwoods' intended move to Puerto Plata mirrored the path of so many other Turks islanders displaced by the 1866 hurricane and its aftermath. As stated above, immigration from the Turks Islands to Hispaniola's northern coast ballooned after the storm. New immigrants joined the hundreds of Turks islanders who already lived in the section known as *Turkilancito* (Little Turks Islands).[65] This community included many of the Astwoods' friends. The Pardos, for instance, had also met tragedy in these years. During the hurricane, the household of eight lost one tank, one outhouse, and sustained £40 worth of damage to their home.[66] Then, in 1871, eleven-year-old Theresa, like George Astwood, passed away.[67] The Pardo family, like so many others, subsequently migrated to Puerto Plata.

Despite the context of yet another exodus from the Turks Islands, it seems that Adolphus and one of his daughters ultimately did not leave home.[68] Puerto Plata's 1871 census listed only one male head of household with the last name Astwood. That man was "Enrique" (Henry).[69] That year, Henry was living in the city's La Marina barrio. His tailoring work provided for six people: his wife, Margarita (Margaret); their three-year-old daughter, Mildred; their newest baby, Miriam; Margaret's mother; and two more minors, Alonzo Rodríguez (age twelve) and Cristina Evertz (age ten). It is unknown whether these children were members of the family or servants in the Astwoods' Dominican home.[70] One year later, on June 26, 1872, the Astwoods' first son, George Adolphus, joined the household, increasing Henry's financial responsibilities and seemingly binding him and the family all the more to Puerto Plata.[71]

In the early 1870s, Henry and Margaret's family might have served as a poetic metaphor for the place and time in which they lived. Still undergoing reconstruction, Puerto Plata, like the Astwoods' union, was a multiethnic fusion just emerging from tragedy and advancing, hopefully, toward a new but still uncertain future. There were signs of progress. Puerto Plata's streets were illuminated with public gas lighting for the first time in 1872.[72] It was the only Dominican city to do so in a country where the War of Restoration had stymied technological advancement. Puerto Plata's principal commercial street ran from the wharf through the center of town, past newly constructed one- and two-story whitewashed wood buildings, including the customhouse and post office.[73] Within a few more steps stood the American and British consulates.[74] The Wesleyan chapel still lay in ruins, but forty-eight society members had collected community funds to erect a wooden shelter where they worshiped.[75]

Puerto Plata also teemed with renewed ethnic diversity when the Astwoods set down roots there. In addition to increased immigration from the British and Danish islands, African American immigrants returned home after the Spanish annexation.[76] Germans, Italians, Spanish, and French merchants came back too in these years, as did vendors from Venezuela, Curaçao, and New Orleans. Soon, upward of four thousand Cuban exiles of the Ten Years' War poured into the city and settled the sector known as Cuba Libre.[77] Cubans and other new settlers found strength in the regional alliances that transformed Puerto Plata into a nucleus of circum-Caribbean *antillanismo* activism that was fiercely anticolonial, resolutely antislavery, and ostensibly color-blind.

Although interethnic alliances did not invert the city's racial and class hierarchies, *antillanismo* ideology did occasion various forms of socialization between Dominicans and Anglophone Protestant migrants like Henry. Along with the Wesleyan school and church, social contact took place through civic events and Masonic brotherhoods. For example, on June 26, 1872, the Wesleyan congregation in Puerto Plata hosted a tea meeting for the purpose of raising money for children's education. One Mr. Castillo hosted the meeting in his home while Rev. Thomas Lawson of Grand Turk presided over the presentation of lectures and songs. Members of Dominican high society attended and gave speeches, including the editor of the newspaper *El Porvenir*. The same later asserted that such tea meetings should become customary (*aclimatarse*) in Puerto Plata because of their progressive goals.[78] Henry Astwood, who had sold tickets for the meeting, also presented a speech, as did Federico Pardo.[79]

Other social connections were forged among men who became Freemasons. In Puerto Plata, many civil servants were Masons. Henry grew closer to such men through his own membership in the organization; he joined the Grand Turk Free Mason lodge in April 1871.[80] Masonic lodges not only provided space for social interaction across ethnic, racial, linguistic, and religious differences, but also enabled specific Antillean political visions of liberty and progress. As posited by Jossianna Arroyo, "for Afro-Caribbean men to belong to Masonic ranks meant building new strategies for freedom."[81] Such freedom strategies reinforced a hopeful view of regional racial politics and helped shape a liberal nationalist ideology that imagined more racially inclusive futures for the Dominican nation and the Antilles at large.

Hope, however, was fragile. Like the infant nation itself, it was to be nurtured and defended against the imminent threats that promptly arrived at the republic's doorstep. In the early 1870s, the Astwoods' new hometown seemed to be under constant siege. Besides smallpox and conflagration scares, war was ever present, as Puerto Plata was the center of resistance against Báez and US annexation.[82] It was off the coast of Puerto Plata that Luperón's *Telegraph* had attacked Báez's forces in 1869.[83] A year later, *puertoplateños* rebelled against Báez again in protest of "the change of their flag" to that of the United States.[84] The insurrection failed, however, and Báez's negotiations with US president Ulysses S. Grant continued. Even the US Commission of Inquiry to Santo Domingo, which Grant sent to survey Dominicans' desire for annexation, noted the city's dissent. The commission, which visited Puerto Plata in February 1871, reported that lower-class Black Dominicans still believed that they would be sold into slavery if the annexation were to occur.[85] Evidently, despite the United States' emancipation of enslaved people during the US Civil War, many *puertoplateños* still did not trust the United States to uphold abolition. Their skepticism proved well placed. With news of anti-Black crimes committed with impunity across the US South and slavery still intact in Cuba and Puerto Rico, Dominicans had no reason to trust that the United States would deal fairly with them once Báez betrayed the nation. A cabal with Americans could just as readily mean the expansion of America's racial model into the republic.

Henry and Margaret Astwood were most likely present for the US commission's visit to Puerto Plata in 1871, although their thoughts on the annexation proposal remain unknown. It is conceivable that, due to their connections to Luperón and their familial and social relations in Puerto Plata, they were against the annexation. They may have even participated in public dissent. It is plausible, however, that at least Henry, like other merchants from the Turks Islands, believed that Báez's regime would improve business relations. If so, Henry may have resented Luperón's campaign. Whatever the case, it is in any event clear that Henry and Margaret were privy to the full spectrum of Dominicans' sentiments on the measure. While people in Puerto Plata objected, opinion was not uniform across the island. Just one hundred miles east of Puerto Plata, the opposite sentiment prevailed in the town of Santa Bárbara de Samaná (known simply as Samaná), where the Astwoods moved circa 1873.[86]

What the White Folks Did Not See: Samaná Americans and the Invisible Institution

Like Puerto Plata, Samaná was a historic port on the northern side of Hispaniola, though this scenic town on the Samaná Peninsula remained a small fishing community whose geopolitical significance to the United States outweighed its economic import. The United States had long coveted the peninsula and its bay. In the years immediately following Dominican independence, US agents sought to use Samaná Bay as a naval port and coaling station.[87] Such designs continued in the 1850s and '60s when US filibusters William and Jane Cazneau arrived on the island and planned to lease the peninsula; European powers sent warships to impede the transaction.[88] Later, after the War of Restoration, Cabral and then Báez used the potential lease of Samaná as a bargaining chip in their negotiations for US support of their respective administrations.[89] In 1869, Grant paid nearly $150,000 with secret discretionary funds for a lease in 1870, but this scheme lasted only a year, since the US Senate never approved the measure.[90] Then in 1873, the Samaná Bay Company, a private American enterprise with direct ties to President Grant and other US government officials, assumed control of the bay with terms similar to those offered previously by the US government, making clear the close-knit partnership between US governmental and commercial power in the region.[91] Though the Samaná Bay Company defaulted on its ninety-nine-year lease, the bay remained a strategic port that the Dominican government used as an incentive to attract

US and European investment and protection for the rest of the century and into the next.[92]

Samaná's large population of African American immigrants was a second reason why US agents felt drawn to the region. This community began when hundreds of US Black émigrés responded to Haitian president Jean-Pierre Boyer's 1824 invitation to migrate to Haiti and settled in the town and its surrounding hills.[93] In the following decades, African Americans maintained their use of English—even while the second generation learned Kreyòl and Spanish. They also reinforced group cohesion through Protestant religion, and, as in Puerto Plata, British Wesleyans established a mission among them.[94] Thus, in the late 1860s and '70s, African American immigrants (who represented the peninsula's majority population) were legible to white US agents through these cultural traits.[95] Agents from the United States who wished to lease or annex the republic, moreover, saw these immigrants as a model for their plans of sending freed African Americans to the Dominican Republic before and after the US Civil War.[96]

Although no surviving documents describe the Astwoods' time in Samaná, these US designs for the region shaped Henry's experiences on the peninsula. Indeed, the fact that he arrived in Samaná in 1873 suggests that Henry may have had ties to the Samaná Bay Company or plans to forge the same. Henry furthermore would have socialized with US Black immigrants through the town's Wesleyan church. Yet, unlike the white US agents and British missionaries whose observations have dominated the written historical record, Henry experienced Samaná as a poor person of color. His outlook thus aligned more closely with the town's US Black immigrant community than with white foreigners.

The same immigrant community possessed a unique religio-racial identity.[97] Prior to their arrival in Samaná, many first-generation immigrants had been members of the independent Black African Methodist Episcopal (AME) denomination in the United States. This religious heritage continued to hold significance for the community even after they transferred their church to the British Wesleyan missionary society in 1838 and remained officially under British leadership thereafter. Since British missionaries visited the community only intermittently, local Black preachers routinely led religious services and maintained African American traditions and traits, such as preaching styles, spirituals, and hymns.[98] In 1873, the immigrant Jacob James led the community of over five hundred people, who felt "perfectly satisfied" that one of their own was appointed to the mission.[99] At fifty-one years old, James reportedly neglected his own homestead for the missionary work in which he served as the preacher for two churches (one in town and the other in the country); held services all day on Sundays in town; ran a Sabbath school that had ninety-nine students and twelve teachers; and generally settled disputes between townspeople.[100] Thus, in contrast with Puerto Plata, where British missionaries were stationed more regularly before the Spanish annexation, the Samaná Wesleyan mission was self-consciously a Black religious space that functioned semiautonomously and formed the basis of African American immigrants' distinct cultural identity.

At the same time, though, US Black immigrants like James negotiated various boundaries of belonging by existing in multiple registers, where they made themselves both legible and illegible to outsiders. As Henry witnessed firsthand, African American immigrants and their Protestant churches in Samaná, as in Puerto Plata, formed a significant part of the region's social milieu, and both individuals and collectives were able to choose when to stress their various subject positions. These facts challenge the prevailing scholarship regarding the Samaná immigrants, which overemphasizes the community's US culture and understates its adaptive strategies.[101] Yet highlighting the community's social embeddedness more accurately reflects both the context from which Henry emerged and the ways that Black Protestantism formed a constitutive part of the era's antiracist (albeit not always anticolonial) freedom struggles.

Jacob James's 1871 interview with the US commission serves as a prime example of the strategic ways that African American immigrants positioned themselves. During the interview, James declared his community racially Black and ethnically American, and drew a further distinction between Samaná and Puerto Plata. "We are all colored people. I am full black," he claimed before adding, "We try to keep our people together here as Americans so that they shall not fall away into the ways of the natives and almost become natives, as they have done too much at Puerto Plata, where they are all mixed up."[102] At face value, this characterization excluded the community from the Dominican Republic's body politic, reifying a distinction that scholars have since preserved.[103] Reading James's words within the context of his whole comments, however, paints a different picture. As Henry would have learned, African American immigrants in Samaná supported US annexation because they believed that US race relations had improved and that the Dominican Republic would become another state of the union.[104] Both Frederick Douglass and his son Charles R. Douglass had assured them of that when the pair traveled with the US Commission of

Inquiry.[105] Furthermore, between 1868 and 1870, new US Black emigrants had settled in Samaná, bringing firsthand experience of social transformations in the United States and the hope, not yet dashed, of Radical Reconstruction.[106] Thus, immigrants like James considered US annexation an alternative to the ideal of self-government. "If this republic could have a government of its own we would be glad," James explained, "but this needs to be rearranged and reconstructed."[107] Within this context, James's identity claims reveal one of the myriad strategies that some Dominicans used to avoid war and conscription, promote commerce, and further personal and communal welfare—even at the cost of sovereignty. This is not to say that James misrepresented himself and his community to the commissioners, but rather that he purposefully chose which details to emphasize.

Other documents from the era suggest that the Samaná congregation was much more embedded in Dominican society than James let on. Indeed, for decades, Protestant immigrants had interacted with Catholic Dominicans and Haitians at various levels of intimacy, creating a sense of "common destiny" for people who considered the island home.[108] Throughout the nineteenth century, for example, trade relations, patronage ties, and military service mitigated (albeit did not eliminate) animosity between Catholics and Protestants living in close proximity. Intermarriage and extramarital sexual relations between these groups also occurred, although the frequency of such unions varied between the two locales and is difficult to ascertain.[109] Yet even in Samaná, where the people avoided mixing, according to James, such unions still occurred, and more consistently so over time.[110] The Samaná Wesleyan mission furthermore served a mixed community. Although the majority of its 235 baptized members in 1873 were of African American descent, James reported that "some *natives* and English folk" had joined the congregation that year.[111] Wesleyan records also show that a few Catholic Dominicans, Haitians, and Cuban émigrés in Puerto Plata also converted to Protestantism during this period.[112] Although converts faced excommunication and social ostracization, these anomalies matter. Their existence shows that Protestant churches provided yet another vector for cross-ethnic Antillean social interaction and cooperation.

The Dominican government also recognized Black Protestants as part of the republic's social fabric. As discussed in chapter 1, nationalist leaders Gregorio Luperón and Ulises Heureaux were educated at the Wesleyan missionary school in Puerto Plata and signed a petition for the Wesleyans' return in 1865. The Dominican state also supported Samaná Protestants by supplying them with lumber to rebuild their chapel in 1866, and it granted

Protestants in the capital a government building.[113] These actions served as proof of Dominican postwar liberalism. Whereas Spain was intolerant of Protestantism and Freemasonry, the Dominican government had reinstituted freedom of conscience. Moreover, many second-generation immigrants had fought in the war against Spain and identified as Dominican citizens. They were, as Jacob James put it, part of "the rising generation, which is taking their [place], [and] knows the maxims and ways of this country."[114] Yes, they and their religious societies were Black and Protestant, but they were also Dominican.

Of all nationalist leaders of the era, this outlook was perhaps best understood by Ulises Heureaux, whose parents were both Protestants. Few details about Heureaux's family are known. However, Wesleyan records show that in 1848, Ulises's Haitian father, Joseph Alexandre Heureaux (aka José Alejandro D'Assas Heureaux Fortune), converted to Wesleyanism in Cap-Haïtien, where he wrote his confession of faith.[115] At that time, Joseph's sister (Ulises's aunt) had already converted to Wesleyanism and had married the British missionary James Hartwell. After Joseph's conversion, Hartwell recommended his brother-in-law for the position of assistant missionary.[116] Ulises Heureaux's mother, Josefa Level, was also a Protestant, albeit not a convert. A mixed-race woman from St. Thomas, she had grown up on an island known for its long history of Black Protestant organization.[117] For his part, Ulises was raised Catholic in Puerto Plata by his adoptive guardian, Roselia Jean Louis, and remained Catholic throughout his life.[118] However, he also maintained correspondence with his parents, and his familial ties to the Wesleyan missions may explain why he remained friendly with Henry Astwood and the republic's Protestant communities later in life.

Such were the Black Protestant social and ideological networks that American and British visitors did not fully understand, and which have largely escaped historians' gaze. The US commission to Santo Domingo, for example, did not know or care to ask African American immigrants in Samaná about their religious outlook and Black activist social sphere. White commissioners furthermore did not track the conversations taking place within Black churches and educational institutions once Frederick Douglass returned to the United States. Nor did they read the letters that African American immigrants wrote to Douglass and their kinfolk on the mainland after the US commission's departure.[119] White observers of Black island life in Puerto Plata and Samaná disdained Black religion and therefore could not perceive the cross-border connections that operated largely outside of their purview. For instance, of the African American immigrant deacon John Hamilton, Jane Cazneau wrote, "This serious individual was as good as a minister, though not exactly ordained and set apart to act in that capacity."[120] In fact, Hamilton had received his ordination from the African American immigrant Isaac Miller, who had received his own ordination at the hands of bishops Richard Allen and Robert Morris of the AME Church.[121] Cazneau, however, did not recognize the AME Church as the source of Hamilton's religious authority. Likewise, the British Wesleyans were mainly unaware of such connections. For Henry Astwood, though, these ties were a part of life—as was whites' racial stigma.

As a member of the Wesleyan congregations in Puerto Plata and Samaná, Henry confronted anti-Black discrimination on several occasions. He likely knew, for example, that white Wesleyan ministers on Grand Turk had approved Jacob James for the lowly ministerial role as catechist in 1868 only after subjecting him to an extensive examination.[122] James was never ordained to a higher role despite serving the Wesleyans for decades. The Wesleyan leadership also denied James's son, Jacob Paul, entrance to the Wesleyan seminary in Jamaica.[123] This and other discriminatory actions led both father and son to seek reaffiliation with the AME Church by the early 1880s.[124] Moreover, Henry was probably present at Puerto Plata when the visiting Wesleyan minister Thomas Lawson drilled the town's congregation about whether they had any desires to follow a local white Baptist missionary in forming a Union Church. The response: "No, we have not."[125] Only partially satisfied, Lawson left that meeting determined to find a white minister for the Black congregation. Later, he planned to make the church's only white member take charge of the society.[126] This man lasted only a year in leadership, during which he went about "revolutionizing everything for whites" and causing "no little pain" within the congregation.[127] Henry Astwood, like other members of the Puerto Plata congregation, endured the insult.

Yet Henry also knew that, even while confronting whites' derision, Black Protestants found ways to benefit from or escape the gaze of white foreigners. In Samaná, for example, James and other churchgoers forged a strategic relationship with the Samaná Bay Company in 1873 that resulted in the church receiving lumber, an organ, and a melodeon from the company.[128] The following year, Julia Ward Howe, the famed author of "Battle Hymn of the Republic" and wife of Samaná Bay Company owner Dr. Samuel Gridley Howe, visited the congregation during her sojourn on the island. As Julia later recounted, she trekked up the side of the mountain to attend an open-air service (held outside the country church building) where she found an all-Black congregation with a "settled pastor" (likely James). The same minister abruptly ended the sermon upon Howe's arrival.[129] While no record provides the precise reason why the minister stopped preaching, it may be inferred that he felt it prudent to change course in the presence of a white woman. Conversely, in the absence of white ecclesiastical oversight, Black Protestants ran things their own way. They did so as Dominicans whose identity claims were never stagnant but had strategically shifted between American, Haitian, Dominican, and even British entities. Such was the "invisible institution"—the Black Protestant practices and ways of being—that Henry and other people of color knew, and that the white folks did not see.[130]

Henry's perspective demands a new narrative: African American immigrants were deeply embedded in Puerto Plata and Samaná societies. Their Protestant churchwork inspired a few Catholics to convert over the years, and many poor Catholic children had been educated in the Wesleyan missionary schools. But during the War of Restoration, British missionaries had fled and never returned. In their place stood Black men, African Americans who had immigrated to the island decades prior, but who had also grown up on the island. These men sought aid from the British Wesleyans, European merchants, American Samaná Bay Company officials, and African Americans on behalf of their communities. Meanwhile, they connected with their Spanish-speaking compatriots through civic organizations. White Americans and Britons laid claim to the congregations by habitually highlighting immigrants' foreignness and their supposed need for white political and religious oversight, and by attempting to direct their worship and finances in various ways. All the while, African American descendants knew well how to negotiate white power in order to make claims of their own. Thus, even though the steepled chapel in Samaná marked the building as a British church, the people inside never forgot who they were, nor their remarkable ability to adapt as needed to local conditions—and neither did Henry Astwood.

Henry would soon find himself adapting in new ways as he quit the island to seek his fortune in the United States. Leaving behind Margaret and his children, Astwood boarded the Union gunboat *Canandaigua* on July 6, 1874, in port that summer to escort the Samaná Bay Company back to the United States.[131] Báez had fallen out of power earlier that year, and the new president, Ignacio María González, had revoked the company's contract. For nationalists in Puerto Plata, things were looking up, although in

Samaná the atmosphere was surely less optimistic. Henry, however, would not be around to debate the particulars of these political events nor see their outcome. He joined the *Canandaigua*, earning his passage as landsman and tailor, but then jumped ship when he reached New Orleans in December 1874.[132] After years in the Turks Islands and the Dominican Republic, Henry would now use his Antillean experiences to remake himself in the US-Caribbean city, where he would gain prominence like never before.

The Emergence of H. C. C. Astwood: A Preacher-Politician in Reconstruction-Era Louisiana

By 1874, the city of New Orleans, like the Dominican northern coast, had seen its fair share of tragedy and transformation. A cosmopolitan port, New Orleans had been the wealthiest, largest, and fastest-growing city in the US South prior to the US Civil War.[133] It was also one of the most diverse and culturally distinct cities in the United States due to its large free Black community and Caribbean immigrant population. The city's French heritage and relatively high degree of racial and cultural intermixing set it apart and perpetuated its multitier caste system. This system allotted Afro-Creoles, a mixed-race class of free people (*gens de couleur*), an intermediary space between white and enslaved Black people. The US Civil War and Reconstruction, however, dramatically transformed social life and racial dynamics in New Orleans. Besides the physical and psychological effects of war, race and class structures were irrevocably altered. Southern whites lost political influence in the immediate aftermath of the war as northern Republicans took over state governance. Under Republicans, emancipated Blacks gained freedom and notable, albeit still limited, civil rights. Simultaneously, mixed-race Afro-Creoles scrambled to secure an elevated place above the formerly enslaved population within a volatile atmosphere in which the former caste system was quickly disappearing.

Henry arrived in New Orleans at a pivotal moment during Reconstruction when white attacks against Black people became even more brazen as the Republican Party retreated from radical reform. White Southerners saw the emancipation of formerly enslaved people and the granting of civil rights to the same as an affront to their traditional grasp on power. In Louisiana, as elsewhere, white men took action to "redeem" the South by organizing white supremacist groups such as the Ku Klux Klan, the Knights of the White Camelia, and the White League to combat radical Republican politics. These groups' vigilante violence terrorized Black communities. Just before Astwood's arrival, for example, the 1873 Colfax Massacre, described as "the single most deadly incident of the Reconstruction era," led to the deaths of over one hundred African Americans in New Orleans, most of them members of Louisiana's Black militia.[134] The next year, whites in New Orleans staged a coup d'état on September 14, 1874, ousting the Republican governor, William P. Kellogg.[135] While white violence raged, the election of Ulysses S. Grant to a second presidential term signaled white Northerners' changed attitudes toward the South. As elderly abolitionists died, a new generation of white Northerners espoused racist policies in order to reunite with the South.[136] Concurrently, a series of Supreme Court decisions based on cases emanating from Louisiana further curtailed protections for Black freed people.[137] The *Slaughterhouse* cases essentially made citizenship rights a matter of state discretion, while the *U.S. v. Cruikshank* decision (which resulted from the Colfax Massacre) maintained that the federal government could only prohibit violations of Blacks' rights perpetrated by states, not by individuals. Louisiana Black Republicans protested these Supreme Court rulings, yet there, as elsewhere, their objections went unheard.

Such injustice shaped Henry's opportunities in Louisiana. He later recalled how, upon his arrival, he found work as a cutler and foreman in New Orleans for a man named Mr. Cozan, who paid him the lofty sum of $9 a week.[138] The White League, however, demanded that Cozan discharge him. Henry then remained unemployed for three months before he found work as a teacher in St. Helena Parish. The gig paid $60 per month, but when he received his earnings at the end of the quarter, he had to settle debts for his room and board. This standard practice was a common way for employers to both bamboozle workers and keep them from leaving by paying wages only quarterly. The school closed soon thereafter, and Astwood could find no work until February 1876, when he transferred to another school in Carroll Parish. Thus, like so many other laborers of the era, Henry bounced from job to job unsure of what his wages would be and vulnerable to exploitation. For Henry, who also worried about supporting his family back in Puerto Plata, the financial setbacks felt all the more catastrophic.

Facing such racial discrimination and financial hardship, Henry joined the struggle for Black civil rights, working as an agent for the Black Republican strongman Pinckney Benton Stewart (P. B. S.) Pinchback, an important figure in Reconstruction history. Born in 1837 in Georgia to a white man and an enslaved woman, Pinchback eventually made his way to New Orleans, where he became a Civil War hero.[139] After the war, he worked with Henry Clay Warmoth, the Republican from Missouri who became governor of Louisiana in 1868. Pinchback, in turn, was elected to the state senate that year. Like Warmoth, Pinchback is remembered for his shady politics, through which he soon amassed wealth and political power.[140] In 1871, he became Louisiana's second Black lieutenant governor, and consequently served as the state's interim governor while Warmoth was undergoing impeachment proceedings in December 1872.[141] Pinchback was also elected to the US Senate that year, but Democrats in Louisiana protested his seat and, despite Republicans' counterattack, he never held office.

Although it is unclear how they met, Astwood became acquainted with Pinchback within months of arriving in New Orleans. Pinchback's newspaper, the *Weekly Louisianian*, which the statesman founded in the 1870s, listed Astwood as its agent in St. Helena in 1875. Astwood also appeared that year in a December article, as he served as secretary of a committee whose purpose was "to take into consideration the seating of senator P. B. S. Pinchback, protection of the colored voter, and the calling of a colored state convention."[142] The same committee voted to send two statements to Washington, D.C. The first was a memorial in praise of Pinchback. The second, for which Astwood wrote the preamble, summarized the atrocities committed against people of color in Louisiana and demanded redress. Astwood continued his political activities in Carroll Parish, where he became the parish's delegate to the Republican state nominating convention and served as its deputy US marshal in 1876.[143]

Henry's political work made him a target of white violence. Indeed, in one highly publicized instance during the presidential campaign of 1876, white Democrats almost murdered Henry in broad daylight. That day Republicans were hosting a rally at St. James Chapel in Monroe when suddenly one hundred Democratic "bulldosers," who used violence to suppress the Black vote, surrounded the assembly and pointed their guns at Henry, the first speaker. In response, Henry proclaimed that any place where a public speaker was surrounded by armed opponents intent on preventing or silencing free speech was naturally uncivilized.[144] Outraged by this Black man's brio, several white Democrats spat back, "You are a goddamn liar!" Astwood doubled down on his resolve, telling his hecklers that "they could assassinate him, but should not trample on his manhood."[145] Although Astwood escaped with his life, several Republican leaders and constituents faced greater misfortune. In the following days, white Democrats in Monroe ruthlessly murdered Black and white Republicans. They also jailed groups of Black people to prevent them from voting. Conditions became so violent that armed sentries ringed Astwood and other Republican leaders around the clock until they could leave Monroe under federal guard.

Despite the ongoing risk to his life, Henry only became more involved in politics after the disputed 1876 election. Henry recounted the threats to his life and voter intimidation patterns before the US Senate investigating committee in December 1876.[146] Then, in April 1877, Henry formed part of the delegation that beseeched the federal commission (created by the Electoral Commission Act) to protect Black people by seating both the Republicans' gubernatorial candidate, Stephen B. Packard, and presidential hopeful Rutherford B. Hayes.[147] These activities, however, did little to change the election's outcome or Henry's fate. The informal deal of 1877 that placed Hayes in office but removed federal troops from the US South ultimately affected Astwood's livelihood: "The campaign of 1876 did away with schools in the parishes," he later reflected. Then, when Packard lost the disputed 1876 gubernatorial race due to the same deal, Astwood lamented, "I lost my entire salary as enrolling clerk of the senate, having me in debt for board at $20 a month during that protracted struggle."[148] Penniless and homeless, Astwood's only solution was to abandon Carroll Parish for more fruitful employment in New Orleans.

In this moment of crisis, Henry turned once again to the church, an institution that had served him well in the Turks Islands and the Dominican Republic. In Louisiana, Henry experienced independent Black churches as a critical center of Black political life. Such churches often served as meeting places for Black politicians, many of whom were also ministers. Black churches also became even more pivotal spaces for civil rights work after 1877 when African Americans lost federal backing and access to voting. From the start, Henry established himself as a model preacher-politician in St. Helena, where he delivered several sermons in 1875.[149] Then, in 1876–77, he joined New Orleans's leading AME Church, St. James. Founded in 1848 by free people of color who received a special charter from the state legislature, St. James served as a principal site for Black Republican organization in the city during Reconstruction (figure 2.1). The church was also closely affiliated with Black secret fraternities. The Prince Hall Grand Lodge of Louisiana (Eureka Grand Lodge)—whose members included leading political figures such as Pinchback, Oscar J. Dunn, and James Lewis—used St. James as a meeting place.[150] Lodge members had actually founded the church.[151] Members of the Magnolia Lodge #1990 of the Grand United

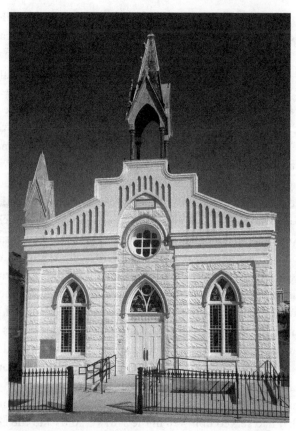

FIGURE 2.1. Historic Saint James AME Church, ca. 2015, New Orleans, LA. Photo: Reverend Otto Duncan. Used with permission.

Order of the Odd Fellows (GUOOF), which Henry soon joined, were also associated with St. James.[152] Thus, church work offered Henry additional ways to involve himself in local politics and embedded him within the cluster of powerful Black men in New Orleans. Although Democratic newspapers constantly ridiculed Henry and other Black ministers and politicians, Henry carried on, risking such derision at best, and death at worst.[153]

Over the next years, Henry served in many religio-political roles in New Orleans. In 1877, for example, he spoke out against Black emigration to West Africa, stating that the "colored race could do better at home" and making him a vocal critic of the AME Church's rising star Henry McNeal Turner, who would later become a famous bishop and political spokesman.[154] Henry moreover opposed the segregation of public schools, which undermined Black citizenship and belonging while also representing a palpable reversal of advancements under Reconstruction.[155] Like other Black Republicans across the South, Henry did not cower from politics after Hayes's compromise. He led the church committee that welcomed Pinchback to St. James to discuss the political situation, chaired the Young Men's Progressive Association, and also began to preach in the AME Church.[156] This work landed him other leadership roles: member of the Colored Convention held at Common Street Baptist Church in April 1879; judge for the AME Church's Sunday School Union the same month; secretary of the Garrison Memorial meeting held at Central Church a few months later; and correspondent for the *Christian Recorder*.[157] By 1880, the *Weekly Louisianian* had given Henry the sobriquet "Mr. H. C. C. Astwood, the 'Tireless,'" so busy was he with local political matters.[158] His work in the church was also rewarded when bishop Thomas Marcus Decatur Ward ordained Astwood a deacon at St. James in 1880.

Inasmuch as St. James and the GUOOF granted Henry access to the city's light-skinned Black Protestant elite, he also moved seamlessly among the Francophone Catholic Afro-Creole class.[159] That aristocratic class of free Black New Orleanians (including some Haitians) were artisans, professionals, and businessmen who had lived in New Orleans and knew each other prior to the Civil War.[160] A few of them, such as Francis Dumas and Charles Sauvinet, were Civil War veterans. After the war, they saw themselves as the logical inheritors of political power and the natural leaders of newly freed, uneducated Black people. The vast majority of these men and women were light in complexion; a few even passed for white. Those of great means had even attended college in the US North or in Paris and, like Astwood, were multilingual, speaking both English and French. Undoubtedly, Astwood believed that he could profit from associating with this crowd of well-heeled Black Southerners. Within such circles, his light skin tone and Caribbean background—and particularly his experiences in Puerto Plata—likely gained him some attention. Henry could speak Spanish and possibly some French at this point in his life, and displayed recognizable tropes as a man accustomed to the halls of power. From his years among people working for the Antillean Confederation, he knew the discourse of *liberté, egalité, et fraternité* infused in Afro-Creole Reconstruction-era thought regarding "public rights."[161] He was also familiar with navigating a dominant Catholic culture in a Caribbean context. Thus, just as Astwood had consorted with leading Catholic Dominicans in Puerto Plata, he assumed a liminal place on the borders of high Afro-Creole society in New Orleans.

Henry's standing among the Afro-Creole elite solidified all the more through familial ties when on May 11, 1878, he married the Afro-Creole bachelorette Alice Ternoir.[162] This was Astwood's second marriage, and he was still married to Margaret, a fact that Astwood concealed at the time of the wedding and which he calculated was worth the social tsk-tsking that he would later endure. The Ternoirs had deep roots in New Orleans's political, financial, and military life. Twenty-two when she wed Henry, Alice was the daughter of brickmason Leon Francois Ternoir and Elizabeth Barthé, both recognized members of the Afro-Creole class who could trace their heritage to France.[163] Of particular note, Alice's paternal great-grandfather Jean Ternoir was born in Saint-Étienne and had partnered with Marie St. Jean, a free woman of color, upon his move to New Orleans at the end of the eighteenth century. Their son Jean Pierre, Alice's paternal grandfather, had fought in the Battle of New Orleans. This pedigree made the Ternoir family connection advantageous to Henry, a social striver who through Alice's family gained further renown among the Afro-Creole class.[164]

Nevertheless, controversy marred the Astwood-Ternoir marriage from the start. Within a few weeks of the wedding, Pinchback confronted Henry about a letter penned by Charles R. Douglass, son of Frederick Douglass, that had arrived at the *Louisianian*. Appointed US consul to Puerto Plata in 1875, the younger Douglass had met Henry's first wife, Margaret, who had implored him to find out what had happened to Henry.[165] Douglass now charged Astwood with already being a married man and with abandoning a wife and four children in the Dominican Republic.[166] Astwood's denial notwithstanding, James Lewis, a Civil War veteran, respected Black Republican, and Pinchback confidant, began investigating Astwood's background.[167] Perturbed by how quickly Henry had insinuated himself into St. James church and Freemason groups, Lewis—himself an influential member of St. James and the grand master of the Eureka Prince Hall lodge—felt especially concerned for the Ternoirs given that Alice was already pregnant with a son before the nuptials.[168] For Lewis, Henry's marriage to Alice showcased yet another aspect of Astwood's predatory nature. Greedy for power and social standing, Henry had bamboozled the Ternoir family, taken advantage of their daughter, impregnated her before marriage, and then been exposed as a bigamist with a secret family back in the Caribbean.[169] Moreover, he had carried out his elaborate ruse while serving at the helm of New Orleans's most prominent Black institutions. Frustrated by Astwood's deceit, Lewis reached out to Charles Douglass directly, urging, "If [Astwood] is not what he is represented, we would like to know it."[170] For Lewis, and by extension the Ternoirs and other Afro-Creole families, Astwood's deceptions and outright lies placed Alice and the community writ large in a perilous position.

Yet, even though Douglass confirmed that Astwood was indeed a married family man, seemingly nothing could prevent Henry from continuing his upward trajectory in New Orleans. This was in part because of the incriminating information that Henry had accumulated working in Black Republican circles. Pinchback, for instance, suppressed Astwood's scandal, much to Lewis's ire, aware that Henry possessed condemnatory evidence regarding Pinchback and the Fifth Congressional District.[171] Accordingly, others who feared Astwood's possible public ripostes silenced further rumors lest their own misdeeds come to light.[172]

For his part, Astwood deflected accusations by pointing out that Charles Douglass had no business passing judgment on Henry's personal affairs. He even dared write Douglass that Margaret was the mother of his children, sidestepping altogether that the couple remained lawfully married in the Caribbean. Instead, Henry emphasized that throughout his time in Louisiana, he had tried to earn enough to provide for his children, making himself seem ever the devoted father as opposed to a deceitful bigamist.[173] Astwood played the same tune for his partners in New Orleans, including Pinchback and other AME leaders, but Douglass saw clearly through his subterfuge. If other powerful Black Republicans did the same in New Orleans, it is not apparent. Astwood's inability to penetrate the Eureka Prince Hall lodge, however, points to fissures that he could not readily smooth over with charm and charisma.

Having married into Afro-Creole society and with Black Republicans fearing that he would expose their secrets, Astwood found that his social striving paid off handsomely. First, Pinchback appointed Henry to the customhouse's revenue department in 1878, although the position did not last.[174] Next the US congressman and former associate judge of the Louisiana Supreme Court, John E. Leonard, found Astwood a position as bailiff in the US circuit court that same year. The bailiff work paid the sum of $48 monthly, the delight of which increased all the more when Pinchback secured Astwood an undisclosed job paying $100.[175] Then, in 1879, Henry joined the *Weekly Louisianian* as assistant editor, a position that enabled him to learn a trade that would serve him later in life and that made fortunes for some of the most powerful African American men of the era.[176]

Astwood's last few years in New Orleans evidenced his place among the city's Black and Afro-Creole elite. In 1878, for example, Astwood enrolled at Straight College, a historically Black institution, where he socialized with other distinguished Black students and alumni.[177] One year later, he was among the orators who spoke at the inauguration of the clubhouse of the Americus Club, one of the most exclusive Afro-Creole leagues in the city and an organization that worked "to cultivate literary tastes, to promote rational discussion, and to sponsor public debates and lectures."[178] Henry also remained involved with the Republican party, the *Weekly Louisianian*, the AME Church, and the GUOOF. In 1880, he served as a delegate for New Orleans's Fourth Ward to the Republican state convention held in the same city, and campaigned for presidential candidate James A. Garfield.[179] In April of that year, he was promoted to local editor of the paper.[180] He worked as the corresponding secretary for the AME Church's New Orleans annual conference in 1881 and was superintendent of the Union Sunday School.[181] Throughout 1881 and 1882, he served as district secretary for the Odd Fellows.[182] From these powerful perches, Astwood tightened his grasp of local power levers among the Black and Afro-Creole classes, whose civil rights efforts he both straddled and endeavored to fuse through his work.

Efforts toward building a united front among the Black and Afro-Creole elites were most apparent in the pages of the *Weekly Louisianian*, which beginning in 1881 ran a French section. Many New Orleans newspapers ran bilingual prints, but it was only under Astwood's directorship that the *Weekly Louisianian* endeavored to do so. As Astwood explained in a francophone article, the editorship added the French section due to the support that the paper received from all people of color in the city.[183] A few francophone articles, including a piece by Rodolphe L. Desdunes (who was also an Odd Fellow), followed Astwood's note.[184] For his part, Desdunes supported the *Louisianian*'s "cardinal goal" of "liberating oppression wherever it reign."[185] The first page of the next issue was printed entirely in French, a practice that continued throughout Astwood's two-year tenure as editor. French articles expounded upon *l'équité universelle* and *fraternité*.[186] They also included news of St. Domingue (Haiti and Dominican Republic), South America, Africa, and France.[187] One issue posted a francophone invitation for the city's people of color to meet at St. James AME Church "to organize an Association for the defense of the rights of man."[188] Such articles demonstrate Astwood's attempts to broaden the appeal of Pinchback's paper to the Afro-Creole elite and thereby unite the city's two classes of Black elites in the fight for social reform. By infusing the paper with his own cosmopolitanism, Henry moreover edited it to reflect New Orleans's status as a significant Caribbean epicenter for regional debates over race and politics.

Yet, even as Astwood gained ground among the Afro-Creole class, his growing reputation and Caribbean background soon led to other opportunities, albeit in the midst of a national tragedy. On a day that should have been joyous, July 4, 1881, a twofold celebration of the nation's independence and the dedication of a newly constructed AME schoolhouse that would serve the city's Black population, Astwood stood solemnly before the St. James congregation. The assassination of President Garfield overshadowed the day's events and likely expedited Astwood's decision to end his eight-year sojourn in the United States.[189] After Garfield's death, Astwood, Pinchback, and other Republicans left New Orleans for Washington, DC, where they vied for promotions within the Republican Party.[190] With his background living in Puerto Plata and his lingual dexterity, Astwood seemed the perfect candidate for foreign service posts in Cuba, Trinidad, and the Dominican Republic. Despite additional protests raised by Charles R. Douglass over Astwood's bigamy and US citizenship status, the new US president, Chester A. Arthur, appointed Astwood as US consul to Santo Domingo in February 1882.[191] This position brought Astwood back to the island where his first family resided, and it brought the Dominican capital its first Black US consul.

Once in Santo Domingo, Henry relied on the reputation he had built for himself in New Orleans as a politician, preacher, and family man. Accordingly, he assumed responsibility for his Dominican children soon after arrival, although he never resumed a relationship with their mother, Margaret. Then, during his first leave of absence in March 1883, he brought Mildred, Miriam, and George to the United States, where the children met Alice and their infant half-sister, Relana Evelina.[192] Henry also enrolled Mildred in Straight College at that time.[193] Later that year, Alice and his children from both marriages traveled with Henry back to Santo Domingo, where the family lived for the next decade, during which Henry would have four more children with Alice, whom he presented as his legitimate first wife.[194] By cultivating an image as a respectable patriarch, Henry justified his consular appointment to those who would doubt his fitness for office, whether because of his personal intrigues or his color.

Conclusion

Henry was a prudent social climber whose singular life experience is instructive on the era's racial and political climate. As a migrant who moved between the Turks Islands, Puerto Plata, Samaná, and New Orleans, Astwood learned how to navigate multicultural spaces. In these port towns, he participated in various public lectures, Masonic clubs, Black Protestant church meetings, Republican politics, and print culture. He did so not as a white traveler snidely observing people of color, but as an individual embedded in these communities. Whereas whites drew ethnic distinctions between people of color, Henry knew that the social networks between the sundry groups to which he belonged formed part of a collective fight for social equality and self-determination. A sense of a collective fight or common destiny that prevailed in the aforementioned towns did not mean that people of color ignored the ethnic distinctions between themselves. Rather, it indicated the social and familial connections that people forged across ethnic lines that blended their various political causes. Henry's early life attested to this fact.

Yet Astwood's unique biography, as recounted here and in chapter 1, also encapsulates the fragility of Black citizenship, and indeed Black life, in the postemancipation period. Astwood faced physical violence and death in the collective fight for Black equal rights. These threats were intense in New Orleans in the early 1870s and became even more acute after 1877 with the departure of US federal troops from the South. Still, people of color in New Orleans and elsewhere did not give up the fight for equal rights. By the early 1880s, however, it became even more dangerous to boldly advocate for Black civil rights in the South.

Astwood's consular appointment in 1882 occurred at another moment of intense social transformation in the United States. As the United States' own experiment in racial democracy crumbled, it seemed to many African Americans that racial democracy and Black political authority were possible only in a place like the Dominican Republic.[195] There, in recent years, two Dominican generals of notable African descent, Gregorio Luperón and Ulises Heureaux, had risen to political prominence. Luperón had even become president of the republic for a short period in 1879. These heroes of the War of Restoration hailed from Puerto Plata, the same cosmopolitan town where Astwood had lived for over seven years. Now leaders of the country's liberal party, Luperón, Heureaux, and other liberals espoused a raceless national ideology and sought to transform the country's newfound political stability and sugar economy into a vehicle for social reform. For Black Americans, the United States' debate over Black rights now extended to Santo Domingo, where it appeared that Black men could still "feel [the] full stature of manhood," as Frederick Douglass reportedly once exclaimed.[196]

Yet, for Astwood, this new opportunity in the US foreign service would present a number of challenges. Yes, he had gained one of the few US government positions still available to Black men. This achievement, however, did not mean that the controversy over his personal background would cease. Nor did it indicate that white foreign service officers would respect his advice and political authority as consul. As a preacher-politician and now a US foreign agent, Henry perpetually had a target on his back. He learned from Pinchback and others in New Orleans, though, that his ability to connect with various people of color as well as hobnob with powerful white individuals created advantages in dangerous times, enabling him to dodge personal attacks and devise political stratagems to his advantage. By both necessity and choice, strategic camouflage and subterfuge would become a common practice at his next job. Indeed, the world through Henry Astwood's eyes was never exactly as it appeared to others, but could transform according to his own machinations.

PART II

Black Political Authority

3

THE OTHER BLACK REPUBLIC
Segregated Statecraft and the Dual Nature of US-Dominican Diplomacy

H. C. C. Astwood took charge of the US consular office in Santo Domingo on April 12, 1882, after a weeklong trip aboard the ss *Geo W. Clyde*. Upon his arrival, he found that the office did not measure up to the "dignity and standing of our government."[1] The small room included a table, a bookcase, a pigeonhole rack and stand, a wardrobe, six chairs, a broken safe, and an obsolete map of the United States. These outdated trappings were an apt symbol for a consulate that waned in significance when compared to the other Caribbean posts for which Astwood had been considered but denied.[2] Astwood, however, was determined to make the best of his position. Writing to the State Department that the current office "cannot be further controlled," he set out to find a new location for the consulate.[3] Within weeks, Astwood had moved his headquarters to a "more central and convenient place" on Atarazana Street, no. 24.[4] The two-story residence was "splendidly situated" only a few yards from the wharf and the town's gates.[5] With large wooden doors, eight feet high by five feet wide, sunlight streamed into an expansive front office. Another set of doors led to a yard and kitchen, and on the second floor the building provided a parlor and three bedrooms in which to entertain visitors and shelter residents. Over time, Astwood would work to transform the low status of his Dominican post. But, for now, this breezy residence was the first symbolic step in a series of modifications that the new US consul proposed to improve US-Dominican diplomatic relations, which had languished in the years after the Samaná Bay Company left the island in 1874.

The years 1874 and 1882 were bookends of sorts. First, 1874 marked the close of an era when US annexation of the Dominican Republic sat on the horizon, and it indicated a new start for both the young nation and the young man who would one day assume the US consulship in Santo Domingo. As a former British Caribbean subject who had spent years on the Dominican northern coast before naturalizing in New Orleans, Astwood had quit the peninsula for the United States in 1874. In Louisiana, he had involved himself in Republican politics, African American activism, and Black religious life. He had also married again and started a new family. Now, returning alone to the island after an eight-year hiatus, Astwood was uniquely positioned to discern the structural shifts that had taken place in Dominican society. The most obvious changes were political and economic in nature. After a tumultuous period of civil war in the 1870s, the liberal Partido Azul had at last brought peace. Simultaneously, a revival of the nation's sugar industry beginning in the early 1870s had boosted the Dominican economy and attracted foreign investors. Now, in 1882, Astwood could discern the financial gains that would come from increasing US-Dominican trade relations, and he set about making plans. One more change, however, impeded his progress. Whereas America's gaze had fallen directly on the Dominican Republic in the early 1870s, now in 1882 the US government treated Dominican affairs with an entrenched indifference.

Astwood knew that his government's disregard for the Dominican Republic was racially motivated. For white Americans, the fact that Haiti had governed the Dominican Republic—a land once ruled by Spain—for twenty-two years (1822–44) made the island nation deserving of the United States' tacit scorn. In the early 1880s, this scorn translated into blatant neglect of Dominican affairs. Indeed, as other scholars have argued, disdain for Haiti led to "misrecognition" of the Dominican Republic, and often Americans did not even bother to distinguish between the two nations.[6]

Keeping in mind this racist US gaze upon the island, this chapter accounts for significant shifts in Dominican politics, economy, and US-Dominican diplomatic relations in the early 1880s. It also tracks Astwood's reactions to those shifts. By doing so, it presents a twofold argument. First, it shows how the racist politics of recognition that marked US-Haitian relations in earlier decades still dominated US-Dominican affairs in the early 1880s when the dark-skinned Dominican general Ulises Heureaux came to power for the first time. Such racism prevented Astwood from realizing his hopes for US-Dominican trade and diplomacy. In light of this context, Astwood's handling of various disputes should be analyzed as political maneuvers purposefully crafted in response to the racist barriers he faced. Whereas historians have traditionally read Astwood's consular record solely to glean details about historical events (sometimes without proper acknowledgment), his dispatches also provide a road map to understanding the racialized context that guided Black politicians' actions.[7] This way of reading the consular records reveals that segregated statecraft—defined here as the process by which notions of official and unofficial diplomacy operated along racially bifurcated lines—characterized US-Dominican diplomatic relations during these years.

Second, the concept of segregated statecraft provides a foundation for understanding how the building of US economic empire and the forging of Black political authority in Santo Domingo existed as interdependent processes. Historians have already recognized that US capital fueled Heureaux's authoritarian regime of the 1880s–90s, particularly as it flowed through the sugar industry and government concessions.[8] Scholars, however, have not yet considered how similar dynamics impacted US Black foreign service agents such as Astwood, making the dialectic between US economic empire and Black political authority integral to their Black internationalism.[9] Like Heureaux, who reportedly always kept a copy of Machiavelli's *The Prince* (1532) on his desk, Astwood resorted to underhanded tactics to boost his power.[10] Consequently, as US consul he did more in Santo Domingo than serve as President Heureaux's puppet, as American historian Sumner Welles and at least one other student of history have asserted.[11] Astwood's reports on Dominican politics and economy provided the most in-depth analysis of the country available in English at the time, and he used his trade insights to manipulate three competing groups:

US State Department officials, American capitalists, and Dominican officials. His manipulations depended upon discursive performances of righteous indignation on behalf of US capitalists in Santo Domingo. These performances, while often bombastic, advanced both US capitalists' interests and Astwood's own authority on the island. Simultaneously, they were strategic responses to white US officials who feared Black government, underestimated Black politicians, and devalued African American foreign service agents to the point of historical erasure.

First Impressions: Dominican Politics and Economics within the US Consul's Purview

Upon arriving in Santo Domingo, Astwood needed a crash course on the country's recent political history. Much had changed politically in the years between 1874 and 1882. At the start of 1874, Buenaventura Báez, the conservative authoritarian *caudillo* who had led the US annexation effort, fled the island. With Báez gone, Ignacio María González, whom Báez had appointed governor of Puerta Plata, assumed the presidency. Despite being a conservative, González passed a series of liberal reforms, including the pardoning of Báez's political adversaries and freedom of the press. He moreover revoked the Samaná Bay Company's contract and signed the Dominican Republic's first official treaty with Haiti. These achievements, however, occurred during a world economic crisis that exacerbated regional tensions in the Dominican Republic as well as the new president's financial problems. Thus, within months of assuming office, González faced a rebellion from conservatives (*rojos*) in the city of Santiago. The president quickly squashed the revolt but subsequently grew despotic as he organized his own political party (*verdes*). González's increasing authoritarianism angered liberals (*azules*) who had initially supported him against Báez. Moreover, due to Báez's pillaging of the national treasury, González could not pay money owed to public servants and members of Congress, and he refused to recognize the national debts incurred by General Gregorio Luperón. Consequently, within two years, González's government fell.[12]

Astwood would have learned that seven presidents followed González in rapid succession (indicated here by numbers), instigating a "cycle of colors."[13] First, a leader within the liberal Partido Azul, the Santiago-born Ulises Francisco Espaillat (1), assumed the presidency on March 29, 1876. Yet, despite his reputable administrative skills, by October of the same year both González and Báez returned from exile, joined forces, and overthrew the liberal president. The controversial Báez (2) then returned to power in December 1876 for a fifth and final term that ended violently in March 1878 when yet another *rojo*, Cesáreo Guillermo (3), turned against the old dictator and attacked the capital. With Báez gone, Guillermo established a provisional government in Santo Domingo while his rival, the former president González, did the same in Santiago. With the help of Luperón, who judged González to be the least of two evils, González (4) won in a special election and returned to the presidency in July 1878. The alliance between Luperón and González, however, did not hold. Within months, Luperón established a provisional government in Puerto Plata, and sent his trusted general, Ulises Heureaux, to take over the capital. Learning of this plot, Guillermo took advantage of Luperón's campaign and also attacked the capital. The two bands of troops easily overthrew González. The liberal-*azul* president of the Supreme Court, Jacinto de Castro (5), served in a provisional role until elections could be held. Through a series of militaristic and political maneuvers, including the assassination of the rival candidate, Guillermo (6) at last took control of the presidency in January 1879. Yet, by October, Heureaux once again marched on the capital at the behest of Luperón (7), who, after defeating Guillermo, became provisional president in December 1879.[14]

Looking on from afar, US commentators depicted the political upheaval as part and parcel of an independent Black government, paying no attention to facts and nuance. The headlines in the early 1880s related chaos: "A New San Domingo Revolt," "Troubles in the West Indies," "Consternation in San Domingo."[15] By portraying Dominican politics as a constant state of unrest motivated singularly by Dominican generals' ambitions, American journalists propagated stereotypes of Black misrule, discounted Dominicans' political grievances, and ignored their ideological visions for their nation.[16] They also discouraged US capital since political instability kept investors at bay. Only those with cash to lose would entrust it to the belligerent "mulatto republic" where even the natural world, with its hurricanes and fires, appeared to revolt against foreign interests.[17]

The new US consul in Santo Domingo, however, learned quickly that Dominican officials, fully aware of how Americans described their country, did not care much for hyperbole. In 1880, Dominicans had elected the Catholic priest and liberal Partido Azul member Father Fernando A. Meriño to a two-year presidential term. Meriño was still in office when Astwood arrived, and after the two met, Astwood warned the US State Department about "certain unjust and malicious rumors circulating through the columns of our Jurnals [*sic*]."[18] Meriño and his officials had repudiated the articles, which they believed were intended to injure the government and the Dominican economy. Dominican exiles in St. Thomas and Venezuela and Spanish officials and planters in Cuba and Puerto Rico had circulated the rumors, they accused. These detractors felt threatened by Meriño's liberal government and the rise of the Dominican sugar industry. Such arguments convinced Astwood, who denounced the "groundless" rumors and stressed that "the rights of [foreigners] thus far are respected."[19] The State Department, however, dismissed Dominicans' concerns over disinformation since the papers had only printed what Americans already assumed to be true: the island was in turmoil since the Dominican Republic, like Haiti, was populated by inherently "warring" people.[20]

For Dominican officials, the triangulated relationship between their nation, Haiti, and the United States presented a troublesome situation during a crucial moment of social transition. The Azul government needed financial backing, and in the early 1880s, US capital represented a largely untapped resource for both national loans and investment in Dominican infrastructure. However, American racism presented a severe disadvantage. As Astwood reported, President Meriño's minister of the interior and police, General Ulises Heureaux, spoke candidly to Astwood about the optics at the level of international relations. Since 1869, the United States had maintained a diplomatic legation at Port-au-Prince, but it assigned only a US consulate to Santo Domingo even though the Dominican Republic conducted more trade with the United States than Haiti did. Why was this the case? The Azul government stood ready to grant additional concessions to American investors, but did the United States consider the Dominican Republic beneath Haiti? Heureaux prodded Astwood to press his government for a diplomatic upgrade in order to facilitate trade. "They are hopeful," Astwood reported, "that if they are not accorded the same honors as are extended to Hayti and Liberia, at least, they will be accorded a consul general to represent our government here."[21] The naming of Haiti and Liberia indicated that Meriño, Heureaux, and other Dominican officials understood the racist animus that still guided US policy toward the Dominican Republic.[22] Facing this stigma, Heureaux used economic incentives as a lure; a US diplomatic legation in Santo Domingo would foster greater exchange between the two nations while legitimizing the Partido Azul within a hostile geopolitical arena.

This strategy had a long history on the island. In the years immediately following the Haitian Revolution, Haitian heads of state used economic treaties and merchant contracts to "carve out a new economic space for [Haiti]," even while foreign governments refused Haiti diplomatic recognition.[23] In this hostile environment, international trade was a form of unofficial recognition, and merchants sometimes acted as unofficial government agents.[24] By negotiating with such agents, Haitian leaders flexed their political authority. Dominican leaders developed a similar tactic. While denied US diplomatic recognition from 1844 to 1866, leaders welcomed US commercial agents to Santo Domingo and granted concessions to American speculators with ties to government.[25] In exchange, the same white men represented Dominican affairs to the US government. While always concerned about race, Dominican officials emphasized economic and militaristic advantages, such as the renting of Samaná Bay.[26] Thus, like Haitians, Dominicans responded to diplomatic rejection with material incentives. In the 1880s, both governments maintained this strategy, since official recognition did not equal mutual respect.[27]

The economic lures proved enticing to Astwood, who found himself on the front end of sweeping market shifts that he described enthusiastically in his first dispatches to the US State Department in 1882. A decade earlier, tobacco was the country's primary export. It was harvested in the Cibao, the country's north-central region, and was exported from Puerto Plata to Europe. The 1873 economic crisis that had engendered Báez's fall and crippled González's presidency, however, had also ruined the tobacco industry.[28] By 1882, sugar was quickly taking over the export trade. Unlike tobacco, sugar was produced on large plantations, the majority of which were located in the southeast.

As historians of the Dominican economy have shown, in 1882 Americans did not yet dominate sugar production, but foreigners still owned most plantations.[29] In fact, in 1872, when Astwood was first living on the island, the Cuban planter Carlos Loynaz built the first steam-powered sugar mill in Puerto Plata.[30] Cubans exiled by the Ten Years' War then transformed the Dominican industry with new technologies, as thirty-seven new sugar plantations emerged in the Dominican Republic between 1875 and 1882.[31] Of this number, twenty-eight haciendas existed in the south and were owned by Germans, Italians, Cubans, Americans, and only a few Dominicans (table 3.1). The pattern of foreign ownership would soon intensify after an 1884 crisis in the sugar market when nervous investors and small-time landholders sold off their interests to foreign proprietors, especially Americans, with deeper pockets.[32] But, in 1882, Americans' monopoly over Dominican sugar production had not yet manifested. Seeing the opportunity,

Astwood outlined his views on Dominican-American commercial relations in a detailed 123-page annual report that took months to prepare.[33]

Astwood's trade insights, gleaned from interviews with Dominican officials and the existing tariff law, support what historians have already written about the Dominican economy during this era. At first glance, there is nothing new here. Still, his first annual report is valuable for at least three reasons. First, it provides a snapshot of the Dominican economy in 1882, including significant data points such as the itemization of the nation's principal imports (table 3.2) and exports (table 3.3).[34] Astwood's report furthermore includes a registry of the nation's principal sugar plantation owners with details of their estates (table 3.1).[35] Together, all three tables attest to the United States' growing dominance over the Dominican economy in the early 1880s.[36] For example, regarding exports, Astwood asserted somewhat hyperbolically that the United States was the "sole" consumer of Dominican sugar in 1882, and he estimated $500,000 in revenue from the unexpectedly large sugar crop that year (160,538 lbs.).[37] Americans dominated imports too. For the fiscal year ending June 1882, Astwood reported that total imports amounted to $881,679.18 and calculated that the United States was responsible for more than two-thirds of that sum ($513,619.45).

Second, Astwood's annual report, when coupled with his other dispatches, provides useful portraits of the American entrepreneurs who invested in the Dominican Republic in the 1870s–80s. There were two types of American investors: those who lived on the island and those who invested from abroad. Of the first group, historian Jaime Domínguez has named Allen Howard Crosby the "prototype immigrant entrepreneur."[38] Crosby, who co-owned Loynaz's sugar plantation in Puerto Plata, obtained concessions to build bridges, railroads, and piers, for which he charged for public use.[39] Another exemplar was William A. Read, a Boston-born merchant who moved to the island in 1846 and owned a plantation in Sabana Grande.[40] Regarding the second group, Astwood reported that one Mr. Hall had received a grant to build a railroad between Azua and Santo Domingo and had arrived in the country along with engineers who were already surveying the region. Another investor, Mr. W. M. Hinman of Boston, was seeking to have the port at Azua designated for sugar exportation.[41] Astwood had also connected John Wanamaker of Philadelphia with the government, which had bought military uniforms from the department store owner and was expected to order more. Throughout the 1880s and early 1890s, Astwood would interact with these American capitalists and over a dozen others, interceding between them and the Dominican government.

TABLE 3.1. Sugar Estates by Year, Location, Owner, and Capacity

Year	Place	Name	Owned By	Sugar	Molasses
Southern estates per Astwood (cross-referenced with Cassá), sugar and molasses measured in hogsheads					
1875	San Carlos	Esperanza	Joaquín M. Delgado	1,500	300
1876	San Carlos	Caridad	Evaristo de Lamar and Co.	2,000	400
1877	San Carlos	Bella Vista	Rafael Abréu Hijo	500	220
1877	Macoris	Angelina	Lorenzo Guirdi	700	280
1877	Sabana Grande	Las Damas	William A. Reed	600	250
1878	Pajarito	Asunción	Francisco Bona	500	250
1878	Pajarito	Constancia	Heredico Urcenion	800	220
1878	Pajarito	Sta. Elena	J. P. Sánchez, Vicini, and Damirón	300	100
1878	Azua	Calderon	John Hardy (Fowie, Carrol, and Ricart)	1,500	300
1879	San Carlos	Encarnación	Francisco Saviñón	800	330
1879	Macoris	Porvenir	Santiago W. Mellor	1,500	350
1880	San Cristobal	Providencia	Marcos A. Cabral	150	75
1880	Bani	Carolina	Soler and Machado	160	70
1880	Bani	Concepción	E. Billini and J. Paulino	130	60
1880	San Carlos	La Fé	J. E. Hatten and Co.	2,500	800
1880	Pajarito	San Luis	Cambiaso Bros.	2,500	500
Southern estates "in course of erection" per Astwood (cross-referenced with Cassá), capacity unknown					
1881	Sabana Grande	Dolores	D. Valera de Lamar		
1882	Pajarito	San Isidro	Hatton and Hernández		
1882	Sabana Grande	La Stella	George Stokes		
1882	San Carlos	La Duquesa	Bass and Krosight		
1882	Bani	Ocoa	J. Heredia and Co.		
Additional southern estates "in course of erection" per Astwood, capacity unknown					
1882	Macoris	Colón	Fernandez and Co.		
1882	Azua	Consuelo	Pardo and Solomon		
1882	Azua	Boston	Wm. M. Hinnman		
1882	San Cristobal	Italia	J. B. Vicini		
1882	San Domingo	Jaina Mosa	F. del Monti and Co.		
1882	La Romana	Alta Villa	Caldron		
1882	Macoris	N/A	N/A		

(continued)

TABLE 3.1. (*continued*)

Year	Place	Name	Owned By	Sugar	Molasses

Northern estates not included in Astwood's chart, sugar measured in *quintales* (qq.) and molasses in gins.

Year	Place	Name	Owned By	Sugar	Molasses
1877	Samaná	Gumersinda	J. M. Glass	4,500	20,250
1878	Samaná	El Progreso	B. Grullón	4,500	20,250
1878	Puerto Plata	Providencia	J. W. Barral	3,750	13,500
1879	Puerto Plata	La Rosca	G. Saidt	2,100	8,100
1879	Puerto Plata	La Industria	E. Hachtman and M. Peralta	15,000	52,650
1879	Puerto Plata	La Luisa	F. Finlle and Co.	3,000	10,935
1880	Puerto Plata	El Progreso	Hachtman, Peralta, and Luperón	N/A	N/A
1880	Puerto Plata	La Ubaldina	Francisco Barranco	N/A	N/A
1882	Puerto Plata	San Marcos	Lithgow Brothers	N/A	N/A

Source: Extracted from H. C. C. Astwood to F. T. Frelinghuysen, September 30, 1882, no. 61, DUSCSD, NARA-59; Cassá, *Historia social y económica*, 130, from original source: *Gaceta Oficial*, no. 418, June 17, 1882.

TABLE 3.2. Articles Imported and Consumed for the Year Ending June 30, 1882

Item	Unit	Total	United States	Other Countries
Flour	lb.	12,461	12,020	441
Lard	lb.	239,141	239,141	
Butter	lb.	66,662	66,066	560*
Cheese	lb.	80,663	59,622	31,041*
Codfish	lb.	249,520	247,420	2,100
Kerosene oil	gal.	122,458	122,458	
Shoes	doz.	3,305	1,037	2,268
Rice	lb.	607,414	122,860	484,556*
Merchandise	yds.	4,346,705	1,865,589	2,418,116
Lumber	ft.	1,044,173	786,249	257,924
Sugar	lb.	160,533	160,533	
Provisions general	"general"	461,477	174,581	256,896*
Soap	lb.	405,298	405,094	.200
Bacon	lb.	60,618	60,618	

*Indicates numbers reported that do not add up.
Source: Extracted from H. C. C. Astwood to F. T. Frelinghuysen, September 30, 1882, no. 61, DUSCSD, NARA-59.

TABLE 3.3. Exports for Years Ending June 30, 1881, and June 30, 1882

Item	Unit	Quantity 1881	Value 1881	Quantity 1882	Value 1882	Quantity Increase	Quantity Decrease
Sugar	lb.	8,318,891	342,429.17	11,464,156	554,222.89	3,145,265	
Molasses	gal.	221,644	29,233.11	222,235	49,880.27	591	
Honey	gal.	76,113	27,772.21	86,415	29,811.54	10,302	
Logwood	tons	683¾	7,045.51	527½	7,362.90	43*	
Lignum vitae	tons	1,039½	29,699.16	1,145³/₈	42,358.76	106	
Hides	lb.	60,564	7,662.90	38,580	5,060.34		21,984
Divi divi (tree)	lb.						
Gum	lb.	5,284	1,563.21	1,381	288.75		6,903*
Mahogany	ft.	21,612	1,804.58	1,120	968.90		10,229*
Extract logwood	lb.	9,202	1,022.70				9,202
Fustic (tree)	tons	130³/₅	1,801.71	49³/₈	729.33		51*
Coffee	lb.	40,227	552757	18,170	2,043.11		22,057
Beeswax	lb.	8,941	2,187.63				8,941
Miscellaneous			1,311.07		29,751.87		
Total			471,050.13		719,478.66		

*Indicates numbers reported that do not add up.

Source: Extracted from H. C. C. Astwood to F. T. Frelinghuysen, September 30, 1882, no. 61, DUSCSD, NARA-59.

Third, Astwood's recommendations for American investors betrayed his own views on how to improve Dominican-American commercial relations. Quite candidly and perhaps unsurprisingly, Astwood desired a complete American monopoly over Dominican trade. Besides sugar, Astwood singled out the country's struggling tobacco market and nascent fruit, coffee, and cacao industries as areas for US investment.[42] He hoped that the United States would replace Germany as the primary tobacco consumer and suggested that Dominican fruit and coffee would meet demand Stateside. Infrastructure represented another arena. Sugar and wood could be exported easily if Americans would invest in the building of roads, bridges, and train tracks. Astwood reported that plans were in the works for two railroad lines, one between Samaná and Santiago in the north and Santo Domingo and Azua in the south. He moreover related that a telephone line between the sugar estate La Fe and the capital had recently been installed, putting several plantations in communication with the city. American capital, he surmised, could moreover relieve the country's financial burdens, which he described in detail. These included the circulation of counterfeit money; the outstanding national debt, which amounted to $3 million; the internal debt and the circulation of worthless government bonds to liquidate it; and the government's reliance upon import and export duties and its dependence upon the merchant-controlled *junta de crédito* to collect them.[43] Government officials believed a national bank would correct these issues, and Astwood hoped Americans would hold a controlling interest in this enterprise. Monopoly, in Astwood's mind, would eventually lead to the United States' possession of the island. "Nothing in my judgement will give perfect peace and security to this beautiful island but its occupation in part or whole by the American government," he maintained.[44]

Astwood's viewpoints fit squarely within the context of growing US imperialism in Latin America. However, his hope for a US occupation also reflected an African American ethos that sought racial uplift of independent Black nations even at the risk of Dominican sovereignty. Such had been the case when the African American traveler J. Dennis Harris had proposed Black immigration to Samaná and other Dominican ports in his 1860 travelogue *A Summer on the Borders of the Caribbean Sea*.[45] The same ideas had manifested when many African Americans had rallied behind the annexation cause in the late 1860s and early 1870s.[46] Back then, African Americans had hoped that annexation would make the Dominican Republic's "racial paradise" another state within the union, and usher in US economy and

Protestant religion to Dominicans' benefit.[47] Now in 1882, Astwood wrote in similar ways about the advantages of American trade to Dominican society. US wool, denim, and other fabrics produced at the cotton mills of Wesson, Mississippi, for example, would give a "better appearance" and be "more serviceable" and "to a better advantage" to Dominicans.[48] Santo Domingo's port could become "one of the finest harbours in the West Indies," and "convenient cottages," which could be built along the waterfront, would address the city's housing crisis.[49] A labor shortage in agriculture, moreover, could be solved with formerly enslaved cane planters from New Orleans.[50] In making the pitch for Black immigration and arguing for agricultural diversification and infrastructure development, Astwood acted within a specific US Black thought tradition that diverged from that of white American monoculture extractivism.[51]

However, Astwood's vision for Dominican society clashed with that of many Partido Azul leaders, who shied away from racial language and felt wary of US capital. History justified their suspicions. In the 1870s, American speculators Joseph Warren Fabens and William L. Cazneau had flaunted the concessions Báez had granted them for their support of US annexation.[52] Moreover, Fabens served as Báez's lobbyist in Washington and had also advocated for the fraudulent loan contracted between the dictator and the British subject Edward Hartmont.[53] The Hartmont loan had irrecoverably indebted the Dominican nation, which in 1882 found itself still burdened by this foreign debt.[54] To make matters worse, the United States had refused to recognize money owed to the Dominican government, some $235,432 with interest, for its use of Samaná Bay in 1871 and 1872.[55] In the late 1870s and early 1880s, presidents Espaillat, Meriño, and Luperón each attempted to force the United States to honor its debt, but the US government had ignored them. As recent history had proved, US capitalists and government agents could not be trusted. Thus, in 1882, prominent *azules* disagreed about the extent to which their government should contract with Americans versus European powers such as France, Britain, and Germany.

Other *azules* protested the influx of foreign capital more generally. While Dominican newspapers typically reported positively on the sugar industry, some liberals demurred.[56] The intellectual and "father of Dominican sociology" Pedro Francisco Bonó was chief among the critics who bemoaned "the titles to [Dominican] property transferred almost for free into the hands of new occupants wrapped in the disguise of progress."[57]

Puerto Rican philosopher and educator Eugenio María de Hostos, who spent years in the Dominican Republic, likewise warned about the sugar industry's dependence upon foreign capital and dominance over exports. Sugar made the nation dependent upon a single crop, crippling small-scale production that provided vegetables, fruits, livestock, and other goods for national consumption.[58] In short, the influx of foreign capital stirred anxiety over the republic's future among some liberals.

Astwood would become increasingly aware of pervading anti-American sentiment across the republic, especially as it manifested in the later part of the 1880s. However, over the summer of 1882, an election year in the Dominican Republic, the pathway for American investment seemed cleared as Ulises Heureaux assumed the presidency for the first time. Astwood immediately recognized Heureaux as an ally, for whom he expressed unequivocal praise. Heureaux, in Astwood's estimation, was "a very brave man" whose presidency guaranteed the stability of the nation and advanced American commercial interests.[59] Astwood's approbation of Heureaux derived not only from Heureaux's friendliness to US investors but also from the fact that he knew Heureaux and the Partido Azul's other most prominent Black leader, Gregorio Luperón, from his early years spent between the Turks Islands and Puerto Plata. Astwood kept secret the precise nature of his relationship with Heureaux, and he wrote little about Luperón, a known critic of the United States who was stationed in France in 1882–83 anyway. Still, on more than one occasion, the US consul divulged that he and the new Dominican president were "intimate and confidential friends."[60]

The camaraderie between Astwood and Heureaux served each man's political interests, as they jockeyed for US recognition and symbolic marks of authority. Heureaux's early petition for a US legation in Santo Domingo, for example, demonstrated how he would sometimes use Astwood to present his desires to Washington. In another example, within weeks of his inauguration, Heureaux summoned Astwood to discuss the possible renewal of the Samaná Bay Company's contract for the lease of the northern peninsula.[61] The Samaná lease would provide the Dominican executive with a steady cash stream, and the president wished to know the US government's position on the matter. Ultimately, the communications between Heureaux and the company led nowhere since the United States considered the negotiations to be a private matter outside the political purview of government.[62] But the "highly confidential" talks established a pattern; Heureaux and Astwood contrived many other plans together behind closed doors.[63]

For his part, Astwood used his tie to Heureaux to gain the trust of US capitalists who sought concessions from the Dominican government. Subsequent dispatches also show that the US consul took any issues involving Americans that he could not easily resolve directly to the executive branch. While Heureaux did not always defend Americans (and never publicly), the cooperation between the US consul and the Dominican president precipitated various deals that came to light in the pages of the *Gaceta Oficial*.[64] Leveraging that success, Astwood tried to convince US State Department officials that his unique relationship to Heureaux not only made him indispensable to American commercial and diplomatic interests but also gave the United States a direct path toward monopoly. It took a while for Astwood to realize, however, that State Department officials in Washington did not share the same view.

As the year 1882 drew to a close, the US consul reflected cheerfully upon recent events. The first sugar crop was en route to New York.[65] Astwood had received personal accolades for his handling of an American ship that had capsized within leagues of Santo Domingo's harbor.[66] Heureaux remained in power; he had successfully squashed a revolt emanating from the Cibao. "The prompt manner in which the President acted in disbanding the rebels has added to the confidence and esteem in which he was held by the people. I think we can look forward to peaceful and successful administration," the US consul reported.[67] From Astwood's vantage point, the future looked bright for the Dominican nation.

But then, all of a sudden, the outlook changed as seemingly innocent words uttered by the sitting US president wreaked havoc in Santo Domingo. In his State of the Union address, Chester A. Arthur advised that due to increased commercial relations with Haiti and the Dominican Republic, the United States planned to place the Dominican Republic under the diplomatic jurisdiction of the US Haitian Legation.[68] News of this arrangement reached Santo Domingo in early 1883, prompting Astwood to object most fervently. Dominican officials "construe that [their] Government is rated beneath that of the Government of Hayti of which Republic they had gained their Independence and [it] would now be considered an act of humiliation to be placed Diplomatically beneath that Government," Astwood warned.[69] The new hierarchy would indicate that, in the United States' purview, the Dominican Republic was not only a Black nation akin to Liberia and Haiti, but Hispaniola's other Black republic—Haiti's tagalong younger sibling.

Bartering Black Authority: Concessions, Claims, and Diplomatic Reciprocity

To date, historians have noted but not yet probed a seemingly trivial state of affairs: from November 20, 1883, to June 14, 1904, the United States directed all diplomatic relations with Santo Domingo through its legation in Port-au-Prince, where a series of African American officials served as US minister to Haiti and chargé d'affaires to the Dominican Republic. During the same years, the US government sent four African American consuls to Santo Domingo.[70] This arrangement made sense to American officials heading an underfunded, understaffed State Department leery of Black government. It made less sense to a lettered class of Dominican politicians who scorned their republic's African heritage and tie to Haiti. Perhaps out of deference to the Dominican elite, historians have overlooked this diplomatic faux pas. The early 1880s were, after all, the "awkward years" of US diplomacy, a transformative period when "mistakes and blundering were probably inevitable."[71]

The US State Department in 1880, unbeknownst to most observers at the time, sat on the cusp of a titanic shift in American foreign policy, and on the whole its permanent staff and untrained public servants found themselves woefully unprepared. In 1880, the United States, unlike Europe, did not possess a robust diplomatic corps.[72] The country's three hundred consuls and commercial agents were political appointees, often merchants or denizens of the local government or European powers, who frequently had no experience in foreign affairs. Once in office, they received no formal training, no job security, and scant pay. Accordingly, any given agent abroad found himself "disillusioned to learn that he must spend hours each day at routine paper work in a dull commercial town, and that on his meager salary he was expected to circulate respectably among local merchants and bankers in the interests of American trade."[73] This description sums up much of Astwood's experience.

Despite the poor condition of the US State Department in the early 1880s, there were also clear signs that top-down change was imminent. Between 1881 and 1885, two US secretaries of state, James G. Blaine and Frederick T. Frelinghuysen, sought to expand the United States' influence abroad through international trade policy. Seeking foreign markets for the United States' industrial surplus, they especially targeted Latin America. Upon taking office in 1881, Blaine veiled his economic intentions toward the region by calling for a Pan-American conference, which he planned for November 24, 1882, and to which he invited all Latin American nations except Haiti.[74] The conference, which in Blaine's estimation would exhibit American goodwill abroad by opening up conversations about regional trade and peacekeeping, positioned the United States as a paternalistic authority over nations south of its borders. Latin American statesmen were not fooled and denounced American imperialism, and Haiti's minister to the United States bitterly protested the slight.[75] Fortunately for these dignitaries, Blaine's 1882 Pan-American conference never occurred. After US President Garfield's death, President Arthur appointed a new secretary of state, Frelinghuysen, who withdrew the conference invitations soon after taking office. Instead, Frelinghuysen pursued his own plans for US economic expansion in Latin America: a series of reciprocity trade treaties.

Based on the 1875 Hawaiian reciprocity treaty, Frelinghuysen's trade agreements, at face value, would institute tariff privileges for American manufactured goods in Latin America and provide the same benefits for Latin American raw materials imported into the United States. They would also force Latin American markets to give preference to the United States over Europe. For Frelinghuysen, time was of the essence. Between 1882 and 1885, while Congress debated the extension of the Hawaiian treaty, the State Department opened concurrent discussions for reciprocity treaties with Mexico, Colombia, El Salvador, the Dominican Republic, Spain (Cuba and Puerto Rico), and the British West Indies.[76] Of these territories, only negotiations with Mexico, Spain, and the Dominican Republic produced signed treaties by the end of 1884.[77]

While historians have recognized the United States' imperialist economic threat in studies of the Spanish and Mexican treaties, the Dominican reciprocity treaty has not drawn much scholarly attention.[78] Yet, of the three treaties, the Dominican case most obviously reveals what historians have only recently stated plainly: racism undergirded the United States' capitalist imperialism and fundamentally mattered in the official operation of US diplomacy.[79] Today, it is no shock that white US bureaucrats conceived of Catholic Latin American peoples as inherently inferior to Protestant Anglo-Saxons and believed that US economic supremacy would instill the "proper" racial order over the hemisphere. Throughout the nineteenth century, this white supremacist ideology had driven the official US policy of nonrecognition of Haiti and the Dominican Republic. As stated earlier, island leaders had turned to economic incentives to exercise their political authority within the international arena.[80] By extending diplomatic recognition to these two nations in the 1860s, the United States ostensibly pledged to negotiate on equal terms with the island republics and legally recognize the reciprocal rights of American, Dominicans, and Haitian citizens. Yet the asymmetry of power between the United States and the island republics meant that diplomatic and commercial relations never operated on fair, equal, or reciprocal terms.

Still, for Haitians, Dominicans, and African Americans who had long fought for the diplomatic recognition of Hispaniola's two nations, the idea of reciprocity imbued the trade treaties of the early 1880s with special symbolic meaning. On the surface, trade reciprocity signified the United States' willingness to deal equally with nonwhite peoples during an era of reactionary anti-Black violence in the United States post-Reconstruction.[81] As one African American editorialist explained regarding the reciprocity treaty with Mexico, "When it is remembered that Mexico is a nation composed of peoples so colored that the average man among them would be liable to the insults we as a class are wont to receive, [then the treaty] is not only significant, but shows at once the readiness of the ruling class in our country to shake hands with anybody and everybody with whom it will pay."[82] This was even more true when considering the Dominican Republic, a nation "purely negro," according to the same author. The notion of reciprocity present in both the move toward diplomatic recognition of Haiti and the Dominican Republic in the 1860s and the 1880s trade treaties marked the symbolic rupture of racial barriers on the international stage for the sake of capitalist accumulation. Believing that white Americans' avarice exceeded their racist antagonism, some African Americans saw the treaties as a step in the right direction. Thus, the Dominican case not only exposed the United States' capitalist imperialism but also revealed how African Americans viewed reciprocity treaties as part of the continued fight for Black equality.

Given this context, the United States' formal diplomatic and commercial relations with the Dominican Republic in the early 1880s require an analytical lens that stretches beyond the vantage point of a defective but changing US State Department. Astwood's experiences as US consul must also be reconsidered because all things were empirically not equal. While every US consular agent suffered the underpaid drudgery of their posts, Astwood operated under the additional and perpetual stigma of Blackness—his own and that of the island. In Santo Domingo, moreover, Astwood found himself in an unofficial diplomatic role and in competition with representatives of European nations, white men who received higher pay from their governments and preferential treatment from the deeply class- and color-conscious Dominican elite, not to discount Dominicans' sometimes vehement anti-American sentiment.[83] Thus, Astwood's experiences as US consul did not truly resemble the status quo of US consuls everywhere but instead reflected the United States' diplomatic apartheid.[84]

Segregated statecraft was the natural product of the State Department's racist operations. As the process by which notions of official and unofficial diplomacy operated along racially bifurcated lines, segregated statecraft sheds light on State Department hierarchy. It also exposes the United States' development of free trade imperialism, defined by Naoko Shibusawa as the use of treaties and agreements to impose imperial state power instead of territorial appropriation.[85] Regarding State Department operations, racist attitudes created a duality in which high-ranking white foreign service officers operating in Washington and abroad ran the formal channels of diplomacy. At the same time, Black foreign service officers' activities, while technically sanctioned, nevertheless remained in the shadows. Washington-based officials, American capitalists, and less-well-off white travelers constantly second-guessed Black officials' intentions, dismissed their insight, and reprimanded or praised their actions based on white Americans' pecuniary interests. Within this hostile environment, African American officials advanced reciprocal (i.e., free trade) treaties as part of the struggle for racial equality in the United States. They did so because reciprocal trade connoted racial equality even though international deals often included injurious "unreciprocated privileges."[86] Consequently, Black US agents pushed forward such treaties as they simultaneously pushed back against racism.

Astwood's response to President Arthur's proposal to place the Dominican Republic under the diplomatic charge of the US minister to Haiti demonstrates this troublesome process. The consular record shows that, in order to reverse Arthur's decision and induce the US government to establish a legation in Santo Domingo instead, Astwood proposed a "medium reciprocity treaty" between the United States and the Dominican Republic.[87] This is to say that the idea for the Dominican reciprocity treaty did not originate in Washington. It began eight months prior to formal negotiations as a private discussion between Astwood, Heureaux, and the Dominican minister of finance, Eugenio Generoso de Marchena, and served a dual purpose: (1) to stimulate the Dominican economy, and (2) to counter President Arthur's proposal. In Astwood's calculus, such treaty negotiations necessitated an upgrade of his consular post. The upgrade carried symbolic power—a recognition of Black political authority expressed through Heureaux's presidency and Astwood's position. Thus, Astwood's quest for the treaty and the consular upgrade became a proxy battle in a larger geopolitical war for Black equality.

In this symbolic fight, the building of US economic empire and the bartering of Black political authority existed as interdependent processes, two sides of the same coin. Astwood's dispatches evidence this unhappy dialectic as he made plain his view that US trade relations and diplomatic representation in Santo Domingo were necessarily intertwined. In the same February 16, 1883, letter in which Astwood protested Arthur's proposal, the US consul self-consciously applied for the position of "Minister Resident and consul general" at Santo Domingo.[88] He explained that the growing commercial importance of the island had "forced" him to make the "bold request" to upgrade his post. Then, in a second dispatch on the same date, he floated the reciprocal treaty idea. The treaty would enable US products to enter the Dominican Republic at half the duties of the current tax code, and Dominican products would have the same privilege in the United States. The negotiation of the treaty would also require US diplomatic engagement with Santo Domingo. Simply put, economic and diplomatic reciprocity went hand in hand.

Astwood's attempts in 1883–84 to secure both a reciprocity treaty and diplomatic legation for Santo Domingo evidence his political calculus. He not only asserted his central role in developing the treaty idea but also strategically presented his ideas as in line with US economic interests. "I have been devising plans, which if appreciated by Congress," he proffered, "cannot fail, not only to be beneficial to both countries, but will completely Americanize the commerce of this Republic."[89] He warned that the United States would otherwise lose ground to Europe. His influence with Heureaux, however, had "paralyzed" local efforts to increase European trade. Such self-aggrandizement served a dual purpose. On the one hand, it boosted white US officials' confidence in Astwood's consular work. On the other hand, it forced white US officials to recognize both Astwood's and Heureaux's political authority. The ultimate goal, of course, was to secure reciprocity's symbolic meaning for the Dominican government by convincing Washington to establish a legation in Santo Domingo. Thus, in essence, both Astwood and Heureaux offered an American monopoly in exchange for symbolic political power.

In his writing, Astwood also highlighted certain Dominicans' hostility toward the United States. By doing so, he hinted at a moral logic that was beginning to form in his mind. For example, when the State Department killed discussions regarding the Samaná Bay Company's lease renewal, Astwood lamented the missed opportunity. General Luperón and Dr. Ramón Emeterio Betances, the Afro–Puerto Rican revolutionary and one-time Dominican agent to France, were attempting to secure the Samaná lease for France. "I do not believe that it is the desire of our government to see Foreign nations control further the Antilles," Astwood goaded in early 1883, implicitly citing the Monroe Doctrine.[90] He then described Luperón as a "sharp and shrewd man," who opposed US capitalist investment in the Dominican Republic and "[did] his work rather underhandedly." While in the Dominican Republic such descriptions of politicians did not necessarily carry negative connotations, for US readers Astwood's language recycled old grievances against the general.[91] It moreover hinted that Dominicans who opposed US dominance were somehow devious. This notion mapped onto Americans' racialized moral imagining of the island.

The State Department, however, did not take the bait. Indeed, officials seemed less interested in Astwood's diplomatic insights and more concerned about reining in Astwood's growing sense of self-importance. Two contemporaneous disputes clearly demonstrate Astwood's attempts to control US-Dominican affairs and, alternatively, US officials' attempts to control him.

The first involved the American entrepreneur Allen Howard Crosby, who, during Báez's last presidential term (1876–78), received a concession to build a bridge over the capital's Ozama River.[92] The contract stipulated that a quarter of the bridge's proceeds would go to the *ayuntamiento* (town council), but it did not specify whether that percentage applied to the gross or the net amount. By 1882, the bridge was in operation, and Crosby paid the town council based on the net amount. The council then sued Crosby for the gross amount. The lawsuit produced an official record: hundreds of pages of legal documents that spanned the years 1882–84. Astwood, however, involved himself in an unofficial extralegal process when, at the behest of Crosby, he spoke with Heureaux about "the gravity of the case."[93] Heureaux then pressured the courts to side with Crosby. The justices refused. Astwood protested, to no avail. He then reported the judges' "abuses" to the US State Department.

In the same dispatch in which Astwood detailed the Crosby case, he informed the State Department of another situation in which two American sailors of the schooner *Lizzie Titus* "breached the peace" in Santo Domingo in a typical fashion: they got drunk, insulted some Dominican guards, and were subsequently arrested and put in the stocks overnight. The ship's captain complained to Astwood about the sailors' sentence. The US consul, in turn, wrote to the governor, who dismissed the claim as a police matter. Astwood then elevated his concerns to Minister of Foreign Affairs Segundo Imbert and President Heureaux. Both men referred Astwood once again to the governor. After a brief back-and-forth, the extralegal processes eventually resolved "satisfactorily" in Astwood's estimation, when Imbert finally investigated the matter and "strictly reprimanded" the port authorities.[94]

The US consul's first dispatch regarding these concurrent events revealed his political acumen as he advanced a nuanced argument regarding Black political authority. Astwood knew that he had overstepped his official duties in both cases, so he tailored an excuse: consular regulations were too limited. Consuls abandoned the interests of foreign citizens out of "fear" that their exequaturs would be revoked. Dominican "abuses" against Americans, however, were too "painful" for Astwood, who was "forced" to speak out against "revolutionary republics . . . though it be at [his] official peril."[95] Here, for the first time, Astwood elevated his own virtue while engaging a well-worn racist stereotype about the island: the Dominican Republic, like Haiti, was a revolutionary republic whose Black officials violated white Americans' rights. The US consul then inversed the racialized moral meaning behind the diplomatic concept of reciprocity. If the Dominican Republic desired true diplomatic reciprocity, he argued, then its officials must learn to respect American privileges. "If our relations are reciprocal, our rights must be [as well]," he proffered. He then carefully stressed that "ignorant and incompetent subordinates," not President Heureaux, had committed the abuses, and had left the US consul with no choice but "to appeal for the higher authorities." Thus, Astwood prompted US officials to support both Heureaux's administration and his own extralegal consular actions. His logic suggested that for the United States to dominate the republic, white US officials had to first legitimize and partner with certain Black authorities (i.e., Astwood and Heureaux).

However, Assistant Secretary of State John Davis cared not for Astwood's insight. Alarmed by Astwood's interference in the two disputes, Davis reprimanded his agent: "Your position as consul does not give you the right to appeal in your representative capacity to the Minister for Foreign Affairs."[96] Davis also reminded Astwood that the United States could not intercede on behalf of private citizens' commercial contracts with foreign governments.[97] Any American who invested abroad did so "with full knowledge of the laws and spirit of the people."[98] Put another way, US capitalists should know better that Dominicans' character could not be trusted. Accordingly, Davis's insistence that Astwood follow official proto-col (despite historical precedent) not only enforced the State Department hierarchy but also reinforced the racial hierarchy that Astwood sought to disrupt for his and Heureaux's benefit.[99]

Astwood took note but discursively dodged Davis's reprimand. The US consul received the assistant secretary's instructions in early 1883, about the same time that he learned of the State Department's plan to place the Dominican Republic diplomatically under Haiti. Gently countering Davis in a dispatch dated February 26, Astwood conveniently linked together the recent events. While acknowledging Davis's advice, the US consul decried the "gross injustice" committed against Crosby.[100] He then la-mented the lack of diplomatic representation in Santo Domingo, praised his own efforts regarding the *Lizzie Titus* incident, and reminded Davis of the "necessity of a more effectual commercial treaty to protect [Ameri-can interests]."[101] A week later, Astwood warned again that the Dominican government "receives very unfavorably the rumor of placing this Republic diplomatically under Haiti."[102] Both a reciprocity treaty and an upgrade of his office were in order, he maintained.

For months thereafter, Astwood boldly continued to pursue the reciproc-ity treaty and his application to be minister-resident. In late March 1883, the State Department informed Astwood that it would take both measures under "careful consideration."[103] Davis did not reveal, however, that in actuality Congress had already approved Arthur's recommendation to make the US minister at Port-au-Prince the new chargé d'affaires of the Dominican Republic. Astwood wrote Davis again regarding the two pro-posals in September 1883 upon his return to Santo Domingo from his first leave of absence. In his dispatch, he forwarded a petition signed by twelve American capitalists, most of them sugar estate owners, to make him minister-resident.[104] Maybe now Davis would provide a direct answer to his entreaty? Two weeks later, Astwood forwarded a letter from Imbert regarding the reciprocal treaty, noting again that "the Dominican govern-ment recommends the appointment of a Diplomatic representative to form the basis of the treaty."[105] Perhaps he would finally be appointed to the role. Astwood remained hopeful, but it took the State Department an additional two months before Davis deigned to respond.

Finally, in mid-October, Astwood learned from Davis that he would not be promoted to minister-resident or consul general at Santo Domingo because on February 26, 1883, Congress had appointed the US minister at Port-au-Prince as the new chargé d'affaires.[106] Official diplomatic instructions were sent in November 1883 to John Mercer Langston, the renowned African American lawyer and current US minister to Haiti.[107] Davis also informed Astwood that the new chargé d'affaires would handle the treaty matter going forward.[108] These events troubled Astwood, who, in accepting the news of Langston's appointment, pleaded at least for a pay raise, to no avail.[109] In a subsequent dispatch, the US consul also described, truthfully or not, the Dominican government's heightened anxiety; Imbert had "found it strange" that in December 1883 Langston had not yet applied for his exequatur.[110] At that time, Langston had only just accepted the position and would soon fulfill the obligation. Yet, with this note, Astwood betrayed a real fear that the new chargé d'affaires might not bother to address the Dominican government separately from Haiti at all.

Building a "Moral Foothold": The Ritualistic Performance of Righteous Indignation

At the start of 1884, the possibility of a US legation in Santo Domingo was gone. The new year also brought a crash in the international sugar market, inciting plantation owners to pressure the Dominican government and the US consul for relief. Confronting these setbacks, Astwood ignored Langston's jurisdiction and attempted to control the reciprocity treaty process by involving himself in two parallel disputes. First, he continued to push the Crosby case before the US and Dominican governments. Second, he found a new cause in the obsolete case of E. Remington and Sons, a New York–based firearms company that demanded payment for guns and ammunition sent to Báez in the 1870s. An analysis of both high-profile cases reveals that the reciprocity treaty became the chief objective in a continued symbolic fight for Black political authority.[111] Through performances of righteous indignation in these cases, Astwood engaged in unofficial diplomatic negotiations in order to influence the treaty's outcome and thus enforce his authority.

Shortly after the new year celebrations of 1884, Astwood brought up the Crosby case again. The dispute between Crosby and the *ayuntamiento* had grown even more hostile. According to Astwood, the *ayuntamiento* had attempted to take over the bridge on a legal technicality, but before the courts settled the matter a hurricane washed away the bridge. Crosby then turned to Astwood, who again met with Heureaux. In Astwood's telling,

Heureaux agreed that the hurricane was an act of God and that Crosby should be given more time to complete the bridge. Nevertheless, once again, this unofficial diplomatic process failed to persuade the courts. When Crosby tried to recover his losses by providing a temporary ferry across the river instead of the bridge, the *ayuntamiento* immediately sued him and seized his barge. In a similar process as before, Crosby lost the lawsuit before the Dominican Supreme Court in early 1884.[112]

In handling the Crosby case, Astwood performed various roles as he navigated between three groups of power brokers. To American capitalists in Santo Domingo (e.g., Crosby), Astwood introduced himself as an official who had the ear of the Dominican president. To Dominican officials, he acted as a diplomatic agent imbued with special power to aid or obstruct US-Dominican diplomatic affairs. And, to US officials in Washington, he showed himself to be a stalwart defender of American interests. Well aware of the "heightened sensitivity that international actors have towards both performance and spectatorship," Astwood decried Dominican "abuses" against white American "victims" as he moved between these three groups.[113] This cultural narrative formed part of his strategic performance of righteous indignation that imbued the case with racialized moral meaning.

Astwood's dispatches to Washington especially demonstrate this performance. Although Davis again cautioned Astwood in late December 1883 that the US government could not intervene diplomatically in private contracts, Astwood reiterated that this noninterventionist policy made it "dangerous in the extreme" for US capitalists to invest in the Dominican Republic because, despite Heureaux's leadership, Americans' security depended upon the "good faith" of subordinated Dominican officials, and, he said, the "rights of foreigners are only maintained in the fear of interference by their Governments."[114] He presented the new developments in Crosby's case as his primary example. He then linked the Crosby affair to the idea of diplomatic reciprocity by stating again that the Dominican government's position in the case ran counter to reciprocity.[115] Dominican abuses put potential reciprocal trade relations in jeopardy, Astwood argued, as he attempted to assert influence over the treaty process.

In the same vein, Astwood made similar arguments regarding Crosby to the Dominican government. In early February 1884, he submitted a formal protest and letter to the *ayuntamiento* to Imbert. In his cover letter, Astwood acknowledged his limitations: "As you know this office has no diplomatic functions, consequently I have no authority to discuss the legal questions involved."[116] Still, Astwood pursued the matter, claiming that the extant 1867 US-Dominican treaty gave him such authority even though Crosby's concession had a clause that explicitly prohibited diplomatic interference. Astwood dismissed the inconvenient clause: "where Governments have reciprocal treaties . . . [such clauses] would not hold good."[117] He then alleged that someone in the Dominican government had committed fraud by publishing the terms of Crosby's concession incorrectly in the *Gaceta Oficial*. The protest and *ayuntamiento* letter continued along the same lines. Summarizing Crosby's testimony, the protest appeared as a legal affidavit, with Astwood both assuming the role of Crosby's lawyer and providing the official seal of the US consul. The same document established that the *ayuntamiento* had pursued "illegal and arbitrary proceedings against [Crosby]" and had "continually menaced" and "persistently persecuted" him.[118] It then demanded $100,000 as compensation for damages. The *ayuntamiento* letter then repeated this grievance and the monetary demand. "Mr. Crosby as a foreign citizen is claiming those reciprocal rights ceded by treaty to the citizens of the two Republics residing in their territories," Astwood asserted.[119] He warned that if the town council did not act favorably toward Crosby, he would forward the matter to the US State Department.

For Imbert, Astwood's intentions were transparent and tiresome. Astwood clearly sought to use Imbert's position as minister of foreign affairs to convey the Dominican executive branch's (i.e., Heureaux's) support of Crosby and thereby compel the *ayuntamiento* to accept Crosby's claim. Imbert refused to play this role, returning unopened Astwood's letter to the town council. The Crosby matter was "purely and essentially judicial, outside of the jurisdiction of the Executive Power and still further beyond the attributions and prerogatives of [the American] Consulate," Imbert objected.[120] Preempting Astwood's threat to complain to the US State Department, Imbert then wrote to US Secretary of State Frelinghuysen himself, enclosing his correspondence with Astwood and other evidence of the Dominican Republic's just comportment in the Crosby affair. In his correspondence with Frelinghuysen, Imbert accused Astwood of violating international law, insulting the Dominican government, and creating his own extralegal jurisdiction to contest a case already decided by the Dominican Supreme Court.[121] Imbert's read on Astwood exposed the consul's scheme. When faced with the US State Department's instructions to back down, Astwood used Crosby's case to invent his own jurisdiction and then vaunted the idea of reciprocity to defend his authority to do so.

Unaware of Imbert's correspondence with Frelinghuysen, Astwood continued his attack. First, he accused Imbert of insulting him. "The return of the document unopened is in my opinion not a lack of courtesy to this office only but to the Government which it represents," he protested.[122] Astwood then forwarded all correspondence with Imbert to Washington along with a translation of Crosby's concession.[123] A few weeks later, Astwood pushed the matter even further. Writing to Imbert on Crosby's behalf, Astwood stated that the *ayuntamiento* had summoned Crosby before the Dominican courts and that Crosby could not comply.[124] Astwood then demanded that the *ayuntamiento* and the Dominican judiciary wait until the US State Department had decided whether or not to take action in the case. Imbert retorted that the Dominican government would not recognize Astwood's authority, which was based on a bogus ad hoc jurisdiction.[125] Yet, for his part, Astwood took no responsibility for his actions. Instead, he gaslit his opposition: "I have taken no steps looking to interfere with the working of the courts"; "my whole language was in the spirit of reconciliation rather than aggression"; "I would state that the steps taken by me [were] purely in the interest of peace." It would be "criminal" for Astwood to ignore Crosby's protest, and "still a greater crime" to refuse to raise the issue with the Dominican government, he declared.[126]

By March 1884 it was clear that neither the Dominican nor the US government supported Astwood's viewpoints and actions in the Crosby case. Even so, as Astwood waited for Davis's final response to the matter, he brought the case before Langston during Langston's first visit to Santo Domingo on March 26. Astwood described how, at Langston's invitation, he ferried out to the chargé d'affaires's ship and escorted him to the consulate and then to the presidential palace.[127] Later that night, Astwood introduced Langston to Crosby, who undoubtedly presented his case to the chargé d'affaires. Then, during a two-hour meeting the following day, Heureaux and Astwood tried to convince Langston to endorse their proposal for a new trade reciprocity treaty.[128] Yet, despite friendly relations and lavish praise on all sides, Langston made no promises, and Astwood later noted that the chargé d'affaires's visit, which lasted less than forty-eight hours, had been too short to make any headway on the treaty negotiations.[129] Twelve days later, Astwood boarded a French steamer for Port-au-Prince, where the US consul hoped to meet privately with Langston regarding the reciprocity treaty and yet another American claim against the Dominican government.[130] He likely discussed Crosby too.

Despite all this, the Crosby case made no additional headway. In fact, upon returning to Santo Domingo, Astwood learned of unfavorable developments regarding both Crosby and the reciprocity treaty. First, Davis had finally responded to his dispatches. As expected, the US assistant secretary of state disavowed Astwood's action under the same terms as he had before. Davis moreover rejected the idea that Imbert had insulted the US government and instead insisted that Imbert's responses to Astwood were "courteous and well-tempered."[131] Davis then instructed Astwood to cease advocating for Crosby since any further efforts "would be unavailing." In response, Astwood finally yielded, while still demurring that "the outcome [would] be detrimental to American interests," and that his dispatches "must have been badly worded" for Davis to give him such instructions.[132] Astwood then relayed the details of another small claim against the government, explaining, "these are some of the abuses to which Americans are subjected here" because the US government refused to intervene.[133] The Crosby affair had not engendered the intervention he desired, but perhaps another case would; he would wait and see.

For now, though, Astwood had other concerns. Details regarding his meeting with Langston in Port-au-Prince elude the historical record, but it can be inferred that the two US agents made little progress regarding the reciprocity treaty. Mere days after Astwood returned to Santo Domingo, Heureaux appointed Manuel de Jesús Galván, a Euro-Dominican statesman known for his anti-Haitian views, as plenipotentiary Dominican minister to lead the reciprocity negotiations in Washington.[134] To Astwood, Galván's appointment seemed premature, and he stated as much in a private meeting with Heureaux.[135] The US consul reminded the Dominican president that the US State Department awaited Langston's report on the treaty, and he promised a quick response to the proposal thereafter. Heureaux, however, saw no reason for delay and believed that Galván could speed the process through his friends in Washington. The fifty-year-old Manuel de Jesús Galván, after all, was not just any Dominican statesman. Most known for his literary work *Enriquillo* (1882), which his contemporaries recognized as the first Dominican novel, Galván was also an experienced lawyer who in 1884 served as the president of the Dominican Supreme Court.[136] These credentials made Galván one of the foremost lettered Dominicans of his day.[137] For Astwood, though, Galván represented an obstacle. Not only had Galván blocked progress in Crosby's case as head of the Supreme Court, but his appointment also meant that future treaty discussions no longer fell under Astwood's unofficial purview. This change suggested that Heureaux had lost faith in Astwood and Langston's ability to advance the negotiations. White men in Washington would now settle the official terms of a treaty first discussed between Astwood and Heureaux.

Official treaty negotiations commenced soon after Galván presented his credentials to Secretary of State Frelinghuysen and President Arthur on June 3, 1884.[138] Two weeks later, Galván sent Frelinghuysen an initial draft of the treaty, which was based on the extant US-Mexican treaty. The draft stipulated that the Dominican Republic would grant a 25 percent reduction for three American manufactured goods and admit fifty-nine other American products free of duty. In return, the United States had to reduce duties on three Dominican manufactured goods (brandy, rum, and tobacco products) and admit twenty-one products free of duty.[139] A month passed before Frelinghuysen responded to this proposal with a counter-version of the treaty. In the cover letter to the revised draft, Frelinghuysen informed Galván that he was unprepared to decide on a schedule of products, yet he still provided a summary of modifications he made to Galván's articles.[140] Galván responded to Frelinghuysen a week later, accepting most of Frelinghuysen's amendments and adding a few of his own.[141] It seemed that the negotiations would proceed quickly. But then, just as soon as it had started, correspondence from Frelinghuysen ceased.

Meanwhile, in Santo Domingo, Astwood's unofficial statecraft continued. Throughout the summer of 1884, he voiced indignation at various cases concerning American capitalists and cautioned the US government to proceed carefully with, and perhaps even stall, the treaty negotiations due to social unrest. He contended that the pending Dominican presidential elections of July 1884 had unsettled the nation.[142] On the one hand, Dominicans feared that Heureaux would void the elections and install himself as dictator. On the other hand, the country might elect a "revolutionary Government" that would not respect the acts of the current administration.[143] If the new administration followed in Heureaux's footsteps, it would "inspire confidence" among American capitalists, but the Crosby case had indicated that "good faith" between Americans and Dominicans "was only maintained for fear of international claim."[144] Meanwhile, the Dominican government and sugar planters aimed to "railroad through the commercial treaty," but the Dominican legislature paid no attention to US claims against its government because the US "[would] not interfere."[145] Instead, Dominican officials recognized French and English claims, such as the infamous Hartmont loan.[146] France, moreover, continued to receive "all of the sympathy" regarding concessions while Americans received "abuses" including refusing Crosby a fair trial, pronouncing "null and void" supposed debts owed to US companies, and imposing "heavy port dues" upon US ships.[147] Astwood, however, admonished Heureaux that it was in "bad taste ... to ignore American enterprise and then to expect favorable consideration from our people" in the form of a reciprocity treaty.[148] The implied quid pro quo hinted at Astwood's game: if Heureaux did not support Americans' interests at Astwood's behest in Santo Domingo, Astwood would jeopardize the reciprocity treaty negotiations taking place in Washington.

In actuality, Astwood probably had little influence on Frelinghuysen's decision to stall the treaty negotiations. The value of Astwood's threat, however, lay not in its sincerity but in Dominican officials' perception of its validity. Due to the slow and often indirect means of communication between Washington and Santo Domingo, Dominican officials who eagerly awaited news of the delayed treaty negotiations became increasingly accommodating. Astwood took advantage of this situation in his concurrent unofficial diplomatic negotiations for E. Remington and Sons.

The Remingtons' case was a tricky one. The claim originated during Báez's six-year dictatorship (1868–74) when Dominican Minister of Finance Ricardo Curiel had ordered firearms and ammunition from E. Remington and Sons, which it intended to purchase through proceeds from the rent of Samaná Bay to the American-owned Samaná Bay Company in 1873.[149] But, within the year, Báez's government fell, and in 1874 the Dominican Republic revoked the company's lease and disputed E. Remington and Sons' draft upon its finance department. When the company realized in 1877 that Báez had returned to power, it presented a claim for $23,101.30 to the Dominican government. The Dominican Congress quickly dismissed the debt since the statutes of limitation had run out. It additionally claimed that the Samaná Bay Company, not the Dominican government, owed E. Remington and Sons for the arms.[150] Now, seven years later, E. Remington and Sons had enlisted US Consul Astwood to bring their claim again before the Dominican Congress.[151]

For Astwood, the Remington claim presented a new opportunity to test his methods, but he had to proceed carefully. Back in March, Frelinghuysen had informed both the Remingtons' lawyer and Langston that, as chargé d'affaires, Langston (not Astwood) should present their claim to the Dominican government.[152] Astwood proceeded anyway. During his trip to Port-au-Prince, he spoke with Langston about the Remingtons' claim. Then, as the reciprocity negotiations stalled in Washington, he championed the Remingtons' case in Santo Domingo. Parting ways with Heureaux, he described the claim as a "just" and "honest" one, and suggested that Heureaux had willfully deceived him in repeated promises and failures to present the claim before Congress.[153] "Personally the administration and I are the best of friends," Astwood wrote to the second assistant secretary of state, William Hunter, "but this matter ceases to be personal since it effects the general interest of the people I represent."[154] To Hunter, Astwood stressed that any action in the Remington case would indicate the extent to which the United States had any chance of exerting dominance over the republic. Meanwhile Frelinghuysen and Langston remained ignorant of Astwood's activities.

Ultimately, Astwood's calculations paid off. In late June, the country elected the Heureaux-backed presidential candidate, Gregorio Billini, whom Astwood secretly supported. According to Astwood, Billini endorsed the Remingtons' claim. His brother also served as Dominican consul to the United States in New York, and the pair were friendly to American interests and were especially supportive of the reciprocity treaty and the Remingtons.[155] The opposition candidate, on the other hand, was Segundo Imbert, the former minister of foreign relations who had opposed Astwood in the Crosby case. Billini's election paved the way for Astwood's success. On July 3, Astwood reported that he had gained partial acknowledgment of the Remingtons' claim, which he asserted "would not have been considered but for the pending treaty negotiations" and Billini's support.[156] Three weeks later, on the same date that he advised the State Department to wait until Billini's inauguration to sign the reciprocity treaty, Astwood relayed the details in the Remington affair.[157] The Dominican Congress would accept the claim into the nation's foreign debt, and E. Remington and Sons would receive $46,920.18, less $5,000 for legal expenses.[158] If the Dominican Republic could secure a foreign loan (say from the United States), the Remington claim would be paid in cash. Later, in August, Astwood sent an update. The Dominican Congress's final vote had curtailed the Remingtons' claim by about half, recognizing only the original amount of $23,101.30 (about $690,000 in 2022) without interest.[159] Astwood's protest went unheard. Still, the fact that he had succeeded at gaining the Dominican government's recognition for the claim at all was noteworthy and indicated that Astwood's strategy had at last succeeded.

The final results in the Remington affair confused Langston in Port-au-Prince and State Department officials in Washington. As chargé d'affaires, Langston had written to Imbert twice regarding the matter—once in April and again in June—and had received no response. Then, around the first week of September 1884, Langston received a note from Billini's new Dominican minister of foreign affairs, J. T. Mejía, informing him that Astwood had settled the claim. Writing to Frelinghuysen, Langston fumbled. He could not say exactly how much or when the Dominican government planned to compensate E. Remington and Sons, but he promised Frelinghuysen that he would investigate.[160] This inefficiency, of course, was not a problem of Langston's own making. With his focus on Haiti, Langston simply could not keep up with events in Santo Domingo, and besides, Astwood had taken matters into his own hands. Seven weeks passed before the chargé d'affaires learned the full details from the Dominican Republic's *Gaceta Oficial* and forwarded them to Washington.[161] Astwood, in turn, had achieved what he had hoped for from the start: he had controlled affairs in Santo Domingo as if he, not Langston, were the United States' diplomatic representative to the Dominican Republic.

Conclusion

It is easy to see Astwood's desire for a consular upgrade and defense of American interests in Santo Domingo as signs of his own ambition. This interpretation, while partially accurate, misses the greater context. Astwood, like other African Americans of his day, viewed Hispaniola's other "Black republic" as a potential model for an American racial paradise and a sign of Black political capacity despite hegemonic racist disbelief in Black rule. Astwood, at least at first, believed that US investment in Dominican infrastructure would prove mutually beneficial for the United States and the Dominican Republic. But then the US government placed Santo Domingo under the diplomatic jurisdiction of Port-au-Prince. This move put Astwood on the defensive, and he persistently bartered for an upgrade in his diplomatic post and worked with Heureaux to propose a reciprocity treaty to the United States. It was only after his application for consul general was denied and the reciprocity treaty was taken out of his hands that Astwood attempted to use American claims against the Dominican government to exert his influence over diplomatic relations. His performance of righteous indignation did not gain him any ground in the Crosby case, but the Remington claim succeeded because it aligned with the timing of the reciprocity treaty, a measure that was deeply needed in Santo Domingo due to the 1884 sugar crash. In the end, Astwood astutely read the political scene, and his involvement in unofficial diplomacy earned him the de facto authority he had sought all along. Nowhere in the diplomatic record does it explicitly say that Astwood gamed the system, but the plethora of coinciding factors suggests this clear line of interpretation.

Such "coincidences" continued through the end of the year. After winning the Remington settlement, Astwood boarded a steamer along with Gregorio Luperón bound for New York, where the traveling companions stayed together at the Fifth Avenue Hotel and most likely met with Billini's brother.[162] The group hoped to persuade Frelinghuysen to proceed with the still-stalled treaty negotiations. Consequently, both Astwood and Galván telegrammed the State Department that the former Dominican president, Luperón, wished an audience with Frelinghuysen and President Arthur.[163] Astwood moreover explained that Luperón had formerly been "somewhat antagonistic to American interests based on false impressions," but since arriving in the United States had changed his mind.[164] For his part, Galván, who was also residing on Fifth Avenue, protested against the delay in negotiations and stated that Luperón wished to "efface unfavorable remembrances" of the annexation period.[165] Frelinghuysen and Arthur, however, chose not to meet with Luperón.[166] Meanwhile, Frelinghuysen finally received word from Langston regarding his views on the reciprocity treaty.[167] Around the same time, Astwood gave speeches in favor of the treaty in Boston and New York, and a week later Galván wrote Frelinghuysen yet again about the treaty.[168] It was not until late October, however, after Frelinghuysen learned that the Remington affair had been settled, that Frelinghuysen reignited the reciprocity treaty negotiations with Galván.[169] Negotiations carried on through November. Meanwhile, Astwood defied the consular bureau's instructions to return to Santo Domingo and instead lobbied for both the reciprocity treaty and the Republican presidential candidate James G. Blaine in New Orleans.[170] Frelinghuysen and Galván finally signed the treaty on December 4, and only then did Astwood return to his post via Port-au-Prince, where he met with Langston regarding "official business" that he never disclosed.[171]

All things were not equal, but the deceitful practices of imperial statecraft remained a constant no matter on which side of the segregated line one stood. Blaine lost the US presidential election to the Democrat Grover Cleveland. The new US president withdrew the United States from the reciprocity treaty signed with the Dominican Republic, and ceased negotiations for similar treaties with other Caribbean territories. Despite the drastic implications of this move for the Dominican Republic, Cleveland's administration never informed the Dominican government, Langston, or

Astwood of this development. Such a lack of respect reflected the United States' racist disregard for the "Black" nation even if such attitudes were not explicitly written into the diplomatic record. The United States' historical racist animosity toward the island betrays this fact, just as the context renders visible the condition of segregated statecraft that characterized US-Dominican diplomacy. Similarly, in the same way that the useless dichotomy between formal and informal imperialism in US historiography serves to veil the violence of America's free-trade imperialism, the bifurcation of Black unofficial and white official statecraft, a process engendered by the United States' diplomatic apartheid, served to pathologize one form of imperial state-grift while rendering the other benign.[172]

African American foreign service agents were not immune to the discursive acrobats, even if their racial attitudes toward the island and goals for US diplomacy in the Dominican Republic and Haiti differed from those of most white Americans. Both Astwood and Langston believed that the reciprocity treaty would increase the United States' power in the region. Therefore, they considered it quite simply the right thing to do. Langston expressed this belief in his assessment of the reciprocity treaty. "Rising above this question of imports and exports," Langston stressed, was a question of deep moral significance: "How shall our Government secure by *peaceful* and *honorable* international methods that footing and power and influence in the West India Islands, which naturally belong to it[?]"[173] Perhaps Langston, like other African Americans, hoped that the reciprocity treaty and his own diplomatic appointment would bring prosperity to the island and promote racially democratic feelings in the United States. Maybe his ideas regarding "peaceful" and "honorable" methods of domination meant something other than US racial capitalist imperialism. Or maybe he merely wished that they could mean something different. For African American foreign agents who joined the US imperial project, this was a quandary: How could the United States gain and enforce a "large and desirable moral foothold" abroad in Santo Domingo when the underfunded State Department consistently disrespected the islands' leaders east and west, insisted upon diplomatic apartheid, and undermined all Black men's political authority?[174]

Astwood's dispatches provide one possible answer to this conundrum: there was no escaping the racism or violence of US imperialism. As consul, he had made myriad suggestions to aid the US State Department in its free-trade imperial project, but his efforts had received minimal acknowledgment. So, when forthright accounting and honest analysis of economic opportunity failed to elicit the desired response, Astwood tried a different tactic; he decried the failings of Dominican government and defended US capitalists in their claims against the same. This strategy barely moved the needle in Astwood's favor. Between 1882 and 1884, the "abuses" that Astwood reported were largely ignored by the State Department, and even Astwood's success in the Remington affair elicited only a lukewarm reaction as Langston and Frelinghuysen scrambled to discover the details of the settlement. Moreover, throughout this period, Astwood had stopped short of declaring the Dominican government corrupt or immoral as he maligned the character of subordinate Dominican officers. His routine performance of righteous indignation in dispatches regarding the treatment of US capitalists in Santo Domingo, however, had increased in frequency and intensity over the short course of two years. As Astwood likely recognized—perhaps even a smidgen sooner than Heureaux, Luperón, and other Dominican officials—with a few more tweaks to his method, his seemingly inconsequential ritual in service of white American interests could potentially change the game. In the Black US consul's own words: "I have been devising plans."[175]

4

DEATH AND DECEIT

Black Political Authority and the Forging of US Moral Logic Abroad

The moon seemed unusually shaped to the naked eye on June 28, 1885. A misty haze contorted its body, confusing an observant Frenchman in the city of Santo Domingo, where "strange proceedings" signaled impending doom.[1] About half past nine, gunfire blasted. The staccato bangs seemed not like gunshots but firecrackers or petards—the usual noisy pranks boys pulled during the national holidays. Shouts accompanied the "celebrations" and caused no immediate alarm. The moon gazer was "so far from thinking [of] a surprise."[2] Everything was twisted, inverted, fallacious, untrue.

Half an hour earlier, on the other side of the city, US consul Henry Astwood and his wife Alice walked home from church. Noticing a dozen armed men at the corner of Commercial and Mercedes Streets headed west toward the Spanish consulate, the couple wondered at the sight of so many soldiers. What could their presence at this late hour mean? Daylight would surely bring revelation, just as the safety of shelter brings comfort in times of uncertainty. So, the consul and lady hurried home, shut the door, and retired to bed. Rest, however, eluded them. An hour or so later, the Frenchman's banging at the front door woke them. Soon thereafter, Astwood found himself standing before a terrible scene. On the second floor of Hotel San Pedro, the same building that housed Spain's consulate, the American citizen John J. Platt lay on the floor, mouth agape with clotted blood. With the moon still obscured, only dim candlelight shone upon the distorted corpse—a grisly shape covered in a sticky dark substance. The red fluid pooled all around, portending trouble ahead.

How did the American John J. Platt meet his untimely death? Scholars concerned with the broad sweep of Dominican politics at the end of the nineteenth century have mentioned the killing solely as it related to the rise of General Ulises Heureaux's thirteen-year dictatorship.[3] Although Heureaux's dictatorship technically began when he took office for a second time in January 1887 and ended with his assassination in June 1899, historians consider the two years 1885 and 1886 as a precursor to his authoritarian regime.[4] During these years, Heureaux forced the elected president, Francisco Gregorio Billini, to resign, and pursued and killed anyone who might challenge his authority. By all accounts, Platt was a casualty of this process. He was killed when Dominican troops mistook him for the ex-president Cesáreo Guillermo and accidently shot him dead. For the Dominican state, the case was embarrassing and financially costly. In retrospect, historians have found little reason to belabor the exact details of the affair or question the indemnity that resulted.

Indeed, the results of the Platt affair seem predictable at first glance. As discussed in chapter 3, the United States' insouciance toward Dominican relations in the 1880s meant that the US government viewed the Dominican Republic as diplomatically subsidiary to Haiti. White Americans, moreover, generally did not differentiate between Hispaniola's east and west, and instead accepted the notion of Black misrule across the whole island, a stance also commonly associated with the US South under Radical Reconstruction.[5] Considering the legacy of this white supremacist gaze, it makes sense that Sumner Welles, the first US historian to publish a serious work on Dominican history in 1928, could not conceive of Heureaux's authoritarian regime—or any other Afro-Dominican leadership for that matter—outside of the paradigms of "Black misgovernment" and inherent "Black immorality."[6] It also makes sense that Welles, and subsequent historians who relied on his treatment of the Platt affair, found no reason to study the case in detail. Platt was a white American who died at the hands of the Black Dominican state. Logically, the United States made the Black republic pay for its misdeed.

The moral logic that undergirded the Dominican government's indemnity of $33,000 Mexican silver (about $860,000 US in 2022) to Platt's wife also had a long history on the island and in the Atlantic world. Indemnification under threat of force dated back at least to 1825 when French warships in Haitian waters demanded 150 million francs in reparations for France's lost colony and to recognize Haitian sovereignty. After all, the people had been commodities, and white masters demanded redress. Britain took a similar path, compensating slave owners after emancipation in the Caribbean in 1834. From this period forward, indemnity became the name of the white foreigners' game. In the late nineteenth century, private claims against the Black republics—Haiti and the Dominican Republic—were the means by which foreign nations diplomatically sought retribution for their aggrieved white citizens. The fact that such claims riddle American and European nineteenth-century diplomatic records demonstrates the extent to which foreign nations used private enterprise as a vampiric mechanism to weaken the Haitian and Dominican governments and strengthen their own economic power over the island. The Platt case proved no different.

And yet, the details of Platt's death and the controversy that it sparked in 1885 chip at the veneer of historical continuity. The most remarkable thing about the accident was how much US officials in Washington disregarded this white man's killing. Somehow Platt's death did not an international scandal make—at least not initially. Considering Platt's case within the context of Heureaux's rising dictatorship and US financial imperialism, this chapter examines the invention of a murder in Santo Domingo that US officials in Washington initially deemed unworthy of diplomatic attention. One man, US consul Astwood, believed otherwise.

More than any other case of Astwood's tenure, Platt's death demonstrates the primacy of moral ideology based in Western Christianity to the making and layering of racial, gender, and national categories. Rising to historian Emily S. Rosenberg's call to view political debates as cultural narratives, this chapter analyzes the folktale-like attributes—"the structural continuities over time, the cautionary qualities that come from a severe and committed delineation of 'good' and 'evil' forces, the rich accretion of symbolism"—of Astwood's dispatches regarding Platt.[7] Through such cultural analysis, Rosenberg has claimed that gendered discourse shaped both white supremacy and US dollar diplomacy in the early twentieth century.[8] This chapter similarly analyzes gendered language in the Platt case, but it also takes Astwood's Blackness into account. By doing so, it demonstrates that Christian ideology—specifically the good/evil dichotomy—existed as the fundamental cultural frame in which racialized gendered language operated. As argued in chapter 3, the construction of US economic empire and the bartering of Black political authority existed as two interdependent processes. The Platt affair shows that racialized and gendered moral discourse fueled this dialectic as Astwood exerted influence over the case. Thus, this case ultimately demonstrates that political authority resided in the ability to judge between right and wrong, good and evil.

Astwood successfully wielded the power to discern between right and wrong in the Platt affair. Whereas US state officials preferred to ignore the killing, Astwood insisted on its significance to international relations and demanded redress. To force his way, he deliberately manipulated white Americans' racist fears of Haiti and anxieties over Black rule. He also strong-armed the Dominican state by collecting and fabricating documentation to curate a key takeaway: Black political authority in Santo Domingo had trampled white American rights to the point of fatal oxymoron. Platt's death qualified as accidental murder (a contradiction in terms), an unintentional mistake that had "willfully" violated one of God's most sacred laws: thou shalt not kill.

Following Astwood's paper trail, this chapter reconstructs the political context leading up to the night of Platt's death. It then analyzes Astwood's dispatches regarding the affair and the controversy that ensued. Throughout, this chapter grapples with the United States' historically and persistently racist gaze upon Hispaniola. It also wrestles with Astwood's own racial Blackness. Thus, the following pages expose how Astwood used a racialized and gendered moral dichotomy between good and evil superimposed upon nations in order to construct and enforce a white supremacist US moral logic abroad.

Death of an American: How John J. Platt Met His Untimely Demise

The shooting that resulted in Platt's death on June 28, 1885, an event at least two decades in the making, was the confluence of a convoluted political history, as all national histories are. As elsewhere across the Americas, Dominican variations on the white supremacist myth stifled the national imagination. Despite having just expelled Spain from the island in 1865, Europhile Dominicans still claimed the colonial conquistadors' legacy. Accordingly, as discussed in previous chapters, reactionary conservatives contrived to return Buenaventura Báez to power.[9] Arguably, the story of the white American man's death begins here.

Among the Dominican forces who brought Báez back to power was Pedro Guillermo, an illiterate landowner and military general from El Seibo. Readers unfamiliar with Dominican history may think it strange that Pedro, who was possibly of African descent, fought for reactionary conservatives. However, Europhile lettered elites' philosophical principles did not reflect the disposition of the Dominican masses who followed strongmen into war for a variety of personal and political reasons.[10] Moreover, regionalism remained strong at a time when the country lacked the communication infrastructure, industrial economy, and strong-state apparatus to foster greater national unity.[11] Peasants' subsistence lifestyle, moreover, tied them to local communal lands, and those who worked the *terrenos comuneros*, while sometimes choosing to work on plantations, had no need for a total proletarization of their class.[12] Thus, in the late 1860s and early 1870s, many Dominicans from the southwest and southeast backed Báez, who was from Azua. They believed he would defend their interests against those of liberal northern merchants and ideologues.[13] This context is critical to understanding the political tensions that led to the events of June 28, 1885, when Dominican soldiers—liberals from the Cibao—mistook Platt for Cesáreo Guillermo, Pedro Guillermo's militant son.

History has not looked kindly on the father-son pair from El Seibo. Both were uneducated countrymen who identified as *rojos-baecistas* and systematically assassinated Báez's political enemies. In distinct instances, they both led troops to march on the capital, and both held the office of president for a short time, Pedro in a provisional capacity in 1865.[14] In his autobiography, Partido Azul leader Gregorio Luperón called Pedro a "murderer and criminal," and he harbored particular antipathy against Cesáreo, whom he labeled "a violent man without pity . . . lacking in discipline, without honor, and without morality."[15] During the few months that Cesáreo held the presidency in 1879, Luperón condemned his actions as despotic, "like an overseer to his slaves."[16] Cesáreo filled Santo Domingo's prison with liberals and his pockets with customs revenue. He targeted liberal thinkers, journalists, and gentlemen. In Luperón's words, Cesáreo Guillermo "never had the reputation of a good man because he had never been righteous."[17] The line between Luperón's view of the Guillermos' moral fiber and US historian Sumner Welles's later racist depictions of the Guillermos was thin. Pedro, according to Welles, was an "illiterate negro" who headed "a rabble of armed ruffians."[18] Cesáreo was a "mulatto ... utterly lacking in education" who "possessed no ambitions beyond the lust for power" and who also headed a troop of "the most villainous looking ruffians."[19] For white Americans, such descriptions implied inherent Black immorality. Such stereotypes, as discussed below, were salient in the Platt case.

Cesáreo did not stay in power long. After ten months, Luperón took control of the government, and Cesáreo fled to Puerto Rico. Liberal *azules* then held power for three consecutive presidential terms: Luperón (1879–80), Ferando A. Meriño (1880–82), and Heureaux (1882–84). The same party remained in power when Platt died. The regional and interpersonal rivalries between the *azules* and *rojos* endured as well, as did the threat of Cesáreo's return.

The election of 1884 precipitated both Cesáreo's return and Platt's death. When Heureaux's presidency ended in 1884, Luperón, as party boss, nominated Heureaux's minister of foreign relations, Segundo Imbert, to the presidential ticket.[20] Wishing to maintain influence over the executive branch, Heureaux joined with Meriño to back a different candidate, Francisco Gregorio Billini.[21] Attempts at a truce, the famous "capitulations" signed at Puerto Plata, failed in the spring of 1884.[22] The internal rupture intensified both interpersonal and regional tensions as the northern Cibao supported Imbert and the southeastern provinces sided with Billini. No one could say for sure who would win the contest. From his vantage point in Santo Domingo, however, US consul Astwood predicted fraud: "Billini is supported openly by [Heureaux] and I understand that strenuous measures will be used to force his election."[23] The election held on June 28–30 confirmed the prophetic word. Although scholars have since disputed the extent of Heureaux's fraud, for Astwood the process of voting had been strange.[24] "Parties voting in the country towns can vote all along the line until they reach the city simply by changing their names at each locality," Astwood observed, and Imbert's supporters had been imprisoned in towns close to the capital.[25] Consequently, Billini carried the southeast, but the Cibao voted for Imbert. When Congress at last declared Billini the winner, Astwood appraised the "remarkable election" in which the total votes amounted to three times more than ever polled before.[26]

Reflecting upon the moment years later, Luperón clarified, somewhat remorsefully, how Billini's triumph—or rather, Heureaux's suspected trap—led to Platt's death. After Billini's inauguration, leaders from Santiago and

Puerto Plata declared war against the new president. The Cibao blamed Billini for Heureaux's violation of the vote, although Billini had nothing to do with the alleged fraud.[27] Consequently, Billini's friendship with Heureaux soured. Then, in order to check Heureaux's power, Billini granted Cesáreo clemency and invited him back to the country. Previous Azul governments had charged Guillermo with treason, and his return only heightened tensions.[28] Luperón, who had been abroad in France, went home to Puerto Plata in 1885, where he found the atmosphere "charged with storm."[29] When the political tension mounted even further, Billini resigned after only ten months in office in order to prevent a bloodbath, and Vice President Alejandro Wos y Gil—one of Heureaux's closest allies—assumed the presidency.[30] Then Guillermo, no longer under Billini's protection and fearing for his life under Wos y Gil's government, plotted a revolt. Learning that Guillermo was living with his family in the capital at the Hotel San Pedro, Wos y Gil issued an order for his arrest. As Luperón recounted, "The governor's squad brutally and savagely fired at [Guillermo] in the hotel where he lived, wounding his respectable wife and killing an innocent American."[31] This was the gist of the matter. An obscure American died, and Cesáreo Guillermo escaped to fight another day.

At this point, historians writing about the era typically move on. The people who witnessed Platt's killing and processed the paperwork, however, could not so easily dismiss the tragedy. In the days following the shooting, eyewitnesses recounted the drama in their own words. Their version of events, devoid of historical context and unencumbered with concerns over the nation's autocratic future, focused instead on the immediate actions of men: the ex-president Dominican general, the governor, the soldiers, the doctors, the judge, the US consul, and the moon-gazing Frenchman. These men with ideas—traumatic memories, expert opinions, and crude effigies—wrote themselves at the center of a tragedy as they reconstructed a timeline of an exceptional, possibly transformative event. By doing so, they sought to instill their distinct racialized visions of Dominican society.

SET AT THE FOOT of a rocky hill, the two-story San Pedro Hotel occupied twenty-eight meters of Las Mercedes Street. It stretched back at least thirty-five meters from the road, offering no means of escape for a fugitive—unless in the extreme rear corner of the building, behind the water closet, where the high rocks formed an extremely narrow point, someone could scale the wall. The person would have to be nimble and a man, since "no lady goes there never," but that route could possibly work.[32] In the same vicinity, on the second floor next to the bathroom, a wide terrace presented a second getaway. A little barrack recently constructed next to the hotel would allow "with great difficulties" a pathway to the roof.[33] But, if the building were surrounded by troops, the renegade on the roof would fatally expose himself to the officers and their gunfire; no remedy existed for a bullet that struck true. So, in reality, the building's architecture presented no clear exit other than the most obvious one: the front door.

None of these structural details should have mattered, since the hotel's inhabitants had little reason to concern themselves with clandestine escapes. But then the Guillermos moved in. The Hotel San Pedro (map 4.1) had much to offer the Guillermos. The family rented two bedrooms on the first floor, which the French proprietor Rosa Moniere typically used only for storage. Cesáreo, however, planned for an extended stay. And why not? Not only did the ground floor's courtyard supply respite from the hot summer days, but the second floor—with its large gallery, dining hall, and indoor bathroom—housed various foreign residents including the Platt family, the Spanish consul, an Italian by the name of Boglioni, and the Frenchman Louis Felen Gustave Petitpierre Pellion. The presence of these foreigners imbued the hotel with an added sense of security, since international law prohibited any sort of military invasion in this decidedly non-Dominican space. Thus, the boarders expected no commotion on the evening of June 28.

That night the hotel was nearly empty since most of the residents had left for the theater. About a dozen individuals, including the Guillermos' children, remained behind. Platt had retired early, reading and smoking in his second-floor room at the front of the hotel. The other adults engaged in routine tasks. Cesáreo sat in the courtyard. His wife, María de la Cruz Herrera, positioned nearby, kept watch over their children and nephews, who were singing. Moniere was in her bedroom, and Pellion paced the second-floor gallery. At this point, the Frenchman noticed the strange shape of the moon and retrieved his opera glass for a better look. Then suddenly the mundane turned mysterious. A loud bang cracked through the stillness. The excitement began.

The orders had come from the highest level of government, and Governor Leopoldo Espaillat followed orders, as did his subordinates.[34] The soldiers, young men of lower rank, hailed from Santiago, like the governor, and their names and ages are known: Juan Bautista Peña, also known as Cepea, age thirty-three; Gil Pepín, age twenty-seven; Juan Pablo Pepín,

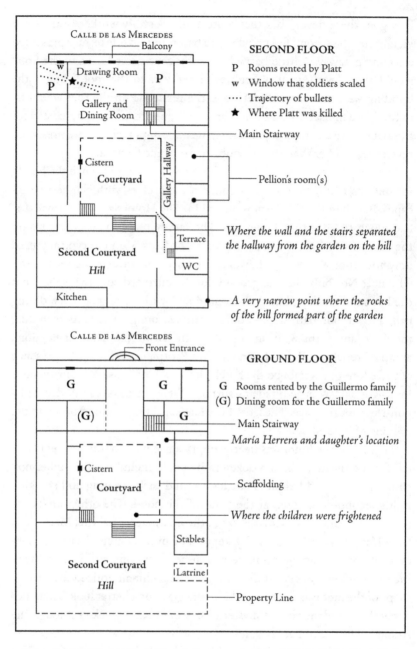

SECOND FLOOR

- **P** Rooms rented by Platt
- **w** Window that soldiers scaled
- ···· Trajectory of bullets
- ★ Where Platt was killed

CALLE DE LAS MERCEDES
Balcony

Drawing Room

P

P

Gallery and Dining Room

Main Stairway

Cistern

Courtyard

Gallery Hallway

Pellion's room(s)

Where the wall and the stairs separated the hallway from the garden on the hill

Second Courtyard

Hill

Terrace

WC

A very narrow point where the rocks of the hill formed part of the garden

Kitchen

GROUND FLOOR

- **G** Rooms rented by the Guillermo family
- **(G)** Dining room for the Guillermo family

CALLE DE LAS MERCEDES
Front Entrance

G

G

(G)

G

Main Stairway

María Herrera and daughter's location

Cistern

Courtyard

Scaffolding

Where the children were frightened

Stables

Second Courtyard

Hill

Latrine

Property Line

MAP 4.1. Schematic rendering of hand-drawn map of Hotel San Pedro by Louis Petit-pierre Pellion, July 3, 1885. Image by Kate Blackmer.

age twenty-seven; Martes de la Rosa, age twenty-four; Augusto Ferreira, age eighteen; Justiano Corniel, no age recorded.[35] This squad may have counted themselves lucky to accompany the governor on such an important mission—the arrest of Cesáreo Guillermo. Neither the soldiers' sentiments nor opinions about the assignment, however, entered the official record. So historians can only guess that, entrusted with an important and possibly dangerous task, they likely felt a mix of nervous anticipation and defiant self-assurance. The knowledge that the governor would enter the hotel first may have been small relief. Cepea and Gil Pepín followed close behind. The procession moved in unison, and each man reportedly witnessed the same scene. They saw Cesáreo lounging with his wife and children in the courtyard. Governor Espaillat approached, and when he stood about ten feet away, Guillermo began to shoot. The soldiers shot back as Guillermo ran away.

At first, the soldiers followed Cesáreo, who bolted up the back stairwell—the one on the left side by the privy—but he was too quick. The men then reversed course. They would ascend the front stairwell and intercept the general in the second-floor hallway. Augusto and Martes remained at the foot of the stairs, guarding the entrance and serving as backup just in case.[36] Later, Pellion accused the troops of scaling the building's front wall to Platt's balcony, driving the man from his room.[37] Meanwhile, the other soldiers advanced quietly up the unlit stairwell. The gallery landing was even more tenebrous since an earlier gust of wind had blown out the candle. . . . Quiet now! And . . . there! In the shadows, a dark *bulto* appeared, a human bulk: Cesáreo Guillermo. Cepea and Gil fired upon the mass.[38] The *bulto* thudded to the ground. The squad descended quickly to inform Espaillat of their feat. A moment later, Espaillat climbed the stairs to examine the corpse, and what he found alarmed him and his men. An unknown white man lay dead in the doorway of the left-side front bedroom, blood coagulating in his mouth. Time stopped . . . and then the world resumed its spinning—for all but the deceased.

Noise! Not the bang of gunshots but the confusion of voices, as men who shouted orders appeared suddenly in the night. The governor directed his soldiers. The messengers made haste. Soon, the judge of instruction (*juez de instrucción*) and mayor (*alcalde*) appeared. Now the doctors arrived. And then, unexpectedly, the US consul and vice consul showed up accompanied by the Frenchman Pellion. From where had they come? Who knows? News traveled too fast—even when one took care to insulate the ensuing investigation. The remaining soldiers resumed the search for Guillermo, but they quickly recognized the exercise in futility and returned to guard the scene. No one had witnessed Cesáreo disappear, but he had indeed escaped. In his wake, new male bodies—one defunct, the rest alive and hectic—crowded the second-floor hall. The cat-and-mouse game had ended. Now the paperwork began.

The judge of instruction, Juan B. Matos, and his lawyer secretary, José María Nouel, arrived a little after ten o'clock to investigate the scene.[39] They took note of the cadaver. The deceased was "white, redheaded, medium height, blonde beard, blue eyes," and wore cashmere "the color of olives" and a small coffee-colored cap.[40] Next they entered the deceased's bedroom. A burning lamp gave off medium light. The iron bed with pink sheets and pillows at the head appeared very neat, "everything in order." Matos sent for the doctor, and after the medical examination, they learned the name and nationality of the dead man: "Juan Plat [sic], North American citizen." Then they continued searching the room and hall. On the stairwell floor and wall, at about three *varas* high, there were bullet holes (a *vara* is about two feet nine inches). Bullets also lodged two *varas* high on the right side of the sitting room doorframe and one and a half *varas* in the door where Platt had fallen. Blood appeared nowhere else in the house except here. Next, Matos and Nouel deposed the governor. At some point, the *alcalde* J. M. Bobea emerged, and together the four men (Matos, Nouel, Bobea, and Espaillat) left the cadaver to search for clues in Guillermo's bedroom. There they found some letters, a Remington pistol, and cartridges. Espaillat kept the letters, but Matos and Nouel did not list who collected the pistol and ammunition. They kept their report short, clean of details deemed unnecessary; the men recorded what they could see.

Yet the official documents written and filed in the weeks and months after June 28 did not fully capture the trauma of that night. Male insight dominated the official record, but women and children had witnessed the tragedy too. María had felt physical pain as she threw her body between the soldiers and her husband, taking a bullet in her right leg. Her eldest daughter had done the same, although the thirteen-year-old received no flesh wound. The soldiers had shot between the women while the Guillermos' youngest children cried. Meanwhile, from her bedroom, Moniere heard the shots and shouting. Heart pounding, she dared to step into the fray; she had nearly been hit by a stray bullet.[41] Later, perceiving a child's wail, the Frenchwoman sent her servant girl to ascertain the situation. The nameless *criada* must have smelled the blood in the hallway before she arrived at the scene. The girl returned surreptitiously to her mistress with news of the American's death. Then Moniere encountered the scene for herself and felt "horrified."[42] Platt lay dead in the doorway of his bedroom, his reading glasses and tobacco at his side. Moniere reported these details two and a half months later to Matos; she was the only woman to testify among a dozen men. And what about the Dominican women who had defended family and home? Matos did not interrogate María or her daughter even after the government's attorney (*procurador fiscal*) ordered him to interview the wounded *señora*.[43] Disposed, not deposed, witnesses to history—the Dominican women who fought for loved ones had no say in the final report; their experiences remained refracted through the eyes of men.

María's physician, Dr. Pedro Antonio Delgado Sánchez, was one such man. Instead of asking María, Matos approached Delgado for a statement on María's health. The physician reported that the bullet had traversed the right calf muscle near the fibula, the peroneus brevis.[44] A convalescing María was on the mend, but a nearly healed leg wound could not solve matters of the heart and mind. Perhaps if María's doctor had been a woman (or a *curandero*, a traditional healer in folk medicine), the physician's report might have noted the psychological or spiritual effects of the tragedy.[45] But, in 1885, medicine, like law and government, remained the domain of men.

And the men knew their business. Matos had called Delgado and his younger colleague Dr. Juan Francisco Alfonseca to examine the corpse the night Platt died. Both were expert physicians. Delgado, who was first trained in Haiti, served as the long-term director of the Dominican Republic's military hospital.[46] Alfonseca, who had apprenticed with Delgado, was the first Dominican to receive a government grant for medical study abroad in Paris.[47] These credentials qualified the physicians to inspect Platt and determine the cause of death. The bullet had "penetrated the upper extremity of the sternum, passed through the trachea and aortic valve, leaving the body on the right side of the spinal column."[48] Death had been instantaneous.

What more could be said? Truly, this was all that could be done. A man had been killed accidentally by Dominican soldiers. No one tried to hide the facts. The following day, Nouel penned the report in beautiful, even script. The governor, doctors, and *alcalde* signed their statements, and Matos handed the paperwork to the *procurador fiscal*, who ordered him to depose the soldiers and María. These orders Matos would follow with "the utmost zeal," except, of course, without bothering to interview María.[49] Meanwhile, Matos prepared to turn Platt's body over to the US consul for burial. But these efforts were too late—or, somehow, not enough. Within two days, US Consul Astwood had already submitted his protest to the minister of foreign affairs, forwarding the same, along with other details, to his superiors in Washington.

Narrating White Sacrifice: Moral Discourse and the Accidental Murder

Who was John J. Platt? This middle-aged journeyman of common name and no rank was likely born in New York around 1850.[50] He held no relation to any influential figure of the era, including the famed New York Republican boss Thomas C. Platt. The plebeian Platt traveled to and from Santo Domingo at least twice in the early 1880s—the last time almost a year before the day of his death.[51] He had a wife named Cordelia and a child named Edward, both of whom lived with him for a time in the Dominican capital. Cordelia and Edward, however, returned to the United States mere months before the shooting.[52] When Platt died, no major US newspapers covered the killing. In Santo Domingo, only one local newspaper reported passively that "on Sunday night, the American citizen J. J. Platt was unfortunately killed [*fue muerto*] in his residence in Hotel S. Pedro."[53] That was it. No servants or relatives collected the body, and no public protests were held. The US consul hosted the white American's funeral in the city's Protestant church and subsequently buried the pale corpse in Santo Domingo's dark soil. He later complained that no high-ranking Dominican official, save Minister of Finance Lucas Gibbes—a Protestant—attended this event.[54] In other words, Platt was a nobody.

Yet, to Astwood, such a subdued response to Platt's fate seemed irreverent, iconoclastic, and indeed immoral. At least, this is what the consul hoped to convey in his letters regarding Platt—an intensity of feeling that magnified at each turn of phrase. Astwood wrote fabrications about what he and everyone else knew, and this was the magic of his statecraft. To reinvent the past was to manifest a nonexistent reality in the present and thereby shape the future. Such work was dangerous business in the nineteenth century, especially for a person of African descent. Astwood, however, operated under the protection of the US flag. Consequently, the day after the shooting, he set pen to paper and addressed the new man serving as Dominican minister of foreign affairs, José de J. Castro. Neither this protest nor its cover letter possessed the bombastic flair of the dispatches that

Astwood would soon craft for State Department officials in Washington. Still, in his first missive to Castro, Astwood fixed his stance, cocked, and fired: "Mr. Platt was deliberately shot."[55]

The ensuing fight was one of letters, not guns. Words written implied threats unverbalized. Astwood rendered Platt's death "careless and unprecedented," and swore to inform the US government.[56] Castro denied Astwood's accusations. The Dominican government was "not to accept the qualification of assassination," since the *procurador fiscal* had not completed the investigation.[57] This dismissal provoked Astwood to write again in a more confrontational tone. In a second letter dated June 30, Astwood charged that Matos's investigation had been "most incomplete" and that Matos had treated the death with "indifference." The officials, moreover, had "abandoned" Platt in his "gore," and the Dominican government displayed no regret. Astwood felt insulted that he had received no official notice and was not invited to take part in the investigation. Castro's response to Astwood's initial letter was the first "official" news of the killing, he accused. Astwood then defended his chosen terminology: "I say murdered, because I can find no other term to apply."[58] The Dominican troops had violated both the nation's Constitution and the US-Dominican treaty that guaranteed American citizens security in life and property. Thus, the Dominican government had created a "breach" that would injure US-Dominican diplomatic relations. To avoid further problems, the Dominican government should offer compensation to Cordelia Platt.

In the battle of words, Castro countered, disavowing Astwood's accusations point by point. The government had indeed attempted to notify Astwood on the fatal night. In the company of a deputy, Castro himself had visited Astwood's residence, but Astwood's wife had informed the two officials that Astwood was already at the hotel. Furthermore, Castro had also twice visited the governor's office that night, where he witnessed Matos briefing President Wos y Gil on the matter. Matos then received "competent orders" to deliver the corpse to Astwood after the investigation. Astwood, nonetheless, had taken and buried Platt's body the next day. Now, four days after the accident, the investigation was still incomplete. From Castro's perspective, the Dominican government had done everything to keep the US consul abreast of the situation, but it could not divulge details of an ongoing inquiry. The minister of foreign relations, however, could and did refute Astwood's second letter. Regarding the security of foreigners, "the deplorable and isolated accident of Mr. Platt may not serve as a cause of doubt." Friendly relations with the United States need not "interrupt nor relax." The Dominican government expected Astwood to persevere "in fomenting these relations," and yes, the Dominican government "accede[d] willingly" to Astwood's request for a copy of the final report.[59]

But Astwood did not back down. Instead, he forwarded this exchange with Castro to the US State Department along with his own testimony. Astwood's June 30 dispatch was sensational to say the least. He employed various rhetorical devices (imagery, hyperbole, allusion, metaphor) to substantiate the lie that the Dominican government deliberately murdered Platt. He offset these shock tactics with a structural symmetry that foregrounded "facts" and lent him credibility. Thus, after a brief introduction in which Astwood lamented "an act, which for audacity, hostility and cruelty, stands without a parallel," he presented his version of events, summarized his conclusions, and offered recommendations.[60] This rhetorical structure, along with the intentional sensationalism, sustained a self-evident dichotomy between good and evil—American innocence and Dominican corruption.

In his testimony, Astwood enumerated facts as a series of offenses. He recounted hearing an incessant knocking that roused his household that night. Upon opening the door, he found Pellion "under the surveillance" of a soldier. The Frenchman then informed Astwood of the killing, and that he, Pellion, "had to force his way" to notify Astwood. If Platt's "murder" served as the first crime, the government's treatment of Pellion added insult to injury. Astwood dressed quickly, and the men proceeded to the residence of US vice consul John Farrand, who then accompanied them to the hotel. Once there, Astwood found himself insulted three, four, and five times over. Not only did he find Platt's dead body sprawled across the bloodstained ground, but Matos was sitting while two doctors examined the corpse in a seemingly unprofessional way, "by simply unbuttoning the collar and exposing the wound . . . leaving the body still in the pool of blood upon the floor." Then, after learning of Platt's cause of death, Astwood requested a written statement from Governor Espaillat. Yet, despite Astwood's repeated reminders throughout the night, Espaillat never produced the document and allegedly sneaked out the next morning "without [Astwood's] knowledge." To compensate for this loss of an eyewitness, Astwood interviewed Moniere, but the landlady "knew nothing of the particulars."[61]

Astwood's outrage continued the following day when he found additional evidence for what he already believed—that the investigation had been inadequate and the doctors incompetent. After the officials left the hotel, Astwood, Farrand, and Preston C. Nason conducted an investigation of their own. Nason, an American capitalist from Boston who had received a landmark concession to develop electric and telephone systems in the republic, possessed no medical or investigatory experience.[62] Still, he led the men in their proceedings. The team found two bullets. One had passed through Platt's body and had lodged in the stone wall of the room's northeast corner (map 4.1). The other bullet was embedded in the room's southeast corner. Confronting the evidence, Astwood determined that the shots were fired "deliberately in the door," and asserted that "this does away with the Governor's theory" that Platt had merely been caught in the crossfire.[63] The US consul then called for Espaillat, who "could not explain" the discrepancy and whom Astwood portrayed as wholly inept in his investigatory work but highly competent when it came to protecting his own interests.

Astwood depicted the Dominican doctors as similarly incompetent. From Astwood's point of view, Delgado and Alfonseca's medical examination was a sham. He described his own team's examination for added proof. Unlike the Dominicans, the Americans moved the corpse to the cot, searched Platt's pockets and found a revolver, and then proceeded to remove Platt's clothing, whereupon they found a second bullet wound. The bullet had penetrated "through the left arm midway between the shoulders and elbow, crushing the bone, passing through the left side and out to the right of the spinal column." This amateur language contrasted with the medical nomenclature that Delgado and Alfonseca had employed. Still, Astwood disparaged the two physicians' analysis. Ignoring their national renown, he claimed, "No important individual was invited to take part in the investigation . . . and I swear the judge or coroner did not put his hands upon the corpse." This fabrication reinforced the notion of Dominican government corruption. Astwood then called for Delgado in order to show him "how incomplete" his and Alfonseca's investigation had been. In Astwood's words, Delgado was "astonished to think they had been so derelict, but said he would add it to the act." Vexed and unimpressed, Astwood intimated that the US government could not trust any document that the Dominican government produced. Instead of waiting for Delgado's updated statement, Astwood sent for another physician, Dr. José de Jesús Brenes, who provided Astwood with a statement to forward to Washington.[64]

In light of the American team's impromptu investigation, Astwood drew a series of conclusions. First, he acknowledged that "the shooting of Mr. Platt was accidental" since the soldiers had mistaken Platt for Cesáreo Guillermo. Second, despite this error, Astwood determined that the killing was still the Dominican government's fault. The soldiers who had "committed the deed in such a lawless manner" had followed government orders. Therefore, according to Astwood, the Dominican government was responsible for damages. Third, the Dominican government had violated foreigners' rights since troops had entered a foreign hotel against the "neutral laws of Nations," which prevented governments from entering foreign private residences without a warrant. "Some respect should have been paid to the lives of foreigners," Astwood chastised. If the soldiers had merely cut off Guillermo's exit instead of entering the hotel, the Dominican government would have captured him, and the United States "would have saved a good and useful citizen." These conclusions escalated the investigation to matters of international relations. Indeed, by including his exchange with Castro in his dispatch to the United States, Astwood meant to highlight the Dominican government's defiance of the "murder" as further evidence of its corruption and thereby sway the US government toward action. The Dominican government had erred, and now the US government should make it pay.[65]

Yet Astwood did not stop there. Convincing the State Department to engage in a dispute with the Dominican Republic over the death of an obscure American citizen required a hard sell—nothing less than the collapsing of time and space. So, to his list of conclusions, Astwood added a denouement. "When you will have read all of the evidence," he foretold, "you will be convinced . . . that 'An American has no rights which a Dominican is bound to respect.'"[66] This forceful dictum self-consciously referenced and rhetorically inversed the landmark 1857 *Dred Scott v. Sandford* decision, in which the US Supreme Court ruled that Blacks had "no rights which the white man is bound to respect."[67] With this deliberate historical allusion, Astwood decried Platt's "murder" and implicitly linked the killing to a second even more cataclysmic affair: the Haitian Revolution.

Well acquainted with US racism, Astwood purposefully preyed on white Americans' fears. As a Black man who had lived in Reconstruction-era New Orleans from 1874 to 1882, Astwood knew that most Americans associated the Dominican Republic with Haiti and had no idea that many elite Dominicans were of European descent. He also knew that Haiti, the site of the Atlantic world's only successful slave rebellion, still vexed white Americans who believed in Black inferiority and feared that any form of Black government would lead to anarchy and the vengeful assassination of whites. These beliefs served as apologia for various injustices: the historical enslavement of Africans; the United States' domineering treatment of the republics south of its borders; and the continued oppression of African descendants in the United States post-1865. Such beliefs had also led to threats against Astwood's life in New Orleans, where the specter of the Haitian Revolution played a central role in redeemer propaganda.[68] Taking advantage of this insight, Astwood appropriated white Americans' prejudicial tropes.[69] Instead of upholding a US racial hierarchy in which whites lorded over Blacks, as during the antebellum period and the infamous Dred Scott trial, he suggested that in the Dominican Republic the opposite was true: Black Dominicans lorded over white Americans.

By deploying this powerful anastrophe, Astwood moralized a seemingly defective situation and simultaneously linked the unnatural circumstance in a supernatural time warp: Santo Domingo in 1885 was the inverse of the United States in 1857 and the ghost of Haiti in 1791. Alternatively stated, the past was present—and the present was white Americans' worst nightmare. Black rule in Hispaniola had prevailed, and it was only a matter of time until the same could be said of the United States. If left unpunished, Platt's murder would establish the "odious" inversion in perpetuity.[70] Then the laws of physics would fail; the advance of time and the distance of geographic space would dissolve. If the United States backed down, then Haiti, the Black republic, would rise.

To bolster this racist narrative, Astwood included the Frenchman's testimony in his dispatch. Pellion superimposed the dichotomy of good versus evil upon racialized bodies and nations in his account of the alleged murder, without ever mentioning race. Instead, Pellion relied on gendered language that invoked common racist stereotypes of deviant Black manhood. His vivid imagery of Dominican soldiers' misconduct, like Astwood's historical allusions, served to emphasize the overall point that Platt's death was a matter of power misapplied to Black men.

The trope of Black misrule abounded in Pellion's testimony. According to him, Dominican soldiers lacked the competency of a regular militia. In fact, the poorly clad troops had not seemed like soldiers at all since they donned rags instead of helmets and uniforms, and one man had paraded about "half bare."[71] Reflecting on their dress, the Frenchman posited that perhaps the soldiers had disguised themselves as poor civilians, but if this was the case, their strategy had failed miserably—even humorously. Indeed, to Pellion, the soldiers' attack would have been "excessively laughable and ridiculous" if Platt had not died. Arresting Guillermo should have been a "game of children" for the "seventy" soldiers (as Pellion counted them), but the men lacked the "necessary order, discipline & coolness indispensable in such matters." This ridicule invoked the trope of bumbling Black soldiers that the French propagated during the Haitian Revolution and that featured in US Civil War and Reconstruction-era minstrel shows, and thus emphasized the Dominican militia's supposed innate inferiority.[72]

Imagery of the soldiers' bestial inhumanity accompanied Pellion's descriptions of their incompetence. The crime scene was "a barbarous one," the "murder" an "act of savagery."[73] The Dominican soldiers were not just inept, they were heathens, "full of rage and fright." Intimations of rape followed. Not only had the soldiers injured María, but in the immediate aftermath of the shooting, Pellion found some soldiers "fixed" in the "complete darkness" of the drawing room along with Cesáreo's wife. One of the soldiers, "a big man" who was "gesticulating and making very much noise," roughly ordered Pellion to return to his room, but he refused. What might have happened if he had not shown up just then? Much later, Pellion noted that María's dress was torn at the hip. Without ever explicitly accusing the soldiers of abusing María, Pellion implied rape by using provocative language and placing the soldiers in the same room as the respectable lady. Pellion suggested that he had prevented other atrocities that evening too. After the incident with María, Pellion stopped some soldiers from forcing Guillermo's daughter out of her bedroom and obliging her to go into another. And when soldiers terrorized the Guillermos' young boys with their rifles, Pellion "protested against this barbarity" and declared it a "question of humanity to not frighten young girls and children." The intimations of rape and the term *humanity* once again recycled common stereotypes of Black men.[74] "In civilized nations," Pellion alleged, the army would have given previous notice to evacuate women, children, and invalids. But, in the Dominican Republic, the supposedly bestial soldiers seemed too consumed by passion, anger, and lust to bother with the "niceties" of war.

Pellion's gendered comparison of Platt and Guillermo further betrayed the racist dichotomy. The night of the shooting, though Cesáreo Guillermo wore dark colors like the attire Platt had donned, Pellion could not understand how one man could be mistaken for the other. The Frenchman described his American neighbor as "little," "fair," and "almost beardless, with a feminine complexion, short hair & with spectacles."[75] Guillermo, on the other hand, was a "very tall, strait, strong man with an enormous Black beard and Black hair." This gendered description conveyed racial meaning even though Guillermo appeared with European features in contemporary depictions (figure 4.1). In his text, the "exceptionally little," effeminate

FIGURE 4.1. "General Cesáreo Guillermo, president of the provisional government of the republic of Santo Domingo." From *La Ilustración Española y Americana* 23, no. 8 (1879): 140.

Platt appeared most like the women and children who needed protection. The Dominican general, in contrast, most resembled the soldiers. These tropes carried moral distinctions as well. Whereas the American was "of a very pacific temper, very laborious, of very good conduct in whatever thing, good-husband and good father," Pellion found no character defense for the general. The absence was conspicuous, since Pellion reiterated that confusing the two men "was entirely impossible." Other than their apparel, Platt and Guillermo had no commonalities. One was a "good" and "industrious young man," the other an outlaw. One lay dead, feet in the doorway of a second-floor bedroom in the Hotel San Pedro. The other had fled the same building with his life intact, leaving an injured wife and children behind for Pellion, a white foreigner, to defend.

The gender-racial-moral stereotypes in Pellion's account served the larger geopolitical dichotomy between Afro-descended Dominicans and white foreigners. For example, Pellion blamed Platt's "murder" upon a "certain class of directing people" whom he believed to rank far above their station.[76] He accused this group of being plagued with "enormous incompetence prohibitive of industry" and being overly excited by their "hereditary antipathy for strangers." These accusations linked Dominican officials to the peasant class—people of majority African descent—whose preference for subsistence living and aversion to plantation wage labor under European or Euro-Dominican landowners was the bane of the foreign-controlled sugar industry.[77] Furthermore, the notion of "hereditary antipathy" referred specifically to Haiti's legal prohibition of white landownership (a law that had long since lost its efficacy in the east).[78] While the Dominican Republic had no such law, Pellion's language fused the two sides of the island together, and thus censured Dominicans for their presumed antiforeign (coded as antiwhite) sentiment. At the same time, Pellion deemed white foreigners "the spring of life & richness of the country."[79] Dominican progress, he affirmed, emanated solely from the French, American, Italian, German, and Dutch communities that had settled in the country. But "the disorder of the men and the disorder of the ideas," which Pellion posited as Dominicans' lack of respect for foreign life and property, "have been the cause of the death of Mr. Platt." In other words, Black misrule had killed Platt. This statement paralleled Astwood's allusions to the Dred Scott trial and the Haitian Revolution and proved Platt's death to be both a powerful metaphor and a matter of moral principle. This case was both figuratively and literally about white life and death in the hands of Black men.

Astwood carried forward this moral logic in his recommendations to the State Department. In general, he advocated for the Platt affair to "be made an example" and advised that the US government settle the case with muscle and money. "If the simple pressure of one of our vessels of war could be had in the investigation of this matter, and if the indemnity demanded be large, it would settle the rights and protection of Americans for all time to come," he suggested.[80] The dual power of gunboat diplomacy and debt (i.e., nascent dollar diplomacy) would impress upon the Dominican government the error of its ways. At the same time, the United States would uphold its duty to defend US citizens abroad.

To emphasize this point, Astwood recommended that the United States pursue a large indemnity for Mrs. Platt. In the process, he turned to numbers and seemingly innocuous "white" lies. According to Astwood, Platt was a twenty-five-year-old "architect" of "rare ability with a bright future before him" who was working on an unspecified contract when he died.[81] These claims were clear falsehoods. At the time of his death, Platt was about thirty-five years old and was likely some kind of low-skilled construction worker, not an architect.[82] Still, Astwood attested that Platt died at "25 years of age instead of 38" and counseled that the "least possible claim for Mrs. Platt and her son . . . should be based on those figures."[83] According to Astwood, Platt could have lived to be seventy years old and would have earned at least $5 per day as an architect. At this rate, the Dominican government owed Mrs. Platt $82,225 (over $2 million in 2022) in restitution, which he deemed "not an extravagant amount for an industrious American to accumulate." Clearly, Astwood's talent was in making the incredible sound reasonable. No amount of money could bring back a life, he argued, but "it is also true that no citizen should be deprived innocently of his life leaving the responsibility to rest upon his unfortunate family." Cordelia Platt deserved compensation, and the US government should ensure that she received it. This argument tapped into new notions of white American manhood where whiteness was central to middle-class men's claims to authority, and it produced a garish image: the abused white American woman, widowed by a revolutionary Black government, required the protection of her manly white republic, whose muscle would guarantee her "life and property" in perpetuity by indebting the corrupt Black nation to the virtuous United States.[84]

Thus, as US consul, Astwood played his role well, epitomizing the foreign class of people who routinely found themselves offended whenever the island's governments did not bend to their pecuniary demands and who justified their complaints in racist terms. However, Astwood was also a Black man. This exception lays bare the stakes of his fight to control the narrative regarding Platt's death. For Astwood, Platt's case was not just about a white man's death at the hands of a Black government. It was a contest for political authority that ironically reflected upon the era's broader debate over Black political capacity.

The Deceit of Tricksters and Badmen: The Price of US Moral Capitalism and the Rise of a Dual Regime

Astwood, of course, was not the only one who peddled moral discourse in order to assert his own power over US-Dominican relations and local politics in Santo Domingo. The US consul's closest Dominican ally, Ulises Heureaux, did the same. According to historian Mu-Kien A. Sang, Heureaux constantly manipulated cultural symbols of righteousness—nationalism, legality, and Catholic morality—in order to control Dominican politics and the nation's finances.[85] He dressed impeccably in martial uniform to assert his national authority, exhibit his patriotism, and counter the stigma associated with his Blackness (figure 4.2). As elsewhere across the Caribbean, the image of the Black soldier both drew on nationalist color-blind citizenship discourse and "fed into those preexisting images and discourses of racial fear" associated with Haiti.[86] To counter such fears, Heureaux turned to religion; in speeches, he "defended the need to not only incentivize and deepen religious sentiment, but also to elevate morality in Dominican society."[87] Thus, both Astwood and Heureaux brokered in moral discourse as they deftly navigated the competing demands of international powers, foreign capitalists, and local patronage networks in Santo Domingo. Their manipulations not only reflected their efforts to command respect, but also to control narrative, money, and political authority in a world where Black politicians found themselves besieged from all sides.

FIGURE 4.2. Ulises Heureaux, president of the Dominican Republic, ca. 1893. Source: Wikipedia.org.

The similarities between Astwood's and Heureaux's tactics require an expanded analysis of the Platt affair, since their methods also matched in other ways. As a politician and then as president, Heureaux knew how to play different private, public, and international contingencies against each other. Similarly, Astwood's negotiations between various groups meant that no single dispatch from the US consul existed in isolation. Each missive formed part of a corpus of writing that altogether demonstrates Astwood's manipulations of private and public interests. As historian Jaime de Jesús Domínguez has argued, "These administrative acts are characterized by the shroud of secrecy that surrounds them, which impedes knowledge of many details and practically renders full comprehension impossible."[88] The Platt case sheds light on this process. Read alongside his reporting of other contemporary events, Astwood's narrative of the killing—his layering of moral, racial, gender, and national dichotomies—partially removes the shroud and reveals the discursive links between race, money, political authority, and constructions of morality.

In this regard, Astwood's linking of Platt's case to the idea of diplomatic reciprocity provides critical insight. As discussed previously, the idea of diplomatic reciprocity signaled the United States' decades-long refusal to recognize Haiti and the Dominican Republic on account of race. Even after the United States officially recognized both countries in the 1860s, the Dominican Republic still struggled to differentiate itself from Haiti in the US mindset. Thus, at the behest of Heureaux, Astwood spent his first year in Santo Domingo attempting to convince the State Department to upgrade his consular office to a diplomatic legation as in Port-au-Prince. When this strategy failed, he proposed a reciprocal trade treaty between the two nations. This context bore upon the Platt case. As Astwood pitched to US officials, Americans should have the right to conduct business as safely in the Dominican Republic as Dominicans did in the United States, but Platt's "murder" violated such reciprocity. Moreover, although European countries enforced reciprocity in Santo Domingo, the United States did not, impeding American trade relations with the island versus other nations. This argument directly invoked the reciprocity treaty, which, as Astwood reminded second assistant secretary of state William Hunter, was "of vital importance to the two Republics."[89] Since neither Astwood nor the Dominican government was aware that President Grover Cleveland had rescinded the treaty after his inauguration in March 1885, Astwood held this claim over Dominican officials as well.[90]

With these claims about reciprocity, Astwood recycled an inherently contradictory script.[91] The Dominican Republic was simultaneously like

Haiti in its violation of white American rights and need for US disciplining, and yet still wholly unlike the Black republic, deserving of separate US diplomatic regard. Astwood's insistence that officials in Washington conduct any negotiations in the Platt case through his office in Santo Domingo rather than via the US minister in Port-au-Prince also played upon this contradiction. On the one hand, Astwood presented himself as the only person who could force allegedly corrupt Dominican officials to pay an indemnity. On the other hand, direct negotiations between Washington and Santo Domingo would equate with a tacit US recognition of a Dominican policy divorced from Haiti. The dual notion of reciprocity—Dominicans as violators of reciprocity and Dominicans as deserving of reciprocity—reflected Astwood's pursuit of four interrelated goals: (1) gain Heureaux and other elite Dominicans the recognition that they sought; (2) hasten US dominance over Dominican affairs; (3) build Astwood's own prestige among both white Americans and Dominicans; and (4) benefit financially from the process. These goals remained constant throughout Astwood's tenure and often affected one another, as the Platt case shows.

A close reading of Astwood's consular dispatches suggests that the Platt affair impacted all aspects of his consular duties and vice versa. Just ten days after the killing, for example, Astwood took credit for brokering a deal between the Dominican government and a US capitalist for a national bank charter, which Astwood declared "the most important concession ever given here."[92] Although no written evidence directly linked the bank concession to Platt's case, the killing provided the US consul with leverage against the Dominican government in private negotiations. Moreover, it reinforced the perception that he successfully controlled US-Dominican relations. The bank charter, along with a railroad concession that Astwood had brokered months prior, would give Americans "complete control of [the country's] commercial affairs," Astwood boasted to officials in Washington.[93] Conversely, business unrelated to the killing also impacted Astwood's effectiveness in Platt's case. In 1885, Astwood received regular payments from the Dominican government for an indemnity to E. Remington and Sons, the New York firearms company whose expired claim Astwood had forced the Dominican Congress to recognize the previous year (see chapter 3).[94] Astwood's demand that the Dominican Republic pay restitution to Mrs. Platt stemmed from this prior experience.

Meanwhile, Astwood continued to antagonize Castro regarding Platt's alleged murder and then used their correspondence to cajole US officials to his side. In a third exchange with Castro, dated July 20, Astwood claimed to feel "especially aggrieved ... not only as the representative of a people, but for [his] individual safety as an American citizen."[95] He then compared Platt's case to three other instances of local shootings in which the assailant had been duly apprehended and punished. The fact that the same could not be said in Platt's case caused him to emote: "What a sad discrimination, Mr. Minister." With this display of righteous indignation, Astwood omitted the fact that only three years earlier, he had recommended a Cuban American plantation owner accused of murdering a Dominican citizen for the office of consular agent at San Pedro de Macorís; the planter, Santiago Mellor, never served time.[96] Brazenly hypocritical, the US consul suggested that the Dominican Republic did not play fair when it came to American claims. Linking the supposed injustice in Platt's case to international trade, he then implied that Dominican immorality had placed the assumedly pending 1884 reciprocity treaty at risk.

As before, Astwood forwarded this letter along with Castro's reply to Washington. This exchange further exposes the US consul's manipulation of Platt's case. Castro had called the US consul's bluff in his response to Astwood; how could the US consul fear for his life and in the same breath "applaud the [zeal] of the judicial authorities" in the three comparable cases, the Dominican minister quipped.[97] "Those examples are an evident proof that justice is fulfilled in the Republic" and should serve as "a guarantee" of the government's impartiality and foreigners' safety. Unrelentingly, Astwood used these very words against Castro in his letter to Washington. "You can see by the Minister's answer how conveniently he tries to construe my letter," he fumed, "[but] no applause was intended by me."[98] By law, Astwood explained, the investigation should have terminated within ten days, but he accused the Dominican government of stalling by offering the excuse that a revolt led by the escaped Cesáreo Guillermo had caused delays. He then decried Dominican evasiveness in the matter and adjudged that the affair would "die out altogether ... if [he] was not so persistent." These allegations enhanced the perception of widespread Dominican corruption, a sense that Astwood reinforced in another dispatch of the same date, in which he upbraided "the greatest frauds imaginable" taking place at the southern Dominican ports of Azua, Barahona, and Petit Trou (Enriquillo).[99] At these locations, ship captains and Dominican port officials committed "highway robbery" by overvaluing cargo and then burning vessels in order to collect payment from American insurance companies. Astwood's emotive language and strategic pairing of dispatches served to fortify his routine negation of the Dominican Republic's capacity for justice, which in turn served as a form of political power. The more Astwood positioned the Platt case fundamentally as a moral dispute, the more he alone could define exactly what morality entailed and thereby reap the associated political and financial benefits.

However, as a Black man, Astwood fought an uphill battle in his quest to secure political authority, as he well knew. Up to this point, Astwood's posturing had been preemptive, a scheme developed in anticipation of Washington's veto. The expected brush-off finally arrived over a month after Platt's death. The case was "shocking" and the victim merited "hearty sympathy," new assistant secretary of state James D. Porter conceded, but the evidence showed Platt's killing "was not murder as there was no malice or forethought against him."[100] Porter instructed Astwood to continue reporting on the case, but also reminded the US consul of his place. "While the Department approves of your zeal and activity in the discharge of what you may suppose to be your duties," Porter admonished, "it regrets to be obliged again to warn you that as a consul your functions are limited to commercial matters." As in prior instances of Astwood's diplomatic interference, the State Department reiterated that Astwood's commission was "not that of a diplomatic officer" and that he had no authority to address the Dominican minister of foreign affairs. The Dominican courts, Porter concluded, should resolve the matter. This curt dismissal was a blow for the US consul, who not only had pushed Platt's case before the Dominican government but had also delivered to Washington the ignominious lie of Black misrule.

Shifting from a preemptive scheme to a reactionary prose, Astwood doubled down on his narrative. "I maintain that Mr. Platt was deliberately murdered," he asserted, and again: "I cannot alter the term murder . . . unless I replace it by the word assassination."[101] The Dominican government, Astwood determined, could never learn of the US government's true attitude toward the Platt matter, or the judge of instruction "would never report."[102] Thus, Astwood intimated that Porter's instructions had been ignorant and nonsensical, and the State Department needed to get with the program. In the Dominican Republic, it had long been the custom that "consuls are called upon to perform all of the functions common to diplomatic representatives."[103] This was true because of the United States' historic refusal to recognize the country. To deprive Astwood of the right to intervene on behalf of Americans now, he exhorted, would be to submit US citizens to "all kinds of oppression" since it would make the US consul the only foreign officer divested of the power to communicate directly with the Dominican government.[104] Consequently, Astwood suggested that it would be better for the US government to let him handle the situation so that Mrs. Platt could be indemnified and Americans "secured in their lives and property." Yet, since his interpretation of the consular regulations was "so foreign to the instructions contained in [the State Department's] communication," he deadpanned, "I would request that you inform me what course I ought to pursue."

Astwood balanced his forceful response to Porter with other coeval dispatches that emphasized his usefulness to the State Department. In one report, he outlined how he had assisted the British subjects of the *Justitia*, a ship captured by Venezuelan revolutionaries that had landed in Santo Domingo, even when the British consul was unwilling to help the men.[105] He deflected accusations that he had misused consular funds in a similar case of assistance to sailors by painstakingly addressing each charge on his account, explaining that his consular salary did not meet the cost of living and bragging that he alone produced the most accurate port statistics available for Santo Domingo. Even the British consul "always takes his statistics from my report," Astwood concluded.[106] Regarding the country's increasingly dire economic situation, Astwood sent a detailed report on the sugar industry and planters' fears of a new export duty. He then reminded the department again that the pending 1884 reciprocity treaty would do much to advance US interests.[107] He also recycled the old proposal for the United States' purchase of Samaná Bay to use as a naval base. "[I am] hoping that the suggestions as they are commercial will not be considered an abuse of my official duties," he proffered at the end of this last dispatch.[108] At each turn, Astwood mitigated his defiance of Porter with evidence that he not only complied with all consular regulations but also produced outstanding advice and results.

Meanwhile, a lightbulb finally clicked on in Washington. Maybe Astwood's persuasions at last took effect, or perhaps the State Department decided that a "completely demoralized" Astwood, as he had described himself, worked against the United States' immediate interests.[109] In either case, Porter's attitude toward Astwood soon flipped. On August 11, the assistant secretary penned a short missive in which he acknowledged Astwood's third exchange with Castro, thanked him again for his "zeal," and authorized him to continue his inquiries.[110] Then, responding to Astwood's justification regarding the accounting irregularities, Porter ordered the consular bureau to "allow the whole amount."[111] Much later, on September 14, Porter instructed Astwood to pursue the indemnity and "at once express to [Castro] the very deep interest which this Government takes in the early and perfect investigation of all facts connected with the death of Mr. Platt."[112] This final order was the reaction that Astwood had wanted all along, and he should have been pleased. Yet Porter's permission arrived much too late. Astwood cursorily acknowledged Porter's instructions in early October.[113] By then, he had already settled Platt's case.

THE END OF THE PLATT affair happened like this. Within days of receiving Porter's August 11 instructions, Astwood engaged Castro once again in a fourth and final exchange that solidified the US consul's triumph over the Dominican government on moral terms. The judge of instruction still had not produced an official report, and the US consul now shot down the "most extraordinary proceedings" with familiar Christian phrases: "If I fail to get the report so as to submit it to my Government, my *only salvation* will be to *lay down my charge*, return to my Government and to the American people with *my hands washed* having done all in my power to rectify the striking down *even until death* of one of its loyal citizens within his own *private sanctum*."[114] Here the US consul assumed the role of the Roman governor of Judea, Pontius Pilate, who washed his hands at Jesus's trial. Platt was the Christ figure, supposedly emblematic of every American citizen whom the Dominican military forces had persecuted even in the inviolable "private sanctum." The phrase "even until death" invoked the biblical verse Philippians 2:8, which describes Jesus's humiliation "even [unto] death on a cross." Other words suggested Astwood's own religious faith and personal righteousness. His "salvation" came only through the "laying down" of his burden. These phrases invoked the Christian belief in casting one's guilt, shame, and anxiety in the physical world upon Jesus Christ, who provides spiritual salvation. Blending Christian spirituality with diplomacy in turn accentuated the Christian moral dichotomy of good and evil layered upon the two nations, a duality that Astwood paired with his ritualistic indignation. "I am becoming incensed, the American people will become incensed, my Government will become incensed," he harangued Castro. His final demand that Castro fast-track the judge's report and terminate "this painful issue upon the basis of common reciprocity" drove home the point. US dominance in this affair and all others was quite simply a matter of good versus evil, and if the Dominican Republic did not acquiesce, it risked financial ruin.

A predictable conclusion followed. Two weeks later and exactly three months to the day from Platt's demise, a copy of Matos's report and the government's judgment finally arrived at the US consul's door. As Astwood expected, the twenty-five-page synthesis of the judge of instruction's investigation presented the obvious verdict: in the case of Platt's killing and the wound to María de la Cruz Herrera's right leg, "no one is responsible and the proceedings are dismissed."[115] Fault lay instead with the dead American, specifically: "the imprudence and inexperience of Mr. Platt to come out of his chamber" during a gunfight. Thus, "this ministry [can] never call, much less qualify, the killing of Mr. Platt as murder." The case should have closed here. Yet the government's verdict ultimately mattered little because the US consul had decided to make something out of the fact that a "good" white American was dead, nay murdered, by the Dominican government. And Astwood never quit. Thus, the US consul's insistence upon his narrative was likewise expected. "There was no indiscretion on the part of Mr. Platt as you say," he rejoined. "The indiscretion was on the part of these officials who shot at an object in a private hotel without identifying it."[116] The only way to preserve "good relations" with the United States was to pursue an "amicable adjustment *without any recourse to litigation or diplomatic correspondence*" (emphasis added). In other words, a backdoor deal was in order. Astwood set his terms even higher than before: the governor and soldiers should be suspended and punished, and Mrs. Platt should receive $5,000 US per annum for the next twenty years, a total of $100,000 (over $2.7 million in 2022). This sum he deemed "just, humane, and magnanimous" and a "guarantee" that "the rights of domicile, life and property be inviolable" in the Dominican Republic. Like his other letters, he forwarded this correspondence to Washington and effectively dared State Department officials to challenge him.

Astwood's deal with Dominican officials ultimately took place without knowledge or approval from Washington. Astwood later justified his actions by presenting a creative interpretation of consular regulations. Consuls, according to Astwood, possessed the power to amicably adjust matters before submitting them for diplomatic discussion. This interpretation clearly flew in the face of Porter's earlier instructions, but Astwood did not care. "If I have erred, it is in judgement, not principle," he concluded.[117] Besides, as Astwood knew, the results spoke for themselves. In the end, the Dominican government had acquiesced to Astwood's demands. Governor Espaillat had been removed from office and sent along with his men to the interior of the country to capture General Guillermo; he was out of sight and mind. While the exorbitant indemnity Astwood demanded was impossible, the Dominican government settled the sum at $33,000 Mexican silver (about $28,500 US in 1885). This amount would enter the foreign debt and, like the Remington claim, be paid at monthly intervals to the US consul, who would forward the money to Mrs. Platt. While the French consul scampered to secure an indemnity for Rosa Moniere as well, Astwood surveyed his handiwork.[118] By allowing the deal, the Dominican government had attempted "to atone for the rashness of its officials."[119] This language of repentance indicated the restoration of moral order; the logic of US capitalism had won. And so too had Astwood. Both the United States and the Dominican Republic had at last recognized Astwood's political authority. The US consul was satisfied.[120]

Soon thereafter, the Dominican government found satisfaction too when Cesáreo Guillermo at last succumbed to military forces. Historians have had much to say on this topic, and so did Astwood, who used the occasion to praise Heureaux. On October 14, the same day that Astwood forwarded President Wos y Gil's sign-off on the Platt indemnity to Washington, he also sent dispatch #283, "Revolt of Cesáreo Guillermo," in which he detailed the fugitive's last battle.[121] Now portraying Dominican soldiers as fully competent, Astwood described how Heureaux had led four hundred men to the southwestern city of Azua, where Guillermo had barricaded the town. Heureaux sent another 250 soldiers to Baní, and Espaillat led a troop of 300 men to San Cristobal. With these forces, the army arrested a few rebels. Then, on October 11, Heureaux surrounded Azua, and Heureaux's and Guillermo's troops battled for three hours before Guillermo made an escape. Still, the government's ultimate victory was "said to be the final overthrow of the General Guillermo's pretensions." Astwood called upon Castro days later and found him with President Wos y Gil, who commended Heureaux's bravery. Astwood also reveled in Heureaux's show of strength. In a separate dispatch, he recounted how, when it was rumored that Pablo Ramírez (Pablo Mamá)—the strongman who controlled Neiba, a town west of Azua—had joined Guillermo's revolt, Heureaux marched one thousand men to Neiba to force Ramírez to capitulate.[122] Then, in early November after more of Heureaux's "rapid movements," Guillermo was dead, and Heureaux was "master of the situation" once again.[123]

The news of Guillermo's death was sensational. Hiding in the brambles in the outskirts of Azua, Cesáreo had called to a young boy to bring him food and water. The boy had run home and reported that he had seen Guillermo in the bushes. The soldiers went quickly to the spot that the boy indicated and surrounded the general, who, realizing he was surrounded, placed his pistol below his right ear and pulled the trigger. When he died, Cesáreo was half naked. His pants had been "torn to pieces," so he donned only his drawers.[124] He had removed his shirt sleeves to bandage his feet. A small handkerchief was wrapped around his head, and his body, like that of Jesus Christ on the cross, was "lacerated in a terrible way." In the end, the government buried Guillermo's broken body in Azua; neither he nor his followers ever rose again. Astwood celebrated the government's triumph by extolling Heureaux, whose power over the government increased with the general's demise. "Too much credit cannot be given to General Heureaux for his activity and bravery in thus defending the peace of his country," the US consul applauded.

These events—Guillermo's suicide and Heureaux's rise to power—reflected upon Platt's case. Although settled with the indemnity, the Platt affair became a point of discussion during the government's celebrations of Heureaux's victory at Azua. "This blow was to have been given on the night of the unfortunate killing of Mr. Platt," one official reminded Astwood. He continued, "I hope now Mr. Consul you are convinced of the necessity of the Government acting [promptly] in this matter."[125] The US minister at Port-au-Prince also wrote about Platt in a dispatch about Guillermo's last stand.[126] And, as Astwood continued to inform on Dominican politics in November and December—reports in which he again praised Heureaux—the Platt claim was entered into the republic's foreign debt. Astwood also received and forwarded to the State Department letters of commendation from US citizens for his role in the process.[127] There is no telling the story of Platt's death without remembering what happened to Guillermo and the Dominican nation as Heureaux came to power.

Yet the same cannot be said in reverse. Historians have long written about Heureaux's rising dictatorship without much attention to Platt's death or Astwood's handling of the case. At first, the Dominican intelligentsia portrayed Heureaux's regime in highly racist terms, featuring anecdotes of brutality that bordered on the absurd. For example, Heureaux ordered the assassination of his brother-in-law, who aided Cesáreo's rebellion, but only after feeding and clothing the prisoner so that his poor appearance would not embarrass the family before the shooting squad.[128] Such stories of the dictator's ruthlessness reinforced stereotypes of Blackness and vice versa. As Anne Eller has written, both Heureaux's Haitian heritage and his dark skin "were not just the topic of ridicule but the essence of the argument for many of his urban opponents."[129] Thus, the elite class hated the Black general, *"el negro mañé,"* and even Luperón later reserved choice words for the "crafty, crooked, corrupted man."[130] At one point, a famous sketch of a lynched Heureaux hung on a wall in the capital (figure 4.3);

FIGURE 4.3. Oil painting of President Heureaux lynched. The inscription translates: "There is no crime without punishment." Photo: Julio Pou, "Fotografía de óleo del presidente Heureaux ahorcado," control 105523, sig. 221, Colección José Gabriel García, AGN, Santo Domingo.

neither the anonymous artist nor public viewers missed the allusion to the concurrent lynchings of Black people across the United States.[131] Rumors also spread that Heureaux was a *brujo* or a shapeshifting *bacá*, terms that signaled the use of Haitian Vodou.[132] And, as political conflict with Haiti increased in the late 1880s, influential men such as Eugenio María de Hostos cursed the birth of "*ese ennegrecedor del quisqueyanismo* (that blackener of quisqueyanism)."[133] This racist hatred translated into historical text after the dictator's assassination in 1899. The tome *Lilí, el sanguinario machetero dominicano* (1901) by Juan Vicente Flores, for example, epitomized the racist invective against Heureaux by his most ardent political enemies.[134] Furthermore, chronicles such as *Cosas de Lilís* by Victor M. Castro (1919) and *Otras Cosas de Lilís* by Gustavo E. Borgés Bordas (1921) ridiculed the Black dictator with jocular anecdotes.

In the United States, the US historian Sumner Welles wrote even more explicit racist descriptions of Heureaux than of the Guillermos. Heureaux, "the savage," was controlled by "his sexual passions, which never were satiated, and his lust for blood."[135] And there was still more: "polished with the veneer of civilization which [Heureaux] had acquired, rapacious, merciless, pitiless, filled with unquenchable daemonic energy, such was the figure which was now for so long to dominate the scene."[136] Welles's view of Heureaux reflected all of the stereotypes white Americans had of authoritative Black leaders. His text, which includes multiple accounts of Black misrule, also revealed his overall bias against Dominicans.

Although historians now recognize the historical racist hatred targeting Heureaux, no one could argue that the dictator was not ruthless; the autocrat himself would have taken offense at any suggestion of softness toward enemies. Yet, just as Heureaux's political maneuvers prompt a reevaluation of Astwood's tactics, Astwood's role in the Platt affair is illuminating since it requires a second look at the racialized contours of both men's battles for political authority and the implications of their fight for the study of history. What does it mean that these two Black men acted similarly and partnered with one another? The affinity between Heureaux and Astwood stemmed partially from the fact that they were both Black leaders facing the same racist world. Astwood's control over the Platt case entangled the Dominican Republic in a geopolitical moral sphere in which the dichotomy of good versus evil was superimposed upon racial, gendered, and national borders. Both he and Heureaux manipulated moral dichotomies in order to assert their authority as men of color, but the game was already set for and against them. "This is no longer a fight about one ambitious person against another," wrote Hostos about Heureaux's regime, "but about decent men against scoundrels."[137]

Conclusion

On November 13, 1885, historical irony abounded. Castro died suddenly by "apoplexy," which any medical professional will say means a stroke. The next day, the US consul reversed script and expressed high esteem for the island nation and its late minister of foreign affairs, whom he had previously condemned. Castro was now "a good man," a person of "great ability," and "a valuable public servant and true friend."[138] Reading these words today, it is not hard to surmise that Castro was suddenly "good" in Astwood's estimation because, just before he died, he had finally capitulated to Astwood.

However, armed with history, context, and rhetoric, an amateur detective might have questioned whether Astwood himself provoked Castro's fatal apoplectic fit. The word *apoplexy*, after all, also signifies a state of intense, almost uncontrollable anger, and the Dominican minister had entertained the US consul just hours before his untimely demise. Astwood swore that when he left Castro's house around 5:00 p.m. on November 13, the bureaucrat "seemed in the best of health."[139] Within hours, though, the man was overcome by a stroke (or rage) and then death. Thus Castro departed this world, leaving his opponent to extend condolences to the Dominican government with this equally ironic phrase: "bowing with you to the will of that Divine Providence who rules the destinies of men and Nations."[140] These words might have been laughable if not for the violence they implied—and if Castro had not died. But he did. The possibility of Castro's murder remains a figment of imagination, a fiction yet to be constructed.

And so we have come full circle, and now the "facts" seem quite plain in retrospect. The Dominican soldiers killed Platt. Like the soldiers, Astwood, Heureaux, and Guillermo were all ruthless Black "badmen" and "tricksters": Astwood cheated two governments; Heureaux cheated a nation; Guillermo cheated death (until he didn't).[141] Castro died, unexpectedly, we believe. Soon thereafter, the Dominican government paid its first installment on the Platt indemnity.[142] Historians moved on.

Yet what happens when everything is twisted, inverted, fallacious, and untrue? When every rumor, story, history—even the facts of death, whether accidental or not—requires careful study? When the dichotomies constructed and manipulated force the all-important question: By whom and for whom was this tale concocted? Then, perhaps, it is crucial to take a second look, to pay attention to the anecdotes and fill in the gaps. It would seem, for example, that the use of a well-worn racist trope would work against the Black US consul's self-interest. But Astwood's cavalier reversal of a painful historic phrase and malicious evocation of the Haitian Revolution was a calculated act of defiant exasperation. "An American has no rights which a Dominican is bound to respect." These words are revolutionary until they are not.

In 1885, Astwood saw the indemnity for Platt's widow as the clearest path toward ensuring his own place in US government and local influence in Santo Domingo. His tactics, however, produced various contradictions. As a Black man and a person with familial ties to the island, Astwood shamelessly employed racist stereotypes of Haiti and "San Domingo" in order to cater to a white US audience and draw State Department officials' attention toward the Platt case. For those who paid attention, rhetorical incongruencies gave his game away. Platt's "murder" was "without a parallel," and yet the killing of a white man in Santo Domingo seemed eerily reminiscent of the Haitian Revolution.[143] Dominicans fulfilled all the racist stereotypes associated with Haitians, and yet "the difference of language, the customs, and the lack of communication" between the two sides of the island required that the US negotiate with Dominican officials via Santo Domingo, not Port-au-Prince.[144] The Dominican Republic of Astwood's creation appeared similar enough to revolutionary Haiti to scandalize the reader and compel officials in Washington to pay attention. This was the bait. The switch came when Astwood then asked the State Department to deal with the Dominican Republic on its own terms. This meant conducting diplomatic affairs directly with Santo Domingo via Astwood, the Black US consul who purported to understand Dominican politics like no one else.

Was Astwood just another Black face wearing a white mask? Maybe. Judging by his words and actions, it is possible that Astwood, like Heureaux, conceded that "the characteristics of a white face are superior to a Black face," as one tale about the dictator goes.[145] But then again, perhaps also like Heureaux, Astwood might have countered, "But when nature gifts a Black man with something notorious and useful for society, that Black man is a *jodien* [fucker] for all you whites. . . . I am not white, but you are mistaken, I am not just one *jodien*. . . . I am hundreds of *jodienes* for the whites of Quisqueya [Hispaniola]."[146] In other words, in this unverifiable anecdote, Heureaux conceded that Blacks were inferior to whites as a rhetorical device that served only to emphasize his main point, which can be paraphrased as follows: You think I'm inferior. Okay, no problem. This inferior Black man is gonna f——— y'all up!

No one recorded the secret conversations between friends and statesmen, so the historian can only surmise the sort of conversations Astwood and Heureaux had behind closed doors. All the same, whether accused *pícaros* (scoundrels) or self-proclaimed *jodienes*, the men whom we then and now label the Black badmen of history knew exactly what they were doing. And, if we are honest with ourselves, so do we. The historian may now move on.

PART III

Social Morality

5

BETWEEN TOLERANCE AND TYRANNY

Protestant Dominicans, Social Morality,
and the Making of a Liberal Nation

In early 1883, US consul Henry Astwood wrote to Benjamin Tucker Tanner, editor of the AME Church's *Christian Recorder*, about his first months in Santo Domingo. Readers of Astwood's missive, which Tanner subsequently published in the newspaper, learned first and foremost that the Dominican Republic was Catholic territory. "Seventeen structures dedicated to this formidable machine of the [Pope] testify to the fealty of the inhabitants," Astwood proclaimed.[1] Among the buildings was the Americas' first cathedral, home to Christopher Columbus's exhumed remains, whose authenticity Astwood verified.[2] It seemed that there was no place for Protestant doctrine within this former Spanish colony, where the people practiced "hereditary Catholicism," in Astwood's view. "Shame to Protestantism, that until now no church edifice of that denomination adorns the precincts of the grand old city," he admonished. "Let African Methodism be the pioneer."[3]

Yet, despite the factual absence of a Protestant chapel in Santo Domingo, Astwood's letter still hinted at a Protestant presence in the city. Indeed, if one looked hard enough, remnants of a former time when Black Methodists convened weekly could be found, "twice a month on moonlight nights" at a private house with a thatched roof and mud floors.[4] The house belonged to François Claudio, who was born on the island but whose grandfather had emigrated from the United States to resettle in Haiti, like thousands of other African Americans in the early 1820s.[5] Nearly sixty years later, Astwood encountered Claudio and other African American descendants upon his arrival in the Dominican capital. At first, Astwood seemed like the ideal person to revive the congregation. Reading the historical record in contra*diction* (to use Lorgia García-Peña's term) to his self-serving narrative, however, challenges any notion that Henry pioneered the city's Protestant church by himself.[6]

Whereas part II of this book analyzed how moral politics influenced the economic and diplomatic aspects of Astwood's consular work, the next few chapters explore moral politics through significant cultural intersections at the Dominican crossroads. This chapter specifically turns to Astwood's social life in Santo Domingo, where he became deeply involved with two local societies: the African Methodist Episcopal (AME) Church and the Grand United Order of Odd Fellows (GUOOF). As discussed in chapter 2, Astwood had joined these organizations while in New Orleans, and in his early consular years he played a foundational role in establishing their presence in the Dominican Republic. Although documentation regarding Astwood's AME and GUOOF work pales in comparison to his consular dispatches (which omit discussion of his social work), the episodic written record enables a fresh look at what sociologist H. Hoetink called the Dominican Republic's "organs of cultural transmission": education, Masonry, religious organizations, the press, and the arts.[7] In the 1880s, shifts in these areas paralleled the economic, political, and diplomatic changes explored in previous chapters. Rather than merely attesting to Astwood's good repute in Santo Domingo, AME and GUOOF records evidence the many ways in which African American descendants formed part of these cultural organs. Such participation impacted the ideological development of Dominican liberalism, specifically the liberal concept of social morality. Thus, following Astwood's paper trail not only provides a more complete picture of late nineteenth-century cultural organs but also requires new analysis of how social morality operated within Dominican society.

Through a counterhegemonic reading of Astwood's social work in Santo Domingo, this chapter tracks the emergence of the AME and GUOOF as Dominican cultural organs. It then argues that African American descendants in the Dominican capital stood at the intersection of varying domestic and foreign notions of social morality. In the Dominican context, the idea of social morality (*moral social*) was first developed by Eugenio María de Hostos, a nineteenth-century positivist thinker who theorized the rational pursuit of modern progress as a moral imperative. For Hostos, the concept of *moral social* was not just a set of liberal principles (i.e., social morals) but a secular way of individual being and acting rightly in society. Hostos's writings on social morality have since become the focus of numerous studies regarding nineteenth-century Latin American thought.[8] Contrary to extant scholarship, however, this chapter interprets social morality as a capacious concept with applicability beyond Latin American positivism. Here, social morality is defined as an expansive transnational public discourse that prescribed moral ways of being for mixed-race societies and served concurrently as a proxy for racial discourse. Thus, on the surface, distinct ideologies of social morality—Latin American positivism, African American Protestantism, US concepts of moral capitalism and Christian diplomacy, and even Dominican Catholicism—seemed compatible with one another.

Operating within this context, US Consul Astwood used transnational understandings of social morality and performances of Black respectability to exude a sense of moral authority in Catholic Santo Domingo. This chapter does not account for all the ways that he did this. Instead, by reading Astwood's record in contra*diction* and fusing the historiographies of Dominican liberalism, US Black internationalism, and US empire, race, and religion, this chapter analyzes how the moral politics of race-making worked locally in Santo Domingo. By doing so, it demonstrates the various convergences between African American descendants, AME leaders, Odd Fellows, Freemasons, positivist liberals, white US capitalists, African American diplomats, and Dominican Catholics that emerged during the 1880s. It also evidences significant divergences. As the last section demonstrates, the ideological distinctions between varying types of social morality in Santo Domingo amplified as Ulises Heureaux grabbed the nation's reins of power and refused to let go.

From the Shadows to the Center: African American Immigrants and Their Children in Santo Domingo

The group of African American descendants that Astwood encountered in the Dominican capital was similar to the US Black immigrant communities that he had lived among in Puerto Plata and Samaná in the 1870s. As argued in chapter 2, in the northern port towns, African American immigrants and their descendants were deeply integrated into Dominican society. Not only did they form economic, political, and even familial relationships with other Dominicans, but their institutions served the local population. As stated previously, liberal leaders Gregorio Luperón and Ulises Heureaux attended the Wesleyan school in Puerto Plata and were thus familiar with African American and British Caribbean Protestants. The Dominican government, moreover, recognized these African American communities by protecting their right to religious freedom and providing material support for their Protestant churches after the War of Restoration. By that time, the congregations in the north operated as de facto autonomous Black religious spaces. These descriptions applied as well to the capital's US Black immigrant community, albeit with one important caveat. Unlike in the north where immigrants and their descendants benefited from British Wesleyan missionaries prior to the war (see the introduction and chapter 1), the capital received no resources from abroad—that is, until Henry Astwood arrived in 1882.

As discussed further below, Astwood's landing in Santo Domingo facilitated a revival within the city's Protestant congregation, reconnecting African American descendants to the AME Church of their forefathers and inaugurating the GUOOF. Due to this influence, Astwood eagerly assumed full credit for the congregation's revival in letters to AME leaders in the United States. Documents from the decade prior to his arrival, however, reveal that precursors to the capital's AME Church and GUOOF society already existed. A counterhegemonic reading of anecdotes regarding the city's African American community attest to this fact, demonstrating the Dominican public's general acceptance of Protestant Dominican citizens and the same Protestants' integration into the capital's mutual aid culture.

What is known about the capital's US Black community in the decade leading up to 1882 derives first from the US governments' 1871 Commission of Inquiry report. The report shows that *capitaleño* Black immigrants such as John Jones, David Brooks, Theodore Hall, and Elijah R. Gross had arrived in Santo Domingo as children or men no older than twenty.[9]

Over the years, they and their offspring learned Spanish, worked in local trades, fought in Dominican wars, and became Dominican citizens. By the 1870s, their children spoke more Spanish than English.[10] Gross, an old man in 1882, informed the commission that he preferred to homeschool his children since Protestant instruction was not allowed in the local Catholic schools, but other immigrants' children such as George Fountain learned to read and write in "Spanish" (i.e., Catholic) schools.[11] While most immigrants remained poor tradesmen and day laborers, a few men participated in the island's government. Gross, for example, served the Haitian government for three years as the postmaster general, and then after Dominican independence was elected a judge under General Pedro Santana, a position that he held for at least nineteen years.[12] Like other Dominican men, the city's Protestant leaders formed a mutual aid fraternity known as the Society of the Bible through which they organized education for their children, cared for orphans and sick members, and collected funds for the burial of their dead.[13] This society, which Claudio and Gross served as president and vice president respectively, was affiliated with their Methodist church, an institution that the Dominican government tolerated before and after Spanish annexation.[14]

In 1872, the community provided further information about their congregation in a letter to AME Church leaders in the United States. Written to persuade US-based African Americans to send financial and ministerial aid, the letter emphasized the immigrants' destitution, sense of religious persecution, and faithfulness to the AME Church, even though they had received governmental concessions and had previously attempted to transfer to the British Wesleyans. As they reported, after a cholera epidemic, the community was quickly disintegrating, and only eighteen of the original immigrants remained. Compounding this loss, the "intolerant" Catholic Church curtailed the "gayety of worship" and had indirectly opposed their organization (probably through noise restrictions).[15] Protestant elders further complained that the Catholic Church "allowed their people to dance, gamble, and indulge in licentionment [sic]," while Protestants prohibited such activities.[16] For these reasons, many of the immigrants' children had left Methodism for Catholicism, much to their parents' chagrin. Thus, the elders appealed to the AME denomination for a preacher who could revive the congregation and counteract Catholic influences. In making this request, they boldly declared their allegiance to the AME Church. "We the members of the African Methodist Episcopal Church of this city emigrated to this country from the United States in the years 1824, 1825, and

1826," they proclaimed. "On arriving here we immediately established our church, under the name BETHEL, and we have kept our language and religion to the present."[17] They then recalled how the AME Church's founder and first bishop, Richard Allen, and Robert Morris (the second bishop) had ordained Isaac Miller, and how Miller had trained and ordained John Hamilton and other immigrant leaders before his death. These facts served to reiterate the community's long-standing loyalty to the AME Church. Taken at face value, the 1872 letter confirmed that immigrants still considered themselves to be part of the AME Church five decades after their arrival. It also undermines the claim that they lived comfortably side by side with Catholic Dominicans.

However, as previously addressed in chapter 2 and as a second 1872 anecdote from Julia Ward Howe suggests, US Black immigrants chose when to stress their various subject positions to outsiders in order to benefit their communities. This fact does not disregard the immigrants' 1872 claims but rather puts them in conversation with other known details about the community. Doing so explains why Astwood's 1882 arrival was such a big deal for the capital's Protestants. It also shows that members of this same congregation formed part of the nation's fraternal "organs of cultural transmission," despite the fact that their leaders and outsiders often stressed their religious and cultural alienation.

Howe's anecdote appeared in her memoir *Reminiscences* (1899) and attested to the immigrants' poverty, religious devotion, and willingness to seek aid outside the AME Church. Howe, who had likewise visited immigrants in the north (see chapter 2), learned about the capital's US Black immigrant community from Claudio, who boarded her incoming ship, the *Tybee*, in February 1872.[18] In describing his community's precarity, Claudio hoped to inspire one of the men aboard the *Tybee* to preach to the struggling congregation, but Julia volunteered for the job instead. Howe, whom Claudio and others apparently permitted in the pulpit, was not the ideal exhorter for this group. Although a few Black women had historically preached in the AME Church by the late nineteenth century, the denomination did not ordain women at that time.[19] Furthermore, Howe was a white woman who believed herself superior to this group of "illiterate negroes."[20] Consequently, her pejorative descriptions of the immigrants' poverty diminished their remarkable perseverance as a religious community through decades of hardship. Howe, for example, noted that most of the members did not have enough money to buy new clothes and shoes.[21] Still, the parishioners had found the means to build a large mahogany pulpit and chancel rail for their dilapidated church building, located in the city's military barracks. They furthermore had no need for the tattered hymnbooks Howe passed out during services, since they had committed the hymns to memory. These details point to the congregation's religious devoutness. They also evince the community's willingness to humor Howe's condescending leadership if it resulted in profit.

Even more to the point, Howe's writings about the Black Protestant community demonstrate that she did not see the full picture of everything that she witnessed. For example, Howe accused white US and British Methodists of neglecting the capital's immigrants, never fathoming that the congregation emanated from a Black institution (i.e., the AME Church). An even more revealing anecdote shows that the congregation's Bible Society was illegible to Howe who, guided by Claudio, visited the group sometime in 1872–73. As Howe recalled, the "secret association" began its ceremony by ringing a bell and addressing her "in a rather high-flown style."[22] Howe professed that she was "much puzzled" by these proceedings and could not imagine how anything she had done could "penetrate the atmosphere of this isolated spot." Unable to respond in Spanish, she expressed her appreciation in French and took her leave. "To this day I have never been able to understand the connection of this association with any Bible society," she later remarked.[23] Howe's belief that the group needed such outside affiliation underscored her inability to comprehend Black leadership independent of white oversight.

Claudio and other members of the Bible Society, however, fully understood their actions and purpose. They formed part of a generation of Dominican men whose mutual aid societies, Masonic lodges, and fraternities contributed to the "altruism, religiosity, patriotism, civility, 'city pride,' [and] love of culture . . . of the Dominican people," according to historian Emilio Rodríguez Demorizi.[24] African American descendants participated in these groups along with Catholic and Sephardic Jewish Dominicans (and possibly even Arab Dominicans) with whom they worked to improve social services for the city's poor (table 5.1).[25] As Mimi Sheller has shown for postemancipation Jamaica, such civic groups fostered democratic alliances as people worked collectively to advance community initiatives.[26] Although Howe noted such interethnic cooperation when she described the Bible Society as "a company of natives of various shades of color," François Claudio and other African American descendants' role in this group proved too confusing for further elaboration.[27] Their assimilation into Dominican civic culture, after all, defied the strict divide that Howe imagined

TABLE 5.1. Known Societies in Which African American Descendants Were Members

African American Descendant	Name of Society	Year Est.	Purpose
Pablo Claudio	Los Hijos del Recreo Dominicano	1875	Recreation
Jacinto Gross	La Misericordiosa	1881	Bury the dead
	Fervorosos del Rosario	1883	Religious, mutual aid
Alejandro R. Gross*	Sociedad Promotora de Inmigración	1890	Promote immigration
Antonio Gross	Los Peregrinos	1883	Mutual aid
Alfredo Hamilton	Socorro entre sus Miembros	1881	Mutual aid
Ángel Jones	Socorro entre sus Miembros	1881	Mutual aid
Clemente Jones	Verdaderos Amigos	1872	Recreation, mutual aid
	Socorro entre sus Miembros	1881	Mutual aid

*Refers to Ricardo Alejandro Gross.
Source: Extracted from Rodríguez Demorizi, *Sociedades*, 94, 96, 99, 102–3, 109.

between "American Blacks" and the high class of "mixed race ... intelligent" Dominicans whose whiteness "so predominates that the leading negro characteristics are rarely observed among them."[28] It also, incidentally, violated what the immigrants and their children wrote about themselves for outsiders' consumption.

On some level, Claudio and other members of the African American community must have registered the multiple contradictions that existed in the ways that they collectively presented themselves to outsiders. The inconsistencies were readily evident. The congregation welcomed Howe to the pulpit although she was a white woman who knew little of the Black history and leadership that sustained the church. The church elders were faithful African Methodists, although they would entertain assistance from anywhere and would not hesitate to join the Wesleyans if they could. Members of the Protestant community described the Catholic Church as intolerant but celebrated the Dominican government's protection of their rights and participated in various civic organizations alongside Catholics. The Bible Society, in turn, was affiliated with the local Methodist Church, but many of its members were Catholic. Together these contradictions reveal how African American immigrants and their descendants, individually and collectively, negotiated externally imposed boundaries of belonging and stretched limited resources in whatever ways kept them afloat. Like other such immigrant groups in the north, they did so by belonging to multiple communities and by making themselves both legible and illegible to others in order to gain material benefits both big and small. Thus, well before Astwood appeared in 1882, *capitaleño* immigrants and their children ran their church and mutual aid societies in ways that ensured their survival within a constantly changing political context. Yet, while African American descendants were deeply integrated into *capitaleño* society, they had not commanded the resources to influence the city's culture in a meaningful way. For this reason, they constantly sought to secure financial resources from abroad as a self-preserving measure.

For Black Protestants in Santo Domingo, such negotiations necessarily continued throughout the 1870s, as more anecdotes from Wesleyan missionary letters make clear. By 1874, with the prospect of US annexation and Buenaventura Báez's regime gone, it became apparent that neither the AME Church nor Julia Howe could provide immediate aid. Consequently, in January of the following year, the congregation petitioned the Wesleyans for help via Reverend Jacob James of Samaná. As mentioned in chapter 2, Astwood likely met James, an African American immigrant and the Wesleyans' appointed catechist in Samaná, while living there circa 1873–74. While Astwood was in New Orleans (1874–82), James served as an intermediary between *capitaleño* African American descendants and the London Missionary Society, which granted James permission to visit the community. James subsequently established the Wesleyan mission among them, presenting their precarious state to London in the same way that immigrants had described themselves to AME leaders in 1872.[29] The congregation, he reported, was nearly dead since John Hamilton had passed away. The next generation had begun to appeal to local Catholic priests to baptize their children and administer Holy Communion, and the now "new" Wesleyan society had only seven members.[30] James hoped that this description would make plain the dire conditions in the Dominican Republic and convince the missionary society to support its newest Caribbean station.

James's letters reveal that the African American descendant community not only hoped to sustain itself but also aimed to transform Dominican society through the Wesleyans' missions as in the north. To this end, James envisioned a Protestant awakening in the city and advised that a church property and an appointed ordained minister would enable Catholic conversions. Thus he surveyed the premises of an old stone building that could be purchased for $45 and used for the chapel, schoolhouse, and mission house in lieu of the current dilapidated church.[31] He additionally estimated that it would take a missionary three years to start the school. In making this pitch, James stressed that Catholic Dominicans would undoubtedly join the new school if it received aid and noted that even the "natives" were "thankful" to now have the Wesleyans among them. This observation reflected the sentiments of at least one government official, the "General Administrator" of the city, who was a Protestant and who wanted the London society to appoint "a native minister, one that can speak Spanish and Inglish [sic]."[32] While James's view was biased (he likely hoped to have his son appointed to the role), his observations reveal a certain level of government backing.[33]

The statement of Joseph A. Prior, a white British missionary to the Turks Islands who visited the capital in 1880, further solidifies this point. Like James, Prior stressed, "Many of the Dominicans speak English and they warmly desire a Protestant Minister and would contribute towards his support."[34] He advised that an English man who could speak Spanish be sent and specified that Heureaux (who was then serving as the capital's governor) wished to reestablish the Wesleyan mission at Puerto Plata and expand the Wesleyans' work throughout the republic. Prior's report suggested that Dominicans who understood English (both African American descendants and some government officials) aimed to reform the capital into a port like Puerto Plata, a bastion of Dominican liberalism where Protestants served the population alongside the Catholic Church. James's subsequent insistence that a "native Minister" be appointed to the capital (i.e., not a British man) would ensure that this effort would remain an Afro-Dominican enterprise.[35]

Nevertheless, as James experienced, the gap between the dreamscape and reality, while not insurmountable, still proved quite vast in the 1870s. Given the government's close ties to the Catholic Church, any sort of improvement to the poor material state of the capital's Protestant congregation and shift in the city's religious composition depended first upon foreign money, which did not surface in the wake of James's preliminary 1875 visit. James's solicitations the following year also yielded no results.[36] Even supplications from the Wesleyans' Bahamas District chair, Reverend Henry Bleby, went unheard. Bleby noted that $300 (or sixty pounds) would enable the society to replace the roof of their church building, which by 1876 "had become so dangerous that the people were afraid to assemble and worship in it."[37] However, the money never came. The following year, 1877, James visited Gross and learned from the now blind elder that the parishioners had begun to repair the roof but lacked the funds to finish the job. Consequently, they had once again written to the "United States" (i.e., the AME Church) for aid.[38] But neither New York nor London sent help in 1878, and repairs stalled. The same held true for the next four years, when James finally urged the British Wesleyan society to formally hand over its mission to the United States. The timing of James's last letter in 1882 was consequential. Astwood arrived in April that year, and it was evident that Heureaux would become the nation's next president, and the Protestants stood to benefit. Having received a letter from Gross explaining the community's intention to transfer to the AME Church under Astwood, James urged London, "If you cannot help them, it is better to give them up."[39]

Astwood's arrival fulfilled the community's longing for ministerial leadership and financial aid, but like the other sources analyzed above, his letters back to the United States require careful scrutiny. Another anecdote regarding Astwood's missionary appointment underscores this point by highlighting the distinct ways in which the capital's African American descendants and US-based African Americans understood his role in Santo Domingo. In July 1883, while on leave in New York, Astwood attended a ceremony for his official charge as the AME Church's missionary to Santo Domingo. The ceremony began with the hymn "Go Preach My Gospel, Saith the Lord," and the sermon delivered by Reverend Goosley of New Jersey was based on a biblical passage carrying a similar message (Mark 16:15–16). Goosley crafted his sermon especially for Astwood, who, he asserted, went "doubly armed" on a Christian mission as consul and AME missionary.[40] He also suggested that the Catholic Dominican Republic would "progress" materially only through Protestant conversion. These proceedings reflected African Americans' belief that it was their God-given duty to evangelize Black people around the world and thus politically unify and materially uplift the same.[41] For *capitaleño* Afro-Americans, however, transferring (back) to the AME Church was a logical response to years of Wesleyan inaction and Astwood's unexpected arrival. Here was a charismatic bilingual preacher whose secular duties as US consul tied him to the country. Astwood, moreover, socialized with Dominican officials, foreign white American capitalists, and US-based AME leaders. For these reasons, Afro-American Dominicans allowed him to pastor their church, and even the Wesleyans felt relieved; "we can hail with joy our American fellow worker," wrote one Turks Islands minister.[42] While such distinctions did not produce conflict immediately, they elucidate why Astwood's missionary letters must be read in contra*diction* to traditional US and Dominican narratives.

In short, Astwood's missionary communications bore the weight of both his own and his audience's conceit. Describing his first encounter with the Protestant community, for example, Astwood emphasized his leadership: "I took hold of the work with the old man [Gross]" and "procured a decent place and started our Sunday school and the church."[43] Accordingly, the congregation left Claudio's hut for a rental space with chairs that Astwood bought on credit. The congregation also bought an organ worth $65 and, as Astwood reported, their expenditures reached $25 per month. Weekly meetings every Sunday and an upswell in attendance enabled the congregants to meet costs. Astwood also used his consular rank and social ties to channel resources to the congregation. When he received no response from AME bishops to a petition for print material in 1882, for instance, he connected with the US-based Foreign Sunday School Association. The organization's president provided the congregation with books and other literature that Astwood received on a regular basis in 1883. A year later, Astwood believed it time to stop renting and finally repair the old church. Comparing himself to the Old Testament prophet Nehemiah, he informed US-based AME leaders of his sense of godly calling: "The Spirit said to me, 'rebuild the walls of Jerusalem.'"[44] He went on to recount how he had selected workers and bought material on credit for the job. "Why or how I began the work, I cannot tell," Astwood mused. "As if by magic the building went on."

Clearly, in letters to the United States regarding his religious activities, Astwood said little of the men and women who joined the Protestant congregation in its new rental space and who directed their time, money, and labor to repair the old church. But, the "magic" consisted of these individuals. A few details betray Astwood's intentional silence on this point. First, the congregation alone supplied the funds for their upkeep. They did so with Sunday offerings that averaged $10 weekly. "We are the more proud because until now, we have not begged for a dollar, every mite given freely upon the table at our Sunday services," Astwood boasted.[45] Second, while Astwood failed to provide the names of the "five carpenters and three masons from within our ranks [and] two outside masons" who completed the church's repairs, his words reveal that eight Protestants and likely two Catholics collaborated on the job. Third, despite the congregation's self-sufficiency, it still needed help to afford the renovation, which cost $1,060. Consequently, a church committee invited Dominican government officials, businessmen, and other prominent society members to witness the public dedication of the AME chapel and offer donations on August 24, 1884 (figure 5.1).[46] The

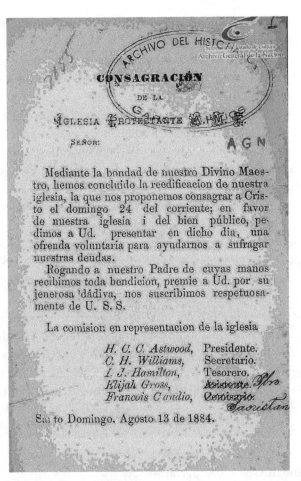

FIGURE 5.1. Invitation to the consecration of the AME Church in Santo Domingo. From "Correspondencia de la comisión de la Iglesia Protestante A.M.E., en la cual solicita ofrenda para cubrir los gastos de reedificación de la misma," control 53420, sig. 30–1–4, Colección José Gabriel García, AGN, Santo Domingo.

attendance of high-class Catholic Dominicans at the consecration service was notable, and Astwood surmised that a church building four times as large would not have contained the people. "What a memorable day! What a grand out pouring of Catholics and Protestants!" he later exclaimed.[47] In his letters, Astwood used both the presence of elite Dominicans and the money raised ($450) to promote his own sense of influence and surmised that a larger church would have quadrupled the donations. Read another way though, these statements show that Dominicans—both Protestants and Catholics—contributed to the rebuilding of the city's Protestant chapel; no foreign money aided the cause.

This alternative reading of Astwood's letters is revealing. The details indicate that the unnamed Dominicans who attended the dedication service in 1884 imagined (however furtively or resolutely) a society in which Catholicism and Protestantism existed side by side. This imagination began during the era of Haitian unification and continued long after Dominican independence. It was present on the northern coast during and after the Spanish annexation. It developed in the thoughts and writings of Antillean liberal intellectuals who traveled across the Anglo-Americas and despised all vestiges of colonial Spain. It percolated in the long-term relationships African American immigrants and their descendants built with their Catholic neighbors and permeated the halls of secret societies, Masonic lodges, and the branches of government.[48] In other words, the reconstruction and consecration of the Dominican capital's AME church was not Astwood's work alone, despite what Astwood boasted in reports to the United States. These events and the change that Astwood instigated within the Protestant community were instead reflective of the society in which they took place. And, in the early 1880s, this society was one in which liberals governed and propagated ideas that made the presence of African American descendants and their Protestant church come into sharper view.

New Organs of Cultural Transmission: The AME and the GUOOF in Dominican Society

The convergence between liberals and African American descendants occurred on two fronts that brought material benefits to the Protestants. First, the few scholars who have acknowledged the existence of the capital's Protestant church in these years have stressed Heureaux's involvement.[49] Heureaux, at Astwood's request, granted the community the land for the renovated church.[50] Emphasis on this partnership, however, does not fully account for the display of widespread support among other Dominicans at the dedication ceremony. Decentering Astwood thus reveals the second front: the positivist moral philosophy developed by the Puerto Rican sage Eugenio María de Hostos. As argued below, Hostonian ideology provided a logic upon which the liberal ideals that most affected Dominican Protestants—the freedom of religion and conscience, the separation of church and state, and the secularization of public education—became a moral imperative among a growing group of lettered Dominican thinkers and influencers. This ideological backdrop made possible the AME Church's and GUOOF's emergence as new organs of cultural transmission.

In the 1880s, Dominican liberals desperately sought to modernize their nation. Their outlook reflected larger currents within Latin American political thought as positivists across the region assumed the basic tenets of scientific racism and considered uneducated populations of Indigenous, Black, and mixed-race people as antithetical to "national progress" and the ideals of Western modernity.[51] Unlike conservatives, who defended old colonial hierarchies that favored the Creole oligarchy and the Catholic Church as pathways to control the masses, liberal positivists fought for economic and social reform. They advocated for policies that would engender free trade, industrialization, scientific innovation, and secular education, and protect freedom of the press, private property, democratic government, and national sovereignty.[52] Such policies would supposedly civilize the masses by creating a proletariat class for agricultural and industrial labor and limited participation in republican government. This shift would then enable the nation to compete economically on the world stage.

In the Dominican Republic, the drive for national progress had many apostles who together created an amorphous body of work classified under the title of Dominican liberalism. The diversity of opinions is especially apparent when considering the political leanings of Partido Azul members. The authoritarian president Ulises Heureaux, for example, was a liberal. So too was Catholic priest and ex-president Fernando Arturo de Meriño. Naturally, both men eventually came to oppose liberal ideas that affected their spheres of influence (state and church). On the other hand, the more socialist-leaning intellectual Pedro Francisco Bonó was critical of *azul* reforms that stripped the peasantry of communal lands, and he too was a liberal. As men visibly of African descent, Heureaux, Bonó, and Luperón were liberals who embraced a Eurocentric view of progress, while ignoring the underlying racist logics that rendered their political leadership inadvisable; most liberals believed that "modernity depended on the appropriate racial mix."[53] Evidently, contradictions abounded. Thus, despite historians' grouping of Dominican liberals together, they had no definite creed since each individual acted upon their varied political and personal interests.

Yet, although Dominican liberals did not always agree on which economic and social policies would most efficiently inspire reform, historians have universally recognized Eugenio María de Hostos as the most influential liberal philosopher of the era.[54] Dominican liberalism was not new to Hostos in the 1880s. He had long supported Luperón's party and was a principal Antillean Confederation ideologue in the previous decade.[55] Indeed, the educator had spent two years in Puerto Plata in the 1870s, arriving mere months before Astwood's departure from Samaná for New Orleans in 1874. Given Puerto Plata's ethnic diversity and regional political activism (discussed in chapter 2), it was an auspicious time for Hostos to be in the town. Surrounded by like-minded friends (including Luperón and Ramón Emeterio Betances), Hostos continued his decade-long advocacy for Puerto Rican and Cuban independence and the Antillean Confederation. He also founded various newspapers that carried his ideals in their names: *Las Dos Antillas, Las Tres Antillas, Los Antillanos*.[56] Beyond the written word, he joined the Liga de la Paz, the city's liberal patriotic society, and participated in local politics in Puerto Plata.[57] It was in Puerto Plata too that Hostos began his initial work on educational reform; he founded the school La Educadora in March 1876.[58] Although Hostos left town soon after establishing La Educadora, these initial experiences on the Dominican northern coast helped to shape his positivist moral philosophy, which he instituted in Santo Domingo after his return to the island three years later.[59]

Like Astwood, Hostos settled in Santo Domingo during his second sojourn on the island. At that time, Cesáreo Guillermo was still in office, but soon Luperón assumed the provisional presidency, gaining Hostos unparalleled influence in the government. Under Luperón, Hostos founded the nation's first normal school on February 18, 1880, in the capital.[60] Then, in November, he established the public law department at the city's Professional Institute, where he had assumed the chair of constitutional and international law a month prior.[61] By then, Meriño was president of the republic; he supported Hostos's pedagogy at first.[62] Influential thinkers including Federico Henríquez y Carvajal, his brother Francisco, and Francisco's wife, Salomé Ureña, who established the Instituto de Señoritas in November 1881, also collaborated with Hostos.[63] Thus, *normalismo*, the contemporary name for the Hostonian movement, charted the educational path for the city's intellectual class and consequently had a substantial impact upon Dominican society in the capital. By the time Hostos committed his philosophy to paper in two tomes that received international acclaim, *Lecciones de Derecho Civil* (1887) and *Moral Social* (1888), *normalismo* had taken the city by storm, deeply influencing the era's liberal discourse.

This educational revolution gave new consciousness to the ideas of national progress and modernity, which, as historian Raymundo González has written, manifested "above all through the rationalist moralization of society."[64] In other words, Hostos propagated a moral philosophy, known as *moral social*, that codified a secular way of being and acting rightly in society. Thus, for *normalistas*, social morality became an academic discipline: "the binding of two sciences: ethics and sociology."[65] Such beliefs reflected the idea that the logics of the natural and social sciences served a higher moral purpose. Acting rightly meant adhering to Western notions of civilization, science, and progress, which they believed would lead a person to fulfill social, political, and economic virtues or obligations (*deberes*) to society.[66] As Hostos wrote, "to be civilized and to be moral is to be the same."[67] Thus, *normalistas* viewed liberal reforms as rational and therefore inherently good, and adherence to this belief was so strong among Hostos and his followers that "the rejection of progress became an immoral or criminal act."[68]

This belief system benefited African American descendants since Hostos's views on Protestantism were more charitable than his writings about the Catholic Church. Hostos depicted the state church as a retrograde institution mired in dogma.[69] Protestants, in contrast, were "superior in public and private morality" to Catholics.[70] This comparison reflected Hostos's beliefs that Protestant societies like the United States had generally embraced science and had adapted to social change while Catholic societies had not. He considered freedom of religion and freedom of conscience to be signs of social progress and therefore believed that the Dominican Republic should become a religiously pluralistic society. Such views did not serve as a wholesale endorsement of Protestantism, which Hostos also saw as in need of evolution. Rather, Hostos ultimately hoped that Catholics and Protestants would work together to construct "social order" and a new "humanistic" religion "radically founded in the philosophical dogma of progress and continual elevation of Humanity."[71] To this end, Hostos praised American freethinkers, suggesting that he would endorse similar humanistic religion in Santo Domingo.[72] In any case, Hostos's elevation of Protestantism above Catholicism not only corresponded with sentiments embraced by the African American immigrant community but also expanded the imaginative possibilities for their descendants' national belonging. The second generation found a new ideological pathway toward inclusion that rationalized their Protestant-Dominican identity, and indeed their very existence in the Dominican capital made Hostos's vision of societal change seem possible.

As stated in the previous section, such ideas indicated liberals' desire to see Puerto Plata's cosmopolitan ethos—of which Protestantism had always formed a part—institutionalized in the capital. Although direct social ties between Hostos and the capital's African American Protestant community in the 1880s are unknown, it is reasonable to assume that some links were made. From his earlier days in Puerto Plata, Hostos would have known about the Wesleyan church and met leading Protestants such as Washington Lithgow, a lay preacher who later served as president of Puerto Plata's municipality, and Charles Fraser, the town's apothecary who taught the Wesleyan church's Sunday school.[73] Such interactions as well as Hostos's multiple visits to New York may have inspired his favorable views on Protestantism. In the capital, moreover, a few known relationships hint at a possible broader social network between *normalistas* and Protestants. Both Lucas T. Gibbes and Emilio Prud'homme, who numbered among the first *normalista* teachers, interacted with the Protestant congregation.[74] Gibbes's father, Lucas Gibbes, the minister of finance and commerce in 1885, was a Protestant and a Freemason who knew leaders of the Afro-American Dominican community. It is also probable that Astwood's son George (Jorge) was one of Hostos's first students at the public law department.[75] These ties likely facilitated public support for the Protestant church's reconstruction in 1884 and the subsequent formation of the GUOOF in December 1885.

As with Astwood's missionary letters, the written testimony of Ángel María Gatón, a founding member of the GUOOF's Dominican chapter, requires reading against the grain. At first glance, Gatón's account reinforces the image that Astwood cultivated of himself. Astwood possessed "great personal charm," "refined intelligence," and a "common-man spirit."[76] His fervent activism on behalf of oppressed Black people in the US South troubled white leaders who "feared the outbreak of a rebellion among the many people ... persuaded by his words" and thus conspired to exile him to Santo Domingo.[77] Such was the man Gatón labeled the "cornerstone," the "first pioneer," and the "founder" of *odfelismo* (Odd Fellowism) in the Dominican Republic. Yet, while Astwood was likely the first person to introduce the idea of a Dominican GUOOF chapter, the formation of fraternities, mutual aid societies, and civic groups was already well established on the island. Thus, Gatón's testimony also evidences how the Odd Fellows stemmed from this cultural practice. Indeed, the Protestant church's old Bible Society formed the backbone of the first GUOOF chapter in Santo Domingo.

This second interpretation requires another look at Astwood's relationship to the city's Protestant church, and his friendship with Claudio in particular. In Gatón's account, Claudio (i.e., not Astwood) was the community's "Dominican pastor" in the early 1880s. As consul, Astwood often attended the Protestant services, and soon began to preach.[78] Protestant Dominicans and North Americans (i.e., white capitalists) who frequented the services enthusiastically received Astwood, who quickly became close friends with Claudio.[79] As Gatón related, Claudio was a "fanatic of mutual aid societies" and led the Amantes de la Biblia, the same Bible Society that he and Gross oversaw back in 1871–72.[80] This group gained many local members, who each paid weekly dues of twenty-five pesos, a substantial sum at the time. After some years, the society had accumulated a large savings fund, and Astwood then proposed affiliating the group with the GUOOF. Reportedly delighted by the idea, the Amantes de la Biblia members voted to become Odd Fellows and resolved to use their savings to rent a meeting space on the corner of Santo Domingo's principal streets, La Separación and La Restauración, for their new club. Thus, the GUOOF began as a multiethnic Dominican institution that reflected the era's liberal ideology, the country's long-term practice of fraternal organization, and the historical social intersections between Protestant and Catholic Dominicans (table 5.2).

Like the AME Church's founding, the inception ceremony for the GUOOF further highlighted such religious intersections. The proceedings occurred over two days, December 8–9, 1885, and interwove Catholic symbolism and religiosity. On the first day, the group formally established the Flor de Ozama Odd Fellow Lodge No. 2638, raising the GUOOF flag above their building on the same day as the Feast of the Immaculate Conception. The next day, a Sunday, the group marched to Santa Barbara Church where the priest, Father Bernardo Pichardo, led a Catholic mass in their honor.[81] Gatón's account of the ceremony emphasized the holiness of the moment. Upon arriving at the parish, the Odd Fellows divested themselves of their regalia, depositing them upon a table prepared for the purpose. Then Father Pichardo gave "an eloquent and beautiful" sermon written especially for the new group.[82] After the ceremony, the Odd Fellows redonned their regalia and promenaded through the capital's principal streets. With this symbolic act, they laid claim to the physical space of the capital as an interreligious, interethnic, and mixed racial group. As with the AME Church's dedication ceremony, Catholic Dominicans' participation in the Odd Fellows organization—and indeed the Catholic priest's consecration of the group—signified a culturally pluralistic future for the Dominican nation. Such events not only reinforced African American descendants' inclusion in the Dominican nation but also enabled them to envision the nation as malleable to their hopes and dreams.

While it is impossible to know the full extent of African American descendants' individual and collective hopes for the Dominican nation,

TABLE 5.2. Analysis of Grand United Order of the Odd Fellows (GUOOF) Membership in Santo Domingo, Dominican Republic

GUOOF Founders, According to Ángel Gatón

Known African American Descendants	With Non-Spanish Surnames	With Spanish Surnames**	
Francisco Claudio	H. C. C. Astwood*	Nicanor Acuña*	Pablo Hernández
Fermín Hamilton	Silvestre Benedicti*	José V. Briñez*	José Hilario
Ángel Jones*	Mateo Decers*	Francisco Cerón	Juan Sánchez
Clemente Jones	Cristián Isrroon*	Federico	Jiménez
Edwin Meller (Miller)	Juan Ismael	Conveniencia*	Antonio
Emil Meller (Miller)	C. H. Williams*	José de Pol*	Küilamo
Adan Rogers*		Julio Erazo	(Güilamo)
		Juan L. Fajardo*	Eugenio
		Tomás García*	Ladrillé
		Ángel Gatón*	Pedro Nataniel
		Francisco Girón*	Rafael G. Neco
			Wenceslao
			Polanco
			Martín Tejada*
			Antonio Vidal

Other Early GUOOF Members, According to Emilio Rodríguez Demorizi

Known African American Descendants	With Non-Spanish Surnames	With Spanish Surnames**	
Simon Hall	Albensí Binett	José Albino	Walter Monsanto
Dundas King	John Costomins	Cornelio Boascón	Adams
Emilio Meyer	Sidney Lockcart	Luis Bron	Rodríguez
	Cristian Peen	Juan Bruno	Senatriz Seno
	John B. Pike	Pablo Elsevy	José Vitoriano
		Isaac Flores	Ángel Yanes
			Cristian Yeron

*Founders omitted in Rodríguez Demorizi's list
**Some of these surnames may have non-Spanish origins

Other Societies Including Two or More GUOOF Members

Name of Society	GUOOF Member	Year Founded	Purpose
Sociedad Jesús en la Peña	Isaac Flores Wenceslao Polanco Juan Bruno Ángel Gatón	1866	Aid the sick, religious

TABLE 5.2. (*continued*)

Recreo Dominicano	Francisco Cerón José Albino	1872	Recreation, intellectual elevation
Verdaderos Amigos	Clemente Jones Eugenio A. Lachillé (Ladrillé) Antonio Güilamo (Küilamo) Martín Tejada Juan L. Fajardo	1872	Recreation, mutual aid
Perla Dominicana	Francisco Girón Ángel Gatón	1873	Moral elevation, recreation
Socorro entre sus Miembros	Francisco Cerón Clemente Jones Julio Erazo Ángel Jones Juan L. Fajardo Federico Conveniencia	1881	Mutual aid
El Pacientísimo Jesús	José Hilario Juan Bruno	1862	Mutual aid, religious

Note: Pablo Claudio and Alfredo Hamilton, whose surnames indicate that they were African American descendants, were members of Perla Dominicana and Socorro entre sus Miembros, but were not named as GUOOF members. Their membership in these organizations further demonstrates African American descendants' participation in Dominican fraternities and mutual aid societies, and suggests theirs and other Dominicans' social and familial ties to GUOOF members.

Source: Extracted from Gatón, *Resumen del origen*, 5; Rodríguez Demorizi, *Sociedades*, 66, 93, 94, 99, 105, 157.

another 1885 anecdote published in the *New York Freeman* provides some hints. Written by Elijah Gross's son, Ricardo Alejandro Gross, the article recounted the events surrounding John Mercer Langston's unexpected arrival in Santo Domingo on October 28 that year. Recently relieved of his position as US minister to Haiti and chargé d'affaires of the Dominican Republic, Langston stopped in the city on his trip back to the United States. Believing that he might know something about the "still pending" US-Dominican reciprocity treaty, someone requested that Astwood organize an impromptu town meeting at the AME Church. Within hours, "prominent members of government and representatives of commercial interests" filled the chapel, and a throng of spectators jammed the sidewalk and streets outside.[83] Gross's report conveyed his enthusiasm for the moment. Echoing Astwood's introduction, Gross described the assembly as "one of the largest and most important gatherings ever seen in this city."[84] He quoted much of Langston's speech verbatim, and he documented the audience's "enthusiastic" approval of the same. He also carefully documented Astwood's symbolic appointment of twelve officiants. First and foremost, Astwood named Lucas Gibbes to preside over the gathering. Second, Astwood designated Ricardo Alejandro as secretary since he had previously served as the city's administrator of customs and as a member of Congress. The remaining ten men acted as "vice-presidents" and included the US vice-consul and the Dutch consul; four planters and merchants from Italy, Venezuela, and the United States; three lay members of the AME Church; and one more Dominican citizen.[85] These officiants symbolically numbered the same as Jesus's disciples, and projected a moral and political hierarchy upon the Catholic country in which African American (i.e., Astwood) and Dominican Protestants (i.e., Gibbes and Gross) presided over the city's "vice-presidents" from Europe, the United States, and Latin America. Insofar as the event also featured the AME Church as a potential center for social and economic reform, Gross's article suggested that African American descendants hoped to influence Dominican culture to a greater extent than historians have previously understood.

Today, Santo Domingo's AME chapel seems a strange place for such a noteworthy event, given that the Dominican Constitution established the Catholic Church as the state's religion. In fact, in traditional Dominican historiography, the AME Church of Santo Domingo did not exist at all; nineteenth-century scholars who mentioned the Protestants always did so without reference to the AME denomination.[86] This racial erasure is revealing. Such silences in the archive indicate that even as Protestants and Odd Fellows emerged as organs of cultural transmission from the shadows of Dominican society into the public eye, they still met stigma on religious and racial grounds. Gross's article, for example, identified no Catholic government officials at Langston's event, signaling their probable absence. Moreover, Euro-Dominican Freemasons had initially protested the GUOOF's founding, stating that only their group had the privilege of hosting secret society meetings. While not explicitly racialized, the protest suggested that high-class Dominicans felt threatened by the new Black-led group; the GUOOF prevailed only after Astwood spoke with Heureaux.[87] Even so, the Dominican Catholic archdiocese's official organ, the *Boletín Eclesiástico*, omitted notice of the group's inception ceremony hosted in

Santa Barbara Church. Thus, while some Dominican elites, especially Heureaux and the *normalistas*, accepted the existence of the AME denomination and a new secret society within the city, there were also clear points of divergence.

Political Divergences: Social Morality and the Contest for Moral Authority

For African American descendants, divisions of race and class presented tacit barriers to social advancement and access to power. Yet racial and class prejudice, while readily evident, was not openly acknowledged. This reality made public claims to morality for dark-skinned people all the more important. As in the United States and elsewhere, immorality was coded as uncivilized and thus racialized as Black. Consequently, as discussed in chapter 4, public displays of Western education, language, demeanor, and dress coalesced into a respectability politics that enabled some African-descended individuals to climb the city's social ladder. Unlike in the United States, where conservative whites attacked African Americans' public and political rights in the 1870s–80s (see chapter 2), in Santo Domingo Afro-Dominicans lost neither civil nor political rights, despite living under dictatorships (Báez and then Heureaux).[88] Moreover, the systematic lynchings of Black people did not occur. Consequently, for Afro-Dominicans, displays of moral rectitude served more as a tactic to gain, sustain, or justify social and political power, as opposed to protection against imminent physical assault. Outward displays of morality could diminish a person's less desirable physical traits and gain them prestige and respect. At the same time, attacks upon a person's character could ruin them socially. Thus, although power differentials remained entrenched along racial and class lines, individuals who secured moral authority could still gain social and political advancements regardless of their color.

In light of this context, the phrase *social morality* is defined here as an expansive public discourse in which all sectors of society engaged in order to gain power. However, while a capacious concept, social morality was not defined and interpreted uniformly across all groups. *Moral social*, as stated above, was a term that *normalistas* used to denote the secular moral relationship between humans and society. Outside of *normalista* circles, however, people in Santo Domingo based their individual and social understandings of morality on Catholic Christianity. Thus, ideological conflicts between Hostos's secular-scientific method and the Catholic Church existed at a fundamental level. American foreigners also had their own ideas about what morality meant in this Catholic land. Be it African American Protestant notions of racial uplift or US financiers' sense of moral capitalism, Americans looked to reform the Dominican nation in their own image. Poor Dominicans, whose voices and syncretic religious practices have received less scholarly attention, likewise understood political and international events through a moral lens that often reflected popular Catholic beliefs as well as principles of Dominican Vodou.[89] Given this context amid ongoing political uncertainty, African American descendants found themselves in a quickly changing social terrain where claiming moral authority, both secular and Christian, became a source of social currency in the contest for political power.

Nowhere was this contest more apparent than in the public discourse over Heureaux's dictatorship, which began with his second presidential bid in 1886–87. As already explored in chapter 4, Heureaux used public displays of morality, Catholic symbology, and magical arts to maintain power.[90] At the same time, his detractors, including Hostos, ridiculed him on both moral and racial grounds. These dynamics came to the fore during Heureaux's 1886 presidential campaign. That year, he ran against Casimiro de Moya, a Euro-Dominican politician who served as vice president during Heureaux's first term (1882–84). According to US Consul Astwood, the contest was "alarming on account of the abusive language indulged in on both sides."[91] Luperón also recognized that "never in the republic was there so much heat in an electoral battle."[92] From the start, de Moya feared that Heureaux would use fraudulent tactics to win.[93] In April Heureaux reported to Luperón that his opponents circled his house shouting racial epithets "all because they [couldn't] stand that we beat them at the elections here in the very capital."[94] The situation became even more worrisome when, after the June election, as predicted, Heureaux was declared the winner. Representing the Cibao, de Moya launched a popular revolt from La Vega the following month. The revolution, which dragged on for months, ended with a victory for Heureaux, who, upon his return to the capital, retreated to the cathedral, where he reportedly "returned thanks to Almighty God for his victory."[95] This display of virtue implied that the outcome of the war was the will of God. Yet Heureaux's triumph over de Moya and installation as president in 1887 marked the beginning of his thirteen-year dictatorship. Later that year, he instigated a constitutional reform extending the presidential term to four years. He then ran for reelection in

1888 when the expanded term applied. Hostos's *Lecciones de Derecho Civil* (1887) was published in protest of these events, as was *Moral Social* (1888).[96]

Yet the contest for moral authority did not merely occur among politicians but was waged by the Catholic Church as well. As Heureaux's power grew throughout 1886–87, the church gained greater political clout in Santo Domingo with the appointment of Meriño as the nation's first Dominican-born archbishop on July 6, 1885. Meriño identified with the liberal Partido Azul and had served as the nation's president in 1880–82. However, judging by the dictatorial methods he employed against opponents during his presidency, his spirit "had more of the conservative than the liberal."[97] Although Báez's enemy in the 1870s, during the 1880s Meriño favored strong government, for the sake of maintaining national peace, over liberal ideals. This conservative outlook impacted his archbishopric. Under Meriño, the Catholic Church advanced its ecclesiastical organization on a national scale. The same year as Meriño's appointment, the Dominican Congress voted to establish a concordat with the Vatican. Although the agreement was never fulfilled, it was not for the Congress's lack of will. Furthermore, between 1865 and 1885, the church had few native priests and lacked an educational system for them.[98] As archbishop, however, Meriño also worked to nationalize the priesthood and served as the director of the capital's seminary and rector of the Professional Institute, through which he increasingly pressured students to accept dogmas in opposition to Hostos's teachings.[99]

Although positivist ideology ran counter to the Catholic Church's teachings across Latin America, in the Dominican Republic, unlike elsewhere, the conflicts were subdued at first. Meriño, well aware of the tensions, did not dare impede Luperón's plans for public education in 1880–82, and after Meriño's presidency he collaborated with Hostos at the Professional Institute.[100] Moreover, although Francisco Xavier Billini, the rector of the city's Catholic school San Luis Gonzaga and a beloved Catholic priest, vehemently opposed the Normal School in 1880, by 1884 he had changed his mind.[101] Billini even adopted the normal system at San Luis Gonzaga and added the *normalista* graduates Lucas T. Gibbes and Evaristo Mejía to his instructor roster.[102] These initial signs of collaboration, however, were short-lived. Soon after Meriño became archbishop, he wrote more forcefully against the *normalistas* in the *Boletín Eclesiástico*, which Meriño founded in 1884. "Some people," he asserted, "in their impious dreams speak deliriously of religion of art, religion of science, religion of duty [*deber*], religion of industry, etc."[103] Such ideas, Meriño concluded, would lead "directly to atheism with their pretenses—fools!" In subsequent issues, he called proponents of liberalism "enemies" and defended Catholic beliefs.[104] "[The church] has not been indifferent to the general movement of social progress," he claimed.[105] But it "cannot accept liberty of thought or of the press with the liberty of meaning presented by the [too] generous liberalism . . . nor does it accept free interpretation of the Bible."[106] The Catholic Church's hostility toward the *normalistas* in prose gave way to more overt displays of aggression in 1887–88 as Heureaux's dictatorship solidified and allied with the church.[107]

These developments did not bode well for the capital's Protestant community, which had benefited both from Heureaux's first presidency and the *normalistas*' teachings. Yet while historians have recognized the ideological struggle between the Catholic Church and the *normalistas*, less has been said about Catholic leaders' position on the Protestants living within their midst.[108] The only study that covers the topic suggests that the nation's Protestant communities were too insignificant to represent a threat to Catholicism.[109] However, ten essays published in the *Boletín Eclesiástico* from May 1886 to February 1888 under the title "A Chapter of Documented History. Protestantism" reveal a certain anxiety among Catholic leaders over the spread of Protestantism in Dominican society. No other non-Catholic religion drew such attention. The essays, which appeared across sixteen issues, not only presented the Catholic Church's historical perspective and theological arguments against Protestantism but also propagated misinformation. Readers learned that Protestants denied the divinity of Jesus, rejected the Bible, and had no true priesthood. The ministers were "no more than lay folks. . . . They are not even Christians."[110] The vendetta against Protestantism included many other sensational phrases: "Protestantism was born with weapons in its hand"; "Protestantism is dead. It committed suicide with its own knife of free interpretation of the Bible"; "Protestantism blew on the Bible and killed it."[111] Together with Meriño's known writings on the subject (he may have been the author of these essays too), the articles exposed not only the Catholic Church's conservatism on religious tolerance but also a sense of alarm over the influences of both Protestantism and positivism within Dominican society. In fact, the *Boletín Eclesiástico* invariably linked the two ideologies together, condemning Protestantism as the religion of science that sought to deny the existence of God.[112] After many of the essays, the journal then printed notes on the history of Santo Domingo's archdiocese, reinforcing the nation's historical ties to the church and Spanish culture. Thus, in the Dominican archdiocese's official publication, the battle against liberalism—beliefs in free thought, freedom of the press, free biblical interpretation, science, and so on—was articulated in these years as a war of Catholic nationalism against Protestant positivism, even though Protestants and *normalistas* held distinct beliefs.

The most logical explanation for the Catholic Church's heightened concern over Protestantism in 1886–88 was the growing population of the capital's AME Church. Although neither the AME Church nor *normalistas* were ever mentioned by name in the *Boletín*, the church used its publication to indoctrinate its people against the local Protestant church, which by all reports was small but thriving. Already in 1885, the Protestant congregation had outgrown its new church building. That year, the congregation appealed to a broad base of potential US donors to finance the construction of an even larger chapel.[113] Hoping to receive donations from white Americans, the petition did not identify the Santo Domingo church as an AME institution. Instead, the congregation referred to themselves as the "Protestant church in this community." They also stressed that their purpose was to convert Dominican Catholics to Protestantism. They furthermore claimed that the new building would be "the first Protestant Church worthy of the name in the oldest city in the New World" and would stand against "the scenes of vice and immorality . . . error and superstition" in the city. Thus, the letter implied that an ecumenical missionary effort among American Protestant churches would lead Catholic Santo Domingo to a supposedly purer form of Christianity. Although the funds for a new church never came through, the letter not only attests to the fact that the AMEs had gained new members but also evidences their position against the Catholic Church in an asymmetrical contest for moral authority.

This contest intensified on the symbolic level as the US-based AME Missionary Board appointed a new missionary to Santo Domingo, and membership continued to grow. Adolphus H. Mevs arrived in Santo Domingo from Port-au-Prince along with his wife, Ellabee, and their infant child on January 23, 1886.[114] A Haitian citizen and member of the AME mission headed by Charles Mossell in Port-au-Prince, Mevs had trained at the AME Church's Wilberforce College for four years before returning to the island. Accordingly, Mevs was among the dozens of Afro-Caribbeans educated at African American institutions such as Wilberforce and Booker T. Washington's Tuskegee Institute.[115] Upon arriving in the Dominican capital, Mevs took over Astwood's duties. Like Astwood, he described the congregation in letters to the United States, reiterating that the church building could not hold its forty-five full members and over one hundred attendees every Sunday. Dozens of Dominican children also took part in the church's Sunday school, despite the fact that the congregation lacked a blackboard, maps, and books for educating the pupils, Mevs reported. Considering this growth among poor Dominicans and Afro-Caribbean labor migrants, Mevs believed that AME leaders "should be proud indeed of this mission and feel much more interested in it than in any of the [AME Church's other missionary stations]."[116] Santo Domingo was a place where Mevs estimated that both the need and potential of Protestant missions were high.

Indeed, Mevs's letters not only signified his optimism regarding membership growth but also articulated an unorthodox vision of Dominican society and the AME Church's future within its moral ecology. In Mevs's view, Port-au-Prince was more modern than Santo Domingo because of its diverse Protestant community and stronger ties to the AME Church in the United States and other parts of the Caribbean.[117] The absence of various Protestant denominations in Santo Domingo meant that "vice and immorality" pervaded the city, and thus Mevs believed that there was a "greater work to be accomplished among this people than among the Haitians." With more foreign missionary investment, Mevs argued, the Dominican Republic could follow the same route toward national progress as Haiti.[118] Such an assessment of Dominican society existed in diametrical opposition to Euro-Dominicans' ideas about Haitians, whom the lettered class demonized as uncivilized because of their Blackness and the revolution that had birthed the hemisphere's first Black republic.

Nevertheless, while Mevs elevated Haiti as a modern state above the Dominican Republic, his perspective was not wholly distinct from that of Euro-Dominican *normalistas*. Like other Westernized intellectuals of the era, AME leaders like Mevs believed that human history proceeded in phases, that societies were in the process of improvement, and that European civilization meant progress.[119] Consequently, missionary duty not only encompassed ministerial functions such as preaching and establishing churches but also included secular labor.[120] To this point, Mevs supplemented his income in Santo Domingo by running a mercantile school where he taught math, English, French, and bookkeeping in the American and European styles to young people.[121] His secular work reflected AME bishop Daniel A. Payne's belief that for a missionary station to be fully self-supporting, it had to encompass a variety of trades, including "a physician, a mechanic, an agriculturist and a linguist, better still, a philological linguist, if one such person could be secured" and "an able corps of teachers [for the] education of heathen children and youth."[122] Given that Hostos's and other *normalistas'* understandings of modern progress emphasized the advancement of society through free thought, science, and industry, their ideas clearly paralleled those of Mevs, Payne, and other AME leaders. The immediate difference was that many *normalistas*, Hostos included, did not see Black people as the harbingers of Western progress in the Dominican Republic and believed that Euro-Dominicans should remain at the head of government and industry. Moreover, they specifically felt wary of the United States both because of its increasing monopolization of the Dominican economy and its imposed racial gaze, which both white and Black Americans applied in their own ways.

But, contrary to Dominican positivists' understandings of the ideal Dominican citizen, the majority of the nation's Protestants were Black men, as were the leaders of the AME denomination in the United States. This racial distinction became even more apparent when, in May 1887, two AME officials from the United States, Bishop Jabez Pitt Campbell and Missionary Secretary Dr. James Matthew Townsend, passed through Santo Domingo on their tour of the island.[123] After meeting with the various government officials and resting in the home of their host, Alice Astwood, Campbell and Townsend led an ordination service in the city's Protestant chapel on Sunday, May 29.[124] The event drew scores of curious onlookers as they left morning mass and gathered outside the small church.[125] The spectators witnessed as five men with ethnic ties to the United States, Haiti, and the Danish Caribbean stood before the African American bishop. Campbell bestowed the second ordination of elder upon Mevs, and the first ordination of deacon upon Claudio. The remaining three men—Adam Rodgers, Charles H. Williams, and Simon Halls—were named local preachers. Rodgers and Williams soon initiated new AME congregations in Barahona and San Pedro de Macorís respectively.[126] Thus, the ordination of these Black Protestant men enabled Dominican Protestant leaders to sustain their church in the capital as well as spread the denomination to other regions of the island with the intention of ministering to both Anglophone Caribbean migrants and Spanish-speaking Dominicans. From the perspective of US-based AME leaders like Campbell and Townsend, it also "crystalized the fragments of the [denomination's] fifty years' labor, anxiety and earnest endeavor" on behalf of the island.[127]

Of course, the vision that US-based AME leaders had of the Dominican Republic and the denomination's potential growth there did not fully reflect the sentiments of African American descendants. As stated above, US leaders did not consider the denomination's ascendancy in Santo Domingo as part of a long-nineteenth-century local history and liberals' current struggle for social reform. Instead, they saw it as a step toward racial unification and uplift, believing that progress would only come to the island's Black republics through the unification of the Black race.[128] As Wilson Jeremiah Moses has stated, this idea of unification was an "authoritarian collectivist" belief that "all Black people could and should act unanimously under the leadership of one powerful man or group of men, who would guide the race by virtue of superior knowledge or divine authority toward the goal of civilization."[129] US-based AME leaders saw such leadership in themselves, the men they ordained, and the smattering of Black politicians in the United States and abroad. This orientation made it difficult for Campbell, Townsend, and other US AME leaders to think of the AME Church's mission in Santo Domingo from the vantage point of the people living there. It was easy for them, however, to find common ground with the Dominican president who fit their image of a strong Black moral patriarch in the secular, if not the religious, sphere.

The similarities in Heureaux's and US AME leaders' political views seem of particular relevance when considering that Campbell and Townsend met with the dictator during their visit. Receiving the pair at the presidential palace, Heureaux reportedly "listened graciously to words appertaining to the duties of a Christian statesman; the influence of Christianity in all nations, and the aim of African Methodism in Santo Domingo."[130] While the conversation between the three men was not recorded, it is reasonable to assume that Campbell and Townsend imparted ideas about racial unification and shared their expansionist vision of the AME Church's future. They likely also commended Heureaux's strongman politics and may have lauded him as a divinely appointed Black leader. After all, an AME "authoritarian political tradition" at the time reflected both Western intellectual views of nationalism and experiential knowledge formed within the Black church.[131] Many AME leaders, in the words of E. Franklin Frazier, acted much like Heureaux: "They were czars, rewarding and punishing their subordinates on the basis of personal loyalties."[132] Of course, such authoritarian tendencies among clergymen naturally conflicted with the democratic processes that formed the basis of collective, dual-gender decision making within Black churches; disputes between pastors and their congregations were not uncommon.[133] What is important here, however, is the symmetries between Heureaux's and US-based AME leaders' political views in the 1880s. Heureaux was head of state, and that fact imbued him with political and moral authority in the minds of African American out-siders who were unaware of the more lurid details of his administration and related to his gentle mannerisms, outward appearance of Black re-spectability, and autocratic rule.

The same applied to Astwood who, while in the United States dur-ing Campbell's and Townsend's visit to Santo Domingo, was regaled with banquets held in his honor in New York and New Orleans. These events demonstrate that friends of Black US government officials viewed them as moral leaders deserving public esteem. The New York gala, hosted by the African American newspaper editor T. Thomas Fortune and William B. Der-rick of the AME Church, was a particularly lavish affair.[134] Held on Friday, May 6, 1887, in the ladies' parlor of the Stevens House, the dinner consisted of an eleven-course meal with wine pairings. The room was draped in Do-minican and American flags, and Astwood's framed picture hung on the wall. The invited guests included twenty prominent Dominicans, African Americans, and white American businessmen invested in Santo Domingo. Among these were the Dominican consul Charles Julian, John Mercer Langston, and Ebenezer D. Bassett.[135] During the event, the guests hon-ored Astwood with speeches, and toasted the Dominican, Haitian, and American presidents. The night ended with a chorus of "For He's a Jolly Good Fellow." A similar, albeit smaller, affair took place two weeks later on May 21 at Dajoie's Creole Restaurant in New Orleans. There, thirty famed Black Republican leaders dined with Astwood, celebrating his work once again with speeches. Numbered among the orators was James Lewis, whose presence indicated that old feuds were forgiven (see chapter 2).[136] These two events demonstrate that Astwood's reputation as a moral politi-cian grew in the United States as he defended US capital invested in the Dominican Republic. Unaware of the various ploys he had used to gain au-thority, people in the United States venerated Astwood for his integrity as consul. The same morality, they believed, had enabled Astwood to retain his consular post even after the Democrat Grover Cleveland assumed the US presidency in 1885.

More than a mere reinforcement of Black respectability politics, the les-son learned here is that a certain logic bound US concepts of Protestant Christian morality to imperial capitalist enterprise. As already discussed in chapter 4, such conquest abroad was gendered as male and raced as white. However, the speeches honoring Astwood also elevated his Black manhood as a symbol of true religio-political authority for all American officials op-erating abroad. Langston's speech was particularly poignant in this regard.

Considering Astwood's consular work, he asserted, "Diplomacy is not dishonesty. Diplomacy is intelligent honesty which defends at once the interests of the government you represent and is not unmindful of the government near which you dwell.... So has [Astwood] represented the Christian spirit of a manly American, strong in the true Christian American spirit as right in diplomacy and consular service.... Christianity is the soul of diplomacy; Christianity is the rock on which diplomacy erects its temple and that temple stands forever."[137] In this view, a man's "Christian spirit" gave him the right to authority abroad despite his race. Christianity, in this case, meant Protestantism and carried with it a US economic mission. Thus, Astwood's AME social work in Santo Domingo justified his authority in the political and business realms. And, as explored further in chapter 7, his success in these areas reflected outwardly upon his supposed true Christian character. In this way, Astwood's consular duties, which primarily consisted of clearing the path for US capitalists in Santo Domingo, was deemed moral work. Such notions of Christian diplomacy washed clean the theft associated with US capitalism and economic imperialism abroad. In a similar way, in later years, the United States would send warships to the Dominican Republic "for their 'moral effect' on the country's leaders."[138]

Unfortunately for Dominicans concerned with US monopolization of the island's economy, notions of US moral capitalism paralleled Heureaux's own visions of the Dominican Republic's economic future. His support for concessions as a modernizing tool led to antiliberal practices that restricted competition for foreigners, and he tended to favor white American investors above all others. The practice of granting concessions to foreign capitalists was hotly debated in the Dominican Congress in the 1880s, but with the government strapped for cash, Dominican politicians found it difficult to relinquish the policy.[139] Heureaux meanwhile personally benefited from a system that reinforced his autocratic leadership; concessions required the approval of the president and Congress and therefore "encouraged corruption."[140] In granting concessions, Heureaux guaranteed that money flowed into the state treasury, which he treated as his personal account and which ultimately sustained his rule. Consequently, "ordinary Dominicans saw foreign concessionaires as props of Heureaux's dictatorship."[141] Thus, as Heureaux funneled money into the Catholic Church to maintain its support and influence among the poor, other sectors of Dominican society revolted.[142] Most notably, Hostos and the young idealists associated with the *normalista* movement became especially ardent opponents of the dictator.

The contest for moral authority between the varying ideologies at play in Santo Domingo disadvantaged the capital's African American descendants, who sat at the juncture between multiple groups. In the early 1880s, Heureaux and the *normalistas* had proven friendly to the Afro-American Dominican community while the Catholic Church had largely overlooked them. Yet, after Heureaux regained the presidency, the Catholic Church linked Protestantism singularly to positivism, implicitly attacking the AME Church's fledgling operation in the *Boletín Eclesiástico*. At the same time, the AME Church's growth in Santo Domingo encouraged US-based AME leaders to see the Dominican Republic as yet another feather in the denomination's missionary expansion hat.[143] The same also venerated Heureaux and Astwood as strong, moral Black men, ignoring their more unsavory activities. The AME Church's self-conscious Blackness, as with Heureaux's skin color, however, stood in polar opposition to Euro-Dominicans' white supremacist sensibilities. Moreover, US notions of Christian diplomacy jeopardized Dominican sovereignty. Thus, Afro-American Dominican institutions—the AME Church and the GUOOF—threatened not only the Catholic Church's but also the *normalistas'* visions of ideal Dominican organs of cultural transmission coded as Hispanic and white. All the while, African American descendants in the capital found themselves caught between the promises of liberal religious tolerance and the impending doom of Heureaux's autocratic tyranny. And, as time moved on, it became less clear who exactly was friend and who was foe. As threats to the Protestant community seemed to emanate from all sides, the practice of forging alliances with multiple sectors of Dominican society became less tenable, as did the possibility of a more religiously and racially inclusive nation. Nevertheless, just like the AME Church and GUOOF, which still exist in Dominican society today, alternative visions of the nation also persevered.

Conclusion

The year Hostos's *Moral Social* was published, Astwood's polemical essay "Shall the Name of the African Methodist Episcopal Church Be Changed to That of the Allen Methodist Episcopal Church?" appeared in the AME Church's academic journal, the *AME Review*. In the essay, Astwood recognized that the AME denomination was founded in reaction and opposition to white discrimination. Still, he argued that the word *African* was no longer needed in 1888 because after the US Civil War Black people were not

Africans but Americans. "Our identity as Africans has been lost; it has been absorbed," Astwood asserted.[144] This claim was highly controversial among African Americans, and historians have since labeled Astwood's opinion as overly optimistic, peculiar, ahistorical, and ignorant.[145] Such judgments, though, have emanated from US-bounded analytical frameworks. Consequently, they have ignored the fact that in writing these words, Astwood was thinking not only of the United States but of the AME Church's mission in the Dominican Republic. With the Caribbean in mind, Astwood claimed that changing the term *African* to *Allen* (after the denomination's founder, Richard Allen) would "better adapt the Church to modifications constantly going on in social and religious relations ... in the West Indies."[146] Thus, more than "projecting his own hopes and ambitions upon [US Blacks], with little understanding of and much opposition to the African sources of their behavior," Astwood was in fact projecting a Dominican vision of racial democracy back upon the United States.[147]

Astwood's 1888 essay proposing a change to the AME Church's name reflected both the hopes and the plights of African Americans' descendants in Santo Domingo. On the one hand, his argument took into account race relations in the Dominican Republic, where the lettered class shunned Blackness. People residing outside of the United States, Astwood argued, did not understand the historical significance of the term *African* for Black Americans. Instead, they viewed it as a mark of racial discrimination. In other words, if church leaders urged converts to turn to God, it was counterproductive to also burden converts with racial distinctions that distracted them from the message of equality and unity in Christ.[148] This argument indicates that Santo Domingo's AME congregation not only hoped to expand their numbers within Dominican society but also saw themselves as part of a broader Dominican movement toward liberal notions of equality. From the perspective of African American descendants, such notions of equality meant freedom of thought, freedom of religion, and freedom to free interpretation of the Bible in the Catholic nation. However, on the other hand, Astwood's proposal also reflected the challenges that the Dominican Protestant community faced in making progress toward these ideals. Certain anxieties over racial Blackness and national belonging are readily apparent in Astwood's essay. Moreover, reading between the lines, there were signs that Christian unity, for Astwood, denoted submission to the AME denomination—not a vision of religious tolerance and Protestant-Catholic cooperation, which had existed in unofficial ways in Santo Domingo and elsewhere on the island since at least 1824.

As the previous pages demonstrate, the capital's African American immigrants and their descendants survived by negotiating various boundaries of race, class, and religion and switching between multiple modes of belonging. In the early 1880s, their community increased in social visibility as they benefited from the Partido Azul's rule, the *normalistas'* ideology, Astwood's presence, and their own long-established social networks. It is this social embeddedness—not actions by Astwood or Heureaux alone—that made the AME Church and the GUOOF organs of cultural transmission. These institutions were never grand in scale. They were, however, symbolically significant. At the Protestant church, Black men preached in Spanish and English to a subsection of Dominican society. The same Black men led the GUOOF, which was truly an interreligious organization. In a country where Europhile elites aligned nationalism with Spanish-Catholic culture, the AME Church and the GUOOF boldly offered an alternative liberal nationalism. This alternative nationalism reflected a broader society in which distinct notions of social morality found pockets of common ground.

Nevertheless, the varying understandings of social morality circulating in Dominican society during the 1880s were ultimately incompatible. Perhaps because of the Catholic Church's overt hostility toward Protestantism, Mevs sought missionary employment elsewhere in 1888.[149] A new AME missionary, Charles Goodin, took charge of the community in 1889. Like Mevs, he tutored to supplement his income, becoming the English teacher to Emilio Prud'homme, Casimiro N. de Moya, and many other Dominicans.[150] Within a year, though, Goodin and the congregation found themselves in a legal dispute with Astwood that reflected the broader contest for moral authority in the capital as Goodin hired *normalista* lawyers, and Astwood turned to Heureaux for support.[151] During the same lawsuit, Astwood asserted that he was the "only *Jefe* [boss]" of the Protestant church, drawing a parallel between his and Heureaux's authoritarian leadership and obfuscating the ways in which African American descendants had been embedded in the capital's social milieu for decades. Meanwhile, the fight for freedom of thought and freedom of religion continued. In June 1889, the *Eco de la Opinión* ran an editorial by the lawyer J. M. Cabral y Báez in which the author revealed that the fight for liberal understandings of religious freedom and democracy did not belong to the capital's Protestant community alone. Cabral y Báez called for the separation of church and state: "An authoritarian church and enemy of free interpretation of the Bible, like the Catholic Church, cannot exist with a truly republican Government," he declared.[152] The ideological convergences between Protestant and positivist liberals, however, threatened not only the Catholic Church but also Heureaux. In turn, the dictator targeted outspoken *normalistas*, whom his forces killed, jailed, and exiled. At the same time, Heureaux reinforced US-based AME leaders' vision of Black political authority by proving himself a friend to the consul-missionary whose narrative about the AME Church and GUOOF in Santo Domingo centered solely on the achievements of one man, himself.

Soon though, Astwood's moral character would become the subject of heated public debate. As head of the AME Church and GUOOF in Santo Domingo, Astwood assumed an outward appearance of moral rectitude that endeared him to white capitalists and African American leaders in the United States. The same Americans celebrated Astwood's "strength of character" and "devotion and sacrifice" on behalf of Dominican society and the US and Dominican governments.[153] Yet, just as soon as a person rose to grace, they could also fall. As Langston said in his 1887 speech praising Astwood, "The moment [a man] ceases to be a man of honor . . . all the confidence of his people in him is at once destroyed. . . . He falls ignominiously from his high position."[154] It is in both the AME Church's and GUOOF's rise in Santo Domingo and Astwood's subsequent downfall (to which chapter 6 turns) that new understandings of how social morality operated in Santo Domingo become apparent as various ideologies of freedom, social progress, and race converged and diverged.

6

"Poor Columbus!" exclaimed the front page of Santo Domingo's *Boletín del Comercio* on May 17, 1888. Sometime prior to publication—days, maybe hours—the newspaper's editor, Miguel Eduardo Pardo, had gotten wind of US Consul Henry Astwood's petition on behalf of an American businessman to lease the mortal remains of Christopher Columbus for public display in the United States. The idea was simple. For 50 percent of the proceeds and not less than $100,000 (about $3 million in 2022) over four years, the Dominican government would guarantee one Hubert Montague Linnell exclusive rights to exhibit Columbus's bones across the United States. The tour would garner international support for the Dominican Republic's side in a dispute with Spain over which country possessed Columbus's true skeleton. More, it would stimulate public interest in solving the matter ahead of the 1892 quadricentennial celebrations of Columbus's arrival in the Americas. Outraged, Pardo linked Linnell's petition to the Spanish controversy, characterizing both as public affronts: "In Spain, they still insist on believing that Columbus's remains are in Cuba, while they are in Santo Domingo, and now they want to disturb [Columbus's] rest." He concluded with a poignant rhetorical flourish: "What would the North Americans say if a foreigner asked them to rent out the mortal remains of Washington to carry them off like an orangutan to some Exhibition?"[1]

Pardo's impassioned response to the Columbus bones scheme reflected heightened anxiety over the racialized international power struggle for control over nationalist Columbus symbology in the years leading up to the quadricentennial celebrations. Pardo directed his outrage at the United States, a country that saw itself as racially superior to Latin America but whose capitalist avarice and imperialism provoked Latin Americans to declare their region's moral superiority.[2] In comparing Columbus to Washington, the *Boletín del Comercio* claimed Columbus's body and memory for the Dominican Republic. It simultaneously accused the United States of taking its capitalist notions too far by exhibiting Columbus like an orangutan—an allusion to African peoples who were put on display at world's fairs. Columbus's true bones, according to the *Boletín*'s logic, rested not in Spain and belonged not to greedy Anglo-Americans or neglectful Spaniards. Columbus belonged instead to Dominicans, Latin American people of spirit, who could distinguish between a sacred insignia—like the one inscribed on the lead box in which Columbus purportedly rested (*Illtre. y Esdo. Varon Dn. Cristoval Colon, D. de la A. Per. Ate.*) (see figures 6.1 and 6.2)—and a "for sale" sign.[3]

Following the *Boletín del Comercio*'s lead, newspapers in the Dominican Republic, the United States, and Latin America portrayed the proposal as an embarrassment unworthy of earnest consideration. Accordingly, articles mocked both the proposal and the US consul involved. Civilian letters to the US State Department protested the slight. Such universal derision protected Columbus's legacy. Still today the proposal's alleged absurdity preserves its obscurity; scholars have mentioned the scandal only briefly in larger histories of US-Dominican affairs.[4]

Nevertheless, like the Platt killing discussed in chapter 4, the Columbus bones scandal and its aftermath are worth retelling, if not for the intrigue of the topic itself, then for what this history teaches about the era's transnational moral politics of race-making. This chapter details the events of the scandal, which began as a private enterprise between a few power brokers in Santo Domingo and ended with Astwood's dismissal. Following the fervent international effort to defame the US consul, the chapter contends that Astwood's blunder was more than an unfortunate episode of diplomacy gone wrong. The proposal challenged the logic of social morality delineated in chapter 5. By doing so, it razed racial and national borders at a symbolic level, exposing the ongoing contest between old and new colonial powers (Spain and the United States) and between their former or potential future dependency in Latin America (Dominican Republic) for control over Columbus symbology. The backlash against Astwood proved that the conflation of two distinct understandings of the human body—sacred and yet for sale—in the figure of Columbus was too absurd for Western societies to take seriously. Ridicule became a race-making ritual that reestablished the supposed proper racial hierarchy within and between nations.

In 1888, most people took for granted the notion that there remained some things outside the realm of commerce: some people, some human bodies, some dead remains too precious to be sold on an open market. Some, but not all. History has a way of producing ironies. In the same year that Brazilian abolition passed, ending slavery in the Americas, a proposal to lease the hemisphere's European discoverer was proffered and immediately disavowed. Put differently, millions of Black people being traded century after century did not seem as absurd as the public exhibition of Columbus's bones. Where, when, and how such distinctions are made—decisions that decipher which class of human beings, living or dead, white or Black, pertain to the realm of "certain things beyond the reach of catchpenny schemes"—is the subject of vast literatures.[5] This chapter focuses instead on what happened to the person who exposed such distinctions as myths. All nationalisms are based on specially curated myths, and all myths require scapegoats.[6]

Relics Found: The Ideological Genealogy and Geopolitics of Columbus's Double Body

The proposal to lease Columbus's remains violated age-old beliefs that infused relics with spiritual meaning. As Patrick Geary has observed, "In order for an object to be venerated as a relic, a new symbolic function had to be assigned [to it]."[7] This spiritual-symbolic function made Columbus's physical bones a "double body" as an emblem of European empire, Christianity, and whiteness.[8] As a relic and a symbol of whiteness, Columbus's double body was supposed to exist outside of the market, which was racialized as

Black. The proposed lease, however, implicitly associated Columbus with supposed profane Black bodies sold into slavery. As discussed below, the fact that relics of the Middle Ages were stolen and covertly traded throws into sharp relief both the fallacy of the sacred-profane divide and the nineteenth-century geopolitical contest over Columbus's remains. This exposure of the Columbus myth threatened both the Dominican Republic's and the United States' national foundational fictions, injuring their stakes in the geopolitical fight.

People who expressed consternation over the proposed leasing of Columbus's bones in 1888 imbued Columbus's bones with social and spiritual meaning that harked back to the Middle Ages and its relics culture. Back then, people believed that the dead bodies of Catholic saints and martyrs possessed power, since they would resurrect upon Jesus Christ's anticipated return to earth. As a dormant live body, relics such as bones, appendages, and hair could defend the living against evil and death. Thus, veneration of saints' mortal remains provided protection to European societies and served as a source of group identity based in an ongoing community of faith (in life and death) during a period of social upheaval and high mortality rates.[9]

This same mechanism operated in the nineteenth century through the veneration of Columbus, or *colonofilia* as historian Christopher Schmidt-Nowara termed it.[10] Although Columbus devotees did not worship Columbus as a saint, some groups sought Columbus's canonization, and homages to Columbus paralleled religious devotion.[11] *Colonofilia* also protected Columbus from the capitalist market since in the nineteenth century people assumed an inherent oppositional relationship between the sacred religious realm and the supposedly profane capitalist market. As Émile Durkheim explained in *The Elementary Forms of the Religious Life* (1912), this construction seemed absolute: "The sacred and the profane are always and everywhere conceived by the human intellect as separate genera, as two worlds with nothing in common."[12] The sacred nature of Columbus's bones originated in the Christian idea that some people—dead or alive—were more holy than others. This hierarchical ordering of human beings meant that the holy bodies of saints could never enter the market and suggested that unholy bodies could.

Relics of the Middle Ages, however, never truly existed outside of the market but remained clandestinely integral to it, generating a peculiar moral politics around the trade in dead human bodies. Indeed, the relic trade burgeoned as European religious devotion imbued saints' mortal remains with immense economic value. Possession of a relic became a sign of both spiritual and social power as monasteries vied with each other for control over certain saints and relics said to have belonged to Jesus. At the same time, the supply of relics in the form of martyrs' bodies decreased due to the decline of Christian persecution.[13] The Catholic Church attempted to organize the transfer and public viewing of relics in monasteries to ease the pressure of supply and demand, but the heightened demand still provoked a robust illicit trade among monks and others. Middlemen, merchants, and thieves obtained relics to sell to elite customers. Pilgrims also bought relics, and whole communities consorted to steal them in the belief that the objects would secure protection for their communities back home.[14] Due to its illegality, the relic trade generated its own moral politics. Documents that detailed the transfer of relics emphasized theft committed out of devotion, *causa devotionis*, in order to disguise theft caused by greed.[15] This discourse assumed that religious fervor motivated the relic trade, divorcing Christian piety from human avarice.

The same moral politics of the relic trade persisted during the modern Atlantic slave trade, which racialized a human hierarchy in relation to the divine. White holy bodies gained status above unholy Black ones. This belief enabled whites to sell Black people on the market with remarkable insouciance. Indeed, so profoundly did people believe in the sacred-profane divide that, in contrast to the relic trade, the Atlantic slave trade took place in plain sight. In this way, enslaved Africans were like living-dead things as opposed to relic objects imbued with dormant life.[16] In other words, whereas the bodies of saints entered the market after death, the bodies of African slaves lost value at the point of death.[17] Various pseudo-scientific beliefs in Africans' nonhumanness or natural human inferiority at the end of the nineteenth century provided further justification for this way of thinking. Such ideas, however, remained fundamentally linked to their religious intellectual origin.[18] Thus, the sacred-profane religious rationale enabled the complete denial of white corruption and, like *causa devotionis*, masked European greed, colonial violence, and slavery's brutality.

The parallels between medieval relic culture and the slave trade manifested in another way too. As discussed in part I, by the late nineteenth century the hemisphere experienced turbulent political, social, and economic shifts that disrupted racial and national borders. Abolition especially threatened racial hierarchy. European superpowers, moreover, began to fear the United States' growing influence in the Caribbean and Latin America. Spain, in particular, had to grapple with its waning colonial power. In this context, defining national identity became not only a political imperative but a moral one as well. To confront the blurring of racial borders, Euro-elites across the Americas and Europe deployed Columbus symbology and its correlating moral politics as renewed foundations for national identity. They also competed for claims to Columbus's mortal remains to assert geopolitical power. Thus, like European towns of the Middle Ages where "the presence of a widely honored saint could provide the means of establishing or maintaining economic power and a competitive position vis-à-vis other cities," American and European countries used Columbus to vie for power within the global racial capitalist system.[19] As a quasi-religious figure, Columbus's double body protected the myth of white supremacy and organized national identity around European cultural dominance. Nations that claimed Columbus gained prestige on the global stage.

The international debate over the discovery of Columbus's bones in the Cathedral of Santa María la Menor on September 10, 1877, set off this geopolitical contest, initiating an intense quarrel over where Columbus's true bones rested. Before 1877, Dominican intellectuals believed that Columbus's remains were in Cuba. They recognized that Columbus's body was first buried along with that of his son Diego in the Capilla de Santa Ana in the Carthusian monastery in Seville. Yet, sometime between 1536 and 1540, Columbus's daughter-in-law (Doña María de Toledo, wife of Diego) transported the remains to Santo Domingo, where the government buried them in the Cathedral of Santa María la Menor. When the Treaty of Basel granted the eastern side of Hispaniola to France in 1795, the general lieutenant of the Spanish Royal Army, Gabriel Aristizábal, decided to relocate Columbus's bones to Cuba so that they would not fall into French hands or, worse still in his eyes, become the possession of Haitian revolutionaries. The government exhumed Columbus's bones and sent them to Havana. For decades, the idea that Columbus was still buried in the Dominican cathedral circulated chiefly as rumor. Then came the discovery of September 10, 1877. Renovations to the cathedral in Santo Domingo led renowned Dominican priest and philanthropist Francisco Javier Billini to uncover a lead box containing human bones and an inscription with Columbus's name. With this discovery, Dominicans claimed that the remains moved to Cuba in 1795 had actually belonged to Diego. News of the discovery spread like wildfire. Over the next months, the Royal Academy of History in Spain disputed the facts. Dominican historians defended the discovery in books, newspapers, and the government's official organ, the

FIGURE 6.1. "The coffin of Christopher Columbus. After the drawing made by R. Cronau on January 11, 1891, in the Cathedral of Santo Domingo." From Cronau, *Discovery of America*, 73.

Gaceta Oficial. The uncovering of the lead container in the Santo Domingo cathedral had opened a metaphorical Pandora's box (figures 6.1–6.3).[20]

From Spain's perspective, the discovery of Columbus's tomb in Santo Domingo threatened its nationalist claims over Columbus's mortal remains and control of his historical memory. As a symbol of colonial empire, Columbus enabled Spain to unify its populace through its status as a world power. While other Western nations' claims on Columbus's historical memory challenged Spain's national image, Spain had invested energy and money in pinning its claim on Columbus. For example, the Spanish Crown had bestowed a title, Duke of Veragua, upon Columbus's descendants. Midcentury paintings depicting Columbus with the Spanish monarchs celebrated the connection. The government named city streets and plazas after Columbus, and as insurrection broke out across eastern Hispaniola, Spain

FIGURE 6.2. Top of the coffin (lead box); the inscription describes Columbus as "Discoverer of America, First Admiral." From Cronau, *Discovery of America*, 74.

erected statues of Columbus in Havana (1862) and Madrid (1863).[21] Thus, the 1877 discovery of Columbus's remains in Santo Domingo presented a political dilemma. If Columbus was not in fact buried in Havana, did Spain still have a right to the explorer's historical memory? Moreover, the discovery exposed Spain to foreign critique. Other European and American states laid claim to Columbus and, in order to forge their own national histories, they vilified Spain by emphasizing the cruelty of its conquistadors, the arrest and humiliation of Columbus in 1500, and the ultimate decline of Spain's empire. Spanish government and intellectual leaders, aware of foreign countries' contempt, interpreted the 1877 discovery as another point where foreign nations might charge Spain with "indifference and ignorance of its own history."[22] Therefore, the Spanish defended even more fiercely their claim to Columbus's bones and his memory. In doing so, they fought for a positive image of Spain's contributions to world history and for a confirmation of Spain's place alongside the modern empires of Europe and the United States.[23]

The United States too had much to gain from *colonofilia*. Although Columbus, a sailor in the service of Spain, never reached continental North America, he became a national symbol for the United States after its founding. In 1792, the United States held its first commemorations of Columbus in Boston, Baltimore, and New York. The country named its capital after Washington and Columbus, and a marble statue of a Native American

FIGURE 6.3. American tourists would have viewed these two empty vaults where Columbus's bones rested in the Cathedral de Santa María la Menor. Dominicans claimed that the one at bottom left, outside the enclosure, held Diego Colón's bones, which Spaniards mistook for Columbus's in 1795. The lead box was found in the vault at right. From Deschamps, *La República Dominicana*, 211.

gazing at Columbus in awe sat at the top of the Capitol Building's steps. Other dedications to Columbus, in marble, paint, and print, abounded in the nation's capital and extended to other parts of the United States. In 1828, for example, Washington Irving published the first major biography of Columbus, the *Life and Voyages of Christopher Columbus*, which became a bestseller. Washington's Columbus inspired a new wave of artists (such as John Vanderlyn and Luigi Persico) to paint and sculpt the explorer, as poets (such as Lydia Huntley Sigourney) penned verses in his homage. As the Civil War broke out, the US government installed bronze doors on Statuary Hall depicting Columbus's life. After the US Civil War, Americans' use of Columbus iconography grew as Irish and Italian newcomers identified with Columbus's religious and ethnic heritage in order to climb up the echelons of whiteness that still painted them as undesirables. During the 1870s, these immigrant communities organized yearly celebrations on October 12 and advocated for the United States to establish the day as a national holiday. By 1877, Americans' patriotic use of Columbus had been firmly entrenched, but Americans realized that Columbus did not belong to them uniquely. Many Americans still identified the explorer with Spain, the former colonial superpower of the Americas, which the United States aimed to supplant. Thus, within the context of late nineteenth-century US expansion, Americans' appropriation of Columbus reflected the country's drive to supersede Spain and establish its own empire in Latin America.[24]

With news of the 1877 discovery, the Dominican Republic entered the geopolitical tug of war over Columbus that Spain and the United States waged both symbolically and discursively. As in the bigger nations, *colono-filia* became central to Euro-Dominican national identity construction.[25] Unlike the other two nations, however, the Dominican Republic could not boast of conquests (colonial, expansionary, or otherwise); Spain, France, and Haiti had all ruled eastern Hispaniola at one time or another. Moreover, the country's African heritage and historical and geographical proximity to Haiti represented a challenge to Euro-Dominican elites' attempts to prove their modernity in the eyes of the United States and Spain. Veneration of Columbus became one way that Dominicans could create a national narrative while signaling to Spain, the United States, and other Western nations that the Dominican Republic was a modern country under white Euro-Dominican power. As Dixa Ramírez has argued, this mindset made Columbus not only a symbol of the Dominican Republic's European heritage, but also a bizarre anticolonial figure through which the Dominican lettered class eschewed the North Atlantic gaze while also maintaining ideologies of Western cultural superiority and white supremacy.[26]

For Dominican elites, claims to Columbus's body mattered all the more since, due to the recent War of Restoration, they did not have full control over the country's still largely unwritten historical narrative or its political future. Spain moreover had burned archival records during the recent war. The lettered class sought to document, narrate, and restore the nation's history through reports and ceremonies regarding the discovery. In this way, Dominicans could "perform their newfound political and cultural agency on the global stage, as they turned Columbus's body into the centerpiece of their country's national archive."[27] Every new publication regarding the event amplified the new archive, which remained a matter of national interest since the country lacked the written sources to prove its historical authenticity. Historical material objects, like Columbus's box casket and bones, filled the gap "that [separated] orality from the written word."[28] At the same time, Dominican elites—intellectuals such as José Gabriel García, Manuel de Jesús Galván, César Nicolás Penson, Salomé Ureña, Manuel Rodríguez Objío, Federico Henríquez y Carvajal, and Josefa Antonia Perdomo—wrote histories, novels, plays, and poetry that established the nation's "foundational fiction."[29] Leaders also scrambled to protect national monuments and raise new ones such as the Columbus statue in the Plaza Colón, commissioned by the city on March 3, 1882, and inaugurated five years later on February 27, 1887, Dominican Independence Day and the discovery's ten-year anniversary.[30] Thus, the 1877 discovery became part of the nation's founding myth as the construction and public consumption of the country's first official narratives and monuments escalated.[31]

All the while, Spain's insistence that Dominicans had fraudulently invented the 1877 discovery played into racist stereotypes about the island.[32] Such charges implied a natural dishonesty or intellectual ineptitude on the part of the Dominican officials who documented the discovery. In light of the racialized geopolitical context, the charges were also meant to deny Dominicans a national history. The frantic production of Dominican history within this context set the stage for the deep indignation that the Dominican press expressed during the Columbus bones scandal of 1888, burdening the event with a racial tenor.

Columbus Exposed: The Violation of the Sacred-Profane Dichotomy

The scandal began when Hubert Montague Linnell visited Santo Domingo during the first quarter of 1888. Upon his arrival, Linnell sought Astwood's aid in facilitating his viewing of Columbus's remains. For Astwood, Linnell's request would have seemed mundane, since Astwood often solicited consent from both the Dominican government and the Catholic Church for that exact purpose. No other American tourist, however, reacted to the visitation in quite the same way as Linnell, who subsequently proposed the official lease and public exhibition of Columbus's bones throughout the United States. Linnell's proposal, and Astwood's subsequent official petition to the Dominican government, incited public outrage during the summer of 1888. The events of the scandal demonstrate the ways that the sacred-profane dichotomy determined the racialized geopolitical contest over Columbus's double body.

Linnell did not leave a large paper trail, and at the height of the scandal some people even questioned whether Linnell ever truly existed. He most certainly did. A New York shipping log recorded one H. M. Linnell, thirty years of age, disembarking in New York harbor on May 15, 1888, after a sojourn in Santo Domingo.[33] This same Linnell was born in Worcester, Massachusetts, in 1860.[34] An electrical engineer by trade, Linnell lived in Connecticut circa 1888 and worked as a business manager for the Schuyler

Electric Light company.[35] The National Electric Light Association nominated Linnell for the position of treasurer in 1885, but besides this distinction Linnell never gained national prominence.[36] After Linnell returned to the United States, he maintained a low profile as the Columbus bones scandal came to light. By then, though, Linnell's involvement in the scheme no longer mattered since the press had pounced on another culprit.

The only extant record of the proposal is included within one of Astwood's consular dispatches. Typed, undated, and unsigned, this copy of the original letter provided no further information about Linnell, although it named him as the plan's originator. Assuming a contractual tone, the letter delineated the terms: "Your petitioner respectfully requests permission to take the remains of Columbus accompanied by both a guard of native soldiers and several priests to the United States for a period of 4 years."[37] Linnell offered to pay for transportation expenses, and promised 50 percent of the net proceeds every six months to the Dominican government. He guaranteed at least $20,000 annually and requested that the Dominican government send eight soldiers and four priests to act as guards for the remains. These twelve men would report to Linnell and would wear "handsome uniforms" and "State robes." Linnell also requested an official document stating that this was the only time that Columbus's bones would leave the country. Whether or not Linnell possessed the financial know-how to make this plan work was beside the point.

Based on this proposal, Astwood drafted and sent a formal petition to the Dominican minister of the interior, Wenceslao Figuereo Cassó, on April 25, 1888. The official letter indicated Astwood's support of the enterprise, making him complicit in the injurious project and serving as the reason why the press blamed him and not Linnell. Still, the plan was Linnell's. Except for the change from "your petitioner" to "Mr. H. M. Linnell," Astwood's petition differed little from Linnell's initial letter. Flowery language at the onset was the only deviation. But even this introduction highlighted Linnell's original point that the project would be "a very valuable advertisement" for the Dominican Republic and would "completely revolutionize [US] public curiosity."[38] By targeting Astwood instead of Linnell, the papers implied that unscrupulous American capitalists were to be expected but official US government agents should know better. Yet given Astwood's racialized position and the history of official US overreach in the region (topics explored in chapters 3 and 4), Astwood's complicity was standard.

Moreover, it was likely the case that neither man sensed his wrongdoing. Both Linnell and Astwood believed that the project would benefit the

Dominican and American governments; their reasons made financial and political sense. Due to the forthcoming quadricentennial celebrations, the demand to view Columbus's remains in the United States would be high. The cost, on the other hand, would be low since Linnell promised to finance the venture. The project, therefore, would not burden either government. Meanwhile, both governments stood to benefit politically from the exhibition's popularity. The Dominican Republic would gain prestige in the United States through Columbus's double body, elevating the country in Americans' racist purview. The United States' recognition that the Dominican Republic possessed Columbus's true bones, moreover, would boost the Dominican claim in its dispute with Spain. The US government would likewise benefit from cooperating in the project, since it would be recognized as the nation that identified Columbus's genuine remains. This role would bolster Americans' claim to Columbus as a national symbol. Thus, the plan was logical.

The Dominican government's response to Astwood's official petition, however, also followed a certain logic, excoriating the proposal in toto. "Profound astonishment, Mr. Consul," Figuereo wrote in a letter dated May 9, 1888.[39] Calling Linnell's proposal a "catch-penny scheme" and "shameful profanation," Figuereo scoffed, "No, Mr. Consul, the government for which I have the honor to speak has sufficient self-respect to spare the civilized world the painful spectacle of an unparalleled simony." Figuereo's forceful rejection of Astwood's petition drove to the heart of the matter. To turn Columbus's remains into a commodified exhibition would breach the presumed strict division between the sacred and the profane.

Besides designating a monetary value to Columbus's body, the proposal also offended at a symbolic level. Dominicans knew that Americans categorized them racially as Black, and evidence of this insult was baked into Linnell's request. The demand that twelve Dominicans—eight soldiers and four priests—accompany the remains to the United States would place the Dominican military and the Catholic Church on display for a white American audience. The habitual display of nonwhite peoples at public exhibitions in Europe and the United States made the racial connotations of the petition obvious. That the soldiers and priests were to wear "showy uniforms" and "canonical vestments" stressed the point.[40] That both soldiers and priests should relinquish their duties to the Dominican government and Catholic Church and come under a white man's "sole control and orders" also suggested a racial ordering that harked back to slavery.[41] Linnell's requested certificate confirming the genuineness and exclusivity of the show, moreover, once again asked the Dominican Republic to prove its claim, discounting the hundreds of pages already written on the topic and raising anew the highly racialized question of fraud.

More contextual information and a close reading of Figuereo's response hint at an additional layer of insult. As already stated, Dominican church and state officials regulated who could view the remains in the cathedral and when. Linnell's proposition sought to bring the tourist attraction directly to Americans in the United States, cutting out Dominican officials. Figuereo hinted at this potential loss of a Dominican enterprise when he wrote that the country felt "justly proud that the remains are ours by [Columbus's] last wishes" and that their display in the United States for money would "bring contempt upon the last descendant of the sons of this land."[42] Could it be that the exhibition of Columbus's remains was not the problem per se, but rather the suggestion that the project should be monetized and that Americans should control the operation instead of Dominicans? The terms that relinquished 50 percent of the proceeds to H. M. Linnell suggested that one US citizen stood to gain as much from the enterprise as the Dominican government. The transfer of a Dominican spectacle to an American would furthermore strip the Dominican Republic of its national patrimony. It would thus inhibit Dominican officials' ability not only to manage Columbus's remains but also to control the messages that tourists received about Columbus and the Dominican nation. Accordingly, by insisting upon the sacred-profane divide, Figuereo defended the Dominican Republic's claim on Columbus and its national honor. His expressed wish that all nations might have the opportunity to "gratuitously" gaze upon Columbus implied that Dominicans knew better how to manage the display of the bones and implicitly questioned the moral fiber of a government that would facilitate their conversion into "an object of traffic."[43]

Figuereo's response set the tone for the public contempt subsequently directed at Astwood through the Dominican press. The *Boletín del Comercio* was the first to warn its readers of the proposal in its May 17 article titled "Poor Columbus!," cited at the beginning of this chapter. "We have heard it said," editor Pardo relayed, "that not very long ago a foreigner had the bizarre idea to propose to the Dominican government that they rent him Columbus's remains . . . for the sum of roughly twenty million pesos monthly!!!"[44] The inaccurate citation of the proposal's terms sensationalized the offense and reflected the *Boletín del Comercio*'s penchant for yellow journalism. But the appearance of Astwood's petition and Figuereo's rejoinder in the June 9 issue of the *Gaceta Oficial* clarified matters.[45] The publication of the two letters side by side in the government's official journal proved that the petition had indeed constituted formal state business, lending the matter legitimacy.

With rumors confirmed, other Dominican newspapers unleashed their anger. Among the few extant newspapers of the era, only the *Eco de la Opinión* offered H. M. Linnell's name up for "Dominicans' execration."[46] Others blamed Astwood. The *Boletín del Comercio* reprinted Astwood's petition and Figuereo's response in its subsequent June issue.[47] In Puerto Plata, *El Porvenir* published an "Energetic Protest."[48] The article, reprinted in the *Boletín del Comercio*, decried Columbus's "martyrdom" and "torment" at the hands of the Spanish and claimed that Spain's insults faded in comparison to "the infamy of desecrating [Columbus's] ashes by handing them to an odious and scandalously degrading trade."[49] The *puertoplateño* paper also characterized the proposal as a national insult, asserting that it had caused "intense indignation in the spirit of all Dominicans zealous for national dignity." In conclusion, it compared Astwood to the American showman Phineas Taylor Barnum and demanded that the Dominican government revoke the "Barnum diplomat's" exequatur. The problem was an issue of exposure. Astwood's actions had exposed the Dominican Republic's need to curry international favor. "If we were Great Britain, France, or Germany, it is sure that no one would have dared to inflict the offense of thinking us corrupt and dishonorable, nor would they have found someone to serve as intermediary," wrote the *Eco de la Opinión*.[50] This statement recognized the racial geopolitics by which the United States considered white European nations morally above "Black" Santo Domingo.

From Dominican ports, the news traveled to Puerto Rico. The *Unidad Nacional* of Mayagüez wrote, "The case is so original, so stupendous, so indignant that truly we can't find words to describe it. What kind of man is this Mr. Astwood and what ideas does he have about the dignity of Hispanic American peoples?"[51] Since the Mayagüez editors assumed that Astwood was white, this question intimated that US racism toward Latin America had influenced Astwood's decision to forward the letter to Figuereo. In other words, instead of attributing the offense to Astwood's Blackness (as US papers soon would), the *Unidad Nacional* blamed US capitalism and suggested that the US government deemed Latin Americans to be ignorant and depraved. "This scandalous event [reveals] how far Yankee mercantilism can go," the paper declared. The denunciation of US capital alluded to its opposite (the Latin American spirit), but it also emphasized the stakes at hand. If the United States could request Columbus's remains with impunity—an act that sought the literal appropriation of the European explorer—then they could also strip Latin Americans of other prized legacies of colonial domination: wealth, Catholicism, and whiteness. Given that the US gaze toward Latin America presumed US superiority, the paper doubted whether the US government would ever recall Astwood. Thus, it implored the Dominican government to deport the US consul or risk "universal censure."

American newspapers, however, were equally quick to denounce the proposal. The *New York Herald* broke the story in the United States on July 24, 1888, citing the *Gaceta Oficial* and reprinting the two letters.[52] The Spanish and French New York papers, *Las Novedades* and *Courrier des États-Unis*, followed suit.[53] Within a week, the story had traveled north to Connecticut, west to Cleveland and Minneapolis, and south to Charleston and New Orleans. US newspapers condemned Astwood. "Diplomatic Disgrace," "Atrocious Impudence," "Must Not Be Dug Up," "A Lively Consul" read the headlines.[54] In many instances, but not all, the newspapers reminded the public that Astwood was Black. The papers of Louisiana were particularly critical, both recalling Astwood's Blackness and bemoaning the fact that he was from New Orleans. "It is with shame and indignation that we are forced to admit that this Consul who has so disgraced his nation is a Louisianian," wrote the *Daily Picayune*.[55] If Dominican and Puerto Rican editors doubted whether Americans would turn a blind eye to the insult, the US press set the record straight. Astwood was the "Barnum" consul, the "highly colored negro" whose idiocy had disgraced the nation.[56]

Disgrace brought otherwise unknown facts to light. In Connecticut, the *New Haven Register* interviewed Stephen Canty, a resident of the town who had visited Santo Domingo some years earlier. Canty provided further information on the schemers. He had little to say about Linnell, whom he described as a "Hartford man" involved with the Schuyler Electric Light company. Canty had much more to say about Astwood. "The kind of man Astwood is may be better imagined than told," he reported.[57] Canty informed the paper that Astwood was a "colored man" and "a poor Methodist minister" at the time of his consular appointment in 1882. "His salary as consul is only $2,500 a year, but it is said that at the present time he is worth at least $75,000," making him a very rich man. This biased account consisted of both hyperbole and truth. For example, Canty wrongly claimed that Astwood was unpopular with the American residents on the island, who had "no dealings with him except when compelled to." That Astwood had been "connected with various money-making schemes of

San Domingo" was true enough, since Astwood regularly represented US businesses before the Dominican government. However, at that point in time, only a few of Astwood's white American contacts in Santo Domingo had reason to doubt his seemingly good intentions on their behalf. Still, Canty's detailed description exuded credibility, obscuring inconsistencies and sensationalizing Astwood's involvement.

Despite its misleading description of Astwood, the *New Haven Register* was one of only a few papers to provide contextual details about the scandal. The presence of the Knights of Columbus, a Catholic fraternity founded in 1882 and headquartered in New Haven, intensified public interest there. In fact, both of the *Register*'s two published articles about the proposal linked the Knights of Columbus to the broader controversy and positioned the organization's members as defenders of Columbus's legacy. For example, the subtitle of the first article read, "Knights of This City to See to It That the Discoverer's Bones Are Not Disinterred and Carted About on an Exhibition Tour."[58] The same article then explained that New Haven's Knights of the San Salvador Council, No. 1, would adopt a resolution to denounce Astwood at its next meeting. Criticisms of Astwood established, the two articles connected the scandal with the debate over the veracity of the bones found in 1877 and the upcoming quadricentennial celebrations of Columbus's discovery in 1892. In one article, the *Register* sided with the Dominican government when it described a casket "found beneath the alter [sic] which established beyond a doubt the fact that it contained the ashes of Christopher Columbus."[59] It went on to explain the history of Columbus's burial and the 1877 debate. The other article focused on the Knights of Columbus's institutional organization and goals for 1892. Expecting membership to rise to ten thousand that year, the fraternity's chapters—all named after historic figures, places, and events associated with Columbus—planned a "monster parade."[60] In setting the record straight about Columbus's remains, describing the two "discoveries" (1492 and 1877), and connecting them to the proximate future (1892), the paper situated the scandal in time and emphasized the significance of Astwood's blunder.

In recounting the 1877 discovery and debate, the *Register* invited white American readers to envision themselves as Columbus's protectors. With words that would have fit well in a travel guide, the paper beckoned Americans to tour the Santo Domingo cathedral to see Columbus for themselves. With a sense of urgency, it then described the perceived insecurity of Columbus's resting place. "For relics of such priceless value," the paper concluded, "they are virtually unprotected. . . . If the bones of Columbus were left exposed like that in the United States, they would be carried away by thieves inside of twenty-four hours."[61] Even though readers could have interpreted these words as a compliment to the Dominican Republic, the paper instead challenged Dominican ownership of the remains, implying that Americans would know better than Dominicans how to care for such important relics. Accordingly, the *Register* claimed that the Knights of Columbus had always "been anxious to obtain some relic directly associated with Columbus."[62] To own Columbus's bones was to claim his double body, dispossessing African descendant Dominicans of his colonial legacy and expropriating it instead for white Americans.

The notion that only white Anglo-Saxon Americans could properly safeguard Columbus's relics betrayed US anxiety over losing out to a Black nation. Indeed, American news about the scandal exposed the shame of being reprimanded by nonwhite people. As the New Orleans *Daily Picayune* lamented, "By the action of its chosen representative the name of the proudest nation on the earth is brought into such extreme depths of degradation and infamy that the officials of a negro republic are shocked and horrified."[63] This sentiment was echoed in Minnesota.[64] The *New Haven Register* furthermore marveled at Figuereo's response, which seemed too refined for an officer of a Black republic. "But didn't the general pay him off in great shape?" it quoted the Knights of Columbus secretary Daniel Colwell. "I will give the coons glory for that."[65] These racist depictions of the Dominican Republic distanced white Americans from supposedly Black Dominicans and served to mitigate the blow of Figuereo's rebuke. For white Americans, Astwood's actions and Figuereo's response had turned international racial hierarchy on its head. Figuereo's letter questioned American morality and accused the US government of defaming Columbus through its mercenary intentions at a time when white Americans believed themselves to be superior on all accounts to African descendants. Thus, rather than capitulate to Figuereo and reevaluate the logic of scientific racism, American newspapers defended the United States' honor by refusing to own up to Astwood's actions. "The United States cannot very well apologize to San Domingo [for] an insult of this kind," stated one newspaper, "but it can show its appreciation of Mr. Astwood's unfitness to represent it abroad by promptly removing him . . . and all other [Black] consuls."[66] Isolating Astwood and emphasizing both his and the Dominican Republic's African heritage reestablished the United States' narrative of white supremacy.

While the scandal played out in the American press, the US State Department tried to get on top of the matter by fielding inquiries and writing urgently to Astwood. Private citizens had reacted to the *Herald*'s news by sending letters to the State Department and demanding Astwood's resignation. Edmund Charles Preiss, for example, wrote to both President Grover Cleveland and Secretary of State Thomas F. Bayard to express his "indignation as a citizen over the unheard of abuse of official privileges."[67] Another "simple American citizen," Amandus Meyer, protested both Astwood's actions and "the mortification of seeing similar unworthy representatives of the United States in the West Indies lower the good name of their country."[68] While both men claimed to "write without influence," Meyer's letter clarified that it was not just Astwood's actions but also his color that amplified the injury for many Americans. The US State Department responded to both men, and while it is not known whether Bayard addressed Meyer's concerns over race, he expressly concurred with Preiss's statements and reassured him that investigations regarding the accuracy of the report were underway.[69]

Assistant Secretary of State George Lockhart Rives wrote Astwood on July 26, 1888. His letter informed Astwood of the *Herald*'s publication, enclosed a copy of it, and affirmed "the deep mortification that has been felt by this Department ... should such a correspondence have actually taken place."[70] Whereas the Dominican and American press had sensationalized the news, the US government left space for Astwood to clarify the situation. This opportunity, however, only further inflamed controversy in Santo Domingo as the Dominican press relentlessly turned to ridicule to make the Black US consul pay for his misdeed.

Columbus Saved: Ridicule as Race-Making Ritual

Still manning his post in August 1888, Astwood came under increased attack from Dominican newspapers. The *Boletín del Comercio*'s editor, Miguel Eduardo Pardo, and editorialist Pedro Obregón Silva, both Venezuelan exiles in Santo Domingo, especially taunted Astwood.[71] The worsening situation in the press reveals how public ridicule—at times bitingly to the point, at other times mysteriously allegorical and chock full of salacious double entendres—dismantled Astwood's well-articulated justifications of his actions by deploying highly racialized and sexualized moral discourse. In doing so, the Dominican press inscribed immorality upon Astwood's foreign Black body.

It also implicitly censured Afro-Dominican President Ulises Heureaux's rule while eschewing the United States' racist imperialist gaze.

The feud between Astwood and the Dominican press began during the first week of August, shifting the media's initial expressions of shock to ridicule of Astwood. Under the gossip section of the *Boletín del Comercio*'s August 2, 1888, issue, a sarcastic article poked fun at the disgraced consul: "CRAZY.—An individual who responds to the name Ache CeCe [the phonetic pronunciation of H. C. C. in Spanish] had a mental breakdown the other day."[72] It reported that Astwood's constant mulling over his "sad situation" had triggered a psychotic episode and supposed that only cigars could help him regain his composure. Two days later, the *Eco de la Opinión* reported more gossip. "They say that Mr. H. C. C. Astwood consul of the USA. is trying to publish a leaflet in defense of the charges the Dominican press has made against him," it stated before admonishing Astwood that "the less said, the better."[73] The *Boletín del Comercio* repeated the *Eco*'s warning a day later, foreshadowing trouble ahead.[74]

Ignoring the newspapers' advice, Astwood circulated a pamphlet retorting to the Dominican press. "Gush for Patriotism and Much Ado about Nothing," explained Astwood's side of the story.[75] Linnell, Astwood claimed, was "considerably interested in the [Dominican Republic's] welfare," and lamented that the world did not know that Columbus's remains lay in "obscurity" in Santo Domingo. Wishing to honor Columbus and the Dominican Republic, Linnell had suggested exhibiting the remains in the United States, which would "give éclat and public acclaim" to the Dominican Republic in its dispute with Spain. The revenues furthermore would have served to erect a mausoleum in Santo Domingo. Since Astwood also wished to honor Columbus, he had discussed the matter with Figuereo. Yet once Astwood had submitted the petition in writing, Figuereo had retained it instead of informing Astwood privately of his offense. Rather than returning the offensive petition to Astwood, Figuereo had forwarded "his celebrated answer and [made] haste in an unusual way to give publicity to the same," Astwood contended. He asserted that only the public could infer Figuereo's sinister intentions. Astwood then attacked the Dominican press, denouncing the newspapers' editors of profiteering from the scandal. "Mercenary minds cannot have other than mercenary motives," he argued. When it came to money, it was these "pretentious scribblers"—not he—whose "good intentions perverted for evil." Astwood posited that the editors cloaked their actions in patriotism when in fact greed fueled their mission: the greater the scandal, the deeper their pockets. Astwood then resolved, "Now Mr. Editor, I have no apology to make for what I have done, believing in my conscience that I have done nothing wrong." Thus, Astwood's pamphlet served as yet another example of his attempts to elevate himself while disparaging as immoral those he viewed as his enemies.

Yet, while Astwood designed the pamphlet as a testament to his benevolence, it also betrayed a certain American arrogance. Astwood's comparison of Columbus's bones to the hypothetical remains of Amerigo Vespucci underscores this point. He wrote:

> If the remains of Amerigo Vespucci were lying in obscurity, in a nook of some one of our Cathedrals in Washington, with no better mausoleum than an ordinary chest for their calm repose, if the Government of the United States were unable, on account of its financial condition to give to the world the proofs of identity or a proper and becoming resting place, I cannot conceive how that Government could be offended if some zealous Italian should petition for the exhibition of the remains in Europe, so as to give to the world a better knowledge and more convincing proofs of the great discoverer's remains, and to invest the necessary and indispensable revenues growing out of the Exhibition to the lifting up of an imperishable monument in honor of his great achievements.[76]

With these words, Astwood highlighted the Dominican Republic's poverty and inability to properly esteem Columbus according to modern Western standards. He also suggested that Americans could give "more convincing" proof than Dominicans on the world stage. These ideas subtly alluded to the racial divide between the two countries. They also divested the Dominican Republic of its symbolic claim on Columbus's bones. "The nationality of Columbus is in no way identified to, or with that of the Dominican Republic," Astwood maintained, "but his fame is dear to every American who breathes the free air of this western hemisphere." Such words questioned the Dominican Republic's right to determine independently the legacy of the remains. Decent people (and nations) would "display patriotism instead of 'bosh,'" by erecting a mausoleum. "Until then, even verbosity should bow its head in silence," Astwood charged.[77]

Yet silent the papers were not. Unsurprisingly, Dominican editors did not reprint Astwood's pamphlet in their columns as he demanded. Instead, they continued their attack on Astwood. The *Boletín* published an incriminating opinion piece on August 16.[78] The *Eco* took a subtler stance and reprinted articles from US newspapers about the scandal.[79] By doing so, it reiterated the need to morally defend the Dominican nation without blaming Astwood outright. One article, for example, repeated the sentiment that Astwood's actions stemmed from American greed: "You would not believe the nerve, and such a complete lack of moral consciousness, if you do not already know how the fever of speculation can lead to so many perversions."[80] Astwood represented the United States, and Figuereo's response served as "a comparative study of characters" between the two men and their nations. The *Eco* also pointed out a silver lining: the US press's response to the scandal indicated that Americans believed the Dominican Republic's claim on Columbus's legitimate remains.[81] In this way, the *Eco* recast Astwood's blunder as a sign of the Dominican Republic's imminent vindication in its fight with Spain.

What exactly Astwood felt upon reading this latest round of attacks remains a mystery, but it is very plausible that they stoked his ire, as evinced by his next actions. On August 19, the *Boletín* reported that the disgraced consul visited its publication office and demanded that Miguel E. Pardo retract the editorial published on August 16, 1888. In demanding the retraction, Astwood likely sought proof of libel that he could then enclose in a letter to the US State Department. Pardo saw through this ruse: "Does [the consul] imagine that we are puppets or instruments of his shameful propositions?"[82] According to the *Boletín*, Astwood even threatened Pardo and Obregón by claiming that "he [would] fix the *matter by another way* if we [did] not change our way of thinking" (emphasis in original). Pardo stood his ground against this warning of violent retaliation, telling Astwood curtly, "A dignified man never retracts; he has an impenetrable shield to cowardice: his honor. Therefore, Mister Astwood 'what is written, remains written.'" Obregón, for his part, mocked Astwood's threats by first admitting that he penned the opinion piece in question and then daring Astwood to face him directly by providing his home address. Not one for half measures, Obregón addressed his challenge "to the Barnum consul."[83] A subsequent editorial, "Al sr. H. C. C. Astwood," left uncapitalized the honorific before Astwood's name, signaling Pardo's and Obregón's forthcoming assault on Astwood's manhood.[84]

Unable to obtain retractions from Dominican newspapers (which would serve as proof of libel), Astwood responded at last to the US State Department on August 21. In this dispatch, Astwood declared his innocence and included three enclosures: a printed copy of Linnell's letter to him, which Astwood had used as a basis for the proposal; the pamphlet circulated to the Dominican press; and a handwritten copy of Astwood's response to the New York press, specifically the *New York Herald*, the *Novedades*, and the *Courrier des États-Unis*.[85] This last document especially made clear the political context in which Astwood operated.

Astwood's letter to the US press recycled prior arguments and presented a few new ones. Like the pamphlet to Dominican newspapers, it reiterated that the preservation of history rested at the heart of the petition. He reminded his US audience that the 1877 discovery of Columbus's bones in Santo Domingo was not common knowledge in the United States and explained that the Dominican government had called for an international conference to investigate the evidence in 1885, but the effort had failed to galvanize international support.[86] "I have always thought that the controversy relative to the identity of Columbus's remains ought to be settled for the benefit of History," he maintained.[87] To this end, Astwood once again related that he had "thoroughly discussed" the matter with the government and had not forwarded the petition until Heureaux had sanctioned the plan. Unlike previous arguments, however, Astwood blamed local politics. As he outlined, 1888 was an election year in the Dominican Republic, and the *Boletín del Comercio* was attempting to turn public opinion against incumbent President Heureaux by inventing a rumor about the "bargain and sale" of Columbus's remains to the United States. However, there was no mercenary agreement of that kind. Astwood condemned the Dominican paper's "disreputable" petty politics, classifying its editors as "anarchists" and "expulsed and renegade Venezuelians [*sic*]."[88] To justify Figuereo's subsequent indignation, Astwood claimed that Figuereo had responded so strongly merely to quell the propaganda. He moreover asserted that there were no bad feelings between him and Heureaux since he had simply followed routine procedures. That the Dominican government remained curiously silent on the matter after Figuereo's initial protest lent this theory some credibility.

Although Astwood addressed this letter to the US press, a translated version also appeared on the front page of the *Eco de la Opinion*'s August 25, 1888, issue.[89] The translation and other adjacent editorials implicitly challenged the *Boletín del Comercio*'s personal attack upon Astwood, demonstrating that at least some Dominicans took umbrage at the *Boletín*'s tone. For example, an article titled "La Prensa" touted journalism's "noble mission to look after the moral and social interests" of society.[90] It then asserted that even when freedom of the press existed in liberal societies, journalists should take care not to scandalize the nation that they aim to defend. Next appeared a letter from Felix E. Soler, who had complained the week prior that "the latest from Obregón offends by its style and disgusts [*repugna*] by its inconsideration."[91] In his August 25 letter, Soler clarified that he had written to curb the *Boletín*'s quarrel with Astwood, since it "teaches nothing, illustrates nothing."[92] His motivation had been the "groan [*gemido*] of an offended society, threatened by more offenses to come." Next, in a preamble to Astwood's letter, the *Eco de la Opinión*'s editors reiterated that they disagreed with Astwood but "could not reasonably deny him columns for the defense he attempts to make."[93] Beneath this, they printed Astwood's cover letter, which characterized the *Eco de la Opinión* as an "impartial" newspaper and asked them to run the piece.[94] The translation came last. Although the *Eco de la Opinión* condemned Astwood's actions, this August 25 issue suggests that not all sectors of Dominican society felt comfortable with the malicious attacks upon his person.

Nevertheless, these overtures did not end matters. On the following day, August 26, an article titled "Morality of the Nations [*pueblos*]" appeared on the *Boletín del Comercio*'s front page. The treatise declared that the Dominican Republic "would remain at the mercy of all the insults, all the harassment, all the violence of foreign nations" if the people did not defend "MORALITY ... as the most holy and the most pious thought, like a religion, in the souls of the nations that adore liberty as they adore God."[95] This piece fused the Hostonian concept of *moral social* (discussed in chapter 5) with Catholic Dominican patriotism, portraying the *Boletín*'s fight with Astwood as a battle for the soul of the Dominican people. Given that the second page of the paper featured at least four articles that addressed the Columbus bones scandal in varying degrees of transparency, the *Boletín* made the lesson clear: Astwood was the immoral foreigner who had violated all notions of social morality operating within Dominican society.

Indeed, the second page of the *Boletín*'s August 26 issue unleashed the full force of the paper's ridicule upon Astwood, insisting upon the separation between the sacred and the profane. Defending the paper, one article asserted the *Boletín*'s pride in being the first to denounce the proposal commercializing the nation's "glorious compatriot" Columbus.[96] Contrasting Astwood's disgrace with Dominican patriotism, the *Boletín* then demanded that the "virtuous Dominican people" judge its actions.[97] Two letters, one each from Pardo and Obregón, followed. Pardo's title, "Valiente Caball...ero!," was a play on the words *cabal*—which in English means a group of plotters against the government, but in Spanish means upright, honest, and sensible—and *caballero* (gentleman).[98] The phrase *caball...ero* also sounded phonetically like "*cabal* Heureaux," suggesting either that

Heureaux had plotted against the nation or that a "brave" cabal should rise against the dictator. The play on words and across languages also set up a contrast of good versus evil superimposed upon people and the nations they represented. Defending his and Obregón's honor as Venezuelan "voluntary exiles" who fought for "liberty," Pardo moreover accused Astwood of degrading the United States: "The bald eagle which holds up its powerful wings in the noble North American seal should not, cannot, does not deserve to raise itself in the bastard banister [*barandilla*] of a dealer in sacred ashes." These words served triple duty: to shame the United States, to belittle Astwood and possibly Heureaux, and to emphasize once again the sacredness of Columbus's remains. Pardo concluded with sexual innuendo: "We desire to know who is the *easy* pen who writes the vigorous thoughts of the Barnum Consul" (emphasis in original). This statement suggested that dubious politics had forced the *Eco* to run Astwood's piece. More importantly, it also threatened to expose secrets, sexual in nature, about Astwood's personal life as yet another form of public humiliation.

Obregón's article also hinted at sexual intrigue, although one would have to be a faithful reader of both the *Boletín* and the *Eco* to fully understand its meaning, since Obregón referred to four previously published articles in his piece titled "Agreed." The other articles included Astwood's response to the New York papers; Soler's first letter of protest; Soler's second letter in the August 25 *Eco*; and an article by a Venezuelan resident, Dr. Pietri, who wrote in support of the *Boletín*'s editors in an earlier August 23 issue. Respecting Astwood's letter, Obregón echoed Pardo's sexual innuendo: "[Astwood's New York correspondence] would also produce in Mr. Soler's society another one of those moans that he has so wrongly officially interpreted, because . . . cries on one side, and moans on the other, and consular grunts as an ultimate low, [ultimately produce] a special *trio* capable of waking the least musical public in the world" (emphasis in original).[99] Obregón's emphasis on "cries, moans, and grunts" implied a lovers' tryst, while the word *trio*, italicized in the paper, held a double meaning by referring to both a musical trio and a love triangle. This sinister characterization of Astwood's letter linked the political to the personal by emphasizing sexually devious behavior that violated modern Christian social mores, which society racially coded as white.

The implicit association between whiteness, morality, and modernity next appeared in Obregón's critique of Soler, the Dominican who dared to chastise Obregón for scandalizing Dominican society. Quick to point out Soler's poor orthography, Obregón wrote, "Now respecting [the accusation] that our discussions 'teach nothing, illustrate nothing' . . . [it is not always possible to teach] the person who does not have capacity to learn, or nerve, or moral interest."[100] Insofar as Soler possibly represented a poorer, phenotypically darker sector of Dominican society, these words implied that the majority of Dominicans were incapable or unwilling to learn Euro–Latin American moral culture. Thus, Obregón condescendingly cautioned "a little more study" before Soler reprimand the press. Obregón also suggested that Soler could stand to learn from Dr. Pietri, a Euro-Venezuelan, who had written in defense of Venezuelan residents in Santo Domingo. "In well constituted and cultured societies," Pietri had instructed, "moral sentiment strengthens and instills in [people's] minds respect and the culture of great principles that are the immovable pillars of all of [the] societies of European civilization."[101] These words attributed inherent morality to European culture. Pietri then warned Dominicans to remember that Venezuelan exiles in Santo Domingo were of European heritage and consequently possessed a high degree of moral culture. "We will not permit that they treat us like Chinese or African emigrants," he vituperated. "We feel grateful for the considerations that distinguish us in this country." Such considerations denoted whiteness, European cultural heritage, high levels of education, and Catholic religion. Without studying and imitating these attributes, Obregón warned, Dominican society "should lose all hope."[102]

Solidifying the racialized divide between the sacred and the profane, the fourth article in the *Boletin*'s August 26 issue, "Díceres"—whose author wrote under the pen name Prometeo [I Promise]—leaked news of various sexual affairs taking place in the capital.[103] In doing so, Prometeo portrayed Astwood as a sexually threatening Black man, and linked him to the 1822 murder of the Dominican "Galindo virgins." This linkage associated Astwood with Haiti and the supposed horror of Black rule. The section targeting Astwood read, "They say that a certain Consul ate ten Editors in only one bite. What a good young man, and so good looking! The person most lustfully [*voluptuosamente*] finished: round neck the color of snow; eyes blue as the sea; mouth of coral broken in two; pale forehead, ears like rose petals . . . and feet of a raped virgin."[104] This vulgar description was meant to belittle and shame Astwood. It exposed a possible extramarital affair, recharacterized Astwood's sexual relationships with Dominican women (including his prior marriage) as rape, and infantilized him as a "young man" rather than a foreign country's professional emissary. Even more significantly, the piece tapped into already circulating racist stereotypes of Haiti through the story of the Galindo virgins. As Sibylle Fischer and Lorgia García-Peña have shown, Dominican intellectuals such as Félix María del Monte and César Nicolás Penson recast Dominican bandits' historic 1822 killing of three sisters as murder and rape committed by Haitian men.[105] Projecting Dominican elites' feelings of disempowerment during Haitian unification onto the bodies of the abused women, the story portrayed Haitians as necrophiliacs possessing "a desire that can only be satisfied by the ultimate act of dehumanization, by transforming the living human body into an inanimate object."[106] This depiction, as Fischer argues, precluded any notion of an alternative future in which Dominicans celebrated the Haitian Revolution's progressive ideals.[107] Read alongside relic culture, though, Haitian desire across "the most significant boundary of all—that between animate and inanimate"—also marked elites' fear of being reduced to the realm of the inanimate and racialized as Black, vendible, and profane.[108] Thus, marking Astwood as a Haitian necrophiliac rapist in 1888 not only employed racist tropes of Black male hypersexuality and Haitian invaders but also depicted him and other Black politicians as dire threats to Euro-Dominican whiteness.

Additional analysis of the "Díceres" column further demonstrates this point. Although many Dominican men of high standing (including Archbishop Meriño) had sexual affairs, Prometeo wed various other local reports of adultery to racial Blackness through Astwood.[109] A poem about an illicit love affair between two young people, news of a woman who shut out her adulterous husband, and gossip about an amateur poet whose love interest shunned him all appeared before the section regarding "a certain Consul," melding them on the page and hopefully also in readers' minds.[110] Another item of gossip read, "They say that the young squire with kinky hair is looking for me. . . . ha! ha! ha!"[111] This likely reference to Astwood emphasized his African features (kinky hair) while belittling his earlier threat against Obregón with laughter, a shot at Astwood's masculinity. Prometeo then ended "Díceres" with another allusion. Directly after portraying Astwood as a rapist, he warned, "Some say that not only a piece, but the whole Cathedral has fallen with yesterday's drizzle." This statement held multiple layers. The cathedral represented Catholic religion and Euro-Dominican virility. The drizzle, however, referred to both the reported gossip and seminal fluid. The implication was that Black men's political desire—portrayed as sexual deviance, weak in form and yet still threatening—had toppled the inherently moral Dominican nation (raced and gendered as Euro-Dominican and male).

Through its strategic targeting of Astwood and extrapolation to Afro-Dominicans, the *Boletín* subtly implicated Heureaux. Additional articles published in late August and September demonstrate the tie. On August 30, the paper divulged Astwood's bigamy in an allegorical tale.[112] On September 2, an article titled "Extrangerismo" underscored the importance of religion, social morality, and hospitality to foreigners who benefited the republic, an implicit critique of Heureaux.[113] Prometeo issued a fresh round of gossip in the same issue, twice alluding pejoratively to Astwood.[114] Then, in a third article, Pardo reported a new bout of bickering between Astwood and the Dominican press. "Let the dance continue!" he declared.[115] And so it did. The front page of the *Boletín*'s September 10 issue, dedicated to the commemoration of the 1877 discovery, depicted a sketch of Columbus and purported that the explorer had lived the "most virtuous life" ever—despite Columbus's own history of adultery (figure 6.4).[116] It then lambasted Astwood's "shameful proposition" and called on Columbus's ashes to "curse" everyone involved with the humiliation. The juxtaposition of praise and curse employed religious language that intensified the contrast between Columbus's alleged Christian morality and Astwood's supposed depravity. Another article in the same issue, dedicated to reprinting an excerpt of Emiliano Tejera's *Los restos de Colón en Santo Domingo* (1878), closed by calling Astwood and Linnell "ignorant cynics and foreign charlatan speculators."[117] In the September 19 issue, Prometeo again wreaked havoc with another parody about a plagiarizing poet visiting the exhibition of Columbus's remains in the cathedral.[118] Then, to close out the month in the September 22 and 27 issues, Obregón penned two reviews of Hostos's *Moral Social* (1888), which tacitly challenged Heureaux's rule.[119] Although these last articles did not mention Astwood specifically, put in context with other articles and the 1888 election, they magnified the idea that both Astwood and Heureaux had violated all notions

FIGURE 6.4. (*opposite*) Front page of the *Boletín del Comercio*, September 10, 1888. The image and the timeline connect the discovery of 1877 to the petition to lease Columbus's bones in 1888. The text translates: "Praise to September 10, 1877! Honor to Quisqueya. The *Boletín del Comercio* offers this number as a tribute of admiration and respect to the discoverers of Columbus's true remains, which rest in the Cathedral of Santo Domingo. Hail to the heroic nation! To the nation that knows how to defend its right with dignity. Hail to the authorities! To the noble authorities who have defended the coffin of the immortal Genovese with vigor and integrity."

SANTO DOMINGO (REPÚBLICA DOMINICANA), SETIEMBRE 10 DE 1888. NÚMERO 135.

EL BOLETIN DEL COMERCIO.

Director-Propietario:
J. B. MAGGIOLO Y CIMELLI

Redactor:
MIGUEL EDUARDO PARDO

1877.   1888.

Cristobal Colon.

Lit.ª de DELLINI y PODMON.

¡¡Gloria a Cristobal Colon!!

¡LOOR AL 10 DE SETIEMBRE DE 1877!

HONOR A QUISQUEYA.

"EL BOLETIN DEL COMERCIO".

ofrenda este número como tributo de admiracion y respeto á los descubridores de los verdaderos restos de COLON—que reposan en la Catedral de Santo Domingo.

¡Salve al heroico pueblo!

AL PUEBLO QUE SABE SOSTENER DIGNAMENTE SU DERECHO.

SALVE Á LAS AUTORIDADES!

¡LAS NOBLES AUTORIDADES QUE HAN DEFENDIDO CON EL TESÓN Y ENTEREZA EL VEREDITO DEL INMORTAL COLON!

of social morality. Thus, even articles explicitly not about the Columbus bones scandal contributed to the two men's demonization.

The continued taunts exhibited the journalists' remarkable fortitude, given the violence Heureaux perpetrated against his enemies. Yet, for all of their bravado, a few articles hinted that Pardo and Obregón braced for backlash. For example, on August 30 Pardo asserted that he was not the author of the Prometeo column, and although he published the clarification only "to placate [his] friends," the short article suggests that his "friends"—if not Pardo himself—felt the need for the distinction.[120] Similarly, in the same issue, the *Boletín*'s owner clarified that Obregón did not serve as an editor or coeditor of the paper.[121] These announcements suggest that Astwood or other people identified in the *Boletín*'s August 26 issue may have attempted to ascertain whether Obregón was Prometeo in order to enact revenge. While the *Boletín* did not mention any overt forms of backlash akin to Astwood's former threats of violence, it is significant that on September 22 Pardo suddenly announced that he would return to Venezuela.[122] Within a month, Obregón had also left the country for St. Thomas, the public reason given being poor health.[123] The sudden departure of both Pardo and Obregón indicates that Astwood or Heureaux may have found a way of intimidating the *Boletín*'s editor and columnist after all. Perhaps not so coincidentally, Obregón was assassinated in Curaçao about a year later.[124] The threats against their lives, however, did not deter Pardo, now stationed in Caracas, from writing some last lines regarding the US consul.

In a final notice published in late September, Pardo informed the Dominican public that Astwood had used Pardo's absence as an opportunity to propagate yet another pamphlet that denounced the editor with obscene language. Pardo asserted that Astwood's "revenge" did not bother him. Characterizing himself as a martyr, Pardo pontificated, "Today, slandered, I will lift my head with more pride than ever. . . . I write these lines only to satisfy cultured Dominican society which deserves all of my respect and distinguished consideration."[125] Pardo's notice appeared next to a reprint of an article written by one Gordiano and published in *El Porvenir*. The article defended Pardo and the *Boletín* against Astwood, portraying the editor as genteel and experienced and the paper as well received within Dominican society compared to Astwood's questionable tracts. "This newspaper has been on top of its game, making itself a faithful echo of what every Dominican thinks," Gordiano contended.[126] Pardo's and Gordiano's articles represented a final attempt to dominate the narrative. Yet, even while they reasserted the *Boletín*'s virtue and Astwood's depravity, the very need to do so implied that they had likely met resistance in the form of Heureaux's intimidation. Indeed, with both men absent from Santo Domingo, news of the Columbus bones scandal and public ridicule of Astwood faded from the Dominican press.

Conclusion

"The cheekiest man on earth has been discovered," declared the *Pittsburgh Dispatch* on Thursday, two weeks after President Grover Cleveland officially dismissed Astwood on December 20, 1888.[127] The article summarized the months-long controversy in a few short sentences. Astwood had attempted to fatten his coffers with proceeds from the lease of Columbus's bones. Instead, the cheeky consul now found himself tossed out on his ear in a most humiliating manner. The newspaper explained that the removal amounted to "the only action that the American Government could take," for it could not have retained the representative who had so disgraced himself, Columbus, and the United States. Other newspapers concurred, reprinting news of the Columbus bones scheme and asserting that Astwood had been fired in order to "appease" the "shade," or curse, of Columbus.[128] Astwood's firing paid the debt owed by his "sacrilegious enterprises, revolting to good taste and common decency, as well as common sense."[129] The US consul's removal was, in short, inevitable, metaphorical retribution from Columbus's ghost.

Just as the drama had intensified in Santo Domingo, the scandal redoubled in American newspapers in September 1888. By then, the State Department, and subsequently the American press, had received Astwood's long explanations of events at hand. Although US newspapers did not publish Astwood's personal secrets, they similarly made quick work of dismissing the consul's claims. The *Herald* explained, "[Astwood's] letter contains so much that is foreign to the subject that its publication in full is impossible" and ill advised.[130] Then, in an article titled "Our Dime Museum Consul" published the following day, it condemned Astwood's plea "weak in both its mental and moral structure."[131] The word *moral* did not carry the same weight as Dominican debates over *moral social*, although the *Herald* did conclude that Astwood's intentions could only be mercenary.

Just as before, other papers followed the *Herald*'s lead. Three days later, *Las Novedades* published short excerpts of Astwood's letter with extended commentary. The only newspaper to bother to reassert Spain as the true possessors of Columbus's skeleton, *Las Novedades* insisted that Astwood could "save himself the trouble of said investigation because it has already been done; the immortal remains of the Discoverer of America rest in the Cathedral in Havana as everyone knows."[132] This statement intended to put to rest the geopolitical contest over Columbus's ashes. To exhibit the bones in the United States would declare the Dominican Republic the true possessor of Columbus's remains and thus verify the island nation's claim to white European heritage. *Las Novedades*'s Spanish editors refused out of hand to legitimize the Dominican Republic's stance.[133] Such cynical assessments of Astwood's logic gave way to more ridicule and rebuke. The *New York Times* compared Astwood to Buffalo Bill, while the *Panama Star and Herald* mockingly accused him of wanting to be president of the Dominican Republic.[134] And, referring to Miguel de Cervantes's dopey character Sancho Panza in *Don Quixote*, *Las Novedades* counseled that it "would have been better for Mr. Astwood to follow Sancho's precept and 'let sleeping dogs rest.'"[135] In sum, *Las Novedades* curtly dismissed the whole sordid saga: "With this we say goodbye to Consul H. C. C. Astwood."[136]

This chapter has deconstructed the various ways that Dominican and American society interpreted Astwood's actions within a transnational context where ideas about race, religion, nation, and empire informed decisions and interactions at all levels, from the macrodiplomatic realm to the granular personal sphere. Indeed, the scandal escalated precisely because of the layering of meaning that made Columbus's double body sacred to multiple nations. Shocked and chagrined in 1888, Americans and Latin Americans universally rejected Astwood's actions, citing both religious and political affronts. They perceived his subsequent removal as vindication of their nations and a defense of the world order as they knew it.

Yet people across the Americas could have reacted differently to the Columbus bones scandal by recognizing Astwood as a product of a long Atlantic world context in which capitalist avarice blurred the boundaries between the sacred and the profane. Such thoughts would have created much cognitive dissonance and called for deeper self-reflection. Both the Dominican Republic's and United States' willingness to invest in Columbus as a national symbol derived from the need to justify the West's history of genocide, exploitation, greed, and trade in human cargo. This fundamental hankering fueled other desires: the United States' imperial aspirations and the Dominican Republic's eagerness for acceptance among the ranks of white nations. Astwood's actions exposed these desires, thereby disrupting popular understandings of Columbus. Instead of recognizing the myth of Columbus for the fiction that it was, it was easier—indeed more logical—for Dominican and American societies to attack Astwood for his supposed foolishness. "Profound astonishment, Mr. Consul," were the words reprinted in newspapers across the Western world.

In an ironic twist of events that even Astwood had not foreseen, pinning the blame on him enabled his enemies in the United States and the Dominican Republic to commodify Columbus in another way—selling the idea of the discoverer as hero and founding father of multiple American nation-states. To understand Astwood on his own terms is to deconstruct this myth. To view Astwood as a product of the late nineteenth-century Atlantic world and grapple with his writings and actions is to contend with everything that his actions reveal—the blurred lines between diplomacy and business, religion and secular society, life and death, Black and white. It is, in fact, to dissect the tropes of the past that the Columbus myth forces upon us all.

7

"THE CHEEKIEST MAN ON EARTH"

H. C. C. Astwood and the Politics of White Moral Exclusivity

When Astwood learned that President Grover Cleveland had officially discharged him on December 20, 1888, he refused to leave office.[1] After holding the Santo Domingo consular office hostage for several months, Astwood returned to the United States in May 1889 only to seek reappointment from newly elected President Benjamin Harrison. He nearly won. For over a year, the US consulship at Santo Domingo remained vacant as illustrious Americans sprang to Astwood's defense. "I again assert that the conduct of the office at San Domingo under Mr. Astwood has been superior to that of any person who has filled his place for the last quarter of the century," declared the US Consular Bureau chief F. O. St. Clair to the secretary of state in April 1890.[2] The Boston shipbuilder and millionaire Nathaniel McKay agreed: "Mr. Astwood has not been guilty of [the] insubordination which you charge against him."[3] Lobbying on Astwood's behalf, St. Clair, McKay, and a host of other American leaders extolled the ex-consul's virtues.

Yet firsthand accounts of Astwood's comportment never presented a balanced picture. In the year following his removal, other prominent men scrutinized Astwood's morality, especially in regard to his handling of their financial transactions. Arguing the counterpoint, Philadelphia department store owner and US postmaster general John Wanamaker lambasted the ex-consul, calling him a "defaulter and an unfaithful servant."[4] Likewise, the wealthy steamship owner William P. Clyde claimed that Astwood's reappointment would "seriously injure American business."[5] Diametrically opposed to St. Clair and McKay's assessments, these deleterious reports ultimately prevented Astwood from regaining his diplomatic position. Moreover, they once again raised questions about Astwood's history and ethics: Was he a misunderstood man of virtue or a scoundrel? Did white American capitalists target the Black US consul, or was it the other way around? These questions mattered acutely to Astwood and his contemporaries. They persist over a century later.

Today, however, ongoing questions over Astwood's moral character matter less than what the debate itself reveals about the era's racialized moral politics. The dispute over Astwood's character indicates the web of US investors in the Dominican Republic who, by controlling the narrative regarding the ex-consul's morality, sought to protect their financial investments. These men—McKay, Wanamaker, Clyde, and a host of others—all supported Astwood at one time or another. Yet, over time, Astwood's inability to satisfy all such investors in Santo Domingo fomented conflict. For years, Astwood had built white Americans' confidence in his trustworthiness as he championed white property and life in the Dominican Republic. When a few investors discovered that the US consul was not as trustworthy as they had first believed, they balked at the notion that a Black man could turn the tables on white Americans with relative impunity. By doing so, Astwood exercised a privilege typically reserved for white elites: the ability to manipulate moral logic. In this way, he challenged white Americans' seemingly exclusive power to determine right and wrong. Protests against Astwood suggest that America's elite class heavily policed this privilege. Yet the many laudatory defenses of his character also indicate that when it came to preserving financial investments abroad, even verifiable facts regarding the ex-consul's duplicity were subject to debate.

This chapter explores Astwood's contested reputation in order to probe the contours of white moral exclusivity, defined here as elite whites' assumed power to decipher right and wrong, fact and fiction. Considering the contentious events surrounding Astwood's dismissal and reapplication to the State Department, it focuses especially on the years 1889–90 when Astwood galvanized prominent white American businessmen and African American journalists and clergy to lobby for his reappointment as US consul to Santo Domingo. By analyzing the moral logic of letters of recommendation filed with the State Department, the chapter also shows how Black men competed for consular positions on moral grounds. To this end, the chapter's last section compares Astwood's reputation to that of his colleagues Frederick Douglass and John Stephens Durham, who also gained federal positions abroad during this period. White capitalists and prominent African Americans judged Protestant Christian manliness as a sign of Black officers' ability to further US business interests abroad and vice versa. By adhering to or defying this image, Black agents like Astwood, Douglass, and Durham shaped white Americans' opinions regarding Black political capacity in the United States. As demonstrated in chapters 3 and 4, they also became complicit in white supremacist US empire-building.

This last chapter further explores African Americans' involvement in the construction of US empire by disentangling the logic of white moral exclusivity as a function of racial capitalist power. As private individuals and government officials attempted to establish the facts and judge Astwood's character, an exercise in moral exclusivity, they exposed the fault lines of America's hypocritical racist ideology. Fiction became fact, and fact was fiction as Americans' moralized conceptions of truth became a moving target paradoxically tied to white Americans' capitalist success abroad. Black officials who sought to control the narratives surrounding their own moral character found that the rules of the game were not universal.

Changing the Narrative: The Self-Righteous Defense of the Black US Consul

Due to the Columbus bones scheme (chapter 6), the State Department wanted Astwood gone, but Astwood's dismissal was not a simple matter. Despite public outcry over the scandal, he had technically committed no fault. Thus, back in July 1888 when the scandal first broke, state officials searched for evidence of other wrongdoing. They found their answer in the indemnity account of Cordelia Platt, whose husband the Dominican militia had accidentally killed back in 1885 (chapter 4). Astwood had not only successfully brokered the indemnity negotiations but had since regularly remitted hundreds of dollars to Cordelia—that is, until 1888. That year, Astwood's drafts signaled that he had misappropriated about $1,700 in funds.[6] Embezzlement was a clear violation of policy and necessitated removal. That was that.

However, the accusation of embezzlement also complicated matters for the State Department because it instigated Astwood's avid defense. Astwood emphatically refused Cleveland's terms of removal in order to keep up appearances.[7] Reputation mattered. Indeed, Astwood's reputation mattered so much in this moment that he, a lowly consular officer, defied a sitting US president. His choice revealed the extent to which compliance with rule of law and federal procedure remained of secondary, or even tertiary, import to people within Astwood's Gilded Age network. Moral character not only determined one's present worth and "future standing," as Astwood put it, but also could reinvent an individual's past, mitigating both accusations of disrepute and, to an extent, the social stigma of one's color.[8] Astwood understood this truism and thus determined that retention of his good name depended upon the retention of his office. For this reason, he ignored the December 20 executive order and employed every conceivable tactic to stall his dismissal.

From December 20, 1888, through March 11, 1889, there were two US representatives in Santo Domingo: the ousted Astwood, who refused to turn over the office, and the vice consul, Juan Antonio Read, whom the State Department recognized as the official interim US consul in the Dominican capital.[9] Dispatches from both men reveal Astwood's multifaceted delay strategy. When Read sought to take over the office, Astwood denied him.[10] When Read cabled the State Department reporting, "Astwood refuses to deliver," Astwood wrote to both Read and the US consular bureau that he would do so only upon taking a leave of absence according to the usual regulations.[11] Astwood additionally provided the State Department with a detailed explanation of the Platt case and a typed letter from the Dominican government attesting to his "good comportment" despite the Columbus bones controversy.[12] When Read subsequently insisted that Astwood comply with Cleveland's executive order, Astwood informed the State Department that Read "refused to accept the office" under his terms.[13] And when Read turned to both the Dominican government and press for aid, Astwood lashed out: "You seem to overestimate your position as a subordinate officer. . . . [Do] not be maddened by your ambition."[14] These tactics stalled Astwood's departure for nearly three months until communication from the US legation in Port-au-Prince reached the Dominican government and forced Astwood's hand. Astwood finally relinquished the consular office on March 11, 1889. By that time, however, a new US president, Benjamin Harrison, held office, and a careful campaign waged by Republican lobbyists raised the possibility of Astwood's reappointment to Santo Domingo.

The lobbyists wrote letters, dozens of them, recommending Astwood again for the Santo Domingo consular post. As an epistolary genre, letters of recommendation do not generally inspire scholarly interest. They are usually dull notes bearing little information, and may be as prosaic and abrupt as a single sentence stating the referee's high regard for the person in question. A few letters submitted for Astwood followed this format, but most did not. Astwood's multiple consular application files in the State Department archive are exceptionally large folders spanning the years 1882–1901 and contain not only the usual humdrum but also letters of protest, affidavits, and personal correspondence. These letters cast the genre of recommendations in a new light, especially when cross-referenced with Astwood's dispatches, Dominican court records, and the *Gaceta Oficial*, where the names of Astwood's capitalist referees often appeared. They demonstrate that white investors' judgment of Black officers' Christian morality was inherently tied to their capitalist success abroad, an association that made the facts of Astwood's embezzlement and contempt of office highly disputable points.

Take Astwood's fantastic reaction to Cleveland's executive order, for example. Was it insubordination or a righteous man's attempt to await vindication as his wealthy American friends sought to remedy the situation? The evidence points both ways. The documents clearly demonstrate that Astwood defied an executive order. However, he based his response on advice he received from his most powerful American business-sector friend, Nathaniel M. McKay.[15] In the days after Astwood received the executive order, McKay coached the consul's next steps. The Bostonian had met with Assistant Secretary of State George L. Rives about the matter. Based on this meeting, McKay advised Astwood to settle Mrs. Platt's claim as soon as possible. He counseled his friend that any explanation to Cleveland, a lame-duck president, would "be the same as writing a letter to a dying man."[16] McKay also divulged that Astwood had enemies at Port-au-Prince, and while McKay did not offer any names, he suggested that Astwood keep his own counsel and not publicize his intentions or actions. Last, McKay urged Astwood to obtain recommendation letters from President Heureaux and Dominican merchants, which McKay pledged to present to the incoming Republican administration. "Do not feel discouraged in the least about the dismissal," McKay reassured Astwood. "Your reputation will stand just as well in the eyes of a Republican administration as before." McKay knew that the US consul would need additional help in protecting his honor. "I will see myself that justice is done you," he promised.[17]

The campaign began slowly. McKay initially believed that his influence with Harrison would result in Astwood's speedy reinstatement. Not only did he cable Walker Blaine, the son of Secretary of State James G. Blaine, with the explicit request to "please have Astwood appointed Consul San Domingo today," but he also sent his Washington-based lawyer to the White House to follow up.[18] Letters to James Blaine also arrived via Connecticut, the headquarters of the Santo Domingo Electric Company and the Blackstone estate, whose owners had business interests in Santo Domingo and believed Astwood the only man "peculiarly fitted for the position."[19] Meanwhile, McKay footed the bill for the Platt indemnity.[20] The effort to amend his record, however, did not prevent Astwood's enemies from colluding against him. Even before Astwood turned over the office on March 11, Philadelphia millionaire John Wanamaker and steamship owner William P. Clyde agreed that they would not support his reappointment.[21] By the end of March 1889, McKay realized that the battle for his friend's reappointment needed more leverage than he could muster alone, and in mid-April he sent for Henry to return to the United States.[22]

With Astwood stationed in New York, McKay and other white businessmen worked quickly to secure his reappointment. The Louisiana Republican State Central committee endorsed Astwood, and McKay continued to write letters to the State Department on Astwood's behalf.[23] Letters of recommendation also arrived from allies in Connecticut, New York, and Boston who represented companies such as Paine's Furniture Company of Boston, the Board of Underwriters of New York, and the Remington Arms Company of New York.[24] In all, thirty-two recommendations filed between May and early October 1889 demonstrated the strength of Astwood's defense. In their letters, the business owners extolled Henry's virtues. Always implicitly and often explicitly, they linked Astwood's moral character to his ability to secure them financial wealth. When Astwood worked in favor of their interests, they opined that he was "a gentleman well suited to the place of United States consul."[25] One blunt statement summed up the consensus among Astwood's elite white supporters: "I am desirous of seeing a capable man in the position on account of my pecuniary interests in [Santo Domingo]."[26]

Meanwhile, Astwood waged his own campaign to improve his image by propagating his side of the story regarding the Columbus bones scandal, shoring up his image as a respectable Black man, and calling upon his white and Black friends to support him. In late June 1889, journalists found Astwood at New York's historic Hoffman House (figures 7.1, 7.2).[27] Astwood, always adjacent to white New York society, drew attention to himself one night by rehashing the story of his removal in his own terms. Although Astwood's version of the events—that the Columbus bones controversy had been set up by Heureaux's enemies—seemed "ludicrous" to the editors of New Orleans's *Daily Picayune*, who reprinted the story, the fact that Astwood spoke his mind at the Hoffman House signaled that he had convinced at least a few influential people.[28] To corroborate his story, Astwood even persuaded H. M. Linnell, the original author of the Columbus bones scheme, to write to President Harrison. "I would state that Mr. Astwood merely acted in this matter as an intermediary for me, a stranger," Linnell explained. Linnell further related his astonishment that politicians had used the scheme "to Mr. Astwood's prejudice" and admitted that he, Linnell, was "solely to blame for Mr. Astwood's connection in the matter."[29] Whether or not Linnell's sentiment was genuine or influenced Harrison at all is unknown, but the fact that this Connecticut investor confirmed Astwood's story at this crucial moment, when before he had remained silent, attests to Astwood's own ferocious attempt to protect his reputation and transform his image among America's white economic and political elite.

Part of Astwood's defense of his own reputation before white audiences involved his long-standing practice of discursively offering racist images of the island of Hispaniola to reinforce his own Black masculine respectability. At the Hoffman House, for example, Astwood differentiated between Hispaniola's two nations by describing Dominicans as "much more conservative" and "enlightened" than Haitians and portraying Haitians as inherently violent people.[30] In another speech before a Boston audience, Astwood rehearsed a biased rendition of Dominican history in which he claimed that the Dominican population consisted of "descendants of the Caribs and the Spaniards, making a race in appearance not unlike the Spaniards themselves."[31] This version of events erased the history of slavery, maroon societies, and Black solidarity on the island, and once again drew sharp divisions between Haitians and Dominicans. The two peoples, Henry maintained, "are distinct in every particular—in language, custom, and their general deportment. The Dominican is kind, hospitable, and *very attentive to strangers.*" These words purposefully linked the two populations' supposed moral propensity to their racial composition. Moreover, the original italicized words underscore the ways in which dominant US

HOFFMAN HOUSE.
(A FAVORITE FAMILY HOTEL.)

400 ROOMS, $2 PER DAY AND UPWARDS.

FIGURE 7.1. Drawing of Hoffman House. From Fontain, *Hoffman House*, n.p.

understandings of Christian morality recognized capitalist enterprise as an inherent virtue tied to race. "Kind" mestizo Dominicans welcomed foreign capital; "revolutionary" Black Haitians did not. Astwood knew that white Americans associated any challenge to the prevailing capitalist system with racial Blackness and immorality, and thus he deflected accusations of his own immorality by reiterating Euro-Dominicans' national narratives and fashioning himself as a champion of US foreign enterprise. By employing racist moral language to differentiate the Dominican Republic from Haiti in these terms, Astwood paved the way for future investment in Santo Domingo. At the same time, he built investors' confidence in his ability to protect their interests and thus reformed his own public image in the United States. In other words, in demonizing Haiti and whitening the Dominican Republic's public profile by portraying it as friendly to foreign capital, Astwood whitened himself and thus improved his image.

This strategy benefited Astwood even though his white supporters did not readily adopt his viewpoints about the island. Indeed, many of the merchants with whom Astwood associated did not differentiate between the

FIGURE 7.2. Drawing of Hoffman House barroom. Astwood may have defended his reputation here. From Fontain, *Hoffman House*, n.p.

two nations of Hispaniola. "It is a singular fact, but it is nevertheless true, that the majority of Americans regard San Domingo and the Republic of Hayti [*sic*] as one and the same country," asserted the *Boston Herald*.[32] In the minds of Astwood's white collaborators, Dominicans, like Haitians, had a penchant for revolution. Tellingly, one of Astwood's Connecticut backers employed common white American stereotypes about the Dominicans' supposed "inflammable and volatile character" and "revolutionary spirit" to describe the Santo Domingo consular office as "anything but a bed of roses."[33] Such letters intimated that the protection of American property depended upon Astwood's continuation in office.

In making this argument, white Americans in no way considered Astwood a social equal. For example, Boston-based lawyer Arthur P. Wilson, whom Astwood had helped gain a concession for a national bank in Santo Domingo, resorted to racial climate science to explain why Henry, a "colored man," was "better adapted to the climate" and thus the right man for the job.[34] Nevertheless, in their letters, white elites did tacitly avow a color hierarchy among Black people. With the same pen and paper, Wilson also listed Astwood's ability to speak Spanish, experience on the island, and "exemplary habits" as evidence of his fitness for the office. The collective emphasis on Astwood's abilities, a theme repeated across the epistolary archive, suggests that Astwood's subservience to white investors' pecuniary goals and verbal disassociation from Haiti defined his moral character in the eyes of his white American associates. Thus, Astwood's rhetoric tapped into a tacit racist principle: some Black people (and nations) were worth keeping around as long as they upheld white supremacist beliefs in their words and actions. Many African Americans rejected this peculiar form of white supremacist performance, an escape valve that remained wholly unavailable to the darkest and poorest class of Blacks. Yet for a few educated individuals of mixed heritage the performance of cultural whiteness became yet another way to survive, if not fight, a racial capitalistic system perpetually stacked against them.

Despite Astwood's denigration of Haiti (a pattern repeated throughout his consular career), he maintained close friendships with influential African Americans who saw both nations of Hispaniola—but especially Haiti—as symbols of Black self-determination. Astwood also defended his honor before these men, and while his racist preference for the Dominican Republic did not differ substantially among his Black friends, their reception of him did. Unlike northeastern white capitalists, African Americans' motivations for standing by Astwood were based on their commitment to racial equality, not their pecuniary interests. Race leaders in the United States regarded Astwood as an equal and saw his removal from office as part of a broader effort to rid the US government of Black representatives. They defended Astwood because they saw accusations against him as racist slander against Black people collectively. Thus, while the white press mocked Astwood's speeches to white audiences, the Black press praised his oratorical ability, and Black churches invited him to speak at various venues.[35] In sermons such as "Christianity against Infidelity" and "The Great Physician," Astwood probably drew from his experiences of living in a Catholic country and suffering multiple health challenges while acting as US consul.[36] These speeches reinforced the notion that Astwood was a righteous man. Thus his Black peers believed in his innocence and sprang to his defense.

Astwood's most vocal Black supporters included Timothy T. Fortune and Jerome Peterson of the *New York Age* as well as several leaders of the African Methodist Episcopal (AME) Church. In the *Age*, editors Fortune and Peterson candidly affirmed his main line of defense. "The spite against Mr. Astwood now existing appears to arise from the failure of certain parties to get the Consul's support and assistance to obtain concessions and privileges from the Dominicans," they explained.[37] Reiterating Astwood's arguments regarding Columbus's remains and the Platt affair, they criticized mainstream newspapers for spreading misinformation. If his enemies had won concessions from the Dominican government, or if Astwood had been a white man, he would not face the same accusations or be subject to the same intense scrutiny. Letters of recommendation from the editors and AME leaders similarly defended Astwood against "trumped up charges" and highlighted his merits, particularly the fact that he had established "the only Protestant Church" in Santo Domingo.[38] By emphasizing Astwood's missionary work, they affirmed that Astwood formed part of a Black elite class that, in their minds, stood as moral examples for African Americans in the United States and African descendants abroad. The long history of Black preachers' involvement in Republican Party politics (chapter 2) lent weight to their claims. Thus, mentioning Astwood's missionary work was also a rhetorical strategy through which African Americans wrote in terms that white politicians recognized. Honorable Black men such as Astwood spoke for "thousands" of African Americans and represented "a large class of people" whose vote they presumably controlled for or against the Republican ticket.[39]

If Black newspaper editors and ministers had their own doubts about Astwood over the summer of 1889, they did not express them in that moment. The AME Church and the *New York Age* continued to support Henry Astwood even after he returned to the United States for good in 1892. Yet the same could not be said of Astwood's white supporters, whose regard wavered throughout those years. Although Astwood consistently aligned himself with white American investors and merchants in their petitions for concessions and lawsuits against the Dominican government, he could not guarantee everyone a profit. His actions generated additional controversy among investors when he seemed to personally benefit from their losses. Astwood's apparent success at the expense of a few white investors did not sit well with those who believed that the color of their skin ensured them a social privilege above people of African descent. Throughout his tenure and especially during the summer of 1889, a handful of individuals protested the Black consul's appointment and critiqued his actions. Their objections provide a clear picture of the moral fault lines of racial capitalist hierarchy.

Protesting Astwood: Political Intrigue and
Moral Logic in Letters of Dissent

Over the summer of 1889, three American entities—the houses of William P. Clyde, John Wanamaker, and Winthrop Cunningham—claimed that Henry Astwood had abused his power as US consul in Santo Domingo. The six letters that these men and their associates sent to President Harrison and Secretary of State Blaine between April and early October 1889 paled in numerical comparison to the thirty-two letters of recommendation sent during the same period. Yet what they lacked in volume, they made up for in both political influence and expressions of rage. Like Astwood's backers, his accusers based their assessment of him on his economic value. They also discursively linked this value to Astwood's moral character. Unlike the recommendation writers, however, the protesters claimed that Astwood had embezzled thousands of dollars from US businesses, and they provided legal and financial records as evidence.

At first glance, the allegation of corruption within the context of Gilded Age politics hardly seems remarkable. This was an era of widespread business fraud, after all.[40] Moreover, due to the era's frequent boom-bust cycles, Americans often framed business success or failure in highly moralized terms.[41] Nevertheless, considering the allegations within the Dominican context has implications for both Dominican and US international politics. On the one hand, it reveals the convoluted ways that Astwood, American capitalists, elite Dominicans, and Heureaux sought to obtain and control money flowing through the Dominican customhouses, particularly capital from the sugar industry. On the other hand, it demonstrates how such political struggles over the Dominican economy guided international politics and reduced discussions regarding Black foreign service agents to a fight between good and evil. Both of these processes, in turn, push scholars to read between the lines of historical documentation to analyze the fight for historical interpretation.

For example, while the charges against Astwood elucidate a complicated web of business and political relations on the island, reconstructing this network and tracing the exact channels through which money flowed within it proves nearly impossible given that recordkeeping ran counter to the secretive nature of backroom dealing. Consequently, speculations of political conspiracy cannot be verified easily, but historians should embrace the likelihood of such nefarious schemes. Such intrigue not only accurately reflects the range of possibilities available to individuals within Astwood's professional circles but also correctly describes the perceptions that people outside of these networks generated for themselves. As in the Gilded Age United States, political conspiracy in Santo Domingo existed both as rumor and assumed reality.[42] The ever-present possibility of corruption meant that the actual facts of an event mattered less than public perception. More than a coherent rendering of historical events, then, the documentation shows that even verifiable corruption on all sides was less important than the stories people told to defend an individual's moral character. Thus, reading the archival record to both speculate about conspiracy and tease apart moral logic provides a clear picture of how competition for economic and political control in Santo Domingo and in the international sphere was ultimately a struggle over the power to determine right from wrong, fact from fiction.

A closer look at Clyde's and Wanamaker's backgrounds, Astwood's involvement with Dominican politics and the sugar industry, and Cunningham's investments in two sugar plantations in 1886 and 1887 sheds light on these dynamics. The various events recounted below not only reveal multiple sites of corruption and possible conspiracy but also demonstrate that the power to determine facts was a struggle for the moral upper hand. Of the three men, William P. Clyde had the longest tie to the island of Hispaniola. Born on November 11, 1839, Clyde grew up working in his father's steamship company, where he distinguished himself in business. In 1878, he opened his own line of steamers, Clyde's Coastwise and West India Steam Lines, which connected eastern US ports to the Caribbean (figure 7.3). For the next two decades, Clyde's line was the only passenger route that linked Santo Domingo to New York.[43] Given Clyde's monopoly over American passenger and freight transport to the island, his and Astwood's social worlds intertwined, although how exactly the two men came to know each other is uncertain. It is certain, however, that Astwood first arrived in Santo Domingo aboard the ss *Geo W. Clyde* in 1882, and he necessarily traveled aboard Clyde's ships even after his removal from office. Furthermore, as consul, Astwood came into frequent contact with Clyde's steamship captains and agents, who in 1883 recoiled at Henry's close adherence to consular rules regarding the clearing of US ships harbored in Dominican waters.[44] Adjustments were made in those early years. In Astwood's words, he successfully convinced Clyde's agents that "the right way is the best way to do business," and the relationship between the men ran more or less smoothly until the last year of Astwood's tenure.[45]

FIGURE 7.3. "Clyde's Steamship Pier, at Foot of Roosevelt Street, New York." From King, *King's Handbook*, 94.

A similar story could be told of John Wanamaker, whose financial dealings in the Dominican Republic have not featured in his biographies. Wanamaker is best remembered as the founder of the United States' first department store, John Wanamaker and Co., which brought various specialty shops under one roof in Philadelphia. His philanthropic work as a religious so-cial reformer has received less attention among scholars, but as Nicole C. Kirk has argued, reflected an ideological fusion of Christianity with capi-talism.[46] As a businessman, Wanamaker believed that seeking money was an honorable pursuit and that one's good character begat wealth. His life served as an example. Born to a religious family of brickmakers in south Philadelphia on July 11, 1838, John began working at age fourteen as an er-rand boy for a local bookstore while simultaneously leading a local Sunday school. He used his knack for business to enhance his religious work and soon became the first paid secretary of the Young Men's Christian Asso-ciation. In 1861, John established a clothing firm with his friend Nathan Brown. This first foray into business, coupled with Wanamaker's religious convictions, led to the establishment of John Wanamaker and Co. in 1875 and inspired his work as a moral reformer. Wanamaker's entrepreneurial success also generated political opportunities. In 1889, due to Wanamaker's

FIGURE 7.4. US postmaster general John Wanamaker. "John Wanamaker 1838–1922, three quarter length portrait, seated, at desk facing right, ca. 1890." Photo: Frances Benjamin Johnston, photographer, Library of Congress, https://www.loc.gov/item/2001703936/.

financial contributions to the presidential campaign, Harrison appointed him as postmaster general (figure 7.4).[47] This role put Wanamaker in a prime position to enforce the Comstock Act (1873), which prohibited the dissemination of birth control through the mail and made Wanamaker a powerful arbiter of all things obscene and immoral as well as a symbol of "holier-than-thou-hypocrisy" and a target for caricaturists (figure 7.5).[48]

Wanamaker moved to Washington, DC, just as Astwood began the fight to save his reputation. In 1889, the two upstarts faced each other as enemies, but this was a new standing in a peripheral relationship that had spanned years. Wanamaker first appeared in Astwood's dispatches on November 22, 1883, when Astwood reported that he had secured Wanamaker a contract in which the latter would supply the Dominican government with all military clothing and accoutrements for two years and ten months. Astwood

THE TWO WANAMAKERS.

SMART JOHN *to* PIOUS JOHN.— I guess you 'll have to look a little extra holy, John, till this Philadelphia trouble blows over !

FIGURE 7.5. Caricature depicting Wanamaker as both "Smart John," a political and business schemer, and "Pious John," a righteous Sunday school teacher. From C. J. Taylor, "The Two Wanamakers," *Puck Weekly*, June 7, 1891.

valued the deal at $50,000 per year.[49] By December of the same year, the Dominican government had nominated Wanamaker's son Thomas to act as its consul in Philadelphia.[50] Three years later, Astwood requested quotes from the house of Wanamaker to furnish the Santo Domingo consular office.[51] The same year, 1886, Astwood began collecting and remitting Dominican customs revenue due to Wanamaker for the military uniforms.[52] Although Wanamaker and Astwood had not met in person, the Philadelphia tycoon knew of the Black US consul through his agent Robert C. Ogden and approved of his work. In April 1886, Wanamaker and Ogden met to discuss Astwood's exemplary consular activity, and the pair subsequently endorsed him for reappointment under President Cleveland's administration.[53] Wanamaker's opinion of Astwood would soon change, but back then he emphatically supported the Black consul.

Winthrop Cunningham's relationship with Astwood began in July of the same year, 1886, but unlike Astwood's partnerships with Clyde and Wanamaker, that with Winthrop Cunningham and Sons soured quickly. Little is known about Cunningham and his New York law firm, which did not gain the fame of Clyde's and Wanamaker's enterprises, but a twenty-three-page affidavit produced by Cunningham's agent Thomas E. Huffington had decided influence over Astwood's fate in 1889. The testimony described Astwood's involvement in the Cunninghams' business affairs in 1886–87 and related various instances of fraud. Astwood, predictably, countered Huffington's testimony with his own version of events. Neither man's interpretation provided an objective record, but probing the two sides of the story reveals how Cunningham, Clyde, and Wanamaker all became embroiled in local political intrigue in Santo Domingo that involved not only the US consular office and its agencies but also powerful sugar industry bosses and the Dominican presidential hopeful, Ulises Heureaux, in 1886.

That year, 1886, at first seemed like it would be a banner year for US Consul Astwood. Since July 1885, he had worked seemingly around the clock to push through the Platt claim. His efforts involved not only compelling Dominican officials to pay a hefty indemnity to Cordelia Platt but also convincing the US State Department that the Dominican government's killing of an unimportant white American citizen warranted diplomatic intervention—and that Astwood, rather than the US minister to Haiti, should lead the negotiations (see chapter 4). Ultimately, the US State Department approved both Astwood's actions and the $33,000 indemnity for Cordelia Platt. The resolution came late in December 1885 and surely pleased no Dominican but was a decided victory for Astwood, who gained support among Americans in Santo Domingo.[54] Between November 1885 and April 1886, over a dozen American capitalists requested that the State Department retain Astwood in office. Clyde sent two letters commending Astwood's "diligence" and describing him as "the most energetic and efficient representative of American interest that has occupied that position within our knowledge or experience extending over some fifteen years."[55] Wanamaker expressed a "conviction that [Astwood's] experience and energy are needed by American interests in Santo Domingo."[56] Other letters hailed from the likes of Horatio Collins King, newspaper editor, lawyer, and judge advocate general of New York; the Board of Underwriters of New York; and the US-owned Stella Sugar plantation.[57] Protest against Astwood during this time emanated solely from Louisiana Democrats whose natural hostility toward Astwood had redoubled when the US consul stumped for Republican Louisiana Governor William Pitt Kellogg during the fall of 1884.[58] Yet, despite the Southerners' opposition, Assistant Secretary of State James Davis Porter was pleased with Astwood and retained him in office.[59] Astwood, who was on leave in the United States from mid-February to early May 1886, returned to Santo Domingo on May 22, secure in his position.

Signs of trouble, however, manifested that summer in a dispute between Astwood and the powerful Dominican sugar cartel. This conflict indirectly kindled the feud between Astwood and Cunningham's agent later in the year. Astwood's conflict with the sugar industry began when, in early June 1886, the Italian Dominican Cambiaso Hermanos company gained a copy of a US consular dispatch dated July 23, 1885, in which Astwood accused Cambiaso Hermanos of export fraud.[60] The Cambiaso brothers, Juan and Luís, were influential merchants and politicians in Santo Domingo, and at the time Juan was serving as the Italian consul to the Dominican Republic.[61] Any suspicion of fraud put not only their business but also Italy's interests at risk. In a threatening letter to the US consul written on June 9, 1886, Juan and Luís demanded that Astwood corroborate his claims, but Astwood refused. The accusations, Astwood asserted, were made under the private seal of the United States, and the Cambiasos had no right to the information. The matter dropped, but for Astwood a pertinent question remained: Who had released the dispatch to the Cambiasos?[62] It was clear that someone had spied on the US consulate, and such espionage had made Astwood an enemy of one of the Dominican Republic's most influential merchant families.

Here is a speculative theory regarding the leaked document. In June 1886, political intrigue plagued Santo Domingo as Heureaux ran for a second presidential term. As during the election of 1884, the heated political race stirred rumors of fraud. This time, however, the rumors also implicated the US consulate. It was no secret that Astwood wished to see Heureaux and his party remain in office.[63] As a foreign consular officer, however, Astwood was not supposed to show bias in Dominican elections. Friends of the opposition candidate, Casimiro N. de Moya, claimed that Astwood was actively using his influence to sway the election in Heureaux's favor.[64] Astwood summarily dismissed de Moya's allegations. Although Astwood sometimes involved himself in Dominican politics, in this case it seems unlikely that he directly interfered in Dominican elections, but indirect meddling also seems plausible. For one, it is possible that Astwood's accusations against the Cambiasos back in 1885 served a political purpose. The Cambiasos counted among the Dominican government's domestic creditors.[65] If the family failed to extend credit to the government, the administration could crack down on export fraud that it would otherwise overlook. This begs the question: Did Astwood ever work with the Dominican executive branch to raise revenue by squashing export fraud? If so, did his involvement prompt Heureaux's enemies in 1886 to spy on the US consulate? Perhaps the leaked document originated with the de Moya campaign. Such backhanded dealing and espionage were common, as was unofficial state-sanctioned violent retaliation. Juan Cambiaso's sudden death a month after demanding Astwood's recantation and weeks before the election raises additional suspicions of foul play.[66] Once again, the historical record leaves more questions than answers.

This speculative approach to the archival record, like the historical context regarding the Cambiaso dispute and the 1886 election, is important to understanding Cunningham's protest against Astwood in 1889. Days after Juan Cambiaso left the physical world behind in July 1886, Cunningham's lawyer Thomas E. Huffington arrived in Santo Domingo.[67] Huffington would become Astwood's most ardent detractor within the year, but neither man knew this at the time. Two opposing records describe their relationship.

According to Huffington's affidavit, he traveled to Santo Domingo in 1886 to secure the transfer of mortgages on Cunningham's investment properties, the sugar plantations Dolores and La Caridad. Huffington carried with him a letter of introduction from Wanamaker to Astwood, who assured him that the two estates were valued at $200,000 and $300,000 respectively. Duly convinced, Huffington contracted the renowned Dominican lawyer and former minister of the interior and police Apolinar de Castro, paid $1,040 for the property transfers, and gave Astwood $25 for his services.[68] He then left the city eight days later, trusting that his employer's affairs were in good hands.[69]

This trust was soon broken. After a few months of silence, in September 1886 Huffington suddenly received letters from Astwood describing lawsuits against the plantations. The Cunninghams instructed Apolinar de Castro via Astwood to do whatever was possible to secure their interests, and Astwood drew drafts on the company's account amounting to $719.58 in Mexican silver to keep lawyer de Castro on retainer. When Huffington returned to Santo Domingo in October 1886, the drafts seemed to add up, more or less, but Astwood's constant demands for more money raised suspicions. Further investigation revealed that the lawsuits were fictitious. Then, in December, La Caridad was sold in a foreclosure that Huffington knew nothing about. Huffington charged Astwood with trying to sell the Dolores estate in a similar scheme.[70] These transgressions exposed other offenses: petty fraud, extortion, blackmail, and embezzlement. Unknown to Huffington at the time, careful comparison of the Cunninghams' accounts with Astwood's consular dispatches demonstrates that the New York firm had actually paid the Platt indemnity on one occasion.[71] In another instance, Astwood blackmailed Huffington for $200, but Huffington refused to pay. Finally, on January 14, 1887, Huffington confronted Astwood at the US consulate about the fraud. The stormy meeting yielded no results, and the New York lawyer immediately cut ties with Astwood and began to plot his revenge.[72]

A cabal formed. Or at least it seemed that way to Astwood, who argued that Americans involved in the Dominican sugar trade had plotted to drive him out of office. From Astwood's viewpoint, the dispute also began with Huffington's arrival back in 1886. In fact, he claimed to have met Huffington, just as Huffington described. Henry, however, asserted that the brokers for La Caridad and Dolores, J. de Rivera and Co., had swindled Cunningham and Sons from the beginning. According to Astwood, the Cunninghams and the sugar planter Alexander Bass had combined their resources to buy La Caridad's mortgage from the bankrupt J. de Rivera and Co. After the deal, the Americans neglected to register the sale with the proper notary, but the Cunningham's lawyer de Castro rectified the mistake by inscribing the mortgage transfer amount of $25,000 in the books. Huffington returned to New York satisfied. Months later, Bass entered a foreclosure on the property. The lawyer sued to protect Cunningham's interest. Then the property manager, the Cuban emigrant Evaristo Lamar, alarmed by Astwood's influence with the notary public and local judge, sought to compromise with de Castro. Lamar's compromise would secure Winthrop Cunningham and Sons' investment by giving the company control over La Caridad's entire sugar crop minus a small commission. According to Astwood, with this compromise in place, Huffington attempted to bribe him to allow export fraud; Huffington would enter a reduced amount of sugar exported at the customhouse and would not give the Dominican government access to his invoices. This scheme mimicked the pattern of irregular export reporting by foreign sugar investors and was just the sort of fraud that Astwood had charged the Italian Dominican Cambiaso brothers with.[73] Astwood refused, and Huffington retaliated by mobilizing a handful of Americans involved in the Dominican sugar industry to petition for Astwood's removal.[74]

Clearly, the events of late 1886–87 varied depending on who related them, Huffington or Astwood. The method of placing blame, however, did not. Both the Cunninghams' agent and the US consul defended their respective positions on moral grounds. In his battle against the US consul, Huffington enlisted James W. Mellor and John Hardy, both sugar planters and US consular agents at San Pedro de Macorís and Azua respectively, and claimed that they represented all Americans in Santo Domingo. Between them, these three men judged Astwood's fitness for office based on both his record of defending the sugar industry's capital and his religious and personal life. For example, Huffington claimed that he had placed his confidence in Astwood upon learning that "he was an ordained Minister of the Gospel and was conducting a Colored Methodist Church in the city."[75] Mellor asserted that Astwood had made business difficult for Americans, and Hardy described the "accusations of a very grave character respecting [his] Family relations" as a "principal cause of the estrangement" with the American community.[76] Of course, there were other issues at stake. Huffington's charges are detailed above. Mellor and Hardy additionally blamed Astwood for not protesting the Dominican government's export tax increase on sugar and not advocating for American planters, whom Dominican officials taxed more than other foreigners.[77] It is also likely that neither man appreciated their subordination to a Black officer. Yet, by employing dichotomous moral discourse that centered on Astwood's family and ministerial work, Huffington and the US agents sought to control the narrative regarding Astwood's character and thus direct the future of the US consular office in Santo Domingo and American enterprise on the island more generally.

Astwood used the same discursive tactic against his adversaries; he charged them with immorality both commercial and personal in nature. According to Astwood, Huffington was "one of that class of pretentious Americans who come down here and officiously tries to injure everyone."[78] Cunningham's lawyer had never paid Astwood for his services and instead sought to remove him from office, all while causing panic in Santo Domingo by selling $50,000 of worthless drafts. Hardy, he asserted, was "personally hostile to myself . . . because he imagines that I am responsible for the export duty."[79] The accusations against Mellor and others were more grave. Mellor had murdered a Dominican man and aided revolutionaries against the Azul government. Former US vice consul John W. Farrand, who had signed the petition along with Mellor and Hardy, was a drunkard and a fornicator. And Alexander Bass, the US sugar plantation owner who had foreclosed on La Caridad, was a "brutal and bad man."[80] Bass, according to Astwood, had his servants, merchants, and business partners testify to their illicit sexual relations with his wife in order to secure a divorce.

In making these allegations, Astwood emphasized the "qualities of strength, aggression, and even violence" that historian Amy Greenberg has associated with white American "martial men," who employed violence as part of their exploitation of Latin America.[81] He additionally pointed out the racial bias involved in accusations against him. As Henry described, one Cuban planter who had colluded with Huffington and Bass condemned the US government for appointing a Black man as consul, and yet could "be found with the lowest, the worst and the most debauched negroes in the cock-pit on every occasion."[82] Astwood's own use of this racist US stereotype of Latin American men in his denouncement of the Cuban planter served to emphasized his own moral standing and "restrained manhood," and thus carried no hint of irony.[83] Restrained men, as Greenberg writes, "grounded their identities in their families, in evangelical practice of their Protestant faith, and in success in the business world."[84] Astwood stressed his adherence to this description. In his words: "I do not drink or gamble. . . . My immorality in San Domingo consists of my exclusive habits from intercourse with these [martial] men."[85]

Henry's allegations did not go without marks of truth. Planters' avarice fueled the exploitative labor practices and customary tax evasion characteristic of the era's sugar industry. Furthermore, historians have remembered at least one of Astwood's sugar industry enemies in 1886, Alexander Bass, as a political suborner and meddler in Dominican affairs.[86] The fact that little information regarding the other named planters exists does not indicate their innocence. As Astwood explained to the US State Department, the planter class expected him to act as "a policeman, the jurors, the judge and finally to declare war against [the Dominican] Government for the most trifling offense."[87] But he could do only so much. Astwood claimed he did everything in his power to protect American interests but could not "legislate for the Dominican Government." Nor could he "protect these parties in their fraudulent transactions." It was the sugar planters, not Astwood, who perpetually attempted to usurp the Dominican authorities and committed a host of sins against God and humanity, he charged.

Recommendation letters corroborated Astwood's claims to restrained manhood in 1887, as various individuals defended him against the sugar cartel. At this time, Astwood's white American supporters included associates of William P. Clyde and John Wanamaker; Samuel F. Purington, a submarine contractor in Santo Domingo; members of the Santo Domingo Electric Company; and many others for whom Astwood had secured Dominican concessions.[88] Nearly all referees portrayed Astwood as a religious man. James Grant, Wanamaker's representative, found Astwood's home to be "hospitable and Christian." For evidence, he offered some insight on Astwood's leadership within the Protestant church.[89] In the fall of 1886, Astwood had repeated a sermon series for Dominicans about marriage by the famed Presbyterian Brooklyn orator Dr. Thomas De Witt Talmage.[90] Grant's report on Astwood not only engaged imperial discourse by elevating white American Protestantism (i.e., Talmage's words in Astwood's mouth) over alleged Dominican sexual deviance but also served as a direct counterexample to the sugar planters' sexual misconduct that Astwood exposed. Purington, for example, felt ashamed that such "disreputable and designing men, some of whom are now openly living with women whom they are not married to," would claim to speak for him and other Americans in Santo Domingo, and called them "defamers of a good official like H. C. C. Astwood."[91] Tellingly, even Nathan Cunningham of Winthrop Cunningham and Sons sided with Astwood and withdrew Huffington's charges that year, although Huffington later argued that he was coerced to do so.[92] In any case, together these positive recommendations with their defense of Astwood's morality—his Protestant Christian leadership and his policing of deviant sexuality and commercial fraud—warranted Astwood's retention in 1887. The same tactics prevailed among Astwood's supporters two years later. "I think the trouble is he is too honest, hence the complaint," concluded E. R. Thompson, the Norwich bank president who continued to defend Astwood in 1889.[93]

Yet, while Thompson and other investors like him remained loyal to Astwood, by 1889 some of Astwood's most earnest advocates, including Wanamaker and Clyde, had turned their backs on him and joined Huffington's side. Why? What happened between 1887 and 1889 to change their minds? At first glance, the short answer is money—or rather, the loss thereof.

A confluence of events between 1887 and 1889 suggests that Astwood truly did embezzle large sums of cash due to Wanamaker and others. As already stated, Astwood had begun collecting Dominican export duties for payment to Wanamaker in 1886.[94] This further enraged the sugar planters who believed that if Astwood had not advocated on Wanamaker's behalf, export taxes on sugar would have been abolished instead of raised.[95] At the same time, Astwood's financial situation in Santo Domingo in 1887–88 came under threat. Besides Huffington's efforts to oust him, a Dominican landowner sued Astwood for payment in a property dispute.[96] Next, the Columbus bones story broke in New York, and Astwood faced additional costs in defending himself against the Dominican and American media. According to Vice Consul Read, Astwood became "extremely embarrassed financially" in 1888, and he began to embezzle and send worthless drafts to parties such as Cordelia Platt to make up the difference.[97] Astwood also tried to make money elsewhere. Besides repeatedly petitioning the US State Department to raise his salary, in 1888 he reportedly invested over $5,000 of his own money to protect a Dominican concession for a railroad granted to an American.[98] No one could say where this money came from. Wanamaker and Ogden, however, later accused Astwood of absconding with over $10,000 worth of Dominican export duties collected on Wanamaker's behalf.[99] Thus, the US postmaster general joined Huffington and the sugar planters in their protest campaign.

Clyde's reversal similarly involved a botched financial deal. Or at least that's the way that Astwood and others relayed the events in letters to the US State Department. Like other such letters, Astwood's side of the story does more to reveal local and international power structures than to clarify verifiable facts. According to Astwood, Clyde's contract with the Dominican government for his steamship monopoly ended sometime in 1887–88. Astwood informed Clyde that he could guarantee renewal via his relationship with Heureaux, but Clyde chose to pursue the contract renewal using the Dutch consul and a Spanish merchant as representatives. The Dominican Congress subsequently rejected Clyde's contract, and he consequently became resentful of Astwood. Such animosity, in Astwood's opinion, was unwarranted. "I had no power to prevent him from placing his matters in the hands of parties who had not sufficient influence to insure him success," he asserted.[100] Astwood again employed moral discourse to explain the situation. Clyde, a "good Republican" in Astwood's estimation, had been led astray by his Democrat captains and pursers who wished to see a "white man who can drink and gamble" in the office of US consul. This was a reasonable explanation, but so too was the possibility that Astwood had colluded with Heureaux to ensure that Clyde's petition failed once it was out of his hands. The archival record is silent.

In any case, as the analysis above has made clear, the issue with Astwood for Clyde, Wanamaker, Cunningham, and the sugar planters in Santo Domingo was not just the money he presumably stole. Their allegations reveal that the struggle for commercial and political power in Santo Domingo was reduced to a fight for the moral upper hand. Further reflections on the island's geopolitical context demonstrate how this case reflected white Americans' larger concerns over the appointment of US Black foreign service agents and the defense of white moral exclusivity.

Standing at the Crossroads: Recommendation and Protest as White Moral Exclusivity

Between 1888 and 1891, US diplomatic relations with the island of Hispaniola centered on Haiti as the United States attempted to negotiate possession of Môle Saint-Nicolas, where the United States hoped to establish a naval base. President Harrison appointed the most famous African American of the time, Frederick Douglass, as US minister to Haiti to lead the negotiations. Haiti welcomed Douglass but readily defended its national sovereignty against US pressure for the *môle*. Meanwhile, Clyde, who had also pressed Haiti for both the *môle* and a monopoly over the island's shipping industry, opposed Douglass's appointment because he believed that Douglass would thwart his profit-making scheme. Unabashedly, Clyde meddled in US politics and Haitian domestic affairs to realize his goals. These events, as recounted in the historiography of the period, had nothing to do with the Dominican Republic, Astwood, or others.[101]

Nevertheless, both the United States' plans and Clyde's ambitions during these years comprehensively involved the whole island. The United States' interest in a naval base shifted (back) to Samaná Bay when it could not obtain the Haitian port, and the Dominican sugar sector's growth meant that a monopoly over the island's US steamship routes promised huge returns for Clyde. Thus, Clyde partnered with Wanamaker to oust Astwood from office, and together they lobbied to have his post filled with their choice candidate: John Stephens Durham.

Clyde and Wanamaker's behind-the-scenes lobbying sheds further light on events in Haiti. Most immediately, it places controversy over Douglass's handling of the Môle Saint-Nicolas discussions in the broader historical context of US-Hispaniola relations. It also further demonstrates that US white society judged Black officers' perceived ability to further US commercial interests abroad as a sign of their morality and vice versa. This exercise in white moral exclusivity not only made Black men dependent upon recommendation letters but also sought to control narratives regarding both Black people's political capacity and history itself. A closer look at recommendations for the man who superseded Astwood (Durham) and controversy over the elderly sage who despised him (Douglass) demonstrates how judgments regarding Black officials' character not only reflected white Americans' financial and imperial interests but also became a battle over the power to determine fact and fiction. This moralized and racialized battle for interpretive power would impact the whole island's fate well beyond 1889.

Comparison of Astwood's, Douglass's, and Durham's experiences requires a brief account of events in Haiti. While Astwood was battling Dominican and New York newspapers in 1888, Haiti became engulfed in civil war. In August that year, President Louis Félicité Salomon resigned amid revolutionary fighting. Two sides in the war then claimed the presidency. General François Denys Légitime in Port-au-Prince represented the southern faction and the most likely candidate. However, his opponent, Louis Mondestin Florvil Hyppolite, controlled Haiti's northern coast, including the important ports of Cap-Haïtien and Môle Saint-Nicolas. It seemed at first that Légitime would win the war since his side had better supplies and had gained recognition from France, Great Britain, and Italy. However, Hyppolite quickly obtained aid from Clyde, who sent arms to his troops in early 1889 in exchange for a future concession for a shipping monopoly over seven Haitian ports and their surrounding lands. The steamship owner also lobbied for US support of the Haitian general. According to Clyde, he convinced President Cleveland to exchange US military aid to Hyppolite for postwar US use of Môle Saint-Nicolas. Reinforced by Clyde and the US Navy, Hyppolite defeated Légitime within months. The civil war ended in August 1889. Hyppolite became president, and the United States and Clyde looked to Haiti to fulfill the new president's old promises.[102]

Yet by late 1889 Clyde had encountered a new kink in his plan. Despite the fact that Clyde, Secretary of State Blaine, and the New York press had lobbied against Douglass's appointment to Haiti, President Harrison had sustained him in the role.[103] Harrison's decision on Douglass motivated Clyde to be all the more forceful in his demands for the Dominican consular post; if he could not win in Port-au-Prince, he would seek to prevail in Santo Domingo.

In his endeavor to prevent Astwood's reappointment, Clyde found a close ally in John Wanamaker. The pair took a two-pronged approach. For his part, Clyde worked his network. He persuaded to his side the submarine contractor Purington and Thomas Collier Platt, the owner of the United States Express Company and political boss of the Republican Party (no relation to John J. Platt).[104] Both men wrote to the White House to protest Astwood's appointment. In a candid letter to Harrison regarding

Astwood's "bad character," Clyde did as well, swearing to "furnish the protest of every American House doing business with Santo Domingo against this appointment."[105] Wanamaker and his associate Ogden likewise attacked Astwood's character and vehemently protested his reappointment in letters to the State Department. Their tactics, however, centered mostly on lobbying for Durham to replace Astwood.

As a candidate for office, Durham had much to offer to northeastern progressive elites like Clyde and Wanamaker. Born in Philadelphia on September 3, 1861, Durham overcame racial and class barriers to distinguish himself in education, first at the common schools of Philadelphia, then at the Institute for Colored Youth, and last at the University of Pennsylvania. He obtained a bachelor of science degree from the university in 1886 and a graduate degree in civil engineering in 1888. While studying, Durham worked in journalism. He edited the *University Journal*, reported for the *Philadelphia Times*, and became the assistant editor of the *Evening Bulletin*, Philadelphia's most popular Republican daily. He occasionally also wrote for the *New York Age*. This work, Durham's near-white complexion, his physical fitness (he played university football), and his knowledge of foreign languages made Durham a favorite among Philadelphia's white leaders, who recommended him first for the position of undersecretary of the legation at London and then later for the Santo Domingo consulate.[106] Thus, long before gaining Wanamaker's approval, Durham already had the support of influential Philadelphians, including the University of Pennsylvania's provost William Pepper, mayor of Philadelphia Edwin H. Fitler, superintendent of public schools James McAllister, and a half dozen other white men.[107] These connections made Durham an attractive choice to Wanamaker, who received a personal letter of recommendation for Durham from Mayor Fitler.[108]

With multiple letters from Philadelphia's elite men, the dots connected quickly for Durham. Ogden sent him to meet with Clyde's brother in Philadelphia, who forwarded a laudatory report to Clyde in New York. Pleased with his brother's assessment, Clyde wrote to Ogden, "we shall be very glad to co-operate with you to the utmost in securing his appointment as Consul to Santo Domingo."[109] Wanamaker forwarded this letter to Blaine along with his own recommendation so that the secretary of state would understand that both the postmaster general and Clyde supported Durham over Astwood.[110] Clyde also sent his own referral to Blaine.[111] Clearly, as with Astwood, Durham's case evidenced the network of elite white men who determined the fate of Black foreign service candidates behind the scenes.

Recommendation letters for Durham also followed the same pattern as those for Astwood; his supporters listed both his professional qualifications and his morality as signs of his fitness for office. For example, Mayor Fitler and Superintendent McAllister wrote of Durham's "traits of mind and character," such as his social work among African Americans, educational and professional success, and "high order of literary ability."[112] Other letter writers mentioned Durham's bilingualism (English and French) and predicted, correctly, that he would learn Spanish quickly.[113] Still others described Durham as "a gentleman of character, cultivation and dignity" and "a man of the highest moral character."[114] Durham's intellectual abilities and perceived morality, in the eyes of Philadelphia's elite, made him "eminently" and "peculiarly fitted" for the Santo Domingo consulship.[115] In Durham, Clyde, Wanamaker, and Philadelphian white society had found the "proper party for the Dominican Consulate" who would unswervingly defend white financial interests.[116]

Such praise, however, came with a cost. As in Astwood's case, Durham's white referees employed moral discourse in order to control both the outcome of the political appointment and the ongoing narrative regarding Black men's political authority. Ogden's candid assessment of Durham in a letter to Wanamaker most clearly exemplified the underlying tenor of these letters. According to Ogden, Durham was a "representative young colored man, with very little of the negro element in his make-up, either physical or mental," and his near-white phenotype afforded Durham the "modesty of true intellectual training."[117] In other words, in Ogden's estimation, Durham's intellectual genius came solely from the European side of his heritage. And while such abilities might be dangerous in a darker-toned man like Astwood, Durham's intellect did not pose a threat to white power because it afforded him a virtuous "modesty" to know his color and keep his place. Ogden surmised that Durham would work in Wanamaker and Clyde's best interest by subordinating his government authority to their business acumen. In this way, Durham would act "in some small degree as a redeemer" for the Black race, who had suffered greatly the "smirched reputations of Langston, Astwood, and other prominent men." In listing the former minister to Haiti, John Mercer Langston, and Astwood as Durham's opposites, Ogden stressed to Wanamaker that Durham was a man whom white elites could trust and control. "If my judgment of [Durham] proves to be wrong," he swore to Wanamaker, "I shall be disposed to sell out all my stock in the colored race."[118]

Like other white people of their time, Ogden and Clyde deemed it their right and duty to judge the morality of nonwhite people. This belief in white moral exclusivity scaled up to nations since racialized moral discourse operated on both interpersonal and symbolic international planes. Clyde's letters to Blaine and T. C. Platt demonstrated the extrapolation. According to Clyde, Astwood's immorality had ruined the United States' reputation in Santo Domingo and had made American trade with the island difficult. As proof, Clyde made the unsubstantiated assertion that even President Heureaux had asked Clyde's managers to transact business with the Dominican government behind Astwood's back—as if Heureaux had known better to seek out a white man for honest trade. Thus, Clyde argued that by appointing someone other than Astwood, the United States would not only gain a coaling port in Samaná but would also teach Dominicans "to respect us, and look up to ours, the leading Republic."[119] The United States, in Clyde's estimation, would then assume its rightful place as the moral arbiter of Hispaniola's two nations and other nonwhite countries in Latin America and Asia. In other words, if men like Astwood challenged white business interests, then the United States would never be able to fully control the nonwhite world. Thus, it was "of the utmost importance" to have men Clyde deemed "honest, intelligent and capable"—adjectives that described Black men's willingness to submit to white power more than a genuine interpretation of the words.

African Americans, of course, knew all about the hypocrisy of white moral discourse, but they also knew how to play the political race game and kept close tally of the score. Their fate was tied to that of the island of Hispaniola, which whites constantly denigrated. Government positions, even "comparatively humble" ones, countered racist stereotypes about Black people and nonwhite nations.[120] Consequently, for Black Americans, it was most important to secure dwindling diplomatic and federal posts, despite the indignities to which whites subjected representative Black men.

For this reason, prominent African Americans wholeheartedly supported Durham while still holding out hope for Astwood's reappointment. For example, in July, AME bishop Jabez P. Campbell, Reverend Levi J. Coppin, and Reverend Benjamin F. Lee, the former president of Wilberforce University and the editor of the *Christian Recorder*, lauded Durham's "intellectual, moral, and general business qualities," and considered him an excellent alternative "in the event that Mr. H. C. C. Astwood should not continue in that office."[121] In late September, *New York Age* editor Peterson, who had sworn that Astwood would receive the post, also hedged his bet.[122] "In case the re-appointment of H. C. C. Astwood . . . is deemed unadvisable," Peterson counseled, "Mr. Durham is an experienced newspaper man of unquestioned integrity, brilliant attainments and forceful character."[123] Such recommendations for Durham adopted an energetic tone equal to those for Astwood. Peterson and celebrated New York lawyer Thomas McCants Stewart reminded Republican Party officials that Durham had contributed to Harrison's recent election through columns in the *Age* and speeches in northeastern states.[124] Lawyer Theophilus J. Minton, furthermore, spoke on behalf of all Black Philadelphians when he affirmed that Durham had the Black community's "fullest confidence and esteem."[125]

Naturally, Black solidarity in the battle for political posts did not eliminate competition between prominent African American men, nor criticism of the administration's ultimate selections. In late September 1889, for example, Astwood visited Washington, DC, in order to defend his bid for the consular post. Once there, he dared to accompany his *New York Age* editor friend Fortune to Douglass's home in Cedar Hill. The pair found Douglass in "very bad humor" on the eve of his departure for Haiti.[126] Fortune, who had always been treated well in Douglass's home, was surprised. Astwood likely was not, although he may have hoped for a better outcome. African American responses to Douglass's appointment had been less sanguine than those for Durham. Some people believed that a younger man should have been chosen for the Haitian post. They also disagreed with Douglass in terms of politics and disliked that he had married a white woman. Others claimed that the Haiti post was not good enough for Douglass.[127] These opinions appeared widely in the Black press and, like recommendation letters, reflected the competition between Black men.[128] Perhaps Astwood believed he and Fortune could smooth things over with the "Old-Man Eloquent" by showing support for his appointment at the eleventh hour. Douglass, however, never liked Astwood and would not be coaxed into assisting him now. He subsequently lodged charges against Astwood at the State Department. Within two weeks of Douglass's departure, rumors circulated that Harrison had rejected Astwood, and consequently Durham prepared to meet with Republican leaders in Washington.[129]

Unfortunately for both Astwood and Durham, Harrison further delayed making a decision between the two candidates. Accordingly, Astwood continued to pursue the post. In an October 1889 letter to Harrison, Astwood acknowledged that his case was closed but requested that Harrison reconsider.[130] Then, in November, Astwood editorialized in the *New York World* that the Republican establishment was mistaken about who the true race leaders were and asserted that Douglass was not an acceptable representative.[131] He warned, "Unless President Harrison, Mr. Blaine, Mr. Wanamaker and others of the cabinet stop fooling with the negro and give him the representation and right to which the Republican party stands pledged, there will be some vacant seats in the White House." This threat of political blowback, however, did not yield the desired results. The first month of 1890 saw no new appointment to Santo Domingo and brought three more petitions from Astwood to Harrison and a few more recommendations from Astwood's supporters to the same.[132] Even Consular Bureau Chief St. Clair wrote that he had previously been ordered to report everything against Astwood, but that he truly believed "Mr. Astwood has done a hundred times more good to our citizens and trade interests, and as a reward has been dismissed."[133] Yet, ultimately, none of these efforts worked.[134] As early as March 1890, Astwood and McKay switched tactics and petitioned for Astwood's appointment to another Caribbean or African position.[135] Then, finally, in May 1890, they learned that Harrison had chosen Durham for the Dominican post, and a defeated Astwood returned to Santo Domingo for his family and possessions.

Yet, as scholars of African American history and US diplomacy know, Astwood was not the only Black officer made to defend his moral character from white Americans' accusations in 1889–91. While Henry tied up his business and family affairs in Santo Domingo, the United States' gaze fell upon Douglass's negotiations for the Môle Saint-Nicolas. The events of Douglass's tenure in Haiti are well known and can be summarized as follows. After Douglass's arrival in Port-au-Prince in October 1889, Clyde's agent unsuccessfully attempted to coerce Douglass to pursue Clyde's interests in Haiti above all other US claims. Douglass refused, and Clyde sought vengeance by sowing doubt about Douglass's loyalty to the United States in the *môle* negotiations. Consequently, Harrison appointed Rear Admiral Bancroft Gherardi to lead the deal. When Gherardi failed, Republicans and the US press blamed Douglass, who resigned from his role as US minister to Haiti on June 30, 1891.[136] According to his opponents, Douglass's race prejudiced him in favor of Haiti, weakening his resolve and making him a traitor to the United States.[137] Never one to mince words, Douglass countered this narrative in the *North American Review*. Like Astwood, he decried the racism, hypocrisy, and immorality of his accusers. Clyde's proposal had "sounded like Satan on the mountain" and was "shameful, dishonest, and shocking."[138] In a clear dispute over who had the moral upper hand, America's greatest moral reformer laid bare a series of facts that implied that the US government had misused him.[139] This insinuation scandalized whites by exposing on the national stage how he had been made a scapegoat. In this brief episode, Douglass and Astwood, alleged enemies from the start, were more alike than they seemed.

Conclusion

Clearly, Douglass's trouble in 1890–91 throws into sharp relief the racist structures stacked against Astwood and helps explain why Astwood maintained the Black press and the AME Church's support throughout his career. However, what does Astwood's story teach us about Douglass, Durham, and the moral politics of US racial capitalism during the period? As the letters regarding Astwood demonstrate, battles for economic and international power were waged at the level of interpersonal relations and involved heartfelt evaluations of an individual's morality. Clyde, Wanamaker, and their agents knew that their opinions counted more than anyone else's due to their whiteness, sex, and wealth, and they took full advantage of their influence. For this reason, Black US agents wrote their own version of history in their dispatches, pamphlets, editorials, and autobiographies, and they used letters of recommendation to defend themselves against the machinations of racist white society. By representing their own viewpoints, genuinely or otherwise, Douglass, Durham, and Astwood became known in the United States as respectable, moral Black race men.

Unlike the others, though, Astwood consistently opted for subterfuge in his exploits abroad (and later in the United States). As stated in the introduction, Astwood's *tigueraje* (trickery) requires a reevaluation of Black international politics and evolving notions of racial solidarity, antiracist activism, and racial uplift in the late nineteenth century. Whereas scholars have analyzed the complicated ways that representative race leaders navigated an era of burgeoning US empire and Jim Crow in order to lift up Black people worldwide, Astwood's history does not fit neatly within common modes of analysis within US Black internationalist thought. His very existence as US consul challenged white supremacist ideology, but his habitual involvement in corruption disrupted notions of US Black respectability and reinforced white supremacy. Accordingly, his actions represented a Black internationalism in constant flux, reflective of his transnational Caribbean context. Even more significantly, the controversy over ex–US consul Astwood's moral character directs scholarly focus toward questions over how Black officials gained authority through narrative making, revealing how the act of fact interpretation itself became a battleground of good versus evil.

Antithetical testimonies regarding Astwood's record in office could not all be true. The dozens of letters posted by influential Americans either highly recommended Astwood or fiercely protested his reappointment to Santo Domingo based on moral grounds. Astwood's unique case demonstrates that such an exercise in white moral exclusivity was a moving target. White Americans who benefited from his *tigueraje* vehemently advocated for his reappointment, while those who felt the sting of betrayal viewed his deceit as proof of Black moral inferiority. Commonality, however, existed in the method if not the details. On both sides, white elites assumed the ability not only to determine Astwood's future but also to interpret the present and past, an action that they moralized as their natural right and ethical obligation. Astwood's story both elucidates this process and reveals its fault lines.

Ultimately, Astwood did not rob thousands of dollars from Clyde as he allegedly did from Wanamaker, Cunningham, and Cordelia Platt. But the problem for Clyde and other white elites was never just about money. In Astwood, they saw a direct challenge to white moral exclusivity. From Clyde's representative viewpoint the problem was this: not only did civil war, Haitian protectionism, and Douglass thwart foreign white power in Haiti, but in eastern Hispaniola a Black US officer had more influence with the Dominican president than white merchants did. And, most importantly, the same Black consul had gained the power to convincingly refashion theft—even theft perpetrated against powerful white Americans—as moral rectitude. In the late nineteenth century, the ability to extract capital through unfair trade, labor exploitation, or downright theft, and label such actions as logical, intelligent, or just, was a privilege tacitly reserved for whites. Astwood, however, disrupted notions of white moral exclusivity since his actions effaced racial lines of distinction by beating American capitalists at their own game.

Although white Americans like Clyde and Wanamaker attempted to reestablish racial boundaries through their letters of protest, in Astwood's case they were only partially successful. By ignoring the US president's instructions, convincingly denying his corruption, and mobilizing white allies, Astwood wrote his own reality into existence; he left the US consular bureau with a clean record. In a similar way (by ignoring contrary evidence, denying systemic corruption, and elevating the colonizers' legacy), the myth of white moral exclusivity also became historical fact.

Conclusion

Given his consistent alliance with white capitalists in Santo Domingo, it is uncertain whether Henry Astwood ever truly believed in the emancipatory movements that made possible his life's trajectory. As argued in chapters 1 and 2, during the 1860s–70s, people of color joined forces across borders to fight for radical visions of Black freedom, anticolonial government, and political belonging within the hemisphere's nation-states. Astwood first learned of the era's transnational political organizing through Protestant church networks between the Turks Islands and the Dominican northern coast. He then embedded himself in activist circles in New Orleans during Reconstruction, risking his life and others' finances for Black suffrage and the dream of social equality. Appointed US consul to Santo Domingo in 1882, Astwood ostensibly carried forth this liberationist spirit to the Dominican capital. Yet Astwood's actions during his consular years indicated that his intentions were less than trustworthy. Habitually labeled a "trickster," "bigamist," "thug," and "blackmailer" by Americans, Dominicans, and other people during his lifetime, Astwood fit the archetype of the Dominican *tíguere*.[1] His true character, a subject of intense debate in the 1880s and 1890s (see chapters 6 and 7), was never fully known, nor could it ever be. It is safe to say, however, that Henry Astwood was not the sort of representative Black man that his contemporaries and historians wished to remember enshrined alongside other great race men of the era like Frederick Douglass.

What then is to be gained from this history of Astwood's early life and consular years? As demonstrated throughout this book, discerning Astwood's character is irrelevant compared to the greater task of unraveling the various schemes in which he was involved. Such analysis provides further insight into the postemancipation Americas, the intricacies of US-Dominican international relations, the rise of US empire in Latin America, and the history of Black US foreign service agents and Black Protestantism in the Caribbean. Significantly, it also highlights the complexity of African American–Dominican diasporic encounters, provoking a reconsideration of late nineteenth-century Black internationalism through the prism of Astwood's political *tigueraje* (trickery). As argued in the introduction, Astwood's political *tigueraje* may serve as an analytical framework for understanding Dominican Blackness and US Black internationalism, demonstrating how trickery factored into Dominican racial identity and Black international politics even to the point of counteracting Black solidarity and liberation. For Astwood, both expressions of racial pride and anti-Blackness existed in flux. This was perhaps reflective of his true attitudes, but more importantly and definitely indicative of a performative strategy that he and other seemingly transgressive Black men used in order to maintain political authority (see chapters 3 and 4).

By focusing on the ways that Astwood commanded such authority by marshaling the era's moral politics of race-making, this book expands understandings of US Black internationalism and redirects scholarly attention to the fundamental question of narrative making. Astwood's US Black internationalism demonstrates that claims to morality based in Protestant and Catholic worldviews formed a currency of power during the late nineteenth century. This currency gave individuals interpretive authority in the hemispheric debate over Black men's capacity for citizenship and political authority. As Astwood manipulated conceptions of good and evil, he gained interpretive power over the past and his present. The various narratives that he constructed—whether fact or fiction, racially liberatory or frustratingly destructive to Black solidarity—held weight in an arena where white people systematically ignored Black voices and destroyed Black property and lives. Thus, the power of Astwood's story lies not within the redemption of the decent man or the condemnation of the scoundrel but rather in the complex ambiguity of a middleman whose *tigueraje* emblematized the transitional time and place in which he lived.

Like other locales across the Americas, Santo Domingo was a hemispheric crossroads at the end of the nineteenth century. Throughout the

1880s, Astwood and his contemporaries—Black and white Americans, Dominicans, Europeans, and Latin American Creoles—strategically engaged moral discourse based in Western Christianity in order to negotiate racial borders, control international policy, and ultimately direct the course of history. By the early 1890s, however, the historical circumstances that had enabled Astwood's figurative seat at the table as a Black man were rapidly disintegrating.

The Vanishing Crossroads

The early 1890s represented a period of nascent US dollar diplomacy in Santo Domingo that drastically transformed US-Dominican relations and hastened the consolidation of US empire in the Caribbean.[2] Along with greater US presence in the region came harsher racial borders and an American ethos of moral capitalism that saw the disintegration of the intersecting domestic and foreign versions of social morality explored in chapter 5. Although dollar diplomacy is typically associated with the administration of US president William Howard Taft (1909–13), this foreign policy actually emerged earlier with the first International American Conference hosted by Secretary of State James G. Blaine during Benjamin Harrison's presidency (1889–93). Also known as the Pan-American Conference, the event held in Washington, DC, in October 1889 (when Astwood was likely in town) sought to impose US dominance over Latin American trade. When Blaine's major goals for the conference fell short, he then turned once again to a series of reciprocity treaties with Latin American nations.[3]

Thus, a second round of reciprocity treaty negotiations took place between the United States and the Dominican Republic nearly a decade after Heureaux and Astwood had first proposed reciprocity in 1882. Yet, unlike the early 1880s when a change in US administration ended the agreement, this time Washington honored its commitment to Santo Domingo. On September 1, 1891, a reciprocity treaty between the two nations at last went into effect. The unanticipated consequence of the new treaty and its threat to Dominican sovereignty soon became clear. The Dominican government lost $100,000 in yearly revenue and suffered the threat of Europe's economic reprisal when the United States hesitated to declare support for Heureaux.[4]

At the same time, other coeval events solidified the United States' control over the country. To Astwood's probable chagrin, William P. Clyde resumed his monopoly over the island's shipping.[5] Meanwhile, John S. Durham led a renewed effort to negotiate the United States' lease of Samaná Bay.[6] Then, within a year, a US corporation, the Santo Domingo Improvement Company (SDIC), took over the republic's foreign debt from the Dutch firm Westendorp and Company.[7] Maintaining control over Dominican finances for the remainder of the century, the SDIC backed Heureaux's dictatorship and called on Washington to enforce its extraordinary rule via diplomacy and military force.[8] These events paved the way for even greater US expansion in the Caribbean in the lead-up to the Spanish-American War (1898).

Astwood was keenly cognizant of these developments. In fact, although his consulship technically ended in 1888, and hopes for its extension shattered in 1890, Astwood returned to Santo Domingo in May 1890, where he lived with his family through the summer of 1892. His presence in the city during these years suggests not only that he witnessed the local effects of the reciprocity treaty, the Samaná Bay negotiations, and the SDIC takeover, but also that he remained marginally involved with US-Dominican diplomatic and commercial affairs. More evidence of Astwood's ongoing participation in US-Dominican relations can be found in the period's US and Dominican state records. His endeavors included dealings with the SDIC, the Santo Domingo Lottery Company, the San Domingo Brewing Company, and the Ozama River bridge project led by Nathaniel McKay.[9] His activities also continued to provoke controversy, leaving a large paper trail. Besides despising Astwood's friendship with Heureaux, the Dominican lettered class dubbed the lottery company a fraud, and by 1893 both the brewing company and the bridge were ensnared in lawsuits. Even the local Protestant congregation in Santo Domingo turned its back on the ex-consul in a lawsuit over African Methodist Episcopal (AME) Church property.

It is likely that these setbacks precipitated Astwood's final return to the United States, where he faced continued objection to his character. As AME leaders promised to investigate rumors of ecclesiastical fraud in early 1893, the other lawsuits in the Dominican capital persisted.[10] Even so, Astwood believed that he still might regain the Santo Domingo consular post that year. The Douglasses and various US businessmen, including the SDIC's president, blocked him.[11] Protests against Astwood even surfaced in the faraway city of Buenos Aires where, at the urgings of José Martí, Argentina's former minister to Washington, Vincente Quesada, published his tome *Los Estados Unidos y la América del Sur: Los yankees pintados por sí mismos* (1893).[12] A scathing treatise on American culture, Quesada's text rehashed

Astwood's complicity in the Columbus bones scandal of 1888 as an example of American avarice.[13]

These final blows to Astwood's reputation gnawed at the image of Black respectability that Astwood had carefully cultivated since the 1870s. Coupled with the broader shift in US racial empire, this loss in actual and symbolic power meant that Astwood could no longer tap into the intersecting notions of social morality in Santo Domingo. Indeed, the ideological convergences between varying notions of social morality were themselves quickly fading as US–Latin American politics shifted. Astwood's cameo in Quesada's work, for example, both censured the ex-consul and evidenced "the emergence of a modern anti-American ... regional identity" in Latin America manifesting in international law and diplomacy.[14] This political regional identity mirrored Latin American leaders' sense of spiritual superiority over Anglo-US materialism, noted in chapter 6. At the same time, US moral capitalism also gained a stronger footing among white Americans as the United States expanded its hemispheric dominance. Men of African descent who had once vied for political authority by straddling the intersection of Latin American and US notions of social morality found that by 1893 the plasticity of the Dominican crossroads had disappeared. In its wake, only the myth remained.

The Myth Enshrined

The turn in US-Dominican affairs is perhaps best captured in the island nation's absence at Chicago's 1893 World's Columbian Exposition, one of the largest quadricentennial celebrations of Columbus's landing in the Americas and a blatant tribute to the myth of white supremacy. Historians have had much to say about the fair's racist politics. Not only were Black Americans excluded from all aspects of the planning, limited to servile employment, and subjected to segregated visiting days, but Africans and other supposedly primitive peoples were exhibited "like an orangutan" (to invoke M. E. Pardo's words in chapter 6) in the section known as the Midway Plaisance.[15] In response, race leaders such as Ida B. Wells and Lettie Trent encouraged African Americans to boycott the fair.[16] Meanwhile, Frederick Douglass curated the Haitian Pavilion, a Greco-colonial building filled with marble statues, paintings, and busts of famous Black men. The pavilion, which stood among European exhibits in the location known as the White City, "showcased the intellectual might, rich history, commercial growth, and future prosperity of Haiti" and was meant to undermine the racist display at the Midway.[17] Thus, African Americans (and subsequent historians) celebrated Haiti's representation at the fair. It is curious, however, that given the Dominican Republic's claim that the country possessed Columbus's true remains, no exhibit was dedicated to Hispaniola's other Black republic.

In contrast to Haiti, the Dominican Republic's representation at the world's fair was remarkably obscure. This was so despite the fact that back in 1891 Frederick A. Ober, the fair's commissioner to the West Indies, had stolen European relics from the island for public display in Chicago.[18] Rather than being housed in a purported Dominican pavilion, Ober's stolen treasures appeared in a replica of La Rábida, the Spanish monastery where Columbus sought succor prior to his voyages.[19] The curated monastery effectively erased Dominicans' claims to the colonial European objects held therein and further propagated the racist dichotomy between Europe and the island.

Ober bluntly delineated the moral logic that undergirded this division in his reflections regarding his 1891 trip to Santo Domingo. Back then Ober had beseeched the Dominican government to erect in Chicago a reproduction of the Homage, Santo Domingo's colonial military tower, which he then planned to fill with relics associated with Columbus. When his plan never came to fruition, Ober fixed the blame on the Dominican government and accused, "I had not counted upon the peculiar trait of the Dominican which (to state it mildly) attaches a mercenary value to patriotism."[20] Upon hearing that the tower would cost $20,000, the Dominican government had requested a loan from the exposition's directors, which Ober dismissed mockingly as a joke. In another troubling twist, President Heureaux had even proposed sending Columbus's disinterred remains to Chicago in exchange for $100,000.[21] In a racist vendetta that echoed the discourse regarding Astwood's proposed lease of the remains in 1888, Ober explained this impropriety by claiming that inferior Black men had enveloped the Dominican Republic in poverty, war, and corruption. Regarding Euro-Dominicans, he moreover lamented the "degradation to which the Sons of Somebody have descended" before asking wryly, "But what can you expect from a people who have been under the iron heel of oppression for many generations, who have been accustomed to look up to, and not down upon, the African sons of nobody?"[22]

Considering Ober's racist outlook, contracting Spain (a white nation) for the reproduction of La Rábida proved more palatable than further negotiations with Dominicans for the Homage. Whereas Ober demanded that the Dominican government pay for the Homage's reconstruction and denied a loan that would have ensured Dominican credit for the building, the fair's managers harbored no reservations about designating $50,000 for La Rábida and another $80,000 to reconstruct in Spain replicas of the *Niña*, *Pinta*, and *Santa María* that eventually docked in Lake Michigan.[23] Ober then expressed no qualms about pillaging Dominican relics for public display in La Rábida while simultaneously disparaging Dominican leaders for their alleged greed.[24] According to time-honored white supremacist logic, Dominican leaders had to be mercenary because of their subordinate status as colonized Black people and because Ober could not logically assume himself and other white Americans to be the same.

Ober's rendering of Dominicans as innately immoral veiled the violence of the United States' imperial enterprise from his American audience. Indeed, by characterizing his barter with Heureaux as a farce, Ober tacitly raised the question of whether the fair's directors would have accepted the Homage replica at all. Whereas La Rábida, a religious symbol, shielded the public from the specter of colonial violence, the Homage, a military building, would have brought that violence to the White City's door. Through the Homage, the city of Santo Domingo—its colonized people of color—gazed back. This image perhaps hit too close to home for white Americans as their government actively exploited the world's fair to expand trade with Latin America.[25] As white Americans consumed La Rábida's religious symbolism, they overlooked the violent economic goals of the genocidal colonial project Columbus began in 1492: the expropriation of land, wealth, and life—first from Indigenous peoples and then from Africans and their descendants. In sum, racialized moral logic enabled colonizers, old and new, to project their own greed upon their victims, thereby masking their own theft by making robbery of imperial subjects an imperative moral virtue. Like African Americans, Haitians, and other people of color, however, Dominicans saw clearly through this ruse.

The Terrible Year of 1893

As thousands of tourists made the pilgrimage to La Rábida in 1893, a war cry leaped from the pages of Santo Domingo's *Listín Diario*.[26] Warning of the US "robbers and assassins" in cahoots with President Heureaux, a "Band of Patriots" called on their fellow citizens to "USE THE RIGHT THAT THEY USE!" and "steal" back the property (Samaná) that had been wrongfully "sold" to the United States.[27] They also explained that Heureaux had recently negotiated new SDIC loans that would drive up the country's debt astronomically. With uncanny prescience, the patriots prophesied that "at the end of a certain time, the Republic will find itself involved in an enormous foreign debt to pay off. Then when these thieves are rich and we are miserable, the government of the United States will ask us guarantee for its subjects, first Samaná Bay, the whole Republic to follow after. You will have no country to give to your children!!!" The patriots then urged the nation to "annihilate" Heureaux and his advisers, whatever the cost. "Dominicans: Remember that we are in the Terrible Year, the year 1893," they urged. "Do the accursed want blood? Then let them drown in their own. . . . Long live the revolution!"

Although the 1893 campaign, an insurrection led by center-island residents against Heureaux's regime, proved short-lived, Anne Eller has argued that the movement known as the revolution of the *bi(e)mbines* or *quisquises* invoked the island's long history of Black fugitivity, African spirituality, and anticolonial resistance.[28] Borderland residents embraced "a 'recombinant mythology' of highlands resistance" and should be understood "not through a lens of absence of capital city control but through the existence of other sovereignties, on their own terms."[29] The notion of "other sovereignties" fueled what Cedric J. Robinson termed the "Black radical tradition" on Hispaniola and across the Atlantic world.[30] Heureaux himself once formed part of this tradition but had ultimately turned his back on the region's historic Black resistance to colonial rule. In this case, he crushed the 1893 revolution within a manner of months and then killed its leaders and his other opponents across the country.[31] Even so, the existence of other sovereignties did not die in 1893. In the following years, opposition to Heureaux and his US backers continued throughout the borderlands and central plains, and in 1899 the dictator ultimately succumbed to assassins' bullets.

The Terrible Year marked the end of an era. Not only did Astwood leave the Dominican Republic for good just months prior to the revolution, but in January 1893 SDIC board members arrived in Santo Domingo for the first time. In many ways, the SDIC's landing, along with the other events of 1890–93, represented the culmination of Astwood's early consular efforts. The caveat, of course, was that none of Astwood's nor Heureaux's visions to improve Dominican society survived. Despite Astwood's machinations, the United States never separated its Santo Domingo consular office from

Haiti during Heureaux's administration.[32] US commercial investments in the country's infrastructure went bust, and Dominican politicians rejected ongoing proposals for African American immigration to the country.[33] It was said too that Dominican officials resented the United States' policy of sending Black consuls. For their part, Black US agents like John S. Durham and Archibald Grimké displayed Astwood's same willingness to cater to white economic and imperial power at the expense of Dominican sovereignty. In 1893, however, there was no need to convince Washington to pay attention to Dominican affairs. Already backing the SDIC, the United States fixed a gimlet eye on the island republic for the remainder of the century. Indeed, the SDIC's experience in the Dominican Republic served as the impetus for Theodore Roosevelt's 1905 corollary to the Monroe Doctrine, which declared that the United States could invade any Latin American nation to correct "wrongdoing."[34] This policy ushered in various US military invasions in the region, including the brutal occupations of Haiti (1915) and the Dominican Republic (1916).

Astwood, like the Dominican crossroads and its dictator, would also soon meet his own demise. Stationed in New York in 1893, Astwood, like other men of his color and class, witnessed the rapid decline in social and economic opportunities for Black people as lynching proliferated in the South and the US Supreme Court upheld Jim Crow segregation in its ruling in *Plessy v. Ferguson* (1896). Astwood never regained a federal government appointment despite further attempts in 1894, 1897, and 1901. He also lost favor within elite white political and commercial circles. Despite all this, Astwood remained a prominent figure in northeastern Black society. He founded his own newspaper, the *Defender*, circa 1894, where he peddled his opinions about US race relations and politics.[35] He also maintained his status as an AME minister and even represented the denomination in its short-lived 1898 mission to Cuba during the Spanish-American War.[36] The trip marked Astwood's last significant sojourn in the Caribbean; he spent the last decade of his life in Philadelphia, where he died of pneumonia in 1908.[37]

In the years after Astwood's death, his US-based children maintained the family's status among the East Coast's African American elite, while others settled in Santo Domingo and other Caribbean towns.[38] Meanwhile, news of Astwood's persistent involvement in various scandals—lawsuits for misappropriation of church money, public disputes, and outlandish comments regarding other African American leaders—faded into obscurity, as did knowledge of his life and contributions to African American and Dominican history.[39] This silence was purposeful, reflective of African Americans' ongoing need for liberatory narratives of Black leaders within the United States' unrelentingly racist context. The unsurprising revelation of Astwood's post-Dominican exploits, however, reminds us of the complexity, ambiguity, and *tigueraje* inherent in the broader Black experience. Despite the terrible year of 1893, the triumph of the myth, and the disappearance of the Dominican crossroads with all that it had once represented, Henry Astwood maintained his stance as a middleman and *tíguere* until his last breath.

Notes

PREFACE

1. H. C. C. Astwood to William Hunter, July 13, 1882; February 5, 1883; and March 8, 1884; nos. 21, 74, 148, DUSCSD, National Archives and Records Administration, Record Group 59 (NARA-59).
2. Day, *Cruise*, 246. This preface draws from Day's and Hazard's travel narratives. See also Hazard, *Santo Domingo*, 212–34. For analysis of these, see Deive, *Los dominicanos*, 218–25, 237–42.
3. Naish, *Slavery and Silence*, 137–41.
4. Such fabrications helped to justify the systematic theft of Indigenous and Mexican land. Naish, *Slavery and Silence*, 142, 160–63.
5. Day, *Cruise*, 255.
6. St. John, *Hayti*; Froude, *English in the West Indies*. See also Webb, *Haiti*, 139–88; Byrd, *Black Republic*, 83–93; Tiffin, "Among Head-Hunters and Cannibals"; Thompson, *James Anthony Froude*, 170–72; N. D. Davis, *Mr. Froude's Negrophobia*. For earlier racist tropes of Haiti, see Daut, *Tropics of Haiti*.
7. Day, *Cruise*, 248.
8. Hazard, *Santo Domingo*, 222; Day, *Cruise*, 248.
9. Serrata, "La ciudad como espectáculo," 474–75.
10. For seventeen structures, see H. C. C. Astwood, "Letter from San Domingo," CR, February 22, 1883.
11. García Lluberes, "Nuestra estatua."
12. For Anacaona, see Baez, "Anacaona Writes Back."
13. Wertheimer, *Imagined Empires*, 46; DeGuzman, *Spain's Long Shadow*, 7, 87; Greer, Mignolo, and Quilligan, *Rereading the Black Legend*, 6.

14. Greer, Mignolo, and Quilligan, *Rereading the Black Legend*, 1.
15. Day, *Cruise*, 259–60.
16. DeGuzman, *Spain's Long Shadow*, 66–67.
17. Horacio C. King to [Pres.] Grover Cleveland, April 24, 1886, ACA-B3, ARPO, NARA-59.

INTRODUCTION

1. "Negro Pastor Convicted," *NYT*, May 24, 1901.
2. Gatewood, *Aristocrats*, 247; E. D. Taylor, *Original Black Elite*, 161–62, 193–94; Dickerson, *African Methodist*, 212–13.
3. Candelario, *Black behind the Ears*, 103; Lugo, "Los restos."
4. For an overview, see Dougherty, "New Scholarship"; Wenger and Johnson, *Religion and US Empire*. For key works, see S. A. Johnson, *African American Religions*; Wenger, *Religious Freedom*; Conroy-Krutz, *Christian Imperialism*; Graber, *Gods of Indian Country*; H. D. Curtis, *Holy Humanitarians*.
5. As Daut does for Haiti, I present Santo Domingo as "one node in a broader crossroads of transnational and diasporic [geographies]," but I also consider non-Black visions. Daut, "Haiti as Diasporic Crossroads," 334.
6. For racial capitalism, see Robinson, *Black Marxism*, which has inspired an immense body of scholarship. For a summary of the field, see Robin D. G. Kelley, foreword to Robinson, *Black Marxism*, xi–xvii; Jenkins and Leroy, "Introduction."
7. Melamed, "Racial Capitalism," 78–82.
8. The literature on race and Christianity is vast. For key works in theology and history, see Carter, *Race*, 1–121; Jennings, *Christian Imagination*; S. A. Johnson, *African American Religions*, 13–156; Delgado and Moss, "Religion and Race."
9. Cassá, "El racismo," 64–65.
10. Martínez-Vergne, *Nation and Citizen*, 2, 19–24; Mella, *Los espejos*, 247, 251–55.
11. San Miguel, *Imagined Island*, 50–52; Mayes, *Mulatto Republic*, 17–35. For elsewhere, see scholarship on José Martí: Fountain, *José Martí*, 17–33; Hooker, *Theorizing Race*, 155–57.
12. Rodríguez Almager, "El antillanismo"; Eller, *We Dream*, 234.
13. Torres-Saillant, "Tribulations," 130–31; Hoetink, *Dominican People*, 95–96, 102–3; Eller, *We Dream*, 189–91.
14. For Haiti, see Byrd, *Black Republic*; Polyné, *From Douglass*, 25–55; Pamphile, *Haitians*, 80–89.
15. On borderlands, see García-Peña, *Borders*, 9–12; Candelario, *Black behind the Ears*, 36, 44–57.
16. Frederick Douglass to Nathaniel McKay, July 24, 1893, ACA-B3, ARPO, National Archives and Records Administration, Record Group 59 (NARA-59); Charles R. Douglass to Secretary of State [Frelinghuysen], May 29, 1882, ACA-B3, ARPO, NARA-59.
17. Roberts, *From Trickster*, 17–64, 171–219.
18. Roberts, *From Trickster*, 174. For the trickster during slavery, see 30–61.

19. For religion, see descriptions of the Santería spirit Eleguá and the Vodou lwa Papa Legba in Fernández Olmos and Paravisini-Gebert, *Creole Religions*, 47–48, 125–26. For African American folklore, see Roberts, *From Trickster*, 22–43.

20. Derby, *Dictator's Seduction*, 174, 186–90. See also Hutchinson, *Tigers*, 33.

21. Collado, *El tíguere*, 2.

22. Chetty and Rodríguez, "Introduction," 2.

23. Vinson, "Introduction," 8–9; García-Peña, *Translating Blackness*, 19–20.

24. Chetty and Rodríguez, "Introduction," 2.

25. Jacoby, *Strange Career*, xxvii. Unlike Astwood who lived in the world as a Black man, Ellis used trickery to transgress the color line, passing as a Mexican national.

26. Arnold, "Spider and Rabbit," 273.

27. Byrd, *Black Republic*; Alexander, *Fear of a Black Republic*; Bourhis-Mariotti, *L'union*; Bourhis-Mariotti, *Wanted! A Nation!*

28. For hegemonic Blackness, see García-Peña, *Translating Blackness*, 4, 34–35.

29. Byrd, "Ebenezer Bassett," 68–69.

30. Ramírez, "Mushrooms," 156–59.

31. For US whites' reactions, see Logan, *Diplomatic Relations*; G. S. Brown, *Toussaint's Clause*; White, *Encountering Revolution*; Dillon and Drexler, *Haitian Revolution*; Dun, *Dangerous Neighbors*. Despite an official policy of nonrecognition, trade with the island continued: Gaffield, *Haitian Connections*.

32. Nelson, "U.S. Diplomatic Recognition."

33. Nelson, "U.S. Diplomatic Recognition," 10; Candelario, *Black behind the Ears*, 35–82; Eller, "'Awful Pirates,'" 87–94.

34. Horne, *Confronting*, 195–99.

35. Horne, *Confronting*, 201–3.

36. Torres-Saillant, "Tribulations," 127–29.

37. Ramírez, *Colonial Phantoms*, 3; Love, *Race over Empire*, 7, 25, 38–72.

38. The Santo Domingo consulate upgraded to US Consul General in 1898, but it only separated from Haiti on June 14, 1904.

39. Lee Borges, "República Dominicana," 137–41.

40. For the racialized context, see Blakely, "Blacks in the U.S. Diplomatic."

41. The most comprehensive histories do not provide in-depth analysis of the 1880s: Henríquez Ureña, *Los Estados Unidos*; Welles, *Naboth's Vineyard*; Knight, *Americans*; Tansill, *United States*; Hauch, *La República Dominicana*; Núñez Polanco, *Anexionismo y resistencia*; Sang, *La política exterior*.

42. For white Americans, see Ramírez, *Colonial Phantoms*, 5–9; Eller, "'Awful Pirates,'" 90.

43. García-Peña, *Translating Blackness*, 41.

44. "A Colored President," *NYH*, November 18, 1879.

45. Guyatt, "America's Conservatory," 999.

46. Fanning, *Caribbean Crossing*; Hidalgo, *La primera inmigración*; Winch, "American Free Blacks and Emigration to Haiti"; Stephens, "La inmigración"; Alexander, *Fear of a Black Republic*, 40–46; Bourhis-Mariotti, *Wanted! A Nation!*, 12–31.

47. Byrd, "A Reinterpretation," 198–99.

48. Maffly-Kipp, *Setting Down*, 11.

49. For foundational AME history, see Payne, *History*, 3–18; Smith, *A History*, 13–14; Dickerson, *African Methodist*, 17–55; Newman, *Freedom's Prophet*; Campbell, *Songs of Zion*, 3–32.

50. Payne, *History*, 477; Steward, *Haitian Revolution*, iv–v; Pamphile, *Haitians and African Americans*, 12.

51. Newman, *Freedom's Prophet*, 249–58; Alexander, "A Land of Promise," 108. For a similar presentation in Baltimore, see Jones, *Birthright Citizens*, 35–36.

52. Fanning, *Caribbean Crossing*, 77; Maffly-Kipp, *Setting Down*, 121.

53. Davidson, "Mission, Migration, and Contested Authority," 75.

54. Griffiths, *History of Methodism in Haiti*, 54–56; Davidson, "Mission, Migration, and Contested Authority," 76–77.

55. Griffiths, *History of Methodism in Haiti*, 56.

56. G. A. Lockward, *El protestantismo*, 248.

57. Wilkins, "'They Had Heard,'" 213, 225–26.

58. "What Hinders," *CR*, January 30, 1873.

59. Wilkins, "'They Had Heard,'" 211–13; Bourhis-Mariotti, "Frederick Douglass," 237–39; Bourhis-Mariotti, *Wanted! A Nation!*, 121.

60. Davidson, "'What Hinders?,'" 56–58.

61. Davidson, "Mission, Migration, and Contested Authority," 79–80; Dickerson, *African Methodist*, 101, 147–48.

62. Davidson, "'What Hinders?,'" 56–58.

63. Steward, *Fifty Years*, 149. See also Davidson, "'What Hinders?,'" 64–65; Byrd, *Black Republic*, 54.

64. Martínez-Vergne, *Nation and Citizen*, 7.

65. Martínez-Vergne, *Nation and Citizen*, 20–24, quote on 21.

66. Martínez-Vergne, *Nation and Citizen*, 10–11.

67. A. Lockward, *Intolerancia*, 97–98.

68. A. Lockward, *Intolerancia*, 107–9.

69. G. A. Lockward, *El protestantismo*, 286–87; A. Lockward, *Intolerancia*, 107–13.

70. Ramírez, *Colonial Phantoms*, 124.

71. Schmidt-Nowara, *Conquest*, 53–75; Muñiz, "Unofficial Archive," 53–112; Serrata, "'The True and Only.'"

72. For these works as a constructed archive, see Muñiz, "Unofficial Archive," 113–63.

73. Muñiz, "Unofficial Archive," 162–202; Mella, *Los espejos*, 241–51.

74. A. Lockward, *Intolerancia*, 98.

CHAPTER 1. A SHADOWY PAST: HENRY ASTWOOD AND THE TRANSITION FROM SLAVERY TO FREEDOM

1. For emancipation and its complications, see Lora Hugi, *Transición de la esclavitud*.

2. Abolition dates: Britain (1834), France (1848), Central America (1824), Chile (1823), Mexico (1829), Uruguay (1842), Ecuador (1851), Bolivia (1851), Colombia (1852), Argentina (1853), Peru (1854), Venezuela (1854), Paraguay (1869), Puerto Rico (1873),

Cuba (1886), and Brazil (1888). Andrews, *Afro-Latin America*, 57; Schmidt-Nowara, *Slavery, Freedom, and Abolition*, 113.

3. Doyle, *American Civil Wars*, 1–14.
4. For social equality, see Scott, "Public Rights"; Scott, "Discerning," especially 521–24.
5. Keel, *Divine Variations*.
6. Baptismal record of Clifford Astwood (b. August 20, 1844), file EAP914/2/2/6, ACRTCI, British Library (BL). Decay has effaced the first two names.
7. Visit Turks and Caicos Islands, "Columbus Landfall National Park", Sadler, *Turks Islands Landfall*, 9–26.
8. Salt Cay and Grand Turk measure 5.25 and 7.5 square miles respectively. Lucas, *Historical Geography*, 130–31; C. M. Kennedy, "Other White Gold," 218–19; N. Kennedy, "Impermanence," 80.
9. C. M. Kennedy, "Other White Gold," 220; N. Kennedy, "Impermanence," 82.
10. N. Kennedy, "Impermanence," 83.
11. C. M. Kennedy, "Other White Gold," 221.
12. Sadler, *Turks Islands Landfall*, 65–67; C. M. Kennedy, "Other White Gold," 221.
13. Sadler, *Turks Islands Landfall*, 70; C. M. Kennedy, "Other White Gold," 223–25.
14. Sadler, *Turks Islands Landfall*, 71; C. M. Kennedy, "Other White Gold," 226.
15. C. M. Kennedy, "Other White Gold," 228–29; Sadler, *Turks Islands Landfall*, 71–73.
16. For decades, the Turks and Caicos government did not require the civil registration of births, deaths, and marriages, and incomplete church records beginning in 1799 remain the only means for tracking genealogy.
17. Lightbourn Butz, *Letter Book*.
18. Lightbourn Butz, *Letter Book*, 82. William Amelius Astwood married Caroline Hughes on Grand Turk in 1866. "Married," *RSGTCI*, March 17, 1866.
19. Lightbourn Butz, *Letter Book*, 18.
20. Lightbourn Butz, *Letter Book*, 41, 48.
21. Prince, *History of Mary Prince*, 19.
22. Prince, *History of Mary Prince*, 20.
23. Prince, *History of Mary Prince*, 21. In Haiti, other substances such as lemon or ashes were used as well. Dubois, *Avengers of the New World*, 50.
24. Prince, *History of Mary Prince*, 21.
25. Prince, *History of Mary Prince*, 21–22.
26. Prince, *History of Mary Prince*, 22.
27. Sadler, *Turks Islands Landfall*, 58; C. M. Kennedy, "Other White Gold," 217.
28. Sadler, *Turks Islands Landfall*, 92.
29. Sadler, *Turks Islands Landfall*, 92.
30. Sadler, *Turks Islands Landfall*, 92.
31. Prince, *History of Mary Prince*, 23.
32. Gerbner, "Rebellion and Religion."
33. Nat Turner's rebellion in Virginia and Sam Sharpe's rebellion in Jamaica took place in 1831. Another revolt occurred in Martinique in 1831. Horne, *Confronting Black*

Jacobins, 156; Holt, *Problem of Freedom*, 13–21. For other rebellions, see Dubois and Turits, *Freedom Roots*, 114–20.

34. Dubois, *Avengers*, 99–102.
35. Prince, *History of Mary Prince*, 23.
36. For Christianity and British abolitionism, see Turley, *Culture of English Antislavery*; C. L. Brown, *Moral Capital*; Hempton, "Popular Evangelicalism"; McKivigan, *War against Proslavery Religion*. For a summary, see Dubois and Turits, *Freedom Roots*, 116–19.
37. Neil Kennedy, interview by author, September 25, 2020.
38. Sadler, *Turks Islands Landfall*, 92. For elsewhere, see Holt, *Problem of Freedom*, 61–67; Lightfoot, *Troubling Freedom*, 93–116.
39. Sadler, *Turks Islands Landfall*, 92–93.
40. Sadler, *Turks Islands Landfall*, 92–93.
41. Sadler, *Turks Islands Landfall*, 93.
42. Sadler, *Turks Islands Landfall*, 94.
43. Sadler, *Turks Islands Landfall*, 94.
44. Sadler, *Turks Islands Landfall*, 102–3.
45. Sadler, *Turks Islands Landfall*, 106; W. B. Johnson, *Post-Emancipation*, 11. The Turks and Caicos became an independent colony in 1848. This presidency era lasted until 1873 when the islands became a dependency of Jamaica.
46. Sadler, *Turks Islands Landfall*, 105.
47. William English to the General Secretaries, June 14, 1853, microfiche 1349, WMMS-WI, Library of the School of Oriental and African Studies (SOAS), University of London.
48. Sadler, *Turks Islands Landfall*, 95.
49. Adolphus's probable relatives were William, Thomas, Edward, James, and Tomas J.
50. Henry's siblings: James Alonzo (1837), Jane Meli- [name incomplete] (1839), Isadora Isranna (1840), Joseph (1842), Jane (1847), Theodore Ernest (1849), and Reglan Fitz Clarence (1854). File EAP914/2/2, ACRTCI, BL.
51. Adolphus's partners: Letitia Astwood (mother of William, b. 1841), Chloe Williams (mother of George, b. 1848), Frances Townham (mother of Rodolph Alexandre, b. 1856), and Mary Rose (mother of Agustus, b. 1863). File EAP914/2/2, ACRTCI, BL.
52. For kinship and intimacy, see J. M. Johnson, *Wicked Flesh*.
53. "Sketches of Delegates," *CR*, April 16, 1896; H. C. C. Astwood, "Shall Our Schools Be Mixed or Separated," *AMECR* 3, no. 4 (1887): 369–76.
54. "Shipping and Commercial List," *RSGTCI*, April 9, 1864.
55. After emancipation, the division of the ponds changed from a headright system to leasehold, and the government collected rent. Sadler, *Turks Islands Landfall*, 102.
56. Francis Moon to E. Hoole, April 17, 1862, microfiche 1374, WMMS-WI, SOAS.
57. Gregoria Goins, "'Miss Doc,'" box 36–4, folder 52, p. 156–57, GGP, Moorland-Spingarn Research Center (MSRC) at Howard University, Washington, DC.
58. Archibald Grimké, "Around the Island of Santo Domingo," box 39–19, folder 365, p. 7, AHGP, MSRC.
59. Goins, "'Miss Doc,'" p. 109.

60. Eller, *We Dream Together*, 39.
61. Puig Ortiz, *Emigración*, 28; Horne, *Confronting Black Jacobins*, 155, 163–68; Fleszar, "'My Laborers.'"
62. Findlay and Holdsworth, *History*, 492; G. A. Lockward, *El protestantismo*, 328; Hidalgo, *La primera inmigración*, 169–70.
63. Eller, *We Dream Together*, 94, 118.
64. Eller, *We Dream Together*, 84–85.
65. James H. Darrell to the General Secretaries, March 30, 1861, microfiche 1370, WMMS-WI, SOAS.
66. Eller, *We Dream Together*, 94, 98–100, 113–15, 132–33, and 136–40; Horne, *Confronting Black Jacobins*, 268; Finke González, "Puerto Plata," 123.
67. Eller, *We Dream Together*, 102–3; Horne, *Confronting Black Jacobins*, 267; Martínez-Fernández, "Sword and the Crucifix," 83–84.
68. Eller, "Rumors," 653–79.
69. Darrell to the General Secretaries, March 30, 1861.
70. Moon to Hoole, April 17, 1862.
71. Francis Moon to E. Hoole, March 18, 1863, microfiche 1376, WMMS-WI, SOAS.
72. "Passengers," *RSGTCI*, January 23, 1864; "Shipping and Commercial List," *RSGTCI*, January 30, 1864; "Shipping and Commercial List," *RSGTCI*, May 20, 1865.
73. Moon to Hoole, March 18, 1863.
74. Moon to Hoole, March 18, 1863.
75. Eller, *We Dream Together*, 170.
76. Martin Hood to Captain General, March 2, 1863, microfiche 2023, WMMS-WI, SOAS. See also Horne, *Confronting Black Jacobins*, 267–68, 389; G. A. Lockward, *El protestantismo*, 233–40; A. Lockward, *Intolerancia*, 77–78; Eller, *We Dream Together*, 134.
77. Eller, *We Dream Together*, 155–56, 189; Finke González, "Puerto Plata," 125.
78. James H. Darrell to E. Hoole, September 18, 1863, microfiche 1377, WMMS-WI, SOAS.
79. Francis Moon to E. Hoole, October 17, 1863, microfiche 1377, WMMS-WI, SOAS.
80. Moon to Hoole, October 17, 1863. Controversy over which troops burned the town abounded: Eller, *We Dream Together*, 145, 155–56; Horne, *Confronting Black Jacobins*, 267.
81. Eller, *We Dream Together*, 174. For Cooper, see James H. Darrell to E. Hoole, October 19, 1863, microfiche 1377, WMMS-WI, SOAS.
82. Darrell to Hoole, October 19, 1863.
83. Moon to Hoole, October 17, 1863.
84. For example, see the case of the schooner *Julia* of Nassau and the *Rapid* of Grand Turk: "Santo Domingo," *RSGTCI*, January 9, 1864. For wartime alliances, see Eller, *We Dream Together*, 180, 197, 208–11, 216.
85. "St. Domingo and Hayti," *RSGTCI*, July 9, 1864; "Santo Domingo," *RSGTCI*, April 23, 1864. Moon reported three boats captured in May 1864. Francis Moon to E. Hoole, May 16, 1864, microfiche 1377, WMMS-WI, SOAS.
86. "Santo Domingo," *RSGTCI*, April 2, 1864.
87. "The Dominican Republic," *RSGTCI*, July 30, 1864.

88. Eller, "Rumors"; Eller, *We Dream Together*, 146–47; Horne, *Confronting Black Jacobins*, 268.

89. "The War in St. Domingo," RSGTCI, January 2, 1864. For Spain's depictions, see Eller, *We Dream Together*, 121–22.

90. "The War in St. Domingo," RSGTCI, January 2, 1864.

91. For example, on Haiti, see "St. Domingo and Hayti," RSGTCI, July 9, 1864. Some British missionaries also denigrated Haiti in these years. See, for example, James H. Darrell to the General Secretaries, December 18, 1863, microfiche 1377, WMMS-WI, SOAS.

92. "Santo Domingo," RSGTCI, September 1, 1866.

93. Eller, *We Dream Together*, 150.

94. "Santo Domingo," RSGTCI, August 7, 1864.

95. "The War in St. Domingo," RSGTCI, January 2, 1864.

96. "Santo Domingo," RSGTCI, April 23, 1864. For finances, see also Martínez-Fernández, *Torn between Empires*, 221.

97. "Santo Domingo," RSGTCI, April 23, 1864. See also "Santo Domingo," RSGTCI, April 2, 1864, in which a Havana correspondent reported that Spain's "national vanity" would have to be "subdued" before surrender.

98. "The Dominican Republic," RSGTCI, July 30, 1864.

99. "St. Domingo," RSGTCI, September 17, 1864.

100. "Spain and St. Domingo," RSGTCI, October 1, 1864.

101. "Spain and St. Domingo," RSGTCI, October 1, 1864.

102. "Santo Domingo," RSGTCI, January 7, 1865; "Santo Domingo," RSGTCI, January 14, 1865; "Spain and St. Domingo," RSGTCI, February 11, 1865; "The Abandonment of Santo Domingo by Spain," RSGTCI, February 11, 1865 (reprinted from the *London Times*); "Santo Domingo," RSGTCI, February 17, 1865.

103. "The Re-established Independence of San Domingo," RSGTCI, March 25, 1865 (reprinted from the *New York Tribune*).

104. "Salt," RSGTCI, April 22, 1865; "Speech of His Honor President Moir," RSGTCI, April 29, 1865; "The Apparent End of the Rebellion," RSGTCI, April 15, 1865 (reprinted from the *New York World*).

105. Like Bahamians, white Turks islanders were sympathetic to US Southerners. W. B. Johnson, *Post-Emancipation*, 40–41.

106. "The Black Man's Own Testimony," RSGTCI, September 2, 1865.

107. "The Freedmen," RSGTCI, July 22, 1865.

108. Holt, *Problem of Freedom*, 42–53, 76–78.

109. James Watson, "The Rebellions Contrasted," RSGTCI, January 13, 1866.

110. Watson, "The Rebellions Contrasted," RSGTCI, January 13, 1866.

111. Holt, *Problem of Freedom*, 291, 294.

112. Watson, "The Rebellions Contrasted," RSGTCI, January 13, 1866; James Watson, "The Rebellions Contrasted," RSGTCI, January 20, 1866.

113. Watson, "The Rebellions Contrasted," RSGTCI, January 20, 1866.

114. Workman, "Thomas Carlyle," 77–78.

115. Webb, *Haiti*, 106–22; Smith, *Liberty, Fraternity, Exile*, 136–52 and 159–63; Sheller, *Democracy after Slavery*, 227–33.

116. Webb, *Haiti*, 90–106; Smith, *Liberty, Fraternity, Exile*, 152–58.

117. Webb, *Haiti*, 92, 100.

118. Webb, *Haiti*, 87–137, especially 89, 136–37.

119. Webb, *Haiti*, 88, 106, 111, 119.

120. [Untitled], *RSGTCI*, December 2, 1865. See also [Untitled], *RSGTCI*, December 9, 1865.

121. Thomas Lawson to William Boyce, December 14, 1870, microfiche 1393–1394, WMMS-WI, SOAS.

122. Eller, *We Dream Together*, 231.

123. Luperón, *Notas autobiográficas*, vol. 3, 399; Domínguez, *Notas económicas y políticas*, vol. 2, 430–31.

124. Eller, *We Dream Together*, 230.

125. "Santo Domingo," *RSGTCI*, June 24, 1865; A. Lockward, *Intolerancia*, 82.

126. "Santo Domingo," *RSGTCI*, September 9, 1865.

127. Bosch, *Social Composition*, 180.

128. Many of the Black men and women from the Turks Islands who relocated to Puerto Plata or went back and forth between the two locales over the years spoke Spanish. See comparable case of Debra in Eller, *We Dream Together*, 136.

129. Francis Moon to E. Hoole, January 17, 1866, microfiche 1379–1380, WMMS-WI, SOAS.

130. "To the Secretaries and Committee," February 12, 1866, microfiche 1380, WMMS-WI, SOAS.

131. Moon to Hoole, January 17, 1866.

132. "To the Secretaries and Committee," February 12, 1866.

133. Martínez, *Diccionario biográfico*, 284; G. A. Lockward, *El protestantismo*, 192–95; A. Lockward, *Intolerancia*, 76.

134. "To the Editor," *RSGTCI*, January 6, 1866. The newspaper misspelled *ciudadano*, which appears as *cindadano*.

135. "To the Editor," *RSGTCI*, January 6, 1866.

136. "To the Editor," *RSGTCI*, January 6, 1866.

137. Marriage certificate no. 337 (1866), Henry C. C. Astwood and Margaret J. Francisco, file EAP914/2/1/1, ACRTCI, BL.

138. Julián Francisco of Puerto Plata sometimes lived on Grand Turk. Luperón, *Notas autobiográficas*, vol. 2, 101, 158; Martínez, *Diccionario biográfico*, 180.

139. "Married," *RSGTCI*, April 7, 1866.

140. Luperón had arrived from St. Thomas that week. "Shipping and Commercial List," *RSGTCI*, April 7, 1866.

141. Charles R. Douglass to Secretary of State [Frelinghuysen], May 29, 1882, ACA-B3, ARPO, National Archives and Records Administration, Record Group 59; Baptismal record of Theresa DeLeon Pardo, file EAP914/2/2/6, ACRTCI, BL. This family is not related to the M. E. Pardo mentioned in later chapters.

142. Arthur Sosa and Arthur Nouel, "Censos."

143. "Shipping and Commercial List," *RSGTCI*, April 28, 1866.

144. "Shipping and Commercial List," *RSGTCI*, April 28, 1866.

145. A. J. Astwood, "To the Editor," *RSGTCI*, June 23, 1866.

146. "Santo Domingo—Its Past and Present," *RSGTCI*, September 1, 1866.

147. Astwood, "To the Editor," *RSGTCI*, June 23, 1866; A. J. Astwood, "Notice," *RSGTCI*, June 23, 1866.

148. Astwood, "To the Editor," *RSGTCI*, June 23, 1866.

149. Horne, *Confronting Black Jacobins*, 225–26. Bahamians were also captured: W. B. Johnson, *Post-Emancipation*, 63–65.

150. "Another Vessel Captured by the Spaniards," *RSGTCI*, May 27, 1865.

151. "Santo Domingo—Its Past and Present," *RSGTCI*, September 1, 1866.

152. "Santo Domingo," *RSGTCI*, September 1, 1866.

153. "Santo Domingo," *RSGTCI*, September 1, 1866.

154. "Santo Domingo—Its Past and Present," *RSGTCI*, September 1, 1866.

155. For Cabral, see Martínez-Fernández, *Torn between Empires*, 222–24.

CHAPTER 2. A RECONSTRUCTED LIFE: BECOMING H. C. C. ASTWOOD
IN THE US-CARIBBEAN SPHERE

1. [Untitled], *RSGTCI*, December 29, 1866, page 2, column 1.

2. Thomas Bates to the General Secretaries, October 8, 1866, microfiche 1380, WMMS-WI, Library of the School of Oriental and African Studies (SOAS), University of London.

3. [Untitled], *RSGTCI*, December 29, 1866, page 2, column 1.

4. "Summary of the Conditions," *RSGTCI*, December 22, 1866.

5. Bates to the General Secretaries, October 8, 1866.

6. For these dynamics, see Gaztambide Géigel, "La geopolítica"; Ojeda Reyes, "Betances, Meriño, Luperón"; Ojeda Reyes and Estrade, *Pasión por la libertad*, 3–94; Cordero Michel, "República Dominicana"; Reyes-Santos, *Our Caribbean Kin*, 29–62; Du Bois, *Black Reconstruction*; Foner, *Reconstruction*; Gates, *Stony the Road*.

7. For examples, see Scott and Hébrard, *Freedom Papers*; Jacoby, *Strange Career*.

8. "The Weather—Our Prospects," *RSGTCI*, October 20, 1866; Francis Moon to E. Hoole, January 17, 1867, microfiche 1381, WMMS-WI, SOAS.

9. Bates to the General Secretaries, October 8, 1866; Thomas Bates to Rev. W. Arthur, January 18, 1867, microfiche 1381, WMMS-WI, SOAS.

10. "The Weather—Our Prospects"; Eller, *We Dream Together*, 234.

11. [Untitled], *RSGTCI*, November 3, 1866, page 2, first article; [Untitled], *RSGTCI*, November 24, 1866, page 2, first article.

12. "Arrival of the November Mails," *RSGTCI*, December 8, 1866.

13. Moon to Hoole, January 17, 1867.

14. "The Weather—Our Prospects." See also Bates to Arthur, January 18, 1867.

15. Moon to Hoole, January 17, 1867.

16. "The Weather—Our Prospects."

17. Thomas Bates to Rev. W. Arthur, December 26, 1866, microfiche 1381, WMMS-WI, SOAS.

18. Adolphus Astwood, "To the Editor," *RSGTCI*, March 2, 1867.

19. "Alarm of Fire," *RSGTCI*, January 5, 1867.

20. "The Drought," *RSGTCI*, February 16, 1867; "Water! Water!!,"*RSGTCI*, March 9, 1867.

21. "Daring and Malicious Robbery," *RSGTCI*, May 4, 1867.
22. "Statement of the Condition," *RSGTCI*, January 12, 1867; "Statement of the Condition," *RSGTCI*, February 2, 1867.
23. "Statement of the Condition," *RSGTCI*, March 2, 1867.
24. "Tailoring," *RSGTCI*, February 9, 1867.
25. "Abstract of Minutes of Proceedings," *RSGTCI*, May 25, 1867; "Participo á este respetable público," *El Porvenir*, March 16, 1872.
26. "Advertisement," *RSGTCI*, June 1, 1867; "Advertisement," *RSGTCI*, June 8, 1867.
27. "Port of Salt Cay," *RSGTCI*, April 6, 1867, "Shipping and Commercial List," *RSGTCI*, October 5, 1867; "A Proclamation," *RSGTCI*, August 3, 1867.
28. "Abstract of Minutes of Proceedings," *RSGTCI*, November 23, 1867; "Notice," *RSGTCI*, February 29, 1868.
29. "Marshal's Sale," *RSGTCI*, February 29, 1868.
30. "The Haytien General Salnave," *RSGTCI*, February 9, 1867.
31. "Hayti," *RSGTCI*, March 23, 1867; "Hayti," *RSGTCI*, March 30, 1867; "Hayti," *RSGTCI*, June 29, 1867.
32. M. J. Smith, *Liberty, Fraternity, Exile*, 172–73; "Hayti," *RSGTCI*, October 12, 1867.
33. "St. Domingo," *RSGTCI*, September 21, 1867 (reprinted from the *New York Herald*).
34. "Hayti," *RSGTCI*, November 9, 1867; "Santo Domingo," *RSGTCI*, November 16, 1867.
35. "Hayti," *RSGTCI*, November 9, 1867. See also Martínez-Fernández, *Torn between Empires*, 224.
36. "Santo Domingo," *RSGTCI*, November 30, 1867.
37. "Santo Domingo," *RSGTCI*, November 30, 1867.
38. "A Proclamation," *RSGTCI*, December 7, 1867.
39. Luperón, *Notas autobiográficas*, vol. 2, 101–2.
40. "Santo Domingo," *RSGTCI*, December 14, 1867.
41. B. Vega, *La cuestión racial*, 85–90; Martínez-Fernández, *Torn between Empires*, 224–25.
42. "St. Domingo—the American Gibraltor," *RSGTCI*, August 28, 1869. See also "Santo Domingo," *RSGTCI*, December 11, 1869; "American—St. Domingo," *RSGTCI*, December 18, 1869.
43. "St. Domingo," *RSGTCI*, January 15, 1870.
44. "The Samana Bay Purchase," *RSGTCI*, January 22, 1870.
45. "St. Domingo," *RSGTCI*, April 2, 1870. For a history of the US annexation effort, see B. Vega, *La cuestión racial*, 99–245; Love, *Race over Empire*, 27–72; Hauch, *La República Dominicana*, 192–232; Tansill, *United States*, 338–464.
46. Eller, *We Dream Together*, 233–34; Reyes-Santos, *Our Caribbean Kin*, 29–36; Cordero Michel, "República Dominicana," 225–36.
47. Reyes-Santos, *Our Caribbean Kin*, 44–53; García-Peña, *Translating Blackness*, 60–70.
48. Guerra, "Héroes y parentela."
49. Ojeda Reyes, "Betances, Meriño, Luperón."
50. [Untitled], *RSGTCI*, October 3, 1868, page 2, column 1, second article. See also Eller, *We Dream Together*, 234.
51. Rodríguez Rosario, "Tejiendo lazos," 151–53.

52. "Shipping and Commercial List," RSGTCI, April 18, 1868; "Shipping and Commercial List," RSGTCI, January 22, 1870.

53. "Santo Domingo," RSGTCI, July 11, 1868; "Santo Domingo," RSGTCI, December 11, 1869.

54. "Santo Domingo," RSGTCI, April 2, 1870; "Santo Domingo," RSGTCI, July 10, 1869.

55. "Santo Domingo," RSGTCI, July 10, 1869.

56. "Dominican Republic," RSGTCI, May 22, 1869.

57. "Abstract of Proceedings of the Legislative Council," RSGTCI, December 4, 1869. For provisions, see the note after "Public Meeting," RSGTCI, November 27, 1869.

58. "Public Meeting," RSGTCI, November 27, 1869.

59. The financial crisis ultimately precipitated a reversal of the independent colony status. The Turks and Caicos Islands were attached to Jamaica in 1873.

60. "Marshal's Sale," RSGTCI, July 2, 1870.

61. "In the Court of the Ordinary," RSGTCI, August 13, 1870.

62. "Sketches of Delegates," CR, April 16, 1896.

63. See "Notice," RSGTCI, October 29, 1870; "Notice," RSGTCI, November 5, 1870; "Notice," RSGTCI, November 11, 1870. Assets also included additional acres in the salt ponds, a plantation on Grand Turk, and a store.

64. "Notice," RSGTCI, October 29, 1870.

65. Zeller, "Puerto Plata," 28. The nineteenth-century Dominican intellectual José Ramón López referred jokingly to Puerto Plata as the "capital of Turks Islands." G. A. Lockward, El protestantismo, 151.

66. "Statement of the Condition," RSGTCI, January 12, 1867.

67. Death record of Theresa De Leon Pardo, February 18, 1871, file EAP914/2/2/7, ACRTCI, British Library (BL).

68. "Marshall's Sale," RSGTCI, July 1, 1876; death record of Adolphus Astwood, June 29, 1884, file EAP914/2/2/7, ACRTCI, BL.

69. Arthur Sosa and Arthur Nouel, "Censos."

70. Cristina was Dominican and likely the child of Erminia Evertz, who likely worked with Henry.

71. "George A. Astwood," DRCR.

72. Zeller, "Puerto Plata," 35.

73. Gregoria Goins, "'Miss Doc,'" box 36–4, folder 52, p. 109, GGP, Moorland-Spingarn Research Center at Howard University, Washington, DC. See also Hazard, Santo Domingo, 176–78.

74. Goins, "'Miss Doc,'" p. 110.

75. James Banks and Prezin Handsbury to Wesleyan Methodist Missionary Society, August 12, 1870, microfiche 1391, WMMS-WI, SOAS.

76. Hazard, Santo Domingo, 180–82; Puig Ortiz, Emigración, 27–29; Eller, We Dream Together, 39–40.

77. Zeller, "Puerto Plata," 28; Rodríguez Rosario, "Tejiendo lazos," 167.

78. "Tea-Meeting," El Porvenir, July 5, 1872.

79. "Se avisa al público," El Porvenir, June 21, 1872; Puig Ortiz, Emigración, 138–39.

80. Henry Chas. Clifford Astwood, April 30, 1871, UGLE-FMR.

81. Arroyo, *Writing Secrecy*, 18.

82. "Small Pox at Porto Plata," *RSGTCI*, January 21, 1871; "A Proclamation," *RSGTCI*, June 10, 1871; "Small Pox at Porto Plata," *RSGTCI*, June 17, 1871; "Small Pox," *RSGTCI*, July 22, 1871; "Fire at Porto Plata," *RSGTCI*, September 2, 1871; "The Fire at Porto Plata," *RSGTCI*, September 16, 1871; "The Late Fire in Puerto Plata," *RSGTCI*, September 30, 1871. This event took place a month before the Chicago fire, which was also reported on.

83. "Santo Domingo," *RSGTCI*, July 10, 1869.

84. "Santo Domingo," *RSGTCI*, April 2, 1870.

85. United States Commission of Inquiry to Santo Domingo, *Dominican Republic*, 133.

86. H. C. C. Astwood to Bancroft Davis, February 25, 1882, no. 1, DUSCSD, National Archives and Records Administration, Record Group 59 (NARA-59).

87. B. Vega, *La cuestión racial*, 27–28; Martínez-Fernández, *Torn between Empires*, 29–32, 42.

88. B. Vega, *La cuestión racial*, 41–57, 76–79; Martínez-Fernández, *Torn between Empires*, 45–49; Eller, *We Dream Together*, 51.

89. Hauch, *La República Dominicana*, 198–229; B. Vega, *La cuestión racial*, 76–98.

90. Hauch, *La República Dominicana*, 228–29; B. Vega, *La cuestión racial*, 222, 226–27. Despite this failure, US ships remained in the bay until 1873.

91. Hauch, *La República Dominicana*, 242–44; B. Vega, *La cuestión racial*, 231–32.

92. B. Vega, *La cuestión racial*, 236, 251–53, 277.

93. Hidalgo, *La primera inmigración*; Fanning, *Caribbean Crossing*; Alexander, "Land of Promise"; Maffly-Kipp, *Setting Down*, 109–53; Jackson, "Origins of Pan-African Nationalism," 49–117; Byrd, "Reinterpretation."

94. For Protestantism, see Findlay and Holdsworth, *History*, 262–69, 490–519; G. A. Lockward, *El protestantismo*, 111–23; G. A. Lockward, *Cartas de Cardy*; Hidalgo, *La primera inmigración*, 163–208.

95. There were eight hundred to a thousand residents of majority African American descent. Hazard, *Santo Domingo*, 199. See also Puig Ortiz, *Emigración*, 30–31.

96. Hazard, *Santo Domingo*, 199; Puig Ortiz, *Emigración*, 29–30; Horne, *Confronting*, 290; B. Vega, *La cuestión racial*, 64–73, 112–13.

97. *Religio-racial identity* refers to "understanding individual and collective identity as constituted in the conjunction of religion and race," described in Weisenfeld, *New World A-coming*, 5.

98. For traditions, see M. E. Davis, "That Old-Time Religion," 107–8; M. E. Davis, "La cultura musical," 150–56.

99. Thomas Bates to William B. Boyce, December 16, 1868, microfiche 1384, WMMS-WI, SOAS.

100. Jacob James to the General Secretaries, January 27, 1874, microfiche 1413, WMMS-WI, SOAS; Thomas Lawson to William B. Boyce, December 14, 1870, microfiche 1393–1894, WMMS-WI, SOAS.

101. For examples, see Hoetink, "'Americans,'" 8–21; Wilkins, "'They Had Heard,'" 213; Hidalgo, *La primera inmigración*, 126–27; Fellows, "Double Consciousness."

102. United States Commission of Inquiry to Santo Domingo, *Dominican Republic*, 229–30.

103. Davidson, "Black Protestants," 281.

104. Wilkins, "'They Had Heard,'" 213; Polyné, *From Douglass*, 29, 35–26; García-Peña, *Translating Blackness*, 53.

105. Wilkins, "'They Had Heard,'" 223; Bourhis-Mariotti, "Frederick Douglass," 237–39; Bourhis-Mariotti, *Wanted! A Nation!*, 121.

106. Wilkins, "'They Had Heard,'" 222.

107. United States Commission of Inquiry to Santo Domingo, *Dominican Republic*, 231.

108. Martínez-Vergne, *Nation and Citizen*, 19.

109. For example, see the name "Elizabeth Hernández" in US Senate, *Index to the Executive Documents*, 65.

110. For example, in 1874 James worried about the baptism of illegitimate children likely born to mixed unions whose parents preferred to baptize them in the Catholic Church rather than let them remain unbaptized. Jacob James to the General Secretaries, August 9, 1874, microfiche 1416, WMMS-WI, SOAS.

111. Jacob James to the General Secretaries, September 29, 1873, microfiche 1412, WMMS-WI, SOAS, emphasis added. Conversions were also reported in James to the General Secretaries, January 10, 1883, microfiche 2052, WMMS-WI, SOAS.

112. Henry Belby to W. B. Boyce, June 16, 1874, microfiche 1415–1416, WMMS-WI, SOAS; Henry Belby to G. J. Perks, October 4, 1876, microfiche 1424, WMMS-WI, SOAS.

113. "A Card," *RSGTCI*, January 5, 1867; A. Lockward, *Intolerancia*, 97–98; G. A. Lockward, *El protestantismo*, 285.

114. United States Commission of Inquiry to Santo Domingo, *Dominican Republic*, 230.

115. Joseph A. Heureaux, February 12, 1848, microfiche 1991, WMMS-WI, SOAS.

116. "Character of Joseph Alexandre Heureaux," May 6, 1848, microfiche 1991, WMMS-WI, SOAS; James Hartwell to Rev. and Dear Brethren, May 1, 1848, microfiche 1991, WMMS-WI, SOAS.

117. Sensbach, *Rebecca's Revival*.

118. Sang, *Ulises Heureaux*, 10.

119. Wilkins, "'They Had Heard,'" 213, 225–26; "Communications," *CR*, March 30, 1872; Davidson, "'What Hinders?,'" 60–62.

120. Cazneau, *Our Winter's Eden*, 11.

121. "Communications," *CR*, March 30, 1872.

122. Thomas Payne to W. B. Boyce, October 8, 1868, microfiche 1384, WMMS-WI, SOAS.

123. Jacob James to the General Secretaries, March 21, 1881, microfiche 2047, WMMS-WI, SOAS.

124. Davidson, "Converting," 338–57; Davidson, "Black Protestants," 269–81.

125. Thomas Lawson to the Secretaries of the Wesleyan Missionary Society, November 16, 1870, microfiche 1393, WMMS-WI, SOAS.

126. Lawson to Boyce, December 14, 1870.

127. H. I. Moore to the General Secretaries, July 7, 1873, microfiche 1412, WMMS-WI, SOAS.

128. James to the General Secretaries, September 29, 1873; Henry Belby to William B. Boyce, May 17, 1875, microfiche 1418–1419, WMMS-WI, SOAS.

129. Howe, *Reminiscences*, 363.

130. This term traditionally refers to Black religion in the antebellum US South. For a summary, see Raboteau, *Canaan Land*, 43–59.

131. Guyatt, "America's Conservatory," 974.

132. Department of the Navy to Charles R. Douglass, February 24, 1890, ACA-B3, ARPO, NARA-59.

133. Nystrom, *New Orleans*, 7.

134. Nystrom, *New Orleans*, 158. See also Keith, *Colfax Massacre*; Lane, *Day Freedom Died*; Tunnell, *Crucible of Reconstruction*, 189–93; J. G. Taylor, *Louisiana Reconstructed*, 267–71.

135. Nystrom, *New Orleans*, 160–85.

136. Foner, *Reconstruction*, 524–27.

137. Foner, *Reconstruction*, 529–31.

138. H. C. C. Astwood to Charles R. Douglass, May 29, 1878, ACA-B3, ARPO, NARA-59.

139. Nystrom, *New Orleans*, 101–3.

140. Nystrom, *New Orleans*, 102.

141. Oscar Dunn was the first Black lieutenant governor.

142. "Our Agents," WL, December 4, 1875; "Proceedings of the Committee," WL, December 4, 1875.

143. "Political Matters," *New Orleans Republican*, May 18, 1876; "H. C. Astwood (colored)," *Times-Picayune*, December 23, 1876.

144. "Mounted and Armed Men," *Janesville Gazette*, November 22, 1876.

145. "Shotgun Suffrage," *New Orleans Republican*, November 17, 1876.

146. "The Investigating Committees," *Perrysburg Journal*, December 29, 1876.

147. "Louisiana," *Chicago Daily Tribune*, April 11, 1877.

148. Astwood to C. R. Douglass, May 29, 1878. These were Freedmen's Bureau schools that closed when federal troops withdrew in 1876.

149. "Christmas and Festivities," WL, December 25, 1875.

150. Walkes, *History of the Prince Hall*, 17–21, 25, 53, 314.

151. Walkes, *History of the Prince Hall*, 17–21.

152. For Astwood's membership, see "Odd Fellows' Convention," NYF, October 16, 1886. One of St. James's stained glass windows commemorates the GUOOF and another the Eureka lodge.

153. For example, "The Country Press," *New Orleans Daily Democrat*, November 11, 1877.

154. "The Colored Emigration Scheme Dodge," *New Orleans Daily Democrat*, October 18, 1877. For Turner, see Angell, *Bishop Henry*.

155. "The School Agitation," *People's Vindicator*, October 20, 1877. The Louisiana State Congress legislated school segregation on July 3, 1877.

156. "Our Reception," WL, December 21, 1878; "An Address," WL, December 28, 1878; "Sketches of Delegates," CR, April 16, 1896.

157. "The Colored Convention," *WL*, April 26, 1879; "Sunday-School Union," *WL*, April 26, 1879; "Proceedings of the Garrison Memorial Service," *WL*, June 28, 1879; [Untitled], *WL*, October 25, 1879, page 3, column 3.

158. "Personals," *WL*, February 21, 1880.

159. For light-skinned, see Bennett, *Religion*, 31. Further investigation confirms Henry's place among Afro-Creoles and refutes earlier claims made in Davidson, "Converting Spanish Hispaniola," 74.

160. For Afro-Creole leaders, see Rankin, "Origins of Black Leadership"; Foner, *Freedom's Lawmakers*.

161. Scott, "Discerning a Dignitary Offense," 526–36.

162. "Marriage License H. C. C. Astwood and Alice Ternoir," April 1, 1878, LPM.

163. "Alice Ternoer in the 1870 United States Federal Census," USC-1870.

164. This information derives from the Ternoir family tree created by Jari Honora, reference associate of the Historic New Orleans Collection. Jari Honora, in discussion with the author, February 3, 2022.

165. Charles R. Douglass to Secretary of State [Frelinghuysen], District of Columbia, February 6, 1882, ACA-B3, ARPO, NARA-59.

166. Three of the children were Henry's. The fourth may have been a child who did not survive, or Margaret's daughter Maria Luisa, born August 18, 1878. "Birth Record, Maria Luisa Astwood," August 18, 1878, DRCR.

167. For Lewis, see Foner, *Freedom's Lawmakers*, 132–33.

168. "Birth Record, Charles Sumner Astwood," July 8, 1878, OP-BR; "Death Record, Charles Sumner Astwood," July 30, 1878, OP-DRC. The child died soon after birth.

169. For charges, see Charles R. Douglas to Frederick Douglass, Washington, DC, October 4, 1893, FDP-GC, Library of Congress.

170. James Lewis to Charles R. Douglass, New Orleans, Louisiana, June 18, 1878, ACA-B3, ARPO, NARA-59.

171. James Lewis to Charles R. Douglass, New Orleans, Louisiana, July 31, 1878, ACA-B3, ARPO, NARA-59.

172. Many men of social standing had children out of wedlock or second families, and it was not unusual for them to "divorce" their wives and remarry in the way that Astwood had. For another contemporary example, see the story of "Aunt Lucket" in Goins, "'Miss Doc,'" pp. 51–54.

173. Astwood to C. R. Douglass, May 29, 1878.

174. Lewis doubted that Henry would be received well, and indeed Astwood reported that he was "put off from 1st to 1st" at the customhouse. Astwood to C. R. Douglass, May 29, 1878.

175. Astwood intimated that $100 was paid monthly. Pinchback's newspaper suggested that the work was as a US customs gauger. Astwood to C. R. Douglass, May 29, 1878; [Untitled], *WL*, August 9, 1879, page 3, column 2.

176. [Untitled], *WL*, July 12, 1879, page 3, column 1.

177. Straight University, *Catalogue of Straight University*, 8; Blassingame, *Black New Orleans*, 125–30.

178. Blassingame, *Black New Orleans*, 147; [Untitled], *WL*, October 11, 1879, page 3, column 1.

179. "Republican Convention," *WL*, March 20, 1880; "Republican State Convention," *WL*, May 29, 1880.

180. [Untitled], *WL*, April 10, 1880, page 2, column 1.

181. [Untitled], *WL*, February 5, 1881, page 3, column 2; "Officers and Teachers Meeting," *WL*, June 18, 1881.

182. "Louisiana District Lodge," *WL*, June 16, 1881.

183. H. C. C. Astwood, "Prospectus," *WL*, July 30, 1881.

184. Desdunes is known for his work as a founder of the Comité des Citoyens, which initiated the pivotal *Plessy v. Ferguson* case.

185. R. L. Desdunes, "Guerre à l'injustice," *WL*, July 30, 1881.

186. Adam Lux, "Un appel sérieux," *WL*, August 12, 1881.

187. For examples, see "Les français en Afrique," *WL*, July 30, 1881; "L'Amérique du Sud," *WL*, August 20, 1881; "Le Président de la République française," *WL*, August 20, 1881; "St. Domingue," *WL*, September 3, 1881.

188. "L'appel," *WL*, August 6, 1881.

189. "The Colored People Meet," *Times-Picayune*, July 5, 1881; "How the Presidential Obsequies Was Observed," *WL*, October 1, 1881.

190. "The Louisiana Office-Seekers," *Times-Democrat*, January 10, 1882. For Henry's first attempt, see "A Louisiana Delegation," *National Republican* (Washington, DC), March 28, 1881.

191. C. R. Douglass to Secretary of State [Frelinghuysen], February 6, 1882. Astwood was naturalized in 1876. He had not yet lived in the country for the required five years. "Hy. C. C. Astwood," June 24, 1876, USNRI.

192. "List of Passengers on Board the Steamship *Geo W. Clyde*," March 20, 1883, PLVNY.

193. "Photograph, Straight University," Straight University and Professor H. H. Swain Collection, MSS 908.1.9.4, Williams Research Center, The Historic New Orleans Collection, accessed February 26, 2024, https://catalog.hnoc.org/en-US/web/arena/collections-search#/entity/thnoc-archive/MSS%20908.1.9.4/photographs. Taken between 1883 and 1886, this image shows students in front of Stone Hall (490 Canal St.); the group includes Mildred Astwood.

194. H. C. C. Astwood to William Hunter, August 22, 1883, no. 93, DUSCSD, NARA-59; "Henry Astwood in the 1900 US Federal Census," USFC-1900.

195. García-Peña, *Translating Blackness*, 41, 53.

196. Goins, "'Miss Doc,'" p. 141; Mayes, *Mulatto Republic*, 15.

CHAPTER 3. THE OTHER BLACK REPUBLIC: SEGREGATED STATECRAFT AND THE DUAL NATURE OF US-DOMINICAN DIPLOMACY

1. H. C. C. Astwood to William Hunter, April 14, 1882, no. 3, DUSCSD, National Archives and Records Administration, Record Group 59 (NARA-59).

2. "Case of H. C. C. Astwood," May 31, 1882, ACA-B3, ARPO, NARA-59; Charles R. Douglass to Whom It May Concern, September 19, 1889, FDP-GC, Library of Congress.

3. Astwood to Hunter, April 14, 1882. This paralleled John Mercer Langston's relocation of the US legation in Haiti. See Langston, *From the Virginia Plantation*, 375.
4. H. C. C. Astwood to William Hunter, May 22, 1882, no. 6, DUSCSD, NARA-59. Atarazana Street was located next to the customhouse on the northeast end of the city. Alemar, *Santo Domingo*, 121.
5. H. C. C. Astwood to William Hunter, October 26, 1885, no. 287, DUSCSD, NARA-59.
6. Ramírez, *Colonial Phantoms*, 7–9; Eller, "'Awful Pirates,'" 90.
7. For traditional readings, see Welles, *Naboth's Vineyard*, 461–68; Hauch, *La República Dominicana*, 252; Domínguez, *Notas económicas y políticas*, vol. 1, 95–97, 122, 128, 171–83, 233; Domínguez, *La dictadura*, 18–19, 25, 115–18, 147.
8. Sang, *Ulises Heureaux*, 39, 50–75; Veeser, "Concessions," 747–49.
9. For examples beyond Astwood, see Blakely, "Blacks in the U.S. Diplomatic," 19–21. For a significant counterexample, see Byrd, "Ebenezer Bassett."
10. Hoetink, *Dominican People*, 131, 161.
11. Gow, "The Economic Background," 82–84; Welles, *Naboth's Vineyard*, 463.
12. Moya Pons, *Dominican Republic*, 232–36; Hauch, *La República Dominicana*, 249–55, 266–67; Domínguez, *Notas económicas y políticas*, vol. 2, 541–64; Tejada, "El partido rojo," 29–31.
13. Tejada, "El partido rojo," 22.
14. Moya Pons, *Dominican Republic*, 236–44; Hauch, *La República Dominicana*, 268–78; Domínguez, *Notas económicas y políticas*, vol. 2, 567–612; Hoetink, *Dominican People*, 114–15.
15. "A New San Domingo Revolt," NYT, January 17, 1880; "Troubles in the West Indies," NYT, April 6, 1880; "Consternation in San Domingo," NYT, December 24, 1881; "Executions in Santo Domingo," *New York Tribune*, August 21, 1881; "The West Indies," NYT, February 14, 1882.
16. Franks, "Transforming Property," 87–106; Martínez-Vergne, *Nation and Citizen*, 11–13.
17. "San Domingo's Big Fire," NYT, March 25, 1880; H. C. C. Astwood to William Hunter, February 24–25, 1883, nos. 78, 79; September 12–13, 17, 1883, nos. 99, 100, 103, DUSCSD, NARA-59.
18. H. C. C. Astwood to Second Asst. Secty. of State, May 12, 1882, no. 5, DUSCSD, NARA-59.
19. Astwood to Second Asst. Secty. of State, May 12, 1882.
20. William Hunter to H. C. C. Astwood, June 8, 1882, no. 6, USSDCI, NARA-59.
21. Astwood to Second Asst. Secty. of State, May 12, 1882.
22. Blakely, "Blacks in the U.S. Diplomatic," 14.
23. Gaffield, *Haitian Connections*, 14.
24. Gaffield, *Haitian Connections*, 10.
25. For example, see B. Vega, *La cuestión racial*, 25–26.
26. B. Vega, *La cuestión racial*, 39–98.
27. García Muñiz and Borges, "U.S. Consular Activism," 35.
28. Hauch, *La República Dominicana*, 251.
29. Hoetink, *Dominican People*, 7; Franks, "Transforming Property," 121–25.
30. Most historians credit another Cuban, Joaquín M. Delgado, with the first steam sugar mill, founded in 1874. I follow García Muñiz's interpretation in *Sugar and*

Power, 202. For Delgado, see Sánchez, *La caña*, 29; Bosch, *Social Composition*, 205; Sang, *Ulises Heureaux*, 42; Cassá, *Historia social y económica*, 131; Knight, *Americans*, 23.

31. Bryan, "Transition to Plantation Agriculture," 85–87; Domínguez, *Notas económicas y políticas*, vol. 1, 303–12; Castillo, "Formation," 215–16; García Muñiz, *Sugar and Power*, 201–2; Bosch, *Social Composition*, 205.

32. Bryan, "Transition to Plantation Agriculture," 105; Castillo, "Formation," 217–20, 224–25; Sang, *Ulises Heureaux*, 44, 230–32.

33. This document includes Astwood's assessment and a translation of the Dominican tariff law. H. C. C. Astwood to [Sec. of State] Frederick T. Frelinghuysen, September 30, 1882, no. 61, DUSCSD, NARA-59.

34. See also Domínguez, *Notas económicas y políticas*, vol. 1, 179, 183.

35. Astwood to Frelinghuysen, September 30, 1882. See also Domínguez, *Notas económicas y políticas*, vol. 1, 95; Cassá, *Historia social y económica*, 130; Sang, *Ulises Heureaux*, 230–32.

36. Domínguez, *Notas económicas y políticas*, vol. 1, 176–86; Sang, *Ulises Heureaux*, 48.

37. Astwood to Frelinghuysen, September 30, 1882; Domínguez, *Notas económicas y políticas*, vol. 1, 184.

38. Domínguez, *Notas económicas y políticas*, vol. 1, 305.

39. García Muñiz, *Sugar and Power*, 202n3; Domínguez, *Notas económicas y políticas*, vol. 1, 305; Baud, *Historia de un sueño*, 36–46.

40. United States Commission of Inquiry to Santo Domingo, *Dominican Republic*, 239; Hoetink, *Dominican People*, 214n26; H. C. C. Astwood to William Hunter, January 1, 1885, no. 202, DUSCSD, NARA-59.

41. H. C. C. Astwood to William Hunter, April 14, 1882, no. 4, DUSCSD, NARA-59.

42. Astwood to Frelinghuysen, September 30, 1882.

43. Astwood to Frelinghuysen, September 30, 1882. For these dynamics, see Domínguez, *Notas económicas y políticas*, vol. 1, 239–91; Rosa, *Las finanzas*, 32–74.

44. H. C. C. Astwood to William Hunter, November 27, 1882, no. 62, DUSCSD, NARA-59.

45. Harris, *Summer*, 62–63, 153–60.

46. Pitre, "Frederick Douglass," 463–64; Polyné, *From Douglass*, 38–43; Guyatt, "America's Conservatory," 990; Davidson, "Converting," 62–64.

47. Guyatt, "America's Conservatory," 975–76, 999–1000; García-Peña, *Translating Blackness*, 41.

48. Astwood to Frelinghuysen, September 30, 1882. For cotton, see also B. Vega, *La cuestión racial*, 89.

49. Astwood to Frelinghuysen, September 30, 1882.

50. Heureaux later rehashed plans for US Black immigration. Welles, *Naboth's Vineyard*, 466–67; Hoetink, *Dominican People*, 189–90.

51. For concurrent immigration to Haiti, see "Emigration to Hayti," CR, February 3, 1881.

52. Tansill, *United States*, 343–46; Hauch, *La República Dominicana*, 193–94; B. Vega, *La cuestión racial*, 41–63, 70–73, 85–90, 104–8, 116–18, 129–32, 145–49.

53. Tansill, *United States*, 347–50; Hauch, *La República Dominicana*, 196; Knight, *Americans*, 13; B. Vega, *La cuestión racial*, 107–8.

54. Domínguez, *Notas económicas y políticas*, vol. 2, 645–46.

55. Hauch, *La República Dominicana*, 229, 280–82.

56. For example, see Castillo, Brea, and Henriquez y Carvajal, *En la elaboración del azúcar*.

57. Luperón, *Notas autobiográficas*, vol. 3, 149. Cited also in Hoetink, *Dominican People*, 11.

58. Hoetink, *Dominican People*, 12–13; Martínez-Vergne, *Nation and Citizen*, 42.

59. Astwood to Hunter, November 27, 1882.

60. H. C. C. Astwood to [Sec. of State] Frederick T. Frelinghuysen, September 30, 1882, no. 42, DUSCSD, NARA-59; H. C. C. Astwood to William Hunter, June 16, 1884, no. 166, DUSCSD, NARA-59.

61. Astwood to Frelinghuysen, September 30, 1882; Welles, *Naboth's Vineyard*, 463–64.

62. William Hunter to H. C. C. Astwood, October 27, 1882, no. 17, USSDCI, NARA-59.

63. Astwood to Frelinghuysen, September 30, 1882.

64. For concessions, see Sang, *Ulises Heureaux*, 248–57.

65. H. C. C. Astwood to William Hunter, December 21, 1882, no. 66, DUSCSD, NARA-59.

66. William Hunter to H. C. C. Astwood, November 11, 1882, no. 19, USSDCI, NARA-59.

67. Astwood to Hunter, December 21, 1882.

68. Arthur, *Collected State of the Union Addresses*, 57.

69. H. C. C. Astwood to William Hunter, February 16, 1883, no. 75, DUSCSD, NARA-59.

70. Astwood (1882–89), John S. Durham (1890–91), Campbell L. Maxwell (1892–93), Archibald Grimké (1894–98), Campbell L. Maxwell (1898–1904). The post was elevated to consul general in 1898.

71. Pletcher, *Awkward Years*, 21.

72. Pletcher, *Awkward Years*, 17–18.

73. Pletcher, *Awkward Years*, 20.

74. Logan, *Diplomatic Relations*, 365–67.

75. Scarfi, "La emergencia," 87; Logan, *Diplomatic Relations*, 366.

76. Pletcher, *Awkward Years*, 179.

77. Pletcher, *Awkward Years*, 302.

78. Pletcher, *Awkward Years*, 180–81, 287–88; Márquez Colín, "El tratado"; Wible and Hoover, "Economics."

79. Horne, "Race from Power"; Shibusawa, "U.S. Empire," 875; Kramer, "How Not to Write," 917.

80. Logan, *Diplomatic Relations*, 205–9; Nelson, "U.S. Diplomatic Recognition"; Plummer, *Haiti*, 32–33, 36–45; B. Vega, *La cuestión racial*, 19–26.

81. Gaffield, *Haitian Connections*, 7.

82. "The President's Message," CR, December 13, 1883.

83. García Muñiz and Borges, "U.S. Consular Activism," 35–36; US Department of the Interior, *Official Register of the United States*, 28; H. C. C. Astwood to James D. Porter, April 14, 1886, DUSCSD, NARA-59.

84. For treatment of Black agents, see Blakely, "Blacks in the U.S. Diplomatic," 14–23.

85. Shibusawa, "U.S. Empire," 863–66.

86. Shibusawa, "U.S. Empire," 866.

87. H. C. C. Astwood to William Hunter, February 16, 1883, no. 76, DUSCSD, NARA-59.

88. Astwood to Hunter, February 16, 1883, no. 75.
89. Astwood to Hunter, February 16, 1883, no. 76.
90. H. C. C. Astwood to William Hunter, February 26, 1883, no. 85, DUSCSD, NARA-59.
91. Hoetink, *Dominican People*, 136; García-Peña, *Translating Blackness*, 47; B. Vega, *La cuestión racial*, 134.
92. For Crosby's concession, see "Buenaventura Baez," *Gaceta Oficial*, April 28, 1877, in Segundo Imbert to Exco. Sor. Secretario de Estado [Frelinghuysen], February 15, 1884, NLDR, NARA-59.
93. H. C. C. Astwood to William Hunter, October 31, 1882, no. 50, DUSCSD, NARA-59.
94. H. C. C. Astwood to William Hunter, November 17, 1882, no. 57, DUSCSD, NARA-59.
95. Astwood to Hunter, October 31, 1882.
96. John Davis to H. C. C. Astwood, December 7, 1882, no. 23, USSDCI, NARA-59.
97. For another example, see Logan, *Diplomatic Relations*, 358–60.
98. Davis to Astwood, December 7, 1882.
99. For precedent, see García-Muñiz and Borges, "U.S. Consular Activism," 35–46.
100. H. C. C. Astwood to William Hunter, February 26, 1883, no. 82, DUSCSD, NARA-59.
101. Astwood to Hunter, February 26, 1883.
102. H. C. C. Astwood to William Hunter, March 8, 1883, no. 91, DUSCSD, NARA-59.
103. John Davis to H. C. C. Astwood, March 24, 1883, USSDCI, NARA-59.
104. H. C. C. Astwood to William Hunter, September 27, 1883, no. 109, DUSCSD, NARA-59. These parties included Evaristo de Lamar, Allen Howard Crosby, Joaquin M. Delgado, John Hardy, George K. Zammiz, James W. Mellor, John W. Ferrand, W. W. White, E. H. Hotchkiss, W. Y. Miler, W. A. Read, and George Stokes.
105. H. C. C. Astwood to William Hunter, October 8, 1883, no. 111, DUSCSD, NARA-59.
106. John Davis to H. C. C. Astwood, October 19, 1883, no. 36, USSDCI, NARA-59.
107. For Langston, see Langston, *From the Virginia Plantation*; Padgett, "Diplomats to Haiti," 281–86; Cheek, "Forgotten Prophet"; Fulton, "John Mercer Langston"; Bourhis-Mariotti, *L'union*, 145–51; Bourhis-Mariotti, *Wanted! A Nation!*, 110–14; Byrd, *Black Republic*, 63–71. For instructions, see [Sec. of State] Frederick T. Frelinghuysen to John Mercer Langston, November 12, 1883, no. 1, DIDS, NARA-59.
108. [Sec. of State] Frederick T. Frelinghuysen to John Mercer Langston, November 13, 1883, no. 2, DIDS, NARA-59; William Hunter to H. C. C. Astwood, November 15, 1883, no. 37, USSDCI, NARA-59.
109. H. C. C. Astwood to William Hunter, November 22, 1883, no. 117, DUSCSD, NARA-59.
110. H. C. C. Astwood to William Hunter, December 6, 1883, no. 122, DUSCSD, NARA-59.
111. Astwood involved himself in other concurrent squabbles, but none were like these cases that appeared before the Dominican Congress and Supreme Court.
112. H. C. C. Astwood to William Hunter, January 17, 1884, no. 132, DUSCSD, NARA-59.
113. Rosenberg, "Revisiting Dollar Diplomacy," 171.
114. John Davis to H. C. C. Astwood, December 25, 1883, no. 41, USSDCI, NARA-59; Astwood to Hunter, January 17, 1884.
115. H. C. C. Astwood to William Hunter, February 15, 1884, no. 136, DUSCSD, NARA-59.
116. H. C. C. Astwood to Segundo Imbert, February 4, 1884, included in Astwood to Hunter, February 15, 1884.

117. Astwood to Imbert, February 4, 1884, included in Astwood to Hunter, February 15, 1884.

118. "Civil Protest by Allen Howard Crosby," February 2, 1884, included in Astwood to Hunter, February 15, 1884.

119. H. C. C. Astwood to the Ayuntamiento of Santo Domingo, February 4, 1884, included in Astwood to Hunter, February 15, 1884.

120. Segundo Imbert to H. C. C. Astwood, February 12, 1884, included in Astwood to Hunter, February 15, 1884.

121. Imbert to Exco. Sor. Secretario de Estado [Frelinghuysen], February 15, 1884.

122. H. C. C. Astwood to Segundo Imbert, February 12, 1884, sig. 708393, SERE, Archivo General de la Nación (AGN).

123. H. C. C. Astwood to William Hunter, February 18, 1884, no. 138, DUSCSD, NARA-59.

124. H. C. C. Astwood to Segundo Imbert, March 7, 1884, sig. 708393, SERE, AGN.

125. These words are based on Astwood's citation of them in his letter. H. C. C. Astwood to Segundo Imbert, March 15, 1884, sig. 708393, SERE, AGN.

126. Astwood to Imbert, March 15, 1884.

127. H. C. C. Astwood to William Hunter, March 28, 1884, no. 149, DUSCSD, NARA-59.

128. Astwood to Hunter, March 28, 1884.

129. For commendations, see John Mercer Langston to [Sec. of State] Frederick T. Frelinghuysen, April 9, 1884, DUSMDR, NARA-59; Astwood to Hunter, March 28, 1884. For Astwood's assessment, see H. C. C. Astwood to William Hunter, April 23, 1884, no. 152, DUSCSD, NARA-59.

130. Astwood to Hunter, April 23, 1884.

131. John Davis to H. C. C. Astwood, April 9, 1884, no. 50, USSDCI, NARA-59.

132. H. C. C. Astwood to William Hunter, May 10, 1884, no. 162, DUSCSD, NARA-59.

133. Astwood to Hunter, May 10, 1884.

134. Acto de 25 de abril de 1884, Legado 1702153, PDLR, AGN.

135. H. C. C. Astwood to William Hunter, May 6, 1884, no. 160, DUSCSD, NARA-59.

136. For Galván's biography, see Martínez, *Diccionario biográfico-histórico*, 187; Fernández and Tamaro, "Biografía."

137. Even Astwood confessed that Galván was "one of the best [Dominican] legal minds." Astwood to Hunter, May 6, 1884.

138. Manuel de Jesús Galván to Secretario de Estado, May 30, 1884, NLDR, NARA-59; [Sec. of State] Frederick T. Frelinghuysen to Manuel de Jesús Galvan, May 31, 1884, M99, NFLDS, NARA-59.

139. Manuel de Jesús Galván to [Sec. of State] Frederick T. Frelinghuysen, June 16, 1884, NLDR, NARA-59.

140. [Sec. of State] Frederick T. Frelinghuysen to Manuel de Jesús Galvan, June 9, 1884, M99, NFLDS, NARA-59.

141. Manuel de Jesús Galván to [Sec. of State] Frederick T. Frelinghuysen, July 17, 1884, NLDR, NARA-59.

142. Astwood to Hunter, May 6, 1884; Astwood to Hunter, June 16, 1884; H. C. C. Astwood to William Hunter, July 3, 1884, no. 169, DUSCSD, NARA-59.

143. Astwood to Hunter, May 6, 1884.

144. Astwood to Hunter, January 17, 1884. See also Astwood to Hunter, May 10, 1884.
145. Astwood to Hunter, May 6, 1884; Astwood to Hunter, May 10, 1884.
146. Astwood to Hunter, July 3, 1884; H. C. C. Astwood to William Hunter, July 25, 1884, no. 182, DUSCSD, NARA-59.
147. Astwood to Hunter, May 6, 1884; Astwood to Hunter, May 10, 1884; H. C. C. Astwood to William Hunter, May 17, 1884, no. 163, DUSCSD, NARA-59.
148. Astwood to Hunter, May 6, 1884.
149. Curiel was also involved in the Harmont loan: Hoetink, *Dominican People*, 24.
150. *Colección de leyes*, 160–62.
151. Astwood to Hunter, July 25, 1884.
152. [Sec. of State] Frederick T. Frelinghuysen to John Mercer Langston, March 18, 1884, no. 6, DIDS, NARA-59.
153. Astwood to Hunter, May 6, 1884; Astwood to Hunter, June 16, 1884.
154. Astwood to Hunter, June 16, 1884.
155. H. C. C. Astwood to William Hunter, July 25, 1884, no. 178, DUSCSD, NARA-59; Astwood to Hunter, July 25, 1884.
156. Astwood to Hunter, July 3, 1884.
157. Astwood to Hunter, July 25, 1884.
158. Astwood to Hunter, July 25, 1884.
159. H. C. C. Astwood to William Hunter, August 16, 1884, no. 185, DUSCSD, NARA-59.
160. John Mercer Langston to [Sec. of State] Frederick T. Frelinghuysen, September 9, 1884, no. 12, DUSMDR, NARA-59. For response, see [Sec. of State] Frederick T. Frelinghuysen to John Mercer Langston, October 2, 1884, no. 14, DIDS, NARA-59.
161. John Mercer Langston to [Sec. of State] Frederick T. Frelinghuysen, October 27, 1884, no. 16, DUSMDR, NARA-59.
162. "Local Gossip," *New York Globe*, September 13, 1884.
163. H. C. C. Astwood to William Hunter, September 11, 1884, telegram, DUSCSD, NARA-59; Manuel de Jesús Galván to [Sec. of State] Frederick T. Frelinghuysen, September 14, 1884, telegram, NLDR, NARA-59.
164. H. C. C. Astwood to William Hunter, September 12, 1884, DUSCSD, NARA-59.
165. Manuel de Jesús Galván to [Sec. of State] Frederick T. Frelinghuysen, September 11, 1884, NLDR, NARA-59.
166. William Hunter to H. C. C. Astwood, September 15, 1884, telegram, USSDCI, NARA-59.
167. William Hunter to John Mercer Langston, September 17, 1884, no. 12, DIDS, NARA-59.
168. "Our Hub Letter," *New York Globe*, September 20, 1884; "Local Gossip," *New York Globe*, September 17, 1884; Manuel de Jesús Galván to Secretario [de Estado (Frelinghuysen)], October 2, 1884, NLDR, NARA-59.
169. [Sec. of State] Frederick T. Frelinghuysen to Manuel de Jesús Galvan, October 28, 1884, NFLDS, NARA-59.
170. "Local Gossip," *NYF*, November 29, 1884; H. C. C. Astwood to William Hunter, November 18, 1884, DUSCSD, NARA-59.
171. H. C. C. Astwood to William Hunter, December 24, 1884, no. 198, DUSCSD, NARA-59. For signing, see Pletcher, *Awkward Years*, 198.

172. Kramer, "How Not to Write," 912.
173. John Mercer Langston to [Sec. of State] Frederick T. Frelinghuysen, August 4, 1884, no. 11, DUSMDR, NARA-59, emphasis added.
174. Langston to Frelinghuysen, August 4, 1884.
175. Astwood to Hunter, February 16, 1883, no. 76.

CHAPTER 4. DEATH AND DECEIT: BLACK POLITICAL AUTHORITY AND THE FORGING OF US MORAL LOGIC ABROAD

1. H. C. C. Astwood to William Hunter, June 30, 1885, no. 243, DUSCSD, National Archives and Records Administration, Record Group 59 (NARA-59).
2. Pellion's testimony, July 3, 1885, included in Astwood to Hunter, June 30, 1885.
3. Welles, *Naboth's Vineyard*, 457; Domínguez, *La dictadura*, 17.
4. Domínguez, *La dictadura*, 17–38; Sang, *Ulises Heureaux*, 29–30.
5. Fredrickson, *Black Image*, 259; Gates, *Stony the Road*, 102–3.
6. Welles, *Naboth's Vineyard*, 449.
7. Rosenberg, "Revisiting Dollar Diplomacy," 170.
8. Rosenberg, "Revisiting Dollar Diplomacy," 173–74.
9. Eller, *We Dream Together*, 181–84, 231–32.
10. Bosch, *Social Composition*, 202–3; Moya Pons, *Dominican Republic*, 220. For the rationale of Báez's supporters, see Bosch, *Social Composition*, 185–87; Tejada, "El partido rojo," 23–24.
11. Bosch, *Social Composition*, 186; Hoetink, *Dominican People*, 50–63.
12. Castillo, "Formation," 228–29; Hoetink, *Dominican People*, 3–5.
13. Bosch, *Social Composition*, 187–88.
14. For these events, see Domínguez, *Notas económicas y políticas*, vol. 2, 430–608; Welles, *Naboth's Vineyard*, 301–8, 430–35.
15. Luperón, *Notas autobiográficas*, vol. 3, 22–23.
16. Luperón, *Notas autobiográficas*, vol. 3, 23.
17. Luperón, *Notas autobiográficas*, vol. 3, 23.
18. Welles, *Naboth's Vineyard*, 302.
19. Welles, *Naboth's Vineyard*, 433–34.
20. Luperón, *Notas autobiográficas*, vol. 3, 147–55.
21. Luperón, *Notas autobiográficas*, vol. 3, 154–55; Hoetink, *Dominican People*, 118.
22. Luperón, *Notas autobiográficas*, vol. 3, 155–63.
23. H. C. C. Astwood to William Hunter, June 16, 1884, no. 166, DUSCSD, NARA-59.
24. For controversy, see Sang, *Ulises Heureaux*, 31–32.
25. H. C. C. Astwood to William Hunter, July 3, 1884, no. 169, DUSCSD, NARA-59.
26. H. C. C. Astwood to William Hunter, July 25, 1884, no. 178, DUSCSD, NARA-59.
27. Luperón, *Notas autobiográficas*, vol. 3, 172.
28. Domínguez, *Notas económicas y políticas*, vol. 2, 647.
29. Luperón, *Notas autobiográficas*, vol. 3, 172.
30. Domínguez, *Notas económicas y políticas*, vol. 2, 648.
31. Luperón, *Notas autobiográficas*, vol. 3, 179.

32. Louis Petitpierre Pellion's testimony, July 3, 1885, included in Astwood to Hunter, June 30, 1885.

33. Pellion's testimony, July 3, 1885, included in Astwood to Hunter, June 30, 1885.

34. For Espaillat, see Martínez, *Diccionario biográfico*, 165.

35. "Copia de la sumaria instruida con motivo de la muerte del súbito norteamericano Sr. J. J. Platt" ("Copy of Proceedings of the Court of Inquiry"), included in H. C. C. Astwood to William Hunter, September 28, 1885, no. 273, DUSCSD, NARA-59. Gil and Juan Pablo were likely related to Pedro Pepín, the governor of Santiago and Heureaux's confidant, whom Welles ridiculed as an "illiterate negro." Welles, *Naboth's Vineyard*, 545; Hoetink, *Dominican People*, 108, 131; Martínez, *Diccionario biográfico*, 377–79.

36. "Copy of Proceedings of the Court of Inquiry," included in Astwood to Hunter, September 28, 1885.

37. Pellion's testimony, July 3, 1885, included in Astwood to Hunter, June 30, 1885.

38. Testimonies of Juan Bautista Peña and Gil Pepín in "Copy of Proceedings of the Court of Inquiry," included in Astwood to Hunter, September 28, 1885.

39. Nouel was the son of the famed priest Carlos R. Nouel. Hoetink, *Dominican People*, 128.

40. For these details and others in the paragraph, see "Copy of Proceedings of the Court of Inquiry," included in Astwood to Hunter, September 28, 1885.

41. Moniere's testimony in "Copy of Proceedings of the Court of Inquiry," included in Astwood to Hunter, September 28, 1885.

42. Astwood's description of Moniere in Astwood to Hunter, June 30, 1885.

43. "Copy of Proceedings of the Court of Inquiry," included in Astwood to Hunter, September 28, 1885.

44. Delgado's statement, July 27, 1885, in "Copy of Proceedings of the Court of Inquiry," included in Astwood to Hunter, September 28, 1885.

45. For *curandero*, see Deive, *Vodú y magia*, 327–31. Note: only two years earlier, the national medical board, over which Delgado undoubtedly presided, had approved the country's first female physician, the African American Dr. Sarah Marinda Fraser, who was also Charles R. Douglass's sister-in-law. Gregoria Goins, "'Miss Doc,'" box 36–4, folder 52, pp. 149–51, GGP, Moorland-Springarn Research Center at Howard University, Washington, DC; Mayes, *Mulatto Republic*, 34.

46. For biography, see "El Doctor Delgado," EDLO, July 14, 1894.

47. Stern, "Dr. Juan Francisco Alfonseca y Arvelo"; Hoetink, *Dominican People*, 146.

48. "Copy of Proceedings of the Court of Inquiry," included in Astwood to Hunter, September 28, 1885.

49. José de J. Castro to H. C. C. Astwood, June 30, 1885, included in Astwood to Hunter, June 30, 1885.

50. "John Platt," NYSC.

51. "List of Passengers on Board the Steamship *George W. Clyde*," February 12, 1883, PLVNY; "List of Passengers on Board the Steamship *Geo W. Clyde*," June 30, 1884, PLVNY.

52. "List of Passengers on Board the Steamship *Geo W. Clyde*," April 30, 1885, PLVNY.

53. "Sueltos," BDC, July 1, 1885.

54. Astwood to Hunter, June 30, 1885.
55. H. C. C. Astwood to José de J. Castro, June 29, 1885, included in Astwood to Hunter, June 30, 1885.
56. Astwood to Castro, June 29, 1885, included in Astwood to Hunter, June 30, 1885.
57. Castro to Astwood, June 30, 1885, included in Astwood to Hunter, June 30, 1885.
58. Astwood to Castro, June 30, 1885, included in Astwood to Hunter, June 30, 1885.
59. José de J. Castro to H. C. C. Astwood, July 2, 1885, included in Astwood to Hunter, June 30, 1885.
60. Astwood to Hunter, June 30, 1885.
61. Astwood to Hunter, June 30, 1885.
62. H. C. C. Astwood to William Hunter, November 11, 1883, no. 116, DUSCSD, NARA-59; Sang, *Ulises Heureaux*, 248.
63. Astwood to Hunter, June 30, 1885.
64. Astwood to Hunter, June 30, 1885.
65. Astwood to Hunter, June 30, 1885.
66. Astwood to Hunter, June 30, 1885.
67. US Supreme Court, *Dred Scott Decision*.
68. Byrd, *Black Republic*, 47–48.
69. For such tropes, see Gates, *Stony the Road*, 126–29.
70. Astwood to Hunter, June 30, 1885.
71. Pellion's testimony, July 3, 1885, included in Astwood to Hunter, June 30, 1885.
72. Dubois, *Avengers*, 221; Toll, *Blackening Up*, 120–24.
73. Pellion's testimony, July 3, 1885, included in Astwood to Hunter, June 30, 1885. For a parallel discussion, see S. E. Johnson, *Fear of French Negroes*, 64.
74. For stereotypes, see Gates, *Stony the Road*, 136–48.
75. Pellion's testimony, July 3, 1885, included in Astwood to Hunter, June 30, 1885.
76. Pellion's testimony, July 3, 1885, included in Astwood to Hunter, June 30, 1885.
77. Castillo, "Formation," 227–29; Bryan, "The Question of Labor," 236–37; S. E. Johnson, *Fear of French Negroes*, 64–65.
78. White landowners in the east became Haitian citizens during unification in order to keep their land. Ardouin, *Études sur l'histoire*, vol. 9, 134–35; Andrew Walker, email message to author, September 27, 2021.
79. Pellion's testimony, July 3, 1885, included in Astwood to Hunter, June 30, 1885.
80. Astwood to Hunter, June 30, 1885.
81. Astwood to Hunter, June 30, 1885.
82. "List of Passengers on Board the Steamship *Geo W. Clyde*," June 30, 1884, PLVNY; H. C. C. Astwood to William Hunter, January 1, 1885, no. 202, DUSCSD, NARA-59.
83. Astwood to Hunter, June 30, 1885.
84. Bederman, *Manliness*, 3. See also Rosenberg, "Revisiting Dollar Diplomacy," 171–75.
85. Sang, *Ulises Heureaux*, 106. See also Hoetink, *Dominican People*, 106, 126.
86. Ferrer, *Insurgent Cuba*, 48 (quote), 61–70, 158; S. E. Johnson, *Fear of French Negroes*, 49–50.
87. Sang, *Ulises Heureaux*, 112.
88. Domínguez, *La dictadura*, 14.

89. H. C. C. Astwood to William Hunter, August 27, 1885, no. 265, DUSCSD, NARA-59.

90. H. C. C. Astwood to José de J. Castro, July 6, 1885, sig. 708394, SERE, Archivo General de la Nación (AGN).

91. For such contradictions, see Gates, *Stony the Road*, 127–28.

92. H. C. C. Astwood to William Hunter, July 7, 1885, no. 245, DUSCSD, NARA-59.

93. Astwood to Hunter, July 7, 1885.

94. H. C. C. Astwood to José de J. Castro, July 11, 1885, and July 13, 1885, sig. 708394, SERE, AGN.

95. H. C. C. Astwood to José de J. Castro, July 20, 1885, included in H. C. C. Astwood to William Hunter, July 23, 1885, no. 257, DUSCSD, NARA-59.

96. H. C. C. Astwood to John Davis, October 10, 1882, no. 46, DUSCSD, NARA-59; H. C. C. Astwood to William Hunter, November 15, 1882, no. 54, DUSCSD, NARA-59.

97. José de J. Castro to H. C. C. Astwood, July 22, 1885, in Astwood to Hunter, July 23, 1885.

98. Astwood to Hunter, July 23, 1885.

99. H. C. C. Astwood to William Hunter, July 23, 1885, no. 256, DUSCSD, NARA-59.

100. James D. Porter to H. C. C. Astwood, July 27, 1885, no. 75, USSDCI, NARA-59.

101. H. C. C. Astwood to William Hunter, August 17, 1885, no. 260, DUSCD, NARA-59; H. C. C. Astwood to William Hunter, September 15, 1885, no. 269, DUSCSD, NARA-59.

102. Astwood to Hunter, August 17, 1885.

103. Astwood to Hunter, September 15, 1885. See also Gaffield, *Haitian Connections*, 10; García Muñiz and Borges, "U.S. Consular Activism," 35.

104. Astwood to Hunter, August 17, 1885.

105. H. C. C. Astwood to William Hunter, August 18, 1885, no. 263, DUSCSD, NARA-59.

106. H. C. C. Astwood to William Hunter, August 27, 1885, no. 266, DUSCSD, NARA-59.

107. Astwood to Hunter, August 27, 1885.

108. Astwood to Hunter, August 27, 1885.

109. Astwood to Hunter, September 15, 1885.

110. James D. Porter to H. C. C. Astwood, August 11, 1885, no. 79, USSDCI, NARA-59.

111. Handwritten note included in Astwood to Hunter, August 27, 1885.

112. James D. Porter to H. C. C. Astwood, September 14, 1885, no. 83, USSDCI, NARA-59.

113. H. C. C. Astwood to William Hunter, October 10, 1885, no. 278, DUSCSD, NARA-59.

114. H. C. C. Astwood to José de J. Castro, September 10, 1885, in Astwood to Hunter, September 15, 1885, emphasis added.

115. "Copy of Proceedings of the Court of Inquiry," included in Astwood to Hunter, September 28, 1885.

116. H. C. C. Astwood to José de J. Castro, September 28, 1885, in Astwood to Hunter, September 28, 1885.

117. H. C. C. Astwood to William Hunter, October 8, 1885, no. 277, DUSCSD, NARA-59.

118. Victor Huttinot to Alfred Deetjen, November 25, 1885, sig. 708394, SERE, AGN.

119. Astwood to Hunter, October 8, 1885.

120. For Astwood's "satisfaction," see H. C. C. Astwood to William Hunter, October 14, 1885, no. 284, DUSCSD, NARA-59.

121. H. C. C. Astwood to William Hunter, October 14, 1885, no. 283, DUSCSD, NARA-59.

122. H. C. C. Astwood to William Hunter, November 13, 1885, no. 289, DUSCSD, NARA-59.

123. Astwood to Hunter, November 13, 1885.

124. Astwood to Hunter, November 13, 1885.

125. Dominican Minister of Justice, cited in Astwood to Hunter, October 14, 1885.

126. John E. W. Thompson to [Sec. of State] Thomas F. Bayard, October 27, 1885, no. 2, DUSMDR, NARA-59.

127. For the accolades, see H. C. C. Astwood to William Hunter, October 15, 1885, no. 285, DUSCSD, NARA-59. See also J. P. Paulison, Charles Dennis, and others to [Pres.] Grover Cleveland, November 15, 1885; Robert Deeley to [Sec. of State] Thomas F. Bayard, November 18, 1885; J. D. Jones to [Sec. of State] Thomas F. Bayard, November 19, 1885, all in ACA-B3, ARPO, NARA-59.

128. Written by Dominican exile Juan María Jiménez, this anecdote was published in various countries and reprinted in Luperón, *Notas autobiográficas*, vol. 3, 347; and Welles, *Naboth's Vineyard*, 447–48.

129. Eller, "Raining Blood," 451.

130. Luperón, *Notas autobiográficas*, vol. 3, 155, 204.

131. Cestero, *La sangre*, 28; Eller, "Raining Blood," 451.

132. Luperón, *Notas autobiográficas*, vol. 3, 343; Deive, *Vodú y magia*, 192; Cestero, *La sangre*, 35–36; Eller, "Raining Blood," 451.

133. Rodríguez Demorizi, *Hostos en Santo Domingo*, vol. 2, 222. "Quisqueya" is a term for Hispaniola.

134. Flores, *Lilí*. See also Cassá, "Juan Vicente Flores," 9–24; Cordero Michel, "Lili."

135. Welles, *Naboth's Vineyard*, 449.

136. Welles, *Naboth's Vineyard*, 449.

137. Rodríguez Demorizi, *Hostos en Santo Domingo*, vol. 1, 286; Domínguez, *La dictadura*, 25.

138. H. C. C. Astwood to Alfred Deetjen, November 14, 1885, sig. 708394, SERE, AGN.

139. Astwood to Hunter, November 13, 1885.

140. Astwood to Deetjen, November 14, 1885.

141. For badmen and tricksters, see Roberts, *From Trickster*, 13.

142. H. C. C. Astwood to James D. Porter, January 15, 1886, no. 308, DUSCSD, NARA-59.

143. Astwood to Hunter, June 30, 1885.

144. Astwood to Hunter, June 30, 1885.

145. A. Vega, *Anecdotas*, 41.

146. A. Vega, *Anecdotas*, 41.

CHAPTER 5. BETWEEN TOLERANCE AND TYRANNY: PROTESTANT
DOMINICANS, SOCIAL MORALITY, AND THE MAKING OF A
LIBERAL NATION

1. H. C. C. Astwood, "Letter from San Domingo," CR, February 22, 1883.

2. For the debate over Columbus's relics, see chapter 6. See also Schmidt-Nowara, *Conquest*, 69–80; Muñiz, "Unofficial Archive," 53–112; Serrata, "'True and Only.'"

3. Astwood, "Letter from San Domingo."
4. Astwood, "Letter from San Domingo."
5. "The Foreign Missions of the AME Church," *CR*, January 19, 1888.
6. García-Peña, *Borders*, 1–2.
7. Hoetink, *Dominican People*, 138–64.
8. For recent examples, see Castillo Pichardo, "Hostos en Santo Domingo"; Alcántara Almánzar, "Hostos"; Avelino, "Hostos"; Rojas Osorio, "Eugenio María de Hostos"; Sánchez Álvarez-Insúa, "Moral Social"; Ward, "From Sarmiento"; Gutierrez Laboy, *Hostos*.
9. United States Commission of Inquiry to Santo Domingo, *Dominican Republic*, 251–54.
10. United States Commission of Inquiry to Santo Domingo, *Dominican Republic*, 255.
11. United States Commission of Inquiry to Santo Domingo, *Dominican Republic*, 255, 268.
12. United States Commission of Inquiry to Santo Domingo, *Dominican Republic*, 254; Hoetink, *Dominican People*, 21.
13. United States Commission of Inquiry to Santo Domingo, *Dominican Republic*, 255–56.
14. United States Commission of Inquiry to Santo Domingo, *Dominican Republic*, 268.
15. "Communications," *CR*, March 30, 1872.
16. "Communications," *CR*, March 30, 1872; Hoetink, *Dominican People*, 21.
17. "Communications," *CR*, March 30, 1872.
18. Howe dates this event to 1873, but it was likely 1872. Howe, *Reminiscences*, 349–50.
19. Dickerson, *African Methodist*, 53–54, 78–80, 229–33.
20. Howe, *Reminiscences*, 351.
21. Howe, *Reminiscences*, 350.
22. Howe, *Reminiscences*, 353.
23. Howe, *Reminiscences*, 354.
24. Rodríguez Demorizi, *Sociedades*, 3.
25. For Sephardic Jews and Masonry, see Hoetink, *Dominican People*, 25–26.
26. Sheller, *Democracy after Slavery*, 161–66.
27. Howe, *Reminiscences*, 353.
28. Howe, *Reminiscences*, 366.
29. Jacob James to the General Secretaries, June 20, 1875, microfiche 1419, WMMS-WI, Library of the School of Oriental and African Studies (SOAS), University of London.
30. Jacob James to the General Secretaries, January 18, 1875, microfiche 1417, WMMS-WI, SOAS.
31. James to the General Secretaries, June 20, 1875, microfiche.
32. This official may have been Gross's son, Ricardo Alejandro, who once served as the administrator of customs.
33. For James's son, Jacob Paul James, see chapter 2. See also Davidson, "Black Protestants," 269–81.
34. Joseph A. Prior to M. C. Osborn, April 22, 1880, microfiche 2045, WMMS-WI, SOAS.

35. Jacob James to the General Secretaries, March 21, 1881, microfiche 2047, WMMS-WI, SOAS.

36. Jacob James to the General Secretaries, January 19, 1876, microfiche 1421, WMMS-WI, SOAS; Jacob James to the General Secretaries, June 20, 1876, microfiche 1423, WMMS-WI, SOAS.

37. Henry Bleby to G. J. Perks, October 4, 1876, microfiche 1424, WMMS-WI, SOAS. Claudio later reported that the roof collapsed that year. "The Foreign Missions," CR, January 19, 1888.

38. Jacob James to the General Secretaries, August 23, 1877, microfiche 1426, WMMS-WI, SOAS.

39. Jacob James to the General Secretaries, May 21, 1882, microfiche 2050, WMMS-WI, SOAS.

40. "Ordained," CR, July 26, 1883.

41. S. A. Johnson, *Myth of Ham*, 73–108; Davidson, "'What Hinders?,'" 57–58.

42. John B. Gedye to M. C. Osborn, August 10, 1883, microfiche 2053, WMMS-WI, SOAS.

43. Astwood, "Letter from Santo Domingo."

44. H. C. C. Astwood, "My Dear Dr.," AMECR 1, no. 2 (1884): 176.

45. Astwood, "My Dear Dr.," 175–76.

46. "Consagración de la iglesia protestante," JGG, Archivo General de la Nación.

47. Astwood, "My Dear Dr.," 176.

48. García-Peña, *Borders*, 32–33.

49. A. Lockward, *Intolerancia*, 97–98. See also G. A. Lockward, *El protestantismo*, 285; Willmore, "Esbozo histórico," 260.

50. For this land grant and its complications, see Davidson, "Converting Spanish Hispaniola," 205–337.

51. Martínez-Vergne, *Nation and Citizen*, 13–21.

52. Martínez-Vergne, *Nation and Citizen*, 15.

53. Martínez-Vergne, *Nation and Citizen*, 21.

54. González, "Hostos," 95.

55. Hostos's ideas derived from his personal connection to the Spanish Caribbean and anticolonial activism. Rodríguez Demorizi, *Hostos en Santo Domingo*, vol. 2, 13–26.

56. Rodríguez Demorizi, *Hostos en Santo Domingo*, vol. 2, 19–20.

57. Rodríguez Demorizi, *Hostos en Santo Domingo*, vol. 2, 23.

58. Rodríguez Demorizi, *Hostos en Santo Domingo*, vol. 2, 22.

59. He went to New York and Venezuela, and returned after the Pacto del Zanjón ended the Ten Years' War.

60. Rodríguez Demorizi, *Hostos en Santo Domingo*, vol. 2, 29.

61. Rodríguez Demorizi, *Hostos en Santo Domingo*, vol. 2, 35.

62. Rodríguez Demorizi, *Hostos en Santo Domingo*, vol. 2, 35; González, "Hostos," 98; Domínguez, *La dictadura*, 45.

63. Rodríguez Demorizi, *Hostos en Santo Domingo*, vol. 2, 38–39; González, "Hostos," 95.

64. González, "Hostos," 98.

65. Gutierrez Laboy, *Hostos*, 36.

66. Hostos, *Moral social*, 115–18.

67. Hostos, *Moral social*, 22. See also Gutierrez Laboy, *Hostos*, 34–35.

300 Notes to Chapter 5

68. González et al., *Política, identidad*, 18.
69. Hostos, *Moral social*, 168.
70. Hostos, *Moral social*, 163.
71. Hostos, *Moral social*, 163, 174–76.
72. Hostos, *Moral social*, 176.
73. For Lithgow see A. Lockward, *Intolerancia*, 99–100. For Fraser, see Mayes, *Mulatto Republic*, 15, 34; Bleby to Perks, October 4, 1876.
74. Rodríguez Demorizi, *Hostos en Santo Domingo*, vol. 2, 40 and 66; Lockward, *El protestantismo*, 286–87.
75. Rodríguez Demorizi, *Hostos en Santo Domingo*, vol. 2, 41.
76. Gatón, *Resumen*, 1.
77. Gatón, *Resumen*, 1–2.
78. Gatón, *Resumen*, 2.
79. Gatón, *Resumen*, 2.
80. Gatón, *Resumen*, 2.
81. Gatón, *Resumen*, 4.
82. Gatón, *Resumen*, 4.
83. "Hon. John Mercer Langston," NYF, November 28, 1885.
84. "Hon. John Mercer Langston," NYF, November 28, 1885.
85. The ten "vice-presidents" were US vice-consul J. W. Farrand; Dutch consul and acting British vice-consul J. M. Leyber; sugar planters J. B. Vicini and Alexander Bass; American engineer George Davis; New York agent of maritime exchange Miguel Limardo Pardo; Dominican citizen J. M. Calera; and representatives of the AME Church Francisco Claudio, Charles H. Williams, and Isaiah Hamilton.
86. García, *Compendio*, vol. 2, 122.
87. Gatón, *Resumen*, 3–4.
88. For public rights, see Scott, "Public Rights"; Scott, *Degrees of Freedom*, 42–47.
89. For example, see Eller, "Raining Blood."
90. Eller, "Raining Blood," 434.
91. H. C. C. Astwood to James D. Porter, June 10, 1886, no. 328, DUSCSD, National Archives and Records Administration, Record Group 59 (NARA-59).
92. Luperón, *Notas autobiográficas*, vol. 3, 215.
93. Luperón, *Notas autobiográficas*, vol. 3, 202.
94. Luperón, *Notas autobiográficas*, vol. 3, 204. Meanwhile, Astwood publicly declared his support for Heureaux, raising the opposition's ire: "El Señor H. C. C. Astwood," BDC, June 30, 1886; H. C. C. Astwood to James D. Porter, July 12, 1886, no. 335, DUSCSD, NARA-59.
95. H. C. C. Astwood to James D. Porter, December 3, 1886, no. 365, DUSCSD, NARA-59.
96. Rodríguez Demorizi, *Hostos en Santo Domingo*, vol. 2, 49.
97. Martínez, *Diccionario biográfico-histórico*, 319.
98. Luperón, *Notas autobiográficas*, vol. 3, 139–40; Nouel, *Historia eclesiástica*, vol. 3, 308–35; Martínez-Fernández, "Sword and the Crucifix," 85–88.
99. Martínez, *Diccionario biográfico-histórico*, 320; Moya Pons, "Notas para una historia," 14–15.

100. Hostos nominated Meriño as the rector for the Professional Institute in 1883, and Meriño subsequently assumed the role: Rodríguez Demorizi, *Hostos en Santo Domingo*, vol. 2, 40; Domínguez, *La dictadura*, 45.

101. Rodríguez Demorizi, *Hostos en Santo Domingo*, vol. 2, 38, 48.

102. Rodríguez Demorizi, *Hostos en Santo Domingo*, vol. 2, 48; González, "Hostos," 98.

103. Fernando A. de Meriño, "Mis queridos hermanos," BE 2, no. 30 (October 15, 1885): 233.

104. Fernando A. de Meriño, [Untitled], BE 2, no. 32 (November 15, 1885): 249; Fernando A. de Meriño, "Salud y bendición," BE 2, no. 37 (March 1, 1886): 289.

105. Meriño, [Untitled], BE 2, no. 32 (November 15, 1885): 249.

106. Fernando A. de Meriño, "Salud y bendición," BE 2, no. 39 (April 15, 1886): 309. See also A. Lockward, *Intolerancia*, 101.

107. Domínguez, *La dictadura*, 45–48.

108. A. Lockward, *Intolerancia*, 98–107; Rodríguez Demorizi, *Hostos en Santo Domingo*, vol. 2, 61–63; González, "Hostos," 98.

109. A. Lockward, *Intolerancia*, 100.

110. "Un capítulo de historia documentada. Artículo VII," BE 3, no. 48 (November 30, 1886): 381.

111. "Un capítulo de historia documentada. Artículo VI," BE 2, no. 42 (June 15, 1886): 333; "Un capítulo de historia documentada. Artículo V," BE 3, no. 44 (July 15, 1886): 348; "Un capítulo de historia documentada. Artículo VI . . . (Continuación)," BE 3, no. 46 (September 15, 1886): 365.

112. "Un capítulo de historia documentada. Artículo VIII," BE 4, no. 49 (July 15, 1887): 388.

113. "An Appeal," CR, September 10, 1885.

114. A. H. Mevs, "A Word from the Santo Domingo Mission," CR, July 29, 1886.

115. Guridy, *Forging Diaspora*, 17–60; Byrd, *Black Republic*, 151–54.

116. Mevs, "Word from the Santo Domingo Mission."

117. Other Protestant denominations in Haiti: Anglicans, Wesleyans, and Baptists. For AME missions in Haiti, see Byrd, "Black Republicans, Black Republic," 557–62; Byrd, "Transnational Work of Elevation."

118. For problems regarding AME investment in Caribbean missions, see Davidson, "'What Hinders?,'" 68–72.

119. Moses, *Golden Age*, 20.

120. Little, *Disciples of Liberty*, 62–64.

121. "Escuela Mercantil," BDC, March 30, 1886.

122. Daniel A. Payne, "The Past, Present, and Future of the AME Church," AMECR 1, no. 4 (April 1885): 314.

123. Mossell, *Toussaint L'Ouverture*, 443.

124. Henry Astwood was absent on sabbatical in the United States.

125. "Bishop Campbell's Letter," CR, June 23, 1887.

126. It is likely that Adam Rodgers and Simon Halls were both Dominican descendants of African Americans. Charles H. Williams, however, was most likely from the Danish West Indian island of St. Thomas.

127. Mossell, *Toussaint L'Ouverture*, 442.

128. Moses, *Golden Age*, 21; Davidson, "Organic Union," 580.

129. Moses, *Golden Age*, 21.

130. Mossell, *Toussaint L'Ouverture*, 443.

131. Moses, *Golden Age*, 22.

132. Frazier and Lincoln, *Negro Church*, 49; cited also in Moses, *Golden Age*, 22.

133. Jones, *Birthright Citizens*, 71–88; Myers Turner, *Soul Liberty*, 57–80.

134. "Honoring Consul Astwood," NYF, May 14, 1887.

135. The other named guests were H. M. Joseph of Antigua, W. I. (professor); T. Mc-
     Cants Stewart (lawyer); Chas. L. Reason (professor); Dr. B. W. Arnett, member of
     the Ohio legislature (AME clergy); Prof. C. A. Dorsey; H. L. Bean (investor); Henri
     Herbert of Trenton, NJ; Jerome B. Peterson (NYF editor); James Grant (of Wana-
     maker and Co., Philadelphia); William H. Dickerson (pastor of Siloam Presbyte-
     rian Church, Brooklyn); Charles Julian Jr.; E. G. Morrell (Dominican consulate
     worker); Nathaniel McKay (investor); and Horatio C. King (investor).

136. "Honoring Consul Astwood," NYF, May 28, 1887. Other notables were Ceasar
     Carpentier Antoine, John R. Lynch, and Henry Demas.

137. "Honoring Consul Astwood," NYF, May 14, 1887.

138. Veeser, "Concessions," 744.

139. Veeser, "Concessions," 745.

140. Veeser, "Concessions," 747.

141. Veeser, "Concessions," 747.

142. Sang, *Ulises Heureaux*, 112.

143. Davidson, "'What Hinders?'"

144. H. C. C. Astwood, "Shall the Name of the African Methodist Episcopal Church
     Be Changed to That of the Allen Methodist Episcopal Church?," AMECR 4, no. 3
     (1888): 320.

145. Stuckey, *Slave Culture*, 266–68; Little, *Disciples of Liberty*, 37.

146. "Hon. H. C. C. Astwood," CR, May 5, 1887.

147. Stuckey, *Slave Culture*, 267.

148. Astwood, "Shall the Name . . . ," 320.

149. Davidson, "'What Hinders?,'" 71.

150. G. A. Lockward, *El protestantismo*, 286–87; Domínguez, *La dictadura*, 206.

151. Davidson, "Converting Spanish Hispaniola," 205–266.

152. J. M. Cabral y Baez, "Libertad religiosa," EDLO, June 1, 1889.

153. "Missionary Report," CR, January 8, 1885; "Honoring Consul Astwood," NYF,
     May 14, 1887.

154. "Honoring Consul Astwood," NYF, May 14, 1887.

CHAPTER 6. LEASING COLUMBUS: HOLY RELICS, PUBLIC RIDICULE,
AND THE RECONSTRUCTION OF TWO AMERICAS

1. "¡Pobre Colon!," BDC, May 17, 1888.

2. For well-known essays, see Martí, *Our America*, 84–94; Rodó, *Ariel*.

3. The inscription written out in full is *Illustre y Esclarecido Varón Don Cristóbal Colón, Descubridor de la América, Primer Almirante*. In English: Illustrious and Distinguished Man Don Christopher Columbus, Discoverer of America, First Admiral.

4. For examples, see Candelario, *Black behind the Ears*, 103; Welles, *Naboth's Vineyard*, 463; Domínguez, *La dictadura*, 129.

5. "Secretaría de estado de lo interior," *Gaceta Oficial*, June 9, 1888.

6. For nationalism as "fiction," see Anderson, *Imagined Communities*, 36, 141; for scapegoat, see Girard, *Scapegoat*, 39.

7. Geary, *Furta Sacra*, 6.

8. The literature on Columbus symbology is vast. For Columbus and empire, see Bartosik-Vélez, *Legacy*; Kubal, *Cultural Movements*; Bushman, *America Discovers*; West and Kling, "Columbus and Columbia"; Hall, *Earth into Property*, 53. For Columbus, Christianity, and white supremacy, see Weed, *Religion*, 4–10; McLeod, "Dignity Denied," 47–48; Mignolo, *Idea*, 33, 105. For "double body," see Laquer, *Work*, 10; Hertz, "A Contribution"; Foucault, *Discipline and Punish*, 28.

9. Geary, *Furta Sacra*, 21, 32.

10. Schmidt-Nowara, *Conquest of History*, 55.

11. Vignaud, *L'ancienne*; Schmidt-Nowara, *Conquest of History*, 69; Serrata, "'True and Only,'" 480.

12. Durkheim, *Elementary*, 36.

13. Geary, *Furta Sacra*, 45–46.

14. Geary, *Furta Sacra*, 58, 107.

15. Geary, *Furta Sacra*, 67–69.

16. In using the term *living-dead*, I consciously signal the zombie figure and its connection to Atlantic slavery. See Lauro, *Transatlantic Zombie*, 201. Scholarly literature on enslaved Africans' social death, albeit theoretical abstraction, makes sense within this comparison. For social death, see Patterson, *Slavery*; For critiques, see V. Brown, "Social Death," 1233; Cooper, *Colonialism*, 17.

17. This truism became most heinously apparent in the case of the *Zong*. See Baucom, *Specters*.

18. Keel, *Divine Variations*, 5–6.

19. Geary, *Furta Sacra*, 107.

20. For summaries of the debate, see Schmidt-Nowara, *Conquest of History*, 69–95; Serrata, "'True and Only'"; Muñiz, "Unofficial Archive," 53–125; Moya Pons, *Los restos de Colón*. For historical accounts of the discovery, see Tejera, *Los restos*; Tejera, *Los dos restos*; Cocchia, *Los restos*; López Prieto, *Informe*; Echeverri, *Do existen*; Colmeiro, *Los restos*; Cestero, *Colon*.

21. Schmidt-Nowara, *Conquest of History*, 58.

22. Schmidt-Nowara, *Conquest of History*, 69.

23. Schmidt-Nowara, *Conquest of History*, 78.

24. Bartosik-Vélez, *Legacy*, 66–67, 84–87; Bushman, *America Discovers*, 131–45; Ramírez, *Colonial Phantoms*, 116; Trouillot, *Silencing*, 124–32.

25. Ramírez, *Colonial Phantoms*, 114–15.

26. Ramírez, *Colonial Phantoms*, 124.

27. Serrata, "'True and Only,'" 474.

28. Muñiz, "Unofficial Archive," 60.

29. Sommer, *One Master*, xii–xiv; Candelario, *Black behind the Ears*, 58–59; Muñiz, "Unofficial Archive," 123–30.

30. "Fragmento de acta," March 3, 1882, sig. C708873, JGG, Archivo General de la Nación (AGN). See also García Lluberes, "Nuestra estatua."

31. Muñiz, "Unofficial Archive," 60.

32. Schmidt-Nowara, *Conquest of History*, 69–80.

33. "List of Passengers on Board the Steamship *Geo W. Clyde*," May 15, 1888, PLVNY.

34. "H. M. Linnell in the 1880 US Federal Census," USC-1880; H. M. Linnell, 1865, MASC.

35. "Columbus' Sacred Ashes," *New Haven Register*, July 26, 1888.

36. National Electric Light Association, *Proceedings*, 111–12.

37. Hubert Montague Linnell to H. C. C. Astwood, n.d., in H. C. C. Astwood to George Lockhart Rives, August 21, 1888, no. 462, DUSCSD, National Archives and Records Administration, Record Group 59 (NARA-59).

38. "The Bones of Columbus," NYH, July 24, 1888; "Traducción," *Gaceta Oficial*, June 9, 1888.

39. "Traducción," *Gaceta Oficial*, June 9, 1888.

40. "The Bones of Columbus," NYH, July 24, 1888.

41. "The Bones of Columbus," NYH, July 24, 1888.

42. "The Bones of Columbus," NYH, July 24, 1888; "Traducción," *Gaceta Oficial*, June 9, 1888.

43. "Traducción," *Gaceta Oficial*, June 9, 1888.

44. "¡Pobre Colón!," BDC, May 17, 1888.

45. "Traducción," *Gaceta Oficial*, June 9, 1888.

46. "Contraste," EDLO, June 9, 1888.

47. "Dos Circulares," BDC, June 14, 1888.

48. "Protesta Energética," BDC, June 28, 1888, reprinted from *El Porvenir*.

49. "Protesta Energética," BDC, June 28, 1888, reprinted from *El Porvenir*.

50. "Contraste," EDLO, June 9, 1888.

51. "Grosera Proposición," BDC, July 5, 1888, reprinted from *Unidad Nacional*.

52. "The Bones of Columbus," NYH, July 24, 1888.

53. "Un Barnum Consular," *Las Novedades*, July 26, 1888; Astwood to Rives, August 21, 1888.

54. "Must Not Be Dug Up," *New Haven Register*, July 26, 1888; "Atrocious Imprudence," *Daily Picayune*, July 27, 1888; "Diplomatic Disgrace," *Daily Picayune*, July 27, 1888; "A Lively Consul," *Daily Capitolian Advocate*, July 27, 1888.

55. "Diplomatic Disgrace," *Daily Picayune*, July 27, 1888.

56. "A Lively Consul," *Daily Capitolian Advocate*, July 27, 1888.

57. "Columbus' Sacred Ashes," *New Haven Register*, July 26, 1888.

58. "Must Not Be Dug Up," *New Haven Register*, July 25, 1888.

59. "Columbus' Sacred Ashes," *New Haven Register*, July 26, 1888.

60. "Must Not Be Dug Up," *New Haven Register*, July 25, 1888.

61. "Columbus' Sacred Ashes," *New Haven Register*, July 26, 1888.

62. "Must Not Be Dug Up," *New Haven Register*, July 25, 1888.

63. "Diplomatic Disgrace," *Daily Picayune*, July 27, 1888.

64. "The Climax of Disgrace," *Star Tribune*, August 1, 1888.

65. "Must Not Be Dug Up," *New Haven Register*, July 26, 1888.

66. "The Remains of Columbus," *Weekly Times Democrat* [New Orleans], August 4, 1888.

67. Edmund Charles Preiss to Secretary of State [Bayard], July 25, 1888, USSDMC, NARA-59.

68. Amandus Meyer to [Sec. of State] Thomas F. Bayard, July 26, 1888, USSDMC, NARA-59.

69. See note in Preiss to Secretary of State, July 25, 1888.

70. George Lockhart Rives to H. C. C. Astwood, July 26, 1888, no. 148, USSDCI, NARA-59.

71. Pardo was likely the same Venezuelan novelist who wrote the canonical text *Todo un pueblo* (1899). An advertisement supports this claim. See "Miguel Eduardo Pardo. Artista Venezolano," *EDLO*, August 4, 1888. Silva was most likely a prominent merchant.

72. "Gacetillas," *BDC*, August 2, 1888.

73. "Sueltos," *EDLO*, August 4, 1888.

74. "Gacetillas," *BDC*, August 5, 1888.

75. "Gush for Patriotism and Much Ado about Nothing," in Astwood to Rives, August 21, 1888.

76. "Gush for Patriotism and Much Ado about Nothing," in Astwood to Rives, August 21, 1888.

77. "Gush for Patriotism and Much Ado about Nothing," in Astwood to Rives, August 21, 1888.

78. A copy no longer exists, but reference to it is made in Miguel Eduardo Pardo, "Entre la espada y la pared," *BDC*, August 19, 1888.

79. "De 'El Courrier des Etats Unis,'" *EDLO*, August 18, 1888; "The World de N. York," *EDLO*, August 18, 1888.

80. "De 'El Courrier des Etats Unis,'" *EDLO*, August 18, 1888.

81. "Cristobal Colón," *EDLO*, August 18, 1888.

82. Miguel Eduardo Pardo, "Entre la espada y la pared," *BDC*, August 19, 1888.

83. P. Obregon S., "Al Barnum Consular," *BDC*, August 19, 1888.

84. P. Obregon S., "Al sr. H. C. C. Astwood," *BDC*, August 23, 1888.

85. Astwood to Rives, August 21, 1888.

86. For the invitation, see "Expediente Relativo al Congreso histórico," December 24, 1884, sig. 708393, SERE, AGN.

87. Astwood to Rives, August 21, 1888.

88. Here, Astwood referenced the contemporaneous 1886 Chicago Haymarket incident in which eight American anarchists were convicted of bombing the police during a labor protest, and accused the *Boletín*'s Italian owner of making "revolutionary innuendos." See Messer-Kruse, *Haymarket Conspiracy*; Avrich, *Haymarket Tragedy*.

89. "Traducción-Original Inglés," *EDLO*, August 25, 1888.

90. "La Prensa," *EDLO*, August 25, 1888.

91. "Una súplica," *EDLO*, August 18, 1888.

92. Felix E. Soler, "Sr. Director," *EDLO*, August 25, 1888.

93. "Despues de haber reproducido," *EDLO*, August 25, 1888.

94. H. C. C. Astwood, "A los Editores de 'El *EDLO*' y de 'El Teléfono,'" *EDLO*, August 25, 1888.

95. "Moralidad de los pueblos," *BDC*, August 26, 1888.

96. "Desacreditado!," *BDC*, August 26, 1888.

97. "Desacreditado!," *BDC*, August 26, 1888.

98. Miguel Eduardo Pardo, "Valiente Caball . . . ero!," *BDC*, August 26, 1888.

99. P. Obregon S., "Convenido," *BDC*, August 26, 1888.

100. P. Obregon S., "Convenido," *BDC*, August 26, 1888.

101. J. Pietri, "Contestación," *BDC*, August 23, 1888.

102. P. Obregon S., "Convenido," *BDC*, August 26, 1888.

103. "Díceres" is a play on words and may translate as the indicative *él dice* (he says), or *cosas que él dice* (things that he says), or as the imperative *tú di* (say it!) or *cosas que tú tienes que / deberías decir* (things that you have to or should say). Thanks to Wendy Muñiz for this insight.

104. Prometeo, "Díceres," *BDC*, August 26, 1888.

105. S. Fischer, *Modernity Disavowed*, 174–79; García-Peña, *Borders*, 23–27.

106. S. Fischer, *Modernity Disavowed*, 178.

107. S. Fischer, *Modernity Disavowed*, 178–79.

108. S. Fischer, *Modernity Disavowed*, 178.

109. For Meriño, see A. Lockward, *Intolerancia*, 98.

110. One of these possibly referred to the Pérez-Sanlan case recounted in Domínguez, *La dictadura*, 27–33.

111. Prometeo, "Díceres," *BDC*, August 26, 1888.

112. The article retold the story of Montrealer Emma Mundford, who "sold" her husband to a woman named Clara Brown. The story not only insulted Astwood's manhood by foregrounding women as bartering over his person but also revealed his history of bigamy, a fact that Dominican society had previously ignored. "Rareza y fenómenos," *BDC*, August 30, 1888. This story reappears in Quesada, *Los Estados Unidos*, 25–26.

113. "Extrangerismo," *BDC*, September 2, 1888.

114. Prometeo, "Chismografia Popular," *BDC*, September 2, 1888.

115. "Siga la danza," *BDC*, September 2, 1888.

116. "Cristoval Colon," *BDC*, September 10, 1888.

117. "Los restos de Colon," *BDC*, September 10, 1888.

118. Prometeo, "Prometeo. Volantes," *BDC*, September 19, 1888.

119. P. Obregon S., "Moral Social," *BDC*, September 22, 1888; P. Obregon S., "Moral Social," *BDC*, September 27, 1888.

120. Miguel Eduardo Pardo, "Aclaratoria," *BDC*, August 30, 1888.

121. J. B. Maggiolo y Gimelli, "Sépase," *BDC*, August 30, 1888.

122. Miguel Eduardo Pardo, "Despedida," *BDC*, September 22, 1888.

123. "Despedida," *BDC*, October 18, 1888.

124. "Asesinato de Obregón," *EDLO*, April 6, 1889.

125. Miguel Eduardo Pardo, "El Barnum Consular," *BDC*, September 27, 1888. This was not the first time Pardo characterized himself as a martyr. See also "El martir de la Sociedad," *BDC*, August 23, 1888.

126. Gordiano, "El Boletín del Comercio," *BDC*, September 27, 1888.

127. "The Bones of Christopher Columbus," *Pittsburgh Dispatch*, January 3, 1889.

128. "Under the Title of Scandalous Business," *Galveston Daily News*, December 31, 1888. See also "A Gladstone Breeze," *Boston Daily Advertiser*, January 3, 1889; "A Scandalous Story," *Daily Evening Bulletin*, January 3, 1889; "Telegraphic Notes," *Daily Evening Bulletin*, January 3, 1889; "Astwood Removed," *Boston Daily Advertiser*, January 4, 1889; "Consul Astwood," *Evening Bulletin*, January 4, 1889; "Why He Was Removed," *Galveston Daily*, January 4, 1889; "Christopher Columbus!," *Weekly Courier-Journal*, January 7, 1889.

129. "Under the Title of Scandalous Business," *Galveston Daily News*, December 31, 1888.

130. "Consul Astwood's Defense," *NYH*, September 7, 1888.

131. "Our Dime Museum Consul," *NYH*, September 8, 1888.

132. "El Cónsul Astwood y los restos de Colón," *Las Novedades*, September 13, 1888.

133. For *Las Novedades*'s history, see Aponte, *La presencia dominicana*, 7–13.

134. *New York Times* cited in "Agua Va!," *Las Novedades*, September 13, 1888; "Caro le ha costado Astwood," *Panama Star and Herald*, September 22, 1888.

135. "Agua Va!," *Las Novedades*, September 13, 1888.

136. "El Consul Astwood y los restos de Colon," *Las Novedades*, September 13, 1888.

CHAPTER 7. "THE CHEEKIEST MAN ON EARTH": H. C. C. ASTWOOD
AND THE POLITICS OF WHITE MORAL EXCLUSIVITY

1. Executive Order, December 20, 1888, DUSCSD, National Archives and Records Administration, Record Group 59 (NARA-59).

2. F. O. St. Clair to [Sec. of State] J. G. Blaine, April 8, 1890, ACA-B3, ARPO, NARA-59.

3. Nathaniel McKay to William F. Wharton, February 28, 1890, ACA-B3, ARPO, NARA-59.

4. John Wanamaker cited in Nathaniel McKay to H. C. C. Astwood, July 21, 1891, ACA-B3, ARPO, NARA-59.

5. William P. Clyde to [Sec. of State] J. G. Blaine, telegram, October 9, 1889, ACA-B3, ARPO, NARA-59.

6. For Astwood's records, see George L. Rives to H. C. C. Astwood, July 28, 1888, no. 151, USSDCI; Astwood to Rives, September 3, 1888, no. 463, DUSCSD. For summaries of these events, see Juan Antonio Read to Department of State, March 15, 1889, no. 495, DUSCSD; Juan Antonio Read to Department of State, March 26, 1889, no. 500, DUSCSD; "History of Consul Astwood's Connection with the Platt Claim," May 5, 1889, vol. 5, no. 20, USCBR; "Dismissal of H. C. C. Astwood," May 5, 1889, vol. 5, no. 21, USCBR. All NARA-59.

7. Instead of dismissing Astwood outright, Cleveland granted him a leave of absence contingent on Astwood respectfully resigning his office on December 31, 1888. Astwood refused, stating that he would prefer to stay in office until the end of Cleveland's term and soliciting an in-person hearing to explain his case. This defiance provoked the State Department to recommend his prompt removal, which came via executive order in December. See George L. Rives to H. C. C. Astwood, October 29, 1888, no. 159, USSDCI; Astwood to Rives, November 28, 1888, no. 475, DUSCSD; Astwood to Rives, January 19, 1889, no. 182, DUSCSD. All NARA-59.

8. Astwood to Rives, January 19, 1889.

9. Juan Antonio Read was the son of William A. Read, a white American landowner in Santo Domingo. See chapter 3.

10. H. C. C. Astwood to George L. Rives, January 23, 1889, no. 483, DUSCSD, NARA-59.

11. Juan Antonio Read to Secretary of State [Bayard], telegram, January 21, 1889, DUSCSD, NARA-59; H. C. C. Astwood to Juan Antonio Read, January 18, 1889, included in Astwood to Rives, January 23, 1889.

12. H. C. C. Astwood to George L. Rives, January 23, 1889, no. 484, DUSCSD, NARA-59; M. M. Gautier to H. C. C. Astwood, January 21, 1889, included in H. C. C. Astwood to George L. Rives, January 25, 1889, no. 485, DUSCSD, NARA-59.

13. H. C. C. Astwood to George L. Rives, February 7, 1889, no. 486, DUSCSD, NARA-59.

14. H. C. C. Astwood to Juan Antonio Read, February 8, 1889, included in H. C. C. Astwood to George L. Rives, February 12, 1889, no. 487, DUSCSD, NARA-59.

15. McKay was the younger brother of the famed shipbuilder Donald McKay. In 1888, Nathaniel waged a political battle against President Cleveland, who had vetoed his bill for the relief of his and Donald's company. Angered over the veto, Nathaniel had raised support for the Republican Benjamin Harrison in the 1888 presidential race. McKay's relationship with Astwood began when Henry helped Nathaniel to obtain a Dominican concession to build a bridge over the Ozama River. For bio, see McKay, *Nathaniel McKay*, 1–2. For veto, see Cleveland, *Public Papers of Grover Cleveland*, 299–303.

16. Nathaniel McKay to H. C. C. Astwood, January 14, 1889, ACA-B3, ARPO, NARA-59.

17. McKay to Astwood, January 14, 1889. For another example, see Nathaniel McKay to H. C. C. Astwood, January 29, 1889, ACA-B3, ARPO, NARA-59.

18. Nathaniel McKay to W. Blaine, April 3, 1889, ACHA-B4, ARPO, NARA-59; Joseph K. McCammon to W. Blaine, April 6, 1889, ACHA-B4, ARPO, NARA-59.

19. Ira L. Peck to [Sec. of State] J. G. Blaine, April 10, 1889, ACHA-B4, ARPO, NARA-59. See also L. D. T. Blackstone to [Sec. of State] J. G. Blaine, April 6, 1889, ACHA-B4, ARPO, NARA-59.

20. See note in "Report: Dismissal of H. C. C. Astwood from the Consulate at San Domingo," May 20, 1889, ACA-B3, ARPO, NARA-59. Astwood also used McKay to settle the Dominican Republic's indemnity on a separate US claim. See E. R. Thompson to [Sec. of State] Thomas F. Bayard, March 5, 1889, no. 32, DUSMDR, NARA-59.

21. Robert C. Ogden to John Wanamaker, March 8, 1889, ACA-B3, ARPO, NARA-59.

22. Nathaniel McKay to [Sec. of State] J. G. Blaine, April 17, 1889, ACA-B3, ARPO, NARA-59.

23. W. P. Kellogg, James Lewis, and A. R. Blaunt to [Sec. of State] J. G. Blaine, May 28, 1889, ACA-B3, ARPO, NARA-59; Nathaniel McKay to [Sec. of State] J. G. Blaine, July 26, 1889, ACA-B3, ARPO, NARA-59.

24. For such letters, addressed to Secretary of State Blaine, President Harrison, and others, see E. R. Thompson to J. G. Blaine, May 1, 1889; C. P. Cogswell to J. G. Blaine, April 10, 1889; Ira L. Peck to J. G. Blaine, April 10, 1889; L. D. T. Blackstone to J. G. Blaine, April 6, 1889; Ogden Pell to J. G. Blaine, May 27, 1889; Edgar R. Champlin to J. G. Blaine, July 1, 1889; A. P. Wilson to John D. Long, July 5, 1889; J. S. Paine to J. G. Blaine, July 3, 1889; W. Irving Comes and James Whitlock to Benjamin Harrison, July 9, 1889; Hartley Graham to Benjamin Harrison, July 10, 1889, all in ACHA-B4, ARPO, NARA-59. See also Chas. C. Haskell to J. G. Blaine, May 17, 1889; Chas. C. Haskell to W. Blaine, June 6, 1889, both in ACA-B3, ARPO, NARA-59. Note that Hartley Graham bought E. Remington and Sons in 1888.

25. Paine to [Sec. of State] J. G. Blaine, July 3, 1889.

26. Champlin [Sec. of State] to J. G. Blaine, July 1, 1889.

27. Elite Americans and internationals often stayed at the hotel, which also served as the headquarters for the Democratic Party. Fontain, *Hoffman House*; "Col. Williams Reviewed," *NYA*, May 7, 1887.

28. "Astwood in New York," *Daily Picayune*, June 26, 1889.

29. H. M. Linnell to [Pres.] Benjamin Harrison, September 13, 1889, ACA-B3, ARPO, NARA-59.

30. "Astwood in New York," *Daily Picayune*, June 26, 1889.

31. "The Dominican Republic," *NYA*, July 27, 1889, reprinted from the *Boston Herald*.

32. "The Dominican Republic," *NYA*, July 27, 1889, reprinted from the *Boston Herald*. See also Ramírez, *Colonial Phantoms*, 2.

33. Cogswell to [Sec. of State] J. G. Blaine, April 10, 1889.

34. Wilson to Long, July 5, 1889.

35. "Bridge Street A.M.E. Church," *NYA*, June 29, 1889. See also "Bridge Street A.M.E. Church," *NYA*, June 1, 1889; "Services at Bethel Church," *NYA*, June 1, 1889; "Rambling Notes," *NYA*, July 8, 1889; "Brooklyn Briefs," *NYA*, July 13, 1889; "Brooklyn Briefs," *NYA*, July 27, 1889; "The Ocean Grove Jubilee," *CR*, July 18, 1889.

36. "Services at Bethel Church," *NYA*, June 1, 1889; "Brooklyn Briefs," *NYA*, July 13, 1889.

37. "Fair Play for Astwood," *NYA*, January 19, 1889.

38. Jerome Peterson to [Pres.] Benjamin Harrison, September 16, 1889, ACA-B3, ARPO; W. B. Derrick to [Pres.] Benjamin Harrison, July 7, 1889, ACHA-B4, ARPO. See also J. M. Townsend to [Sec. of State] J. G. Blaine, May 26, 1889, ACA-B3, ARPO; H. M. Turner, W. B. Derrick, and others to [Pres.] Benjamin Harrison, September 16, 1889, ACA-B3, ARPO. All NARA-59.

39. James A. Handy to [Sec. of State] J. G. Blaine, July 25, 1889, ACHA-B4, ARPO, NARA-59; Turner, Derrick, and others to Harrison, September 16, 1889.

40. For these dynamics, see Balleisen, *Fraud*, 3–241, especially 75–76. For contemporary embezzlement, see Unterman, "Boodle over the Border."

41. Levy, "Freaks of Fortune."

42. Derby, "Beyond Fugitive Speech," 126–27.

43. Logan, *Diplomatic Relations*, 406–7.
44. H. C. C. Astwood to William Hunter, November 22, 1883, no. 119, DUSCSD, NARA-59.
45. H. C. C. Astwood to William Hunter, January 14, 1884, no. 129, DUSCSD, NARA-59.
46. Kirk, *Wanamaker's Temple*, 7.
47. Kirk, *Wanamaker's Temple*, 17–60.
48. Fischer, "'Holy John,'" 451.
49. H. C. C. Astwood to William Hunter, November 22, 1883, no. 116, DUSCSD, NARA-59.
50. H. C. C. Astwood to William Hunter, December 6, 1883, no. 121, DUSCSD, NARA-59.
51. H. C. C. Astwood to James Davis Porter, July 12, 1886, no. 336, and October 1, 1886, no. 335, DUSCSD, NARA-59.
52. Affidavit of J. E. Huffington, September 25, 1889, ACA-B3, ARPO, NARA-59.
53. John Wanamaker to James Davis Porter, April 24, 1886, ACA-B3, ARPO, NARA-59.
54. H. C. C. Astwood to James Davis Porter, December 29, 1885, no. 296, DUSCSD, NARA-59.
55. William P. Clyde to [Sec. of State] Thomas F. Bayard, April 26, 1886, and July 12, 1886, ACA-B3, ARPO, NARA-59.
56. Wanamaker to Porter, April 24, 1886.
57. Board of Underwriters to [Pres.] Grover Cleveland, November 15, 1885; Robert Deeley and Co. to [Sec. of State] Thomas F. Bayard, November 18, 1885; John D. Jones to [Sec. of State] Thomas F. Bayard, November 19, 1885; Horatio Collins King to [Pres.] Grover Cleveland, April 24, 1886; John Paulison to [Sec. of State] Thomas F. Bayard, April 26, 1886, all in ACA-B3, ARPO, NARA-59.
58. N. C. Blanchard and others to [Sec. of State] Thomas F. Bayard, April 15, 1886, ACA-B3, ARPO, NARA-59.
59. Halford, "Matters Diplomatic," 381.
60. H. C. C. Astwood to James Davis Porter, June 10, 1886, no. 327, DUSCSD, NARA-59.
61. Juan Cambiaso immigrated to eastern Haiti in 1841 and helped create the Dominican Navy after 1844. In 1881, he and Luís owned a sugar refinery near the Ozama River and invested in Dominican commercial houses. Sang, *Ulises Heureaux*, 58.
62. H. C. C. Astwood to James Davis Porter, June 24, 1887, no. 395, DUSCSD, NARA-59.
63. H. C. C. Astwood to James Davis Porter, June 10, 1886, no. 328, DUSCSD, NARA-59.
64. H. C. C. Astwood to James Davis Porter, July 12, 1886, no. 355, DUSCSD, NARA-59.
65. Sang, *Ulises Heureaux*, 59.
66. H. C. C. Astwood to James Davis Porter, July 5, 1886, no. 333, DUSCSD, NARA-59.
67. Affidavit of J. E. Huffington, September 25, 1889.
68. For Apolinar de Castro, see Martínez, *Diccionario biográfico-histórico*, 113.
69. "List of Passengers on Board the Steamship *George W. Clyde*," August 11, 1886, PLVNY.
70. Franks notes that local actors used such fraud to thwart the Dominican government's and US planters' control of land. It is possible that Astwood's motives were similar. Franks, "Transforming Property," 151.
71. H. C. C. Astwood to James Davis Porter, September 21, 1886, no. 351, DUSCSD, NARA-59.

72. Affidavit of J. E. Huffington, September 25, 1889.

73. H. C. C. Astwood to William Hunter, July 23, 1885, no. 256, and October 30, 1885, no. 362, DUSCSD, NARA-59.

74. H. C. C. Astwood to James Davis Porter, May 7, 1887, DUSCSD, NARA-59.

75. Affidavit of J. E. Huffington, September 25, 1889.

76. James W. Mellor to the Secretary of State [Bayard], February 19, 1887; John Hardy to James Davis Porter, July 28, 1887; John Hardy to [Sec. of State] Thomas F. Bayard, October 4, 1887, all in DUSCSD, NARA-59.

77. H. C. C. Astwood to James Davis Porter, June 28, 1887, no. 396, and July 30, 1887, no. 406, DUSCSD, NARA-59.

78. H. C. C. Astwood to James Davis Porter, August 19, 1887, no. 408, DUSCSD, NARA-59.

79. Astwood to Porter, July 30, 1887.

80. Astwood to Porter, May 7, 1887.

81. Greenberg, *Manifest Manhood*, 12.

82. Astwood to Porter, May 7, 1887.

83. For stereotype, see Greenberg, *Manifest Manhood*, 91–106, especially 103.

84. Greenberg, *Manifest Manhood*, 11.

85. Astwood to Porter, May 7, 1887.

86. Martínez-Vergne, *Nation and Citizen*, 43–44.

87. Astwood to Porter, July 30, 1887.

88. Astwood to Porter, May 7, 1887; Chas. C. Haskell to John Sherman, April 29, 1887, ACA-B3, ARPO, NARA-59.

89. James Grant to [Sec. of State] Thomas F. Bayard, April 29, 1887, included in Astwood to Porter, May 7, 1887.

90. For bio, see Milkman, "Thomas Dewitt Talmage."

91. S. F. Purington to [Sec. of State] Thomas F. Bayard, May 5, 1887, included in Astwood to Porter, May 7, 1887.

92. Cunningham and Sons to [Sec. of State] Thomas F. Bayard, May 6, 1887, included in Astwood to Porter, May 7, 1887; Affidavit of J. E. Huffington, September 25, 1889.

93. E. R. Thompson to [Sec. of State] Thomas F. Bayard, April 29, 1887, included in Astwood to Porter, May 7, 1887.

94. Astwood did not report these monies in any dispatch. He drew on State Department funds for Wanamaker only once for rent and miscellaneous expenses. See H. C. C. Astwood to James Davis Porter, July 7, 1887, no. 400, DUSCSD, NARA-59.

95. John Hardy to H. C. C. Astwood, 28 July 1887, no. 30, DUSCSD, NARA-59; John Hardy to Thomas F. Bayard, October 4, 1887, no. 34, DUSCSD, NARA-59.

96. "Poder Judicial," *Gaceta Oficial*, February 16, 1889.

97. Read to Department of State, March 26, 1889.

98. Read to Department of State, March 26, 1889. For Astwood and railroads, see Baud, *Historia de un sueño*, 66–73.

99. Robert C. Ogden to John Wanamaker, September 24, 1889, DCA-B34, ARPO, NARA-59.

100. H. C. C. Astwood to [Pres.] Benjamin Harrison, January 27, 1890, ACA-B3, ARPO, NARA-59.

101. References to Astwood are few: Himelhoch, "Frederick Douglass," 168n21; Volwiler, *Correspondence*, 76n29.

102. Logan, *Diplomatic Relations*, 397–457. See also Byrd, "Ebenezer Bassett," 51–53; Bourhis-Mariotti, *Wanted! A Nation!*, 129–30.

103. Healy, *James G. Blaine*, 188. For press, see Blight, *Frederick Douglass*, 693; Byrd, "Ebenezer Bassett," 51; Bourhis-Mariotti, *Wanted! A Nation!*, 126–28.

104. T. C. Platt to [Pres.] Benjamin Harrison, September 13, 1889; S. F. Purington to [Sec. of State] J. G. Blaine, September 14, 1889, both in ACA-B3, ARPO, NARA-59.

105. William P. Clyde to [Pres.] Benjamin Harrison, September 12, 1889; William P. Clyde to [Sec. of State] J. G. Blaine, October 14, 1889, both in ACA-B3, ARPO, NARA-59.

106. For Durham, see Wynes, "John Stephens Durham"; Padgett, "Diplomats to Haiti." For London, see William Pepper to [Sec. of State] J. G. Blaine, March 16, 1889; Sims Jr. to [Sec. of State] J. G. Blaine, March 18, 1889; Gibson Peacock to [Sec. of State] J. G. Blaine, March 18, 1889, all in DCA-B34, ARPO, NARA-59.

107. Pepper to Blaine, March 16, 1889; Edwin H. Fitler to [Sec. of State] J. G. Blaine, September 17, 1889; Mac Alister [*sic*] to Anonymous, September 19, 1889, all in DCA-B34, ARPO, NARA-59. McAllister signed his name "Mac Alister."

108. Edwin H. Fitler to John Wanamaker, September 17, 1889, DCA-B34, ARPO, NARA-59.

109. William P. Clyde to Robert C. Ogden, September 22, 1889, DCA-B34, ARPO, NARA-59.

110. John Wanamaker to Secretary of State [Blaine], September 28, 1889, DCA-B34, ARPO, NARA-59.

111. William P. Clyde to [Sec. of State] J. G. Blaine, October 14, 1889, DCA-B34, ARPO, NARA-59.

112. Fitler to J. G. Blaine, September 17, 1889; Mac Alister [*sic*] to Anonymous, September 19, 1889.

113. See, for example, Thomas Cooper to [Sec. of State] J. G. Blaine, September 17, 1889; and Robert C. Ogden to John Wanamaker, September 25, 1889, both in DCA-B34, ARPO, NARA-59.

114. Charles Emory Smith to the President [Harrison], September 18, 1889; John R. Lynch to the President [Harrison], September 17, 1889; Gibson Peacock to [Sec. of State] J. G. Blaine, October 8, 1889, all in DCA-B34, ARPO, NARA-59.

115. Smith to President, September 18, 1889.

116. Robert C. Ogden to John Wanamaker, October 7, 1889, DCA-B34, ARPO, NARA-59.

117. Ogden to Wanamaker, September 25, 1889.

118. Ogden to Wanamaker, October 7, 1889.

119. William P. Clyde to T. C. Platt, September 12, 1889, DCA-B34, ARPO, NARA-59.

120. Douglass, *Life and Times*, 601.

121. Jabez P. Campbell to Robert C. Ogden, July 8, 1889; Levi J. Coppin to Robert C. Ogden, July 8, 1889; Benjamin F. Lee to Robert C. Ogden, July 8, 1889, all in DCA-B34, ARPO, NARA-59.

122. "The San Domingo Consulate," NYA, July 20, 1889; "Editorial Note and Comment," NYA, August 24, 1889.

123. Jerome Peterson to the President [Harrison], September 30, 1889, DCA-B34, ARPO, NARA-59.

124. Peterson to the President [Harrison], September 30, 1889; McCants Stewart to [Sec. of State] J. G. Blaine, October 5, 1889, DCA-B34, ARPO, NARA-59.

125. Theophilus J. Minton to the President [Harrison], September 17, 1889, DCA-B34, ARPO, NARA-59.

126. "Rambles in the South," NYA, October 5, 1889.

127. Himelhoch, "Frederick Douglass," 164–65; Bourhis-Mariotti, *Wanted! A Nation!*, 127.

128. For competition, see Byrd, *Black Republic*, 37–39, 63–64, 104–5.

129. Ogden to Wanamaker, October 7, 1889.

130. H. C. C. Astwood to [Pres.] Benjamin Harrison, October 14, 1889, ACA-B3, ARPO, NARA-59.

131. "Kellogg's Backing," *Daily Picayune*, November 14, 1889, reprinted from the *New York World*.

132. H. C. C. Astwood to [Pres.] Benjamin Harrison, January 10, 1890; H. C. C. Astwood to [Pres.] Benjamin Harrison, January 27, 1890; H. C. C. Astwood to [Pres.] Benjamin Harrison, January 28, 1890; B. W. Arnett, W. J. Gaines, and others to [Sec. of State] J. G. Blaine, January 22, 1890; M. Mark, Thos. Healy, and others to [Sec. of State] J. G. Blaine, January 27, 1890; M. Mark, Thos. Healy, and others to [Pres.] Benjamin Harrison, January 27, 1890, all in ACA-B3, ARPO.

133. F. O. St. Clair to [Sec. of State] J. G. Blaine, April 8, 1890; also F. O. St. Clair to the Secretary of State [Blaine], April 4, 1890, both in ACA-B3, ARPO, NARA-59.

134. "Will Not Be Seated," *Plain Dealer*, May 9, 1890.

135. Other places were Liberia, Vera Cruz (Mexico), Boma (Congo), Demerara (Guyana), Málaga (Spain), Madagascar, and the Turks Islands. See H. C. C. Astwood to Benjamin Harrison, March 4, 1890; Nathaniel McKay and others to [Sec. of State] J. G. Blaine, March 24, 1890, both in ACA-B3, ARPO, NARA-59.

136. For these events, see Bourhis-Mariotti, *Wanted! A Nation!*, 140–47.

137. Himelhoch, "Frederick Douglass," 176–78; Byrd, "Ebenezer Bassett," 59–65.

138. Douglass, *Life and Times*, 616–17.

139. Himelhoch, "Frederick Douglass," 179; Bourhis-Mariotti, *Wanted! A Nation!*, 145–147.

CONCLUSION

1. See, for example, "Taylor and Astwood," *Washington Bee*, January 5, 1895.

2. Veeser, *A World Safe*, 6–7.

3. Veeser, *A World Safe*, 32; Logan, *Diplomatic Relations*, 431.

4. Veeser, *A World Safe*, 33.

5. Moya Pons, *Dominican Republic*, 272.
6. Veeser, *A World Safe*, 34–38.
7. Veeser, *A World Safe*, 11–13, 35–37.
8. Veeser, *A World Safe*, 41.
9. For examples, see C. W. Wells to H. C. C. Astwood, March 1, 1893; Directors of the New Jersey and San Domingo Brewing Company to [Pres.] Grover Cleveland, March 8, 1893, both ACA-B3, ARPO, National Archives and Records Administration, Record Group 59 (NARA-59).
10. W. M. H. Butler, "Office of the Home and Foreign Missionary Society," *Voice of Missions* 1, no. 1 (January 1893): 1.
11. Smith M. Weed to Josiah Quincy, May 19, 1893, ACA-B3, ARPO, NARA-59; "Astwood Not a Diplomat," *Washington Bee*, October 7, 1893.
12. Scarfi, "Hacia un orden," 137. Quesada published under the pen name Domingo de Pantoja.
13. Quesada, *Los Estados Unidos*, 49.
14. Scarfi, "Hacia un orden," 127.
15. Reed, *"All the World,"* 145–67; Byrd, *Black Republic*, 130, 129–30; Wells et al., *Reason Why*; Bourhis-Mariotti, *Wanted! A Nation!*, 176–85.
16. Reed, *"All the World,"* 128.
17. Byrd, *Black Republic*, 130.
18. Muñiz, "Unofficial Archive," 192–99.
19. "Shrine of the Fair," *Chicago Daily Tribune*, May 8, 1893. For a full description, see Curtis, *Relics of Columbus*, 69–85, 91, 109.
20. Ober, *Our West Indian Neighbors*, 190.
21. Ober, *Our West Indian Neighbors*, 190. See also Ramírez, *Colonial Phantoms*, 116–17.
22. Ober, *Our West Indian Neighbors*, 183.
23. Coates, "Pan-American Lobbyist," 34; Cassell, "The Colombian Exposition," 119.
24. Ober, *In the Wake of Columbus*, 326–29.
25. Cassell, "The Colombian Exposition," 110.
26. "Shrine of the Fair," *Chicago Daily Tribune*, May 8, 1893.
27. "Palpitante," *Listín Diario*, n.d., newspaper clipping, ACA-B3, ARPO, NARA-59.
28. Eller, "Raining Blood," 449–57.
29. Eller, "Raining Blood," 435.
30. Robinson, *Black Marxism*, 72–73, 169–71.
31. Eller, "Raining Blood," 451.
32. Veeser, *A World Safe*, 41. See also W. F. Powell to John Sherman, March 2, 1898, no. 30, DUSMDR, NARA-59.
33. John S. Durham to William F. Wharton, August 4, 1891, no. 67, DUSCSD, NARA-59.
34. Veeser, *A World Safe*, 4.
35. "The *Defender*," *Leavenworth Herald*, November 24, 1894. Astwood's *Defender* likely ran from 1894 until his son's death in 1911. Few issues exist today.
36. "Astwood Sails for Cuba," *Pennsylvania Times*, August 12, 1898. See also Dodson, "Encounters," 89.
37. "Burial Record of Henry Astwood," August 19, 1908, PNJCTR.

38. Arturo Trinidad, interview with the author, July 30, 2018; Corliss Astwood, phone and email correspondence, October 14, 2019. See also US Black newspapers for Astwood's American children.

39. For examples, see "Is There a Break?," *Washington Bee*, August 26, 1893; "H. C. C. Astwood," *Washington Bee*, July 14, 1894; "Taylor and Astwood," *Washington Bee*, January 5, 1895.

Bibliography

ARCHIVES

Dominican Republic
Archivo General de la Nación (AGN)
 Colección José Gabriel García (JGG)
 Presidencia de la República (PDLR)
 Secretará de Estado de Relaciones Exteriores (SERE)

United Kingdom
British Library (BL)
 Anglican Church Records from Turks and Caicos Islands, Parishes St. Thomas and
  St. Johns, 1799–1922 (ACRTCI)
Library of the School of Oriental and African Studies (SOAS), University of London
 Microfiche of the Wesleyan Methodist Missionary Society, West Indies Correspon-
  dence, Methodist Missionary Society Archives (WMMS-WI)

United States
Library of Congress
 Frederick Douglass Papers, General Correspondence (FDP-GC)
National Archives and Records Administration, Record Group 59 (NARA-59)
 Application and Recommendations for Public Office (ARPO)
  Astwood, Cleveland Administration, box 3 (ACA-B3)
  Astwood, Cleveland-Harrison Administration, box 4 (ACHA-B4)
  Durham, Cleveland Administration, box 34 (DCA-B34)

Despatches from United States Consuls in Santo Domingo, 1837–1906, Microcopy T-56 (DUSCSD)

Despatches from United States Ministers to the Dominican Republic, 1883–1906, M-93 (DUSMDR)

Diplomatic Instructions of the Department of State, 1801–1906, M-77 (DIDS)

Notes from the Legation of the Dominican Republic in the United States to the Department of State, 1844–1906, T801 (NLDR)

Notes to the Foreign Legations in the United States from the Department of State, 1834–1906, M-99 (NFLDS)

US Consular Bureau Report (USCBR)

US State Department Consular Instructions (USSDCI)

US State Department Miscellaneous Correspondence, M179, roll 754 (USSDMC)

Moorland-Spingarn Research Center (MSRC) at Howard University, Washington, DC

Archibald H. Grimke Papers (AHGP)

Gregoria Goins Papers (GGP)

GENEALOGICAL DATABASES

Ancestry.com

1870 U.S. Census, Population Schedules, NARA microfilm publication M593 (USC-1870)

1880 U.S. Federal Census, NARA microfilm publication T9, roll 107 (USFC-1880)

1900 U.S. Federal Census, NARA microfilm publication T623, roll 1443 (USFC-1900)

Dominican Republic, Civil Registration, 1801–2010 (DRCR)

Massachusetts State Census, 1855–1865, microfilm, New England Historic Genealogical Society (MASC)

New York State Census for 1875, microfilm, New York State Archives (NYSC)

Passenger Lists of Vessels Arriving at New York, New York, 1820–1897, NARA microfilm publication M237 (PLVNY)

Pennsylvania and New Jersey, Church and Town Records, 1669–2013 (PNJCTR)

United Grand Lodge of England Freemason Membership Registers, 1751–1921 (UGLE-FMR)

U.S. Naturalization Records Indexes, 1791–1992 (Indexed in World Archives Project), NARA microfilm serial P2087, roll 1 (USNRI)

FamilySearch.org

Louisiana Parish Marriages, 1837–1957 (LPM)

Orleans Parish, Louisiana Birth Records, 1819–1906 (OP-BR)

Orleans Parish, Louisiana Death Records and Certificates, 1835–1954 (OP-DRC)

NEWSPAPERS

Note: This list includes only those newspapers for which abbreviations are used. Other similar sources are designated by title in the notes.

AME Church Review (AMECR)

Boletín del Comercio (BDC)

Boletín Eclesiástico (BE)
Christian Recorder (CR)
Eco de la Opinión (EDLO)
New York Age (NYA)
New York Freeman (NYF)
New York Herald (NYH)
New York Times (NYT)
Royal Standard and Gazette of the Turks and Caicos Islands (RSGTCI)
Weekly Louisianian (WL)

SECONDARY SOURCES

Alcántara Almánzar, José. "Hostos y las ciencias sociales." *Caudal* 3, no. 1 (2004): 47–50.

Alemar, Luis E. *Santo Domingo, Ciudad Trujillo*. Santiago, Dominican Republic: Editorial El Diario, 1943.

Alexander, Leslie M. *Fear of a Black Republic: Haiti and the Birth of Black Internationalism in the United States*. Champaign: University of Illinois Press, 2022.

Alexander, Leslie M. "A Land of Promise: Emigration and Pennsylvania's Black Elite in the Era of the Haitian Revolution." In *The Civil War in Pennsylvania: The African American Experience*, edited by Samuel W. Black, 97–132. Pittsburgh: Pennsylvania Heritage Foundation, 2013.

Anderson, Benedict. *Imagined Communities: Reflections on the Origin and Spread of Nationalism*. London: Verso, 1983.

Andrews, George Reid. *Afro-Latin America, 1800–2000*. Oxford: Oxford University Press, 2004.

Angell, Stephen Ward. *Bishop Henry McNeal Turner and African-American Religion in the South*. Knoxville: University of Tennessee Press, 1992.

Aponte, Sarah. *La presencia dominicana en el periódico* Las Novedades, *1876–1918: De breve mención a propietarios en la ciudad de Nueva York*. New York: CUNY Dominican Studies Institute, 2022.

Ardouin, B. *Études sur l'histoire d'Haïti suivies de la vie du général J. M. Borgella*. Vol. 9. Paris: Dézobry, E. Magdeleine et Ce, Libreries-Editeurs, 1860.

Arnold, James. "Spider and Rabbit: Tricksters as Mediators of Caribbean Cultural Identity." In *Colonizer and Colonized*, edited by Theo D'Haen and Patricia Krüs, 269–76. Amsterdam: Rodopi, 2000.

Arroyo, Jossianna. *Writing Secrecy in Caribbean Freemasonry*. New York: Palgrave Macmillan US, 2013.

Arthur, Chester A. *Collected State of the Union Addresses, 1881–1884*. N.p.: Del Lume Books, 2017.

Arthur Sosa, Luis Héctor, and Vítor José Arthur Nouel. "Censos del honorable ayuntamiento de Puerto Plata, R.D. de los años 1871, 1875 y 1879." Accessed November 11, 2019. http://genealogiadominicana.com/arthur/cpp/portada-cpp.htm.

Avelino, Francisco Antonio. "Hostos: Pensador social." *Clío* 73, no. 168 (2004): 203–44.

Avrich, Paul. *The Haymarket Tragedy*. Princeton, NJ: Princeton University Press, 2020.

Baez, Jennifer. "Anacaona Writes Back: The Columbus Statue in Santo Domingo as a Site of Erasure." *Small Axe* 25, no. 66 (2021): 1–23.

Balleisen, Edward J. *Fraud: An American History from Barnum to Madoff*. Princeton, NJ: Princeton University Press, 2017.

Bartosik-Velez, Elise. *The Legacy of Christopher Columbus in the Americas: New Nations and a Transatlantic Discourse of Empire*. Nashville: Vanderbilt University Press, 2014.

Baucom, Ian. *Specters of the Atlantic: Finance Capital, Slavery, and the Philosophy of History*. Durham, NC: Duke University Press, 2005.

Baud, Michiel. *Historia de un sueño: Los ferrocarriles públicos en la República Dominicana, 1880–1930*. Santo Domingo: Fundación Cultural Dominicana, 1993.

Bederman, Gail. *Manliness and Civilization: A Cultural History of Gender and Race in the United States, 1880–1917*. Chicago: University of Chicago Press, 1995.

Bennett, James B. *Religion and the Rise of Jim Crow in New Orleans*. Princeton, NJ: Princeton University Press, 2005.

Blakely, Allison. "Blacks in the U.S. Diplomatic and Consular Services, 1869–1924." In *African Americans in U.S. Foreign Policy: From the Era of Frederick Douglass to the Age of Obama*, edited by Linda Heywood, Allison Blakely, Charles Stith, and Joshua C. Yesnowitz, 13–29. Urbana: University of Illinois Press, 2015.

Blassingame, John W. *Black New Orleans*. Chicago: University of Chicago Press, 1973.

Blight, David W. *Frederick Douglass: Prophet of Freedom*. New York: Simon and Schuster, 2018.

Borgés Bordas, Gustavo E. *Otras cosas de Lilís*. Santo Domingo: Imp. Montalvo, 1921.

Bosch, Juan. *The Social Composition of the Dominican Republic*. New York: Routledge, 2016.

Bourhis-Mariotti, Claire. "Frederick Douglass and Debates over the Annexation of the Dominican Republic." In *In Search of Liberty: African American Internationalism in the Nineteenth-Century Atlantic World*, edited by Ronald Angelo Johnson and Ousmane K. Power-Greene, 224–50. Athens: University of Georgia Press, 2021.

Bourhis-Mariotti, Claire. *L'union fait la force: Les noirs américains et Haïti, 1804–1893*. Rennes, France: Presse Universitaires de Rennes, 2015.

Bourhis-Mariotti, Claire. *Wanted! A Nation! Black Americans & Haiti, 1804–1893*. Athens: University of Georgia Press, 2023.

Brown, Christopher Leslie. *Moral Capital: Foundations of British Abolitionism*. Chapel Hill: University of North Carolina Press, 2006.

Brown, Gordon S. *Toussaint's Clause: The Founding Fathers and the Haitian Revolution*. Jackson: University Press of Mississippi, 2005.

Brown, Vincent. "Social Death and Political Life in the Study of Slavery." *American Historical Review* 115, no. 5 (2009): 1231–49.

Bryan, Patrick E. "The Question of Labor in the Sugar Industry of the Dominican Republic in the Late Nineteenth and Early Twentieth Centuries." In *Between Slavery and Free Labor: The Spanish-Speaking Caribbean in the Nineteenth Century*, edited by Manuel Moreno Fraginals, Frank Moya Pons, and Stanley L. Engerman, 235–51. Baltimore: Johns Hopkins University Press, 1985.

Bryan, Patrick. "The Transition to Plantation Agriculture in the Dominican Republic, 1870–84." *Journal of Caribbean History* 10 (1978): 82–105.

Bushman, Claudia. *America Discovers Columbus: How an Italian Explorer Became an American Hero*. Hanover, NH: University Press of New England, 1992.

Byrd, Brandon R. *The Black Republic: African Americans and the Fate of Haiti*. Philadelphia: University of Pennsylvania Press, 2020.

Byrd, Brandon R. "Black Republicans, Black Republic: African-Americans, Haiti, and the Promise of Reconstruction." *Slavery and Abolition* 36, no. 4 (2015): 545–67.

Byrd, Brandon. "Ebenezer Bassett and Frederick Douglass: An Intellectual History of Black U.S. Diplomacy." *Diplomatic History* 46, no. 1 (2022): 35–69.

Byrd, Brandon R. "A Reinterpretation of African Americans and Haitian Emigration." In *In Search of Liberty: African American Internationalism in the Ninteenth-Century Atlantic World*, edited by Ronald Angelo Johnson and Ousmane K. Power-Greene, 197–223. Athens: University of Georgia Press, 2021.

Byrd, Brandon R. "The Transnational Work of Moral Elevation: African American Women and the Reformation of Haiti, 1874–1950." *Palimpsest* 5, no. 2 (2016): 128–50.

Campbell, James T. *Songs of Zion: The African Methodist Episcopal Church in the United States and South Africa*. New York: Oxford University Press, 1995.

Candelario, Ginetta E. B. *Black behind the Ears: Dominican Racial Identity from Museums to Beauty Shops*. Durham, NC: Duke University Press, 2007.

Carter, J. Kameron. *Race: A Theological Account*. Oxford: Oxford University Press, 2008.

Cassá, Roberto. "El racismo en la ideología de la clase dominante dominicana." *Ciencia* 3 (1976): 61–85.

Cassá, Roberto. *Historia social y económica de la República Dominicana*. Santo Domingo: Editora Alfa y Omega, 1993.

Cassá, Roberto. "Juan Vicente Flores: El guerrero de la pluma." In *Lilí, el sanguinario machetero dominicano*, 2nd ed, 9–24. Santo Domingo: Archivo General de la Nación, 2006.

Cassell, Frank. "The Colombian Exposition of 1893 and United States Diplomacy in Latin America." *Mid-America: An Historical Review* 67, no. 3 (1985): 110–24.

Castillo, José del. "The Formation of the Dominican Sugar Industry: From Competition to Monopoly, from National Semiproletariat to Foreign Proletariat." In *Between Slavery and Free Labor: The Spanish-Speaking Caribbean in the Nineteenth Century*, edited by Manuel Moreno Fraginals, Frank Moya Pons, and Stanley L. Engerman, 215–34. Baltimore: Johns Hopkins University Press, 1985.

Castillo, José P., Pedro Brea, and Francisco Henriquez y Carvajal. *En la elaboración del azúcar está la salvación del país*. Santo Domingo: Sociedad Literaria Amigos del País, 1877. https://nrs.harvard.edu/urn-3:FHCL:968150.

Castillo Pichardo, José del. "Hostos en Santo Domingo: Periplo de un iluminado." *Clío* 87, no. 196 (2018): 117–52.

Castro, Victor M. de. *Cosas de Lilís*. 2nd ed. Santo Domingo: Editora Taller, C. por A., 1986.

Cazneau, Mrs. William Leslie. *Our Winter's Eden: Pen Pictures of the Tropics*. New York: Author's Publishing Company, 1878.

Cestero, Tulio M. *Colon (su nacionalidad, el predescubrimiento de America, su tumba y el faro commemorativo)*. Buenos Aires: Cervantes de J. Suarez, 1933.

Cestero, Tulio. *La sangre: Una vida bajo la tiranía*. Santo Domingo: ABC Editorial, 2002.

Cheek, William Francis, III. "Forgotten Prophet: The Life of John Mercer Langston." PhD diss., University of Virginia, 1961.

Chetty, Raj, and Amaury Rodríguez. "Introduction." *Black Scholar* 45, no. 2 (2015): 1–9.

Cleveland, Grover. *The Public Papers of Grover Cleveland: Twenty-Second President of the United States, March 4, 1885 to March 4, 1889.* Washington, DC: Government Printing Office, 1889.

Coates, Benjamin A. "The Pan-American Lobbyist: William Eleroy Curtis and U.S. Empire 1884–1899." *Diplomatic History* 38, no. 1 (2014): 22–48.

Cocchia, Rocco. *Los restos de Cristobal Colon en la catedral de Santo Domingo: Contestacion al informe de la Real academia de la historia al gobierno de S. M. el rey de España.* Santo Domingo: Imprenta de García Hermanos, 1879.

Colección de leyes, decretos y resoluciones emanadas de los poderes legislativo y ejecutivo de la Republica Dominicana. Vol. 7. Santo Domingo: Imprenta de Garcia Hermanos, 1884.

Collado, Lipe. *El tíguere dominicano: Hacia una aproximación de cómo son los dominicanos.* 3rd ed. Santo Domingo: Editora Collado, 2002.

Colmeiro, Manuel. *Los restos de Colon: Informe de la Real academia de la historia al gobierno de S. M. sobre el supuesto hallazgo de los verdaderos restos de Cristóval Colon en la Iglesia Catedral de Santo Domingo.* Madrid: Imprenta de M. Tello, 1879.

Conroy-Krutz, Emily. *Christian Imperialism: Converting the World in the Early American Republic.* Ithaca, NY: Cornell University Press, 2015.

Cooper, Frederick. *Colonialism in Question: Theory, Knowledge, History.* Berkeley: University of California Press, 2005.

Cordero Michel, Emilio. "Lili, el sanguinario machetero dominicano de Juan Vicente Flores." *Boletín del Archivo General de la Nación* 31, no. 114 (2006): 111–26.

Cordero Michel, Emilio. "República Dominicana, cuna del antillanismo." *Clio* 71, no. 165 (2003): 225–36.

Cronau, Rudolf. *The Discovery of America and the Landfall of Columbus: The Last Resting Place of Columbus. Two Monographs, Based on Personal Investigations by Rudolf Cronau, with Reproductions of Maps, Inscriptions and Autographs, and of Original Drawings by the Author.* New York: R. Cronau, 1921.

Curtis, Heather D. *Holy Humanitarians: American Evangelicals and Global Aid.* Cambridge, MA: Harvard University Press, 2018.

Curtis, William Eleroy. *The Relics of Columbus: An Illustrated Description of the Historical Collection in the Monastery of La Rabida.* Washington, DC: William H. Lowdermilk, 1893.

Daut, Marlene. "Haiti as Diasporic Crossroads in Transnational African American Writing." In *African American Literature in Transition, 1850–1865,* edited by Teresa Zackodnik, 331–51. Cambridge: Cambridge University Press, 2021.

Daut, Marlene. *Tropics of Haiti: Race and the Literary History of the Haitian Revolution in the Atlantic World, 1789–1865.* Liverpool: Liverpool University Press, 2016.

Davidson, Christina C. "Black Protestants in a Catholic Land: The AME Church in the Dominican Republic 1899–1916." *New West Indian Guide* 89 (2015): 258–88.

Davidson, Christina C. "Converting Spanish Hispaniola: Race, Nation, and the AME Church in Santo Domingo, 1872–1904." PhD diss., Duke University, 2017.

Davidson, Christina C. "Mission, Migration, and Contested Authority: Building an AME Presence in Haiti in the Nineteenth Century." In *Global Faith, Worldly Power: Evangelical Internationalism and U.S. Empire*, edited by John Corrigan, Melani McAlister, and Axel R. Schäfer, 70–96. Chapel Hill: University of North Carolina Press, 2022.

Davidson, Christina C. "An Organic Union: Theorizing Race, Nation, and Imperialism within the Black Church." *Journal of African American History* 106, no. 4 (2021): 577–600.

Davidson, Christina C. "'What Hinders?' African Methodist Expansion from the U.S. South to Hispaniola, 1865–1885." In *Reconstruction and Empire: The Legacies of Abolition and Union Victory for an Imperial Age*, edited by David Prior, 54–78. New York: Fordham University Press, 2022.

Davis, Martha Ellen. "La cultura musical religiosa de los 'Americanos' de Samaná." In *Cultura y folklore de Samaná*, edited by Dagoberto Tejeda Ortiz, 147–212. Santo Domingo: Editora Alfa y Omega, 1984.

Davis, Martha Ellen. "That Old-Time Religion: Tradición y cambio en el enclave 'Americano' de Samaná." In *Cultura y Folklore de Samaná*, edited by Dagoberto Tejeda Ortiz, 97–146. Santo Domingo: Editora Alfa y Omega, 1984.

Davis, N. Darnell. *Mr. Froude's Negrophobia, or Don Quixote as a Cook's Tourist*. Demerara, British Guiana: Argosy Press, 1888.

Day, Susan de Forest. *The Cruise of the Scythian in the West Indies*. London: F. Tennyson Neely, 1899.

DeGuzman, Maria. *Spain's Long Shadow: The Black Legend, Off-Whiteness, and Anglo-American Empire*. Minneapolis: University of Minnesota Press, 2005.

Deive, Carlos Esteban. *Los dominicanos vistos por extranjeros (1739–1920)*. Santo Domingo: Banco Central de la República Dominicana, 2008.

Deive, Carlos Esteban. *Vodú y magia en Santo Domingo*. Santo Domingo: Fundación Cultural Dominicana, 1992.

Delgado, Jessica L., and Kelsey C. Moss. "Religion and Race in the Early Modern Iberian Atlantic." In *The Oxford Handbook of Religion and Race in American History*, edited by Kathryn Gin Lum and Paul Harvey, 40–60. New York: Oxford University Press, 2018.

Derby, Lauren. "Beyond Fugitive Speech: Rumor and Affect in Caribbean History." *Small Axe* 18, no. 2 (2014): 123–40.

Derby, Lauren. *The Dictator's Seduction: Politics and the Popular Imagination in the Era of Trujillo*. Durham, NC: Duke University Press, 2009.

Deschamps, Enrique. *La República Dominicana: Directorio y guía general*. Barcelona: La Vda. de J. Cunill, 1906.

Dickerson, Dennis C. *The African Methodist Episcopal Church: A History*. Cambridge: Cambridge University Press, 2020.

Dillon, Elizabeth Maddock, and Michael J. Drexler, eds. *The Haitian Revolution and the Early United States: Histories, Textualities, Geographies*. Philadelphia: University of Pennsylvania Press, 2016.

Dodson, Jualynne E. "Encounters in the African Atlantic World: The African Methodist Episcopal Church in Cuba." In *Between Race and Empire: African-Americans* and Cubans before the Cuban Revolution, edited by Lisa Brock and Digna Castañeda Fuertes, 85–103. Philadelphia: Temple University Press, 1998.

Domínguez, Jaime de Jesús. *La dictadura de Heureaux*. Santo Domingo: Editora Universitaria, UASD, 1986.

Domínguez, Jaime de Jesús. *Notas económicas y políticas dominicanas sobre el período julio 1865–julio 1886*. Vol. 1. Santo Domingo: Editora de la UASD, 1983.

Domínguez, Jaime de Jesús. *Notas económicas y políticas dominicanas sobre el período julio 1865–julio 1886*. Vol. 2. Santo Domingo: Editora de la UASD, 1984.

Dougherty, Matthew W. "New Scholarship in Religion and United States Empire." *Religion Compass* 13, no. 5 (2019): e12316.

Douglass, Frederick. *Life and Times of Frederick Douglass*. New York: Collier, 1962.

Doyle, D. H., ed. *American Civil Wars: The United States, Latin America, Europe, and the Crisis of the 1860s*. Chapel Hill: University of North Carolina Press, 2017.

Dubois, Laurent. *Avengers of the New World: The Story of the Haitian Revolution*. Cambridge, MA: Belknap, 2004.

Dubois, Laurent, and Richard Lee Turits. *Freedom Roots: Histories from the Caribbean*. Chapel Hill: University of North Carolina Press, 2019.

Du Bois, W. E. B. *Black Reconstruction in America*. New York: Routledge, 2017.

Dun, James Alexander. *Dangerous Neighbors: Making the Haitian Revolution in Early America*. Philadelphia: University of Pennsylvania Press, 2016.

Durkheim, Émile. *The Elementary Forms of the Religious Life*. Translated and with an introduction by Karen E. Fields. New York: Free Press, 1995.

Echeverri, José Manual de. *Do existen depositadas las cenizas de Cristobal Colon? Apuntes al caso en defensa de su conducta oficial*. Santander, Spain: Imprenta de Solinis y Cimiano, 1878.

Eller, Anne. "'Awful Pirates' and 'Hordes of Jackals': Santo Domingo/the Dominican Republic in Nineteenth-Century Historiography." *Small Axe* 44 (2014): 80–94.

Eller, Anne. "Raining Blood: Spiritual Power, Gendered Violence, and Anticolonial Lives in the Nineteenth-Century Dominican Borderlands." *Hispanic American Historical Review* 99, no. 3 (2019): 431–65.

Eller, Anne. "Rumors of Slavery: Defending Emancipation in a Hostile Caribbean." *American Historical Review* 122, no. 3 (2017): 653–79.

Eller, Anne. *We Dream Together: Dominican Independence, Haiti, and the Fight for Caribbean Freedom*. Durham, NC: Duke University Press, 2016.

Fanning, Sara. *Caribbean Crossing: African Americans and the Haitian Emigration Movement*. New York: New York University Press, 2014.

Fellows, Kristin R. "Double Consciousness and an African American Enclave: Being Black and American on Hispaniola." In *Archaeologies of Slavery and Freedom in the Caribbean: Exploring the Spaces in Between*, edited by Lynsey Bates, John Chenoweth, and James A. Delle, 307–28. Gainesville: University Press of Florida, 2016.

Fernández, Tomás, and Elena Tamaro. "Biografía de Manuel de Jesús Galván." In *Biografías y vidas: La enciclopedia biográfica en línea* [online]. Barcelona, 2004. https://www.biografiasyvidas.com/biografia/g/galvan.htm.

Fernández Olmos, Margarite, and Lizabeth Paravisini-Gebert. *Creole Religions of the Caribbean: An Introduction from Vodou and Santería to Obeah and Espiritismo.* 2nd ed. New York: New York University Press, 2011.

Ferrer, Ada. *Insurgent Cuba: Race, Nation, and Revolution, 1868–1898.* Chapel Hill: University of North Carolina Press, 1999.

Findlay, George Gillanders, and William West Holdsworth. *The History of the Wesleyan Methodist Missionary Society.* London: Epworth Press, 1921.

Finke González, Carlos Manuel. "Puerto Plata en la gesta restauradora." *Clío* 74, no. 170 (2005): 115–48.

Fischer, Roger A. "'Holy John' Wanamaker: Color Cartoon Centerfold." *Pennsylvania Magazine of History and Biography* 115, no. 4 (1991): 451–73.

Fischer, Sibylle. *Modernity Disavowed: Haiti and the Cultures of Slavery in the Age of Revolution.* Durham, NC: Duke University Press, 2004.

Fleszar, Mark. "'My Laborers in Haiti Are Not Slaves': Proslavery Fictions and a Black Colonization Experiment on the Northern Coast, 1835–1846." *Journal of the Civil War Era* 2, no. 4 (2012): 478–510.

Flores, Juan Vicente. *Lilí, el sanguinario machetero dominicano.* 2nd ed. Santo Domingo: Archivo General de la Nación, 2006.

Foner, Eric. *Freedom's Lawmakers: A Directory of Black Officeholders during Reconstruction.* Baton Rouge: Louisiana State University Press, 1996.

Foner, Eric. *Reconstruction: America's Unfinished Revolution, 1863–1877.* Updated. New York: Harper Perennial Modern Classics, 2014.

Fontain, F. G. de. *The Hoffman House, C.H. Read and E.S. Stokes Proprietors: Its Attractions.* New York: Photo-Engraving Company, 1885.

Foucault, Michel. *Discipline and Punish: The Birth of the Prison.* Social Theory. New York: Vintage, 1979.

Fountain, Anne. *José Martí, the United States, and Race.* Gainesville: University Press of Florida, 2014.

Franks, Julie Cheryl. "Transforming Property: Landholding and Political Rights in the Dominican Sugar Region, 1880–1930." PhD diss., State University of New York at Stony Brook, 1997.

Frazier, E. Franklin, and C. Eric Lincoln. *The Negro Church in America: The Black Church since Frazier.* New York: Schocken, 1974.

Fredrickson, George M. *The Black Image in the White Mind: The Debate on Afro-American Character and Destiny, 1817–1914.* Middletown, CT: Wesleyan University Press, 1987.

Froude, James Anthony. *The English in the West Indies; or, The Boy of Ulysses.* London: Longmans, Green, and Co., 1888.

Fulton, John Dirk. "John Mercer Langston, United States Minister to Haiti, 1877–1885." Master's thesis, University of Nebraska, 1969.

Gaffield, Julia. *Haitian Connections in the Atlantic World: Recognition after Revolution.* Chapel Hill: University of North Carolina Press, 2015.

García, José Gabriel. *Compendio de la historia de Santo Domingo.* 3rd ed. Vol. 2. Santo Domingo: Imprenta de García Hermanos, 1894.

García Lluberes, Alcides. "Nuestra estatua de Colón." *El faro a Colón* 9, no. 22 (1958): 100–108.

García Muñiz, Humberto. *Sugar and Power in the Caribbean: The South Porto Rico Sugar Company in Puerto Rico and the Dominican Republic 1900–1921*. San Juan: La Editorial Universidad de Puerto Rico, 2010.

García Muñiz, Humberto, and José Lee Borges. "U.S. Consular Activism in the Caribbean, 1783–1903: With Special Reference to St. Kitts-Nevis' Sugar Depression, Labor Turmoil and Its Proposed Acquisition by the United States." *Revista Mexicana del Caribe* 5 (1998): 32–79.

García-Peña, Lorgia. *The Borders of Dominicanidad: Race, Nation, and Archives of Contradiction*. Durham, NC: Duke University Press, 2016.

García-Peña, Lorgia. *Translating Blackness: Latinx Colonialities in Global Perspective*. Durham, NC: Duke University Press, 2022.

Gates, Henry Louis, Jr. *Stony the Road: Reconstruction, White Supremacy, and the Rise of Jim Crow*. New York: Penguin, 2019.

Gatewood, Willard B. *Aristocrats of Color: The Black Elite, 1880–1920*. Fayetteville: University of Arkansas Press, 2000.

Gatón, Ángel María. *Resumen del origen y fundación del odfelismo en la República Dominicana*. Ciudad Trujillo: Imprenta Jackson, 1954.

Gaztambide Géigel. "La geopolítica del antillanismo en el Caribe del siglo XIX." *Memorias* 4, no. 8 (2007): 1–35.

Geary, Patrick J. *Furta Sacra: Thefts of Relics in the Central Middle Ages*. Princeton, NJ: Princeton University Press, 1978.

Gerbner, Katharine. "Rebellion and Religion: Slavery and Empire in Early America." In *Religion and US Empire: Critical New Histories*, edited by Tisa Wenger and Sylvester A. Johnson, 19–40. New York: New York University Press, 2022.

Girard, René. *The Scapegoat*. Baltimore: Johns Hopkins University Press, 1986.

González, Raymundo. "Hostos y la conciencia moderna en República Dominicana." In *Política, identidad y pensamiento social en la República Dominicana*, edited by Raymundo González, Michiel Baud, Pedro L. San Miguel, and Roberto Cassá, 95–104. Santo Domingo: Doce Calles, Academia de Ciencias Dominicana, 1999.

González, Raymundo, Michiel Baud, Pedro L. San Miguel, and Roberto Cassá, eds. *Política, identidad y pensamiento social en la República Dominicana*. Santo Domingo: Doce Calles, Academia de Ciencias Dominicana, 1999.

Gow, Douglas R. "The Economic Background of the Dominican Customs Receivership, 1882–1907." Master's thesis, North Texas State University, 1975.

Graber, Jennifer. *The Gods of Indian Country: Religion and the Struggle for the American West*. New York: Oxford University Press, 2018.

Greenberg, Amy S. *Manifest Manhood and the Antebellum American Empire*. Cambridge: Cambridge University Press, 2005.

Greer, Margaret R., Walter D. Mignolo, and Maureen Quilligan, eds. *Rereading the Black Legend: The Discourses of Religious and Racial Difference in the Renaissance Empires*. Chicago: University of Chicago Press, 2007.

Griffiths, Leslie. *History of Methodism in Haiti*. Port-au-Prince: Imprimerie Méthodiste, 1991.

Guerra, José Antonio. "Héroes y parentela: Los dominicanos en la guerra de Cuba. Apuntes genealógicos." *Boletín del Archivo General de la Nación* 36, no. 131 (2011): 585–604.

Guridy, Frank Andre. *Forging Diaspora: Afro-Cubans and African Americans in a World of Empire and Jim Crow*. Chapel Hill: University of North Carolina Press, 2010.

Gutierrez Laboy, Roberto. *Hostos y su filosofía moral: Acercamiento a Moral Social*. Lajas, Puerto Rico: Sociedad Historica de Lajas, 1992.

Guyatt, Nicholas. "America's Conservatory: Race, Reconstruction, and the Santo Domingo Debate." *Journal of American History* 97, no. 4 (March 2011): 974–1000.

Halford, A. J. "Matters Diplomatic." *International* 3, no. 1 (1897): 380–86.

Hall, Anthony J. *Earth into Property: Colonization, Decolonization and Capitalism*. Vol. 2. Montreal: McGill-Queen's University Press, 2010.

Harris, J. Dennis. *A Summer on the Borders of the Caribbean Sea*. New York: A. B. Burdick, 1860.

Hauch, Charles C. *La República Dominicana y sus relaciones exteriores, 1844–1882*. Santo Domingo: Sociedad Dominicana de Bibliófilos, 1996.

Hazard, Samuel. *Santo Domingo: Past and Present, with a Glance at Hayti*. New York: Harper and Brothers, 1873.

Healy, David. *James G. Blaine and Latin America*. Columbia: University of Missouri Press, 2001.

Hempton, David. "Popular Evangelicalism and the Shaping of British Moral Sensibilities, 1770–1840." *Historically Speaking* 8, no. 6 (2007): 16–19.

Henríquez Ureña, Max. *Los Estados Unidos y la Republica Dominicana: La verdad de los hechos comprobada por datos y documentos oficiales*. Havana: Imprenta el Siglo XX, 1919.

Hertz, Robert. "A Contribution to a Study of the Collective Representation of Death." In *Saints, Heroes, Myths, and Rites: Classical Durkheimian Studies of Religion and Society*, edited by Alexander Riley, Sarah Daynes, and Cyril Isnart, 109–80. London: Paradigm, 2009.

Hidalgo, Dennis. *La primera inmigración de negros libertos norteamericanos y su asentamiento en la Española (1824–1826)*. Santo Domingo: Academia Dominicana de la Historia, 2016.

Himelhoch, Myra. "Frederick Douglass and Haiti's Mole St. Nicolas." *Journal of Negro History* 56, no. 3 (1971): 161–80.

Hoetink, H. "'Americans' in Samaná." *Caribbean Studies* 2, no. 1 (April 1, 1962): 3–22.

Hoetink, H. *The Dominican People, 1850–1900: Notes for a Historical Sociology*. Baltimore: Johns Hopkins University Press, 1982.

Holt, Thomas C. *The Problem of Freedom: Race, Labor, and Politics in Jamaica and Britain, 1832–1938*. Baltimore: Johns Hopkins University Press, 1992.

Hooker, Juliet. *Theorizing Race in the Americas: Douglass, Sarmiento, Du Bois, and Vasconcelos*. New York: Oxford University Press, 2017.

Horne, Gerald. *Confronting Black Jacobins: The United States, the Haitian Revolution, and the Origins of the Dominican Republic*. New York: Monthly Review Press, 2015.

Horne, Gerald. "Race from Power: U.S. Foreign Policy and the General Crisis of 'White Supremacy.'" *Diplomatic History* 23, no. 3 (1999): 437–61.

Hostos, Eugenio María de. *Moral social*. 2nd ed. Madrid: Imprenta de Bailly-Bailliere é Hijos, 1906.

Howe, Julia Ward. *Reminiscences: 1819–1899*. Boston: Houghton Mifflin, 1899.

Hutchinson, Sydney. *Tigers of a Different Stripe: Performing Gender in Dominican Music*. Chicago: University of Chicago Press, 2016.

Jackson, James O'Dell. "The Origins of Pan-African Nationalism: Afro-American and Haytian Relations, 1800–1863." PhD diss., Northwestern University, 1976.

Jacoby, Karl. *The Strange Career of William Ellis: The Texas Slave Who Became a Mexican Millionaire*. New York: Norton, 2016.

Jenkins, Destin, and Justin Leroy. "Introduction: The Old History of Capitalism." In *Histories of Racial Capitalism*, edited by Justin Leroy and Destin Jenkins, 1–26. New York: Columbia University Press, 2021.

Jennings, Willie James. *The Christian Imagination: Theology and the Origins of Race*. New Haven: Yale University Press, 2010.

Johnson, Jessica Marie. *Wicked Flesh: Black Women, Intimacy, and Freedom in the Atlantic World*. Early American Studies. Philadelphia: University of Pennsylvania Press, 2020.

Johnson, Sara E. *The Fear of French Negroes: Transcolonial Collaboration in the Revolutionary Americas*. Berkeley: University of California Press, 2012.

Johnson, Sylvester A. *African American Religions, 1500–2000: Colonialism, Democracy, and Freedom*. New York: Cambridge University Press, 2015.

Johnson, Sylvester A. *The Myth of Ham in Nineteenth-Century American Christianity: Race, Heathens, and the People of God*. New York: Palgrave Macmillan, 2004.

Johnson, Whittington B. *Post-Emancipation Race Relations in the Bahamas*. Gainesville: University Press of Florida, 2006.

Jones, Martha S. *Birthright Citizens: A History of Race and Rights in Antebellum America*. Cambridge: Cambridge University Press, 2018.

Keel, Terence. *Divine Variations: How Christian Thought Became Racial Science*. Stanford, CA: Stanford University Press, 2018.

Keith, LeeAnna. *The Colfax Massacre: The Untold Story of Black Power, White Terror, and the Death of Reconstruction*. Oxford: Oxford University Press, 2008.

Kennedy, Cynthia M. "The Other White Gold: Salt, Slaves, the Turks and Caicos Islands, and British Colonialism." *Historian* 69, no. 2 (2007): 215–30.

Kennedy, Neil. "Impermanence and Empire: Salt Racking in the Turks and Caicos Islands." In *Exploring Atlantic Transitions: Archaeologies of Transience and Permanence in New Found Lands*, edited by Peter E. Pope and Shannon Lewis-Simpson, 80–89. Woodbridge, UK: Boydell Press, 2013.

King, Moses. *King's Handbook of New York City*. 2nd ed. Boston: Moses King, 1893.

Kirk, Nicole C. *Wanamaker's Temple: The Business of Religion in an Iconic Department Store*. New York: New York University Press, 2018.

Knight, Melvin Moses. *The Americans in Santo Domingo*. New York: Vanguard, 1928.

Kramer, Paul A. "How Not to Write the History of U.S. Empire." *Diplomatic History* 42, no. 5 (2018): 911–31.

Kubal, Timothy. *Cultural Movements and Collective Memory: Christopher Columbus and the Rewriting of the National Origin Myth*. New York: Palgrave Macmillan, 2008.

Lane, Charles. *The Day Freedom Died: The Colfax Massacre, the Supreme Court, and the Betrayal of Reconstruction.* New York: Henry Holt, 2008.

Langston, John Mercer. *From the Virginia Plantation to the National Capital.* Hartford, CT: American Publishing Company, 1894.

Laquer, Thomas W. *The Work of the Dead: A Cultural History of Mortal Remains.* Princeton, NJ: Princeton University Press, 2015.

Lauro, Sarah J. *The Transatlantic Zombie: Slavery, Rebellion, and Living Death.* New Brunswick, NJ: Rutgers University Press, 2015.

Lee Borges, José. "República Dominicana: De la restauración a los primeros pasos de la verdadera influencia estadounidense, 1865–1880." *Revista Mexicana Del Caribe* 5, no. 10 (2000): 108–48.

Levy, Jonathan. "The Freaks of Fortune: Moral Responsibility for Booms and Busts in Nineteenth-Century America." *Journal of the Gilded Age and Progressive Era* 10, no. 4 (2011): 435–46.

Lightbourn Butz, Adrienne Antoinette. *The Letter Book of Captain John Lightbourn Sr. and William Astwood.* Pembroke, Bermuda: White Lodge Press, 2013.

Lightfoot, Natasha. *Troubling Freedom: Antigua and the Aftermath of British Emancipation.* Durham, NC: Duke University Press, 2015.

Little, Lawrence S. *Disciples of Liberty: The African Methodist Episcopal Church in the Age of Imperialism, 1884–1916.* Knoxville: University of Tennessee Press, 2000.

Lockward, Alfonso. *Intolerancia y libertad de cultos en Santo Domingo.* Santo Domingo: Distribuidora y Editora de Literatura Evangélica, 1993.

Lockward, George A, ed. *Cartas de Cardy. Primer misionero metodista en Samaná.* Santo Domingo: Educativa Dominicana, 1988.

Lockward, George A. *El protestantismo en Dominicana.* 2nd ed. Santo Domingo: Editora Educativa Dominicana, 1982.

Logan, Rayford. *Diplomatic Relations of the United States with Haiti, 1776–1891.* Chapel Hill: University of North Carolina Press, 1941.

López Prieto, Antonio. *Informe que sobre los restos de Colon presenta al Excmo. Sr. gobernador general D. Joaquín Jovellar y Soler, despues de su viaje á Santo Domino, Don Antonio López Prieto.* Havana: Imprenta del Gobierno y Capitanía General por S.M., 1878.

Lora Hugi, Quisqueya. *Transición de la esclavitud al trabajo libre en Santo Domingo: El caso de Higüey (1822–1827).* Santo Domingo: Academia Dominicana de la Historia, 2012.

Love, Eric T. *Race over Empire: Racism and U.S. Imperialism, 1865–1900.* Chapel Hill: University of North Carolina Press, 2004.

Lucas, C. P. *A Historical Geography of the British Colonies.* Oxford: Clarendon, 1890.

Lugo, Américo. "Los restos de Colón cont." *Clio* 2, no. 12 (1934): 174–80.

Luperón, Gregorio. *Notas autobiográficas y apuntes históricos por el general Gregorio Luperón.* 2nd ed. Vol. 2. Santiago: Editorial El Diario, 1939.

Luperón, Gregorio. *Notas autobiográficas y apuntes históricos por el general Gregorio Luperón.* 2nd ed. Vol. 3. Santiago: Editorial El Diario, 1939.

Maffly-Kipp, Laurie F. *Setting Down the Sacred Past: African-American Race Histories.* Cambridge, MA: Belknap, 2010.

Márquez Colín, Graciela. "El tratado de reciprocidad de 1883: ¿Una oportunidad perdida?" *HMex* 61, no. 4 (2012): 1413–59.

Martí, José. *Our America: Writings on Latin America and the Struggle for Cuban Independence.* Edited by Philip Sheldon Foner. New York: Monthly Review Press, 1977.

Martínez, Rufino. *Diccionario biográfico-histórico dominicano, 1821–1930.* Santo Domingo: Editora de la Universidad Autónoma de Santo Domingo, 1971.

Martínez-Fernández, Luis. "The Sword and the Crucifix: Church-State Relations and Nationality in the Nineteenth-Century Dominican Republic." *Latin American Research Review* 30, no. 1 (1995): 69–93.

Martínez-Fernández, Luis. *Torn between Empires: Economy, Society, and Patterns of Political Thought in the Hispanic Caribbean, 1840–1878.* Athens: University of Georgia Press, 1994.

Martínez-Vergne, Teresita. *Nation and Citizen in the Dominican Republic, 1880–1916.* Chapel Hill: University of North Carolina Press, 2005.

Mayes, April. *The Mulatto Republic: Class, Race, and Dominican National Identity.* Gainesville: University Press of Florida, 2014.

McKay, Nathaniel. *Nathaniel McKay.* Washington, DC: Nathaniel McKay, 1901.

McKivigan, John R. *The War against Proslavery Religion: Abolitionism and the Northern Churches, 1830–1865.* Ithaca, NY: Cornell University Press, 2018.

McLeod, James D. "Dignity Denied: A Theological Anthropology of Whiteness." PhD diss., Garrett Evangelical Theological Seminary, 2015.

Melamed, Jodi. "Racial Capitalism." *Critical Ethnic Studies* 1, no. 1 (2015): 76–85.

Mella, Pablo. *Los espejos de Duarte.* Santo Domingo: Amigo del Hogar, 2013.

Messer-Kruse, Timothy. *The Haymarket Conspiracy: Transatlantic Anarchist Networks.* Champaign: University of Illinois Press, 2012.

Mignolo, Walter. *The Idea of Latin America.* Malden, MA: Blackwell, 2005.

Milkman, Howard Louis. "Thomas Dewitt Talmage: An Evangelical Nineteenth Century Voice on Technology, Urbanization, and Labor-Management Conflicts." PhD diss., New York University, 1979.

Moses, Wilson Jeremiah. *The Golden Age of Black Nationalism, 1850–1925.* Oxford: Oxford University Press, 1978.

Mossell, Charles W. *Toussaint L'Ouverture, the Hero of Saint Domingo, Soldier, Statesman, Martyr; or, Hayti's Struggle, Triumph, Independence, and Achievements.* Lockport, NY: Ward and Cobb, 1896.

Moya Pons, Frank. *The Dominican Republic: A National History.* 3rd ed. Princeton, NJ: Markus Wiener, 2010.

Moya Pons, Frank. *Los restos de Colón: Bibliografía.* Santo Domingo: Academia Dominicana de la Historia, 2006.

Moya Pons, Frank. "Notas para una historia de la Iglesia en Santo Domingo." *Eme Eme* 1, no. 6 (1973): 3–18.

Muñiz, Wendy V. "The Unofficial Archive: A Critique of Archival Culture in the Dominican Republic, 1865–1927." PhD diss., Columbia University, 2017.

Myers Turner, Nicole. *Soul Liberty: The Evolution of Black Religious Politics in Postemancipation Virginia.* Chapel Hill: University of North Carolina Press, 2020.

Naish, Paul D. *Slavery and Silence: Latin America and the U.S. Slave Debate*. Philadelphia: University of Pennsylvania Press, 2017.

National Electric Light Association. *Proceedings of the National Electric Light Association*. Baltimore: Baltimore Publishing Company, 1886.

Nelson, William Javier. "U.S. Diplomatic Recognition of the Dominican Republic in the 19th Century: A Study in Racism." *Afro-Hispanic Review* 10, no. 1 (1991): 10–14.

Newman, Richard S. *Freedom's Prophet: Bishop Richard Allen, the AME Church, and the Black Founding Fathers*. New York: New York University Press, 2008.

Nouel, Carlos. *Historia eclesiástica de la arquidiócesis de Santo Domingo, primada de América*. Vol. 3. Santo Domingo: Editora de Santo Domingo, 1979.

Núñez Polanco, Diómedes. *Anexionismo y resistencia: Relaciones domínico-norteamericanas en tiempos de Grant, Báez y Luperón*. Santo Domingo: Alfa y Omega, 1997.

Nystrom, Justin. *New Orleans after the Civil War: Race, Politics, and a New Birth of Freedom*. Baltimore: Johns Hopkins University Press, 2010.

Ober, Frederick A. *In the Wake of Columbus: Adventures of the Special Commissioner Sent by the World's Columbian Exposition to the West Indies*. Boston: D. Lothrop, 1893.

Ober, Frederick Albion. *Our West Indian Neighbors*. New York: James Pott, 1912.

Ojeda Reyes, Félix. "Betances, Meriño, Luperón: Profetas de La Antillana, Combatientes de Nuestra Libertad." *Ciencia y Sociedad* 29, no. 4 (2004): 648–71.

Ojeda Reyes, Félix, and Paul Estrade, eds. *Pasión por la libertad*. San Juan: Editorial de la Universidad de Puerto Rico, 2000.

Padgett, James A. "Diplomats to Haiti and Their Diplomacy." *Journal of Negro History* 25, no. 3 (1940): 265–330.

Pamphile, Léon Dénius. *Haitians and African Americans: A Heritage of Tragedy and Hope*. Gainesville: University Press of Florida, 2001.

Pardo, Miguel Eduardo. *Todo un pueblo*. Madrid: Editorial-América, 1917.

Patterson, Orlando. *Slavery and Social Death: A Comparative Study*. Cambridge, MA: Harvard University Press, 1982.

Payne, Daniel. *History of the African Methodist Episcopal Church*. Nashville: Publishing House of the A.M.E. Sunday School Union, 1891.

Pitre, Merline. "Frederick Douglass and American Diplomacy in the Caribbean." *Journal of Black Studies* 13, no. 4 (1983): 457–75.

Pletcher, David M. *The Awkward Years: American Foreign Relations under Garfield and Arthur*. Columbia: University of Missouri Press, 1962.

Plummer, Brenda Gayle. *Haiti and the United States: The Psychological Moment*. Athens: University of Georgia Press, 1992.

Polyné, Millery. *From Douglass to Duvalier: U.S. African Americans, Haiti, and Pan Americanism, 1870–1964*. Gainesville: University Press of Florida, 2010.

Prince, Mary. *The History of Mary Prince: A West Indian Slave*. Edited by Sara Salih. New York: Penguin, 2004.

Puig Ortiz, José Augusto. *Emigración de libertos norteamericanos a Puerto Plata en la primera mitad del siglo XIX*. 2nd ed. Santo Domingo: Editora Nacional, 2011.

Quesada, Vincente G. *Los Estados Unidos y la América del Sur: Los yankees pintados por sí mismos*. Buenos Aires: J. Peuser, 1893.

Raboteau, Albert J. *Canaan Land: A Religious History of African Americans*. Oxford: Oxford University Press, 2001.

Ramírez, Dixa. *Colonial Phantoms: Belonging and Refusal in the Dominican Americas, from the 19th Century to the Present*. New York: New York University Press, 2018.

Ramírez, Dixa. "Mushrooms and Mischief: On Questions of Blackness." *Small Axe* 23, no. 2 (2019): 152–63.

Rankin, David C. "The Origins of Black Leadership in New Orleans during Reconstruction." *Journal of Southern History* 40, no. 3 (1974): 417–40.

Reed, Christopher Robert. *"All the World Is Here!" The Black Presence at White City*. Bloomington: Indiana University Press, 2000.

Reyes-Santos, Alaí. *Our Caribbean Kin: Race and Nation in the Neoliberal Antilles*. New Brunswick, NJ: Rutgers University Press, 2015.

Roberts, John W. *From Trickster to Badman: The Black Folk Hero in Slavery and Freedom*. Philadelphia: University of Pennsylvania Press, 1989.

Robinson, Cedric J. *Black Marxism: The Making of the Black Radical Tradition*. 3rd ed. Chapel Hill: University of North Carolina Press, 2020.

Rodó, José Enrique. *Ariel*. 1900. Reprint, Madrid: Editorial Linkgua USA, 2011.

Rodríguez Almager, Carlos. "El antillanismo." *Boletín del Archivo General de la Nación* 43, no. 152 (2018): 477–84.

Rodríguez Demorizi, Emilio. *Hostos en Santo Domingo*. 2nd ed. Vol. 1. Santo Domingo: Sociedad Dominicana de Bibliófilos, 2004.

Rodríguez Demorizi, Emilio. *Hostos en Santo Domingo*. 2nd ed. Vol. 2. Santo Domingo: Sociedad Dominicana de Bibliófilos, 2004.

Rodríguez Demorizi, Emilio. *Sociedades, confradias, escuelas, gremios y otras corporaciones dominicanas*. Santo Domingo: Editora Educativa Dominicana, 1975.

Rodríguez Rosario, Orlando. "Tejiendo lazos de amistad: República Dominicana y la diplomacia mambisa, 1868–1878." *Boletín del Archivo General de la Nación* 44, no. 153 (2019): 149–98.

Rojas Osorio, Carlos. "Eugenio María de Hostos and His Pedagogical Thought." *Curriculum Inquiry* 42, no. 1 (2012): 12–32.

Rosa, Antonio de la. *Las finanzas de Santo Domingo y el control americano*. Santo Domingo: Sociedad Dominicana de Bibliófilos, 1987.

Rosenberg, Emily S. "Revisiting Dollar Diplomacy: Narratives of Money and Manliness." *Diplomatic History* 22, no. 2 (1998): 154–76.

Sadler, H. E. *Turks Islands Landfall: A History of the Turks and Caicos Islands*. Kingston: United Cooperative Printers, 1997.

Sánchez, Juan J. *La caña en Santo Domingo*. Santo Domingo: Imprenta García Hermanos, 1893.

Sánchez Álvarez-Insúa, Alberto. "Moral Social de Eugenio María de Hostos." *Abor Ciencia, Pensamiento y Cultura* 183, no. 724 (2007): 211–16.

Sang, Mu-Kien A. *La política exterior dominicana, 1844–1961*. Santo Domingo: Secretaría de Estado de Relaciones Exteriores, 2000.

Sang, Mu-Kien A. *Ulises Heureaux: Biografía de un dictador*. Santo Domingo: Instituto Tecnológico de Santo Domingo, 1989.

San Miguel, Pedro Luís. *The Imagined Island: History, Identity, and Utopia in Hispaniola.* Chapel Hill: University of North Carolina Press, 2005.

Scarfi, Juan Pablo. "Hacia un orden legal regional: Vincente Quesada y la construcción del derecho internacional latinoamericano." *Revista de Historia de América* 156 (2019): 125–42.

Scarfi, Juan Pablo. "La emergencia de un imaginario latinoamericanista y antiestadounidense del orden hemisférico: De la Unión Panamericana a la Unión Latinoamericana (1880–1913)." *Revista Complutense de Historia de América* 39 (2013): 81–104.

Schmidt-Nowara, Christopher. *Conquest of History: Spanish Colonialism and National Histories in the Nineteenth Century.* Pittsburgh: University of Pittsburgh Press, 2006.

Schmidt-Nowara, Christopher. *Slavery, Freedom, and Abolition in Latin America and the Atlantic World.* Albuquerque: University of New Mexico Press, 2011.

Scott, Rebecca J. *Degrees of Freedom: Louisiana and Cuba after Slavery.* Cambridge, MA: Belknap, 2005.

Scott, Rebecca J. "Discerning a Dignitary Offense: The Concept of Equal 'Public Rights' during Reconstruction." *Law and History Review* 38, no. 3 (2020): 519–53.

Scott, Rebecca J. "Public Rights, Social Equality, and the Conceptual Roots of the Plessy Challenge." *Michigan Law Review* 106, no. 5 (2008): 777–804.

Scott, Rebecca J., and Jean M. Hébrard. *Freedom Papers: An Atlantic Odyssey in the Age of Emancipation.* Cambridge, MA: Harvard University Press, 2012.

Sensbach, Jon F. *Rebecca's Revival: Creating Black Christianity in the Atlantic World.* Cambridge, MA: Harvard University Press, 2005.

Serrata, Médar. "La ciudad como espectáculo: Santo Domingo ante la mirada de los primeros turistas." In *Diálogos culturales en la literatura iberoamericana: Actas del XXXIX Congreso del Instituto Internacional de Literatura Iberoamericana,* 463–77. Madrid: Verbum, 2014.

Serrata, Médar. "'The True and Only Bones of Columbus': Relics, Archives, and Reversed Scenarios of Discovery." *PMLA* 137, no. 3 (2022): 472–88.

Sheller, Mimi. *Democracy after Slavery: Black Republics and Peasant Radicalism in Haiti and Jamaica.* Gainesville: University Press of Florida, 2000.

Shibusawa, Naoko. "U.S. Empire and Racial Capitalist Modernity." *Diplomatic History* 45, no. 5 (2021): 855–84.

Smith, C. S. *A History of the African Methodist Episcopal Church: Being a Volume Supplemental to A History of the African Methodist Episcopal Church.* Philadelphia: A.M.E. Book Concern, 1922.

Smith, Matthew J. *Liberty, Fraternity, Exile: Haiti and Jamaica after Emancipation.* Chapel Hill: University of North Carolina Press, 2014.

Sommer, Doris. *One Master for Another: Populism as Patriarchal Rhetoric in Dominican Novels.* Lanham, MD: University Press of America, 1983.

Stephens, Jean. "La inmigración de negros norteamericanos en Haití en 1824." *Eme Eme* 3, no. 14 (1974): 40–71.

Stern, Herbert. "Dr. Juan Francisco Alfonseca y Arvelo." *El Caribe* (blog), April 21, 2018. https://www.elcaribe.com.do/gente/cultura/dr-juan-francisco-alfonseca-y-arvelo/.

Steward, T. G. *Fifty Years in the Gospel Ministry, from 1864 to 1914*. Philadelphia: A.M.E. Book Concern, 1921.

Steward, T. G. *The Haitian Revolution*. New York: Thomas Crowell, 1914.

St. John, Spenser. *Hayti; or, The Black Republic*. London: Smith, Elder, 1884.

Straight University. *Catalogue of Straight University, 1883–84*. New Orleans: F. F. Hansell, 1884. https://archive.org/details/ScCatalogue18831884/page/n1/mode/2up.

Stuckey, Sterling. *Slave Culture: Nationalist Theory and the Foundations of Black America*. 2nd ed. Oxford: Oxford University Press, 2013.

Tansill, Charles Callan. *The United States and Santo Domingo, 1798–1873: A Chapter in Caribbean Diplomacy*. Baltimore: Johns Hopkins University Press, 1938.

Taylor, Elizabeth Dowling. *The Original Black Elite: Daniel Murray and the Story of a Forgotten Era*. New York: Amistad, 2017.

Taylor, Joe Gray. *Louisiana Reconstructed, 1863–1877*. Baton Rouge: Louisiana State University Press, 1974.

Tejada, Adriano Miguel. "El partido rojo, el partido azul y el partido verde." *Eme Eme* 3, no. 16 (1975): 21–42.

Tejera, Emiliano. *Los dos restos de Christóbal Colón exhumados de la catedral de Santo Domingo en 1795 i 1877*. Santo Domingo: Imprenta de Garcia Hermanos, 1879.

Tejera, Emiliano. *Los restos de Colón en Santo Domingo*. Santo Domingo: Imprenta de García Hermanos, 1978.

Thompson, Thomas W. *James Anthony Froude on Nation and Empire: A Study in Victorian Racialism*. New York: Garland, 1987.

Tiffin, Helen. "Among Head-Hunters and Cannibals: Spenser St. John in Borneo and Haiti." *Kanapipi* 23, no. 2 (2001): 18–30.

Toll, Robert C. *Blackening Up: The Minstrel Show in Nineteenth-Century America*. New York: Oxford University Press, 1974.

Torres-Saillant, Silvio. "The Tribulations of Blackness: Stages in Dominican Racial Identity." *Latin American Perspectives* 25, no. 3 (1998): 126–46.

Trouillot, Michel-Rolph. *Silencing the Past: Power and Production of History*. Boston: Beacon, 1995.

Tunnell, Ted. *Crucible of Reconstruction: War, Radicalism, and Race in Louisiana, 1862–1877*. Baton Rouge: Louisiana State University Press, 1984.

Turley, David. *The Culture of English Antislavery, 1780–1860*. London: Routledge, 1991.

United States Commission of Inquiry to Santo Domingo. *Dominican Republic: Report of the Commission of Inquiry to Santo Domingo*. Washington, DC: Government Printing Office, 1871.

Unterman, Katherine. "Boodle over the Border: Embezzlement and the Crisis of International Mobility, 1880–1890." *Journal of the Gilded Age and Progressive Era* 11, no. 2 (2012): 151–89.

US Department of the Interior. *Official Register of the United States: Containing a List of Officers and Employés in the Civil, Military, and Naval Service on the First of July, 1883*. Vol. 1. Washington, DC: Government Printing Office, 1883.

US Senate. *Index to the Executive Documents Printed by Order of the Senate of the United States for the Third Session of the Forty-First Congress, 1870–71*. Washington, DC: US Government Printing Office, 1871.

US Supreme Court. *The Dred Scott Decision: Opinion of Chief Justice Taney*. New York: Van Evrie, Horton, 1860. https://www.loc.gov/item/17001543.

Veeser, Cyrus. "Concessions as a Modernizing Strategy in the Dominican Republic." *Business History Review* 83, no. 4 (2009): 731–58.

Veeser, Cyrus. *A World Safe for Capitalism: Dollar Diplomacy and America's Rise to Global Power*. New York: Columbia University Press, 2002.

Vega, Augusto. *Anecdotas de Ulises Heureaux (Lilís), 1846–1899*. 2nd ed. Ciudad Trujillo: Impresora Dominicana, 1955.

Vega, Bernardo. *La cuestión racial y el proyecto Dominicano de anexión a Estados Unidos en 1870*. Santo Domingo: Academia Dominicana de la Historia, 2019.

Vignaud, Henry. *L'ancienne et la nouvelle campagne pour la canonisation de Christophe-Colomb*. Paris: Au siège de la Société, 1909.

Vinson, Ben. "Introduction: African (Black) Diaspora History, Latin American History." *The Americas* 63, no. 1 (2006): 1–18.

Visit Turks and Caicos Islands. "Columbus Landfall National Park." Accessed June 2, 2020. https://www.visittci.com/grand-turk/columbus-landfall-national-park.

Volwiler, Albert T., ed. *The Correspondence between Benjamin Harrison and James G. Blaine, 1882–1893*. Philadelphia: American Philosophical Society, 1940.

Walkes, Joseph A., Jr. *The History of the Prince Hall Grand Lodge of Louisiana 1842–1979*. N.p.: Joseph A. Walkes Jr., 1986.

Ward, Thomas. "From Sarmiento to Martí and Hostos: Extricating the Nation from Coloniality." *European Review of Latin American and Caribbean Studies* 83 (2007): 83–104.

Webb, Jack Daniel. *Haiti in the British Imagination: Imperial Worlds, 1847–1915*. Liverpool: Liverpool University Press, 2020.

Weed, Eric A. *The Religion of White Supremacy in the United States*. Lanham, MD: Lexington, 2017.

Weisenfeld, Judith. *New World A-coming: Black Religion and Racial Identity during the Great Migration*. New York: New York University Press, 2017.

Welles, Sumner. *Naboth's Vineyard: The Dominican Republic 1844–1924*. New York: Payson and Clarke, 1928.

Wells, Ida B., Frederick Douglass, Irvine Garland Penn, and Ferdinand L. Barnett. *The Reason Why the Colored American Is Not in the World's Columbian Exposition: The Afro-American's Contribution to Columbian Literature*. Edited by Robert W. Rydell. Urbana: University of Illinois Press, 1999.

Wenger, Tisa Joy. *Religious Freedom: The Contested History of an American Ideal*. Chapel Hill: University of North Carolina Press, 2017.

Wenger, Tisa Joy, and Sylvester A. Johnson. *Religion and US Empire: Critical New Histories*. New York: New York University Press, 2022.

Wertheimer, Eric. *Imagined Empires: Incas, Aztecs, and the New World of American Literature, 1771–1876*. New York: Cambridge University Press, 1999.

West, Delno C., and August Kling. "Columbus and Columbia: A Brief Survey of the Early Creation of the Columbus Symbol in American History." *Studies in Popular Culture* 12, no. 2 (1989): 45–60.

White, Ashli. *Encountering Revolution: Haiti and the Making of the Early Republic*. Baltimore: Johns Hopkins University Press, 2010.

Wible, James R., and Kevin D. Hoover. "The Economics of Trade Liberalization: Charles S. Peirce and the Spanish Treaty of 1884." *European Journal of the History of Economic Thought* 28, no. 2 (2021): 229–48.

Wilkins, Christopher. "'They Had Heard of Emancipation and the Enfranchisement of Their Race': The African American Colonists of Samaná, Reconstruction, and the State of Santo Domingo." In *The Civil War as Global Conflict: Transnational Meanings of the American Civil War*, edited by David T. Gleeson and Simon Lewis, 211–34. Columbia: University of South Carolina Press, 2014.

Willmore, Nehemiah. "Esbozo histórico de la llegada de inmigrantes afro-americanos a la isla de Santo Domingo y Haití." *Boletín del Archivo General de la Nación* 36, no. 129 (2011): 247–75.

Winch, Julie Patricia. "American Free Blacks and Emigration to Haiti." San Germán, Puerto Rico: Centro de Investigaciones del Caribe y América Latina, 1988.

Workman, Gillian. "Thomas Carlyle and the Governor Eyre Controversy: An Account with Some New Material." *Victorian Studies* 18, no. 1 (1974): 77–102.

Wynes, Charles E. "John Stephens Durham, Black Philadelphian: At Home and Abroad." *Pennsylvania Magazine of History and Biography* 106, no. 4 (1982): 527–37.

Zeller, Neici. "Puerto Plata en siglo XIX." *Eme Eme* 5, no. 28 (1977): 27–52.

Anacaona (Taíno princess), xv–xvi

annexation debates (1865–71), 9–11, 14, 57–59, 86; African American support for, 65–66, 96–97; Black immigration proposed, 64, 96–97; Puerto Plata at center of, 62

anti-American sentiment, 98, 103, 104–5, 265

antillanismo movement, 58, 61, 714

Antillean Confederation, 58–59, 75, 174

Aristizábal, Gabriel, 200

Arroyo, Jossianna, 62

Arthur, Chester A., 79, 99, 101, 117; proposal to place Dominican Republic under Haiti legation, 99, 103–4, 107–8

Astwood, Adolphus James, 34–35, 38; as Commercial Agent of the Dominican Republic on Grand Turk, 48–49, 57; and family financial crisis, 57, 59–60; and hurricane of 1866, 55–56

Astwood, Alice Ternoir, 76–77, 79, 120, 187

Astwood, George, 35, 38, 60

Astwood, George Adolphus, 61, 79, 176

Astwood, Henry Charles Clifford (H. C. C.), xvii; activism of, 55, 71–72, 80; argument for removing *African* from AME name, 191–92; as badman figure, 5–6; banquets given for in US, 189; as bigamist, 76–77, 79, 222, 307n112; birth of on Salt Cay, 28–29, 34, 51; against Black emigration to West Africa, 74; on *Canandaigua* (union gunboat), 69–70; capitalists, relations with, 92–93, 229, 232–45; in Carroll Parish, 70–73; children and family, 60–61, 79, 269, 286n166; as clergyman-politician, 1, 3, 73–75, 81; college education, 77–78; colonial slave context of ancestors, 29; embedded in multiple social networks, 79–80; embezzlement alleged against, 231, 232, 239, 246–47, 251; expressions of both racial pride and anti-Blackness, 262; final departure from Santo Domingo (1892), 22; four interrelated

goals pursued by, 144; Haiti denigrated by, 136–37, 155, 234, 237–38; Heureaux, association with, 18–19, 45–46, 98–99, 113–15, 153, 301n94; Heureaux, rejection of, 114–15, 125; Heureaux, similarities with, 18–19, 142–43, 153, 193; historical context of life, 29, 51–52; jobs held by, 57, 60, 71, 77–78; leadership positions in AME Church, 75, 78; leaked document incident, 245–46; legal dispute with AME mission, 193; life trajectory, 2, 18–19, 35, 55; Luperón, association with, 44–46, 63, 98; marriage to Alice Ternoir, 76–77, 79, 120; marriage to Margaret Francisco, 48, 50, 60–61, 79; as middleman, 1–3, 262, 270; missionary appointment, 14–15, 20–21, 169–72; moral authority of, 189, 229, 259–60; moral logic of, 104–5, 262; multiethnic networks of, 55; in New Orleans, 70, 73–79, 86, 167; New York visits, 117, 234; ordained as deacon, 75; parentage of, 29, 34–35; and petition to Wesleyan Missionary Society, 45, 46, 47, 66; in Philadelphia, 269; political acumen of, 106, 116–17; political authority of, 3, 19–20; political positions held in New Orleans, 77–78; as poor person of color in Samaná, 64; predatory nature of, 76–77; under protection of the US flag, 132; protests against in Buenos Aires, 264; and Puerto Plata current affairs, 43–44; purposeful neglect of, 1–2, 269–70; as race leader, 1, 237–38; racialized moral discourse wielded by, 19, 106, 109, 123, 134, 136–38, 149, 154–55, 235–37, 249; religious discourse used by, 148, 170; reputation, importance of, 231, 233; ritualistic performance of righteous indignation, 20, 88, 108–16, 132; sacred-profane divide violated by, 205–13; in Samaná, 63–70; secrecy of, 98, 143, 155; against segregation of public schools, 74–75; sermons given

by, 73, 237, 250; "Shall the Name of the
African Methodist Episcopal Church
Be Changed to That of the Allen
Methodist Episcopal Church?," 191–
92; sketch of, *xvii*; social life in Santo
Domingo, 169, 189–90; as social striver,
76–77; speeches given by, 62; statecraft
of, 113, 132; subterfuge practiced by, 8,
77, 81, 259; and sugar industry, 245–51;
as target of white violence, 72–73, 80;
tenure in Santo Domingo (1882–92),
19–20; as trickster/*tíguere* figure, 5–8,
141–53, 259–60, 261–62, 270; as US
consul to Santo Domingo, 20, 22, 79,
85–119; at *Weekly Louisianian*, 77–78.
See also Columbus lease controversy;
dismissal of Astwood; Platt affair
Astwood, John T., 48
Astwood, Margaret Julia (Francisco), 48,
50, 60–61, 79
Astwood, Mildred Julia, 48, 60, 79
Astwood, Miriam, 60, 79
Astwood, Relana Evelina, 79
Astwood, William, 31–32
Astwood, William Amelius, 31
Astwood, William T., 48
Astwood family, 29–35; feelings toward
Dominican-Spanish war, 40; financial
crisis, 57; males as merchants, clergy,
and judicial magistrates, 34; mercan-
tile relations, 44–45; move to Puerto
Plata, 43–44, 49–52, 60–61; Protestant
church connections, 45. *See also* Turks
and Caicos Islands
azules (Partido Azul), 16, 18, 80, 88, 97,
125–26; and Dominican liberalism, 173,
183, 193

"badman" figure, 5–6, 152, 155
Báez, Buenaventura, 44, 46–47, 57–59, 63,
69; dictatorship of, 58, 89, 97, 114, 181;
Euro-Dominican support for, 124; fall
of, 69, 88, 91; and Remington case, 108,
114; return to power, 88–89

Bahamas, 34
Baptist War (Jamaica), 42
Barbados, 55
Barnum, Phineas Taylor, 209
Barthé, Elizabeth, 76
Bass, Alexander, 249
Bassett, Ebenezer Don Carlos, 7
Batson, Elizabeth, 34–35
Bayard, Thomas F., 213
Bermuda, privateers from, 30
Betances, Ramón Emeterio, 58, 105
Bethel AME Church, 12–13, 164
Bible Society, 163–165, 176, 177; transfer
to AME Church, 169
Billini, Francisco Gregorio, 115–16, 121,
124–26
Billini, Francisco Javier, 183, 200
Black expression, multiplicity of,
6–7
"Black legend" myth, xv–xvi
Black misrule, racist stereotypes of, 20,
89–90, 151, 266; and Platt affair, 121–23,
125, 137–41
Black radical tradition, 268
Black social equality, debate over, 4, 23,
28, 56, 80, 236, 238, 261
Blaine, James G., 100–101, 117, 233, 239,
253, 256, 263
Blaine, Walker, 233
Bleby, Henry, 168
Bogle, Paul, 42
Boletín del Comercio, 195–96, 208–9,
215, 217–18, 223; Prometeo articles,
220–21; ridicule of Astwood in,
213–14
Boletín Eclesiástico, 180–81, 183–84, 191;
"A Chapter of Documented History.
Protestantism," 184–85
Bonó, Pedro Francisco, 97, 173
Bordas, Gustavo E. Borgés, 153
Boston Herald, 236
Boyer, Jean-Pierre, 12, 32, 64
Bremer, John C., Jr., 57
Brenes, José de Jesús, 135

British Caribbean: Slave Emancipation
Act (1833), 33; tensions in, 41–43, 51;
transition from slavery to free labor,
19. *See also* Turks and Caicos Islands
British Empire, 29–30. *See also* Turks and
Caicos Islands
Brown, Nathan, 241
Buenos Aires (Argentina), 264
Bulldog (HMS), sinking of, 42
Byrd, Brandon R., 12

Cabral, José María, 50, 57–59
Cabral y Báez, J. M., 193–94
Cambiaso, Juan, 246
Cambiaso Hermanos company, 245–46,
248
Campbell, Jabez Pitt, 187–89, 256
Canty, Stephen, 210–11
Cap-Haïtien (Haitian port), 38, 42, 57–58,
253
capitalism: American lobbyists, 91, 97;
Astwood's relations with US investors,
92–93, 229, 232–45; Black integra-
tion into as necessity, 28; blamed for
Columbus lease proposal, 209–10;
European powers, 97; Heureaux and
US investors, 87, 98–99, 113–14, 244,
264; at level of interpersonal relations,
259; market racialized as Black, 197–98;
moral, 161, 182, 190, 263; network of investors, 229; and Protestant Christian
morality, 189–91, 241; racial, 2–3, 23,
259; symbolic rupture with racism, 102
carpetbaggers, 72
Castro, Apolinar de, 246
Castro, Jacinto de, 89
Castro, José de J., 132–33, 144–45, 148, 150
Castro, Victor M., 153
Cathedral of Santa María la Menor, xv
17–18, 159, 200–202, *201, 202, 203, 204*
Catholic Church, 16–18; anxieties about
spread of Protestantism, 184–85; *azules*
aligned with, 16; Dominican Republic,
ties with, 159; and Heureaux, 67, 184,

190; Knights of Columbus (US), 211;
moral authority, competition for, 185,
262; and nationalism, 17–18; in New
Orleans, 75; *normalistas*, opposition to,
183–85, 191; peasant class as Catholic, 13,
16–17; Protestant Dominican interaction with Catholics, 66, 69, 163, 167,
170–72, 284n110; Protestants suppressed
by, 14, 163; Santo Domingo, presence
by, 159–60; and social morality, 181–83;
threatened by Afro-American Dominican institutions, 191, 193–94
causa devotionis (theft committed out of
devotion), 199
Cazneau, Jane, 63, 68
Cazneau, William L., 63, 97
Charleston, South Carolina, 32
Chetty, Raj, 6
Chicago World's Fair (1893), *See* World's
Columbian Exposition (1893)
Christian ideology, 2–3, 122–23, 148;
in appointment of twelve "vice-
presidents," 180, 301n85; capitalism
and Protestant Christian morality,
189–90, 241; hierarchical ordering of human beings, 198. *See also*
African Methodist Episcopal (AME)
Church; Catholic Church; Protestant
Dominicans
Christian Recorder, 75, 159–60
Church of England, 13, 35
Cibao region, 36, 47, 91, 99
citizenship, Dominican: birthright, 44;
granted to African American immigrants, 14
civil capacity of Blacks, debate over, 8,
15, 19, 51; and Black social equality, 4,
23, 28, 56, 80, 236, 238, 261; and debate
over Astwood's fitness for office, 22;
fragility of Black citizenship, 80; and
Platt affair, 141; white religion and
racial science, 28. *See also* political
authority, Black; social equality, Black
civil rights work, 71, 73, 80

corruption, 239–240; as moral rectitude, 260

Cosas de Lilís (Castro), 153

Crosby, Allen Howard, 92, 105, 107, 108–16

crossroads, Dominican Republic as, 2, 5–6, 160, 262–63, 265–70, 272n5; decline of, 263–65

Cuba, 37, 58; delegation to (1898), 269; prisoners allegedly sold to, 39; rebellion against Spain, 54; said to be location of Columbus's body, 196, 200–202, 226; Ten Years' War, 4, 61, 91

Cunningham, Winthrop, 239, 240, 244–48, 250–51, 260

Curiel, Ricardo, 114

Daily Picayune (New Orleans), 210, 212

Darrell, James, 37

Davis, John, 106–108; and Crosby case, 111–12

Day, Susan de Forest, xiv

Defender, 269, 315n35

Delgado Sánchez, Pedro Antonio, 131, 135, 295n45

del Monte, Félix María, 221

Demorizi, Emilio Rodríguez, 165

Derrick, William B., 189

Desdunes, Rodolphe L., 78, 287n184

diplomacy, US-Dominican, 19–20, 85–119; American monopoly sought by Astwood, 91–99, 104, 144; Astwood's annual reports, 91–96, 93–94, 95; Astwood's de facto authority, 116–17, 123; Astwood's reports on Dominican politics and economy, 87–88; Astwood's ritualistic performance of righteous indignation, 88, 108–16; Astwood's strategic pairing of dispatches, 104, 115, 145–47; Astwood's trade insights, 57–58, 87, 91–92, 93–94; Astwood's unofficial diplomacy, 99, 102–10, 113, 146; asymmetry of power between United

States and island, 101–2; consular office moved, 85–86; Crosby case, 105, 107, 108–15; Dominican placed under jurisdiction of US Haitian Legation, 90, 99–100, 103–4, 107–8, 268–69; economic concessions offered to US/American speculators, 90–92, 97, 101, 190; European diplomats as competition, 102–3; Heureaux and cooperation of US capitalists, 98–99, 113–14; infrastructure addressed by Astwood, 90, 96, 116; jurisdiction invented by Astwood, 110–11; *Justitia* incident, 147; and Langston, 111–19; limited regulations challenged by Astwood, 106; *Lizzie Titus* incident, 105–6, 107; and national bank charter, 144; nonrecognition of Dominican Republic, 8–11, 21, 101, 146; Ozama River bridge lawsuit, 105, 108–9; petition for US legation, 90, 98; and Platt's death, 122–23; political context prior to Astwood's appointment, 88–89; politics and economics within purview of consulate, 88–99; racialized context of Astwood's political maneuvers, 7, 87, 107, 109; racism as guide to US policy, 5, 9–10, 20, 87, 90, 101–3, 118; segregated statecraft, 20, 87, 103, 118; triangulated relationship with Haiti, 90; untrained US diplomatic corps, 100; upgrade sought by Astwood, 90, 103–4, 107–8, 116, 143; US diplomatic recognition granted in 1860s, 9, 101–2; US indifference and scorn toward, 86–87, 117–18, 121; white capitalists as lobbyists, 91, 97; white European men as competition, 102–3. *See also* consular positions; Platt affair; political authority, Black; reciprocity trade treaties; trade relations; United States; US State Department

dismissal of Astwood, 196; Astwood's refusal to surrender post, 22, 228, 231, 232; Black opposition to reinstatement,

256–57; Black supporters, 237–38; calls for during Columbus controversy, 209–10, 212, 225; clean record of service, 260; by Cleveland, 225, 228, 231; in context of Gilded Age politics, 239–40; defended against, 228–29, 232; embezzlement alleged, 231, 232, 239, 246–47, 251; leave of absence granted, 231, 309n7; letters of recommendation, 22, 230, 232–33, 236–39; and McKay's advice, 232–33; opposition to reinstatement of, 238, 239–52, 256–57; reapplication to State Department, 230; white supporters, 232–38, 244–45

Domínguez, Jaime de Jesús, 92, 143

Dominican Republic: all colors represented in government, 11; annexation debates (1865–71), 9–11, 14, 54, 57–59, 62; annual deficit with Spain, 1860s, 40; anti-American sentiment, 98, 103, 104–5, 265; Astwood's in-depth analysis of, 87–88; birthright citizenship, 44; as both Black and of lesser importance than Haiti, 10–11; "capitulations" (1884), 124; Catholic Church, ties with, 159, 168, 184–85; civil and political rights of Black people, 14; Constitution, 44, 180; "cycle of colors" regimes, 88–89; debt incurred by, 264; decolonial struggle, 4–5; dictatorship of Báez, 58, 89, 97, 114, 181; dictatorship of González, 88; dictatorship of Heureaux, 16, 18, 121–22, 151–53, 155, 161, 181–84, 190–91, 219, 264, 268–69; Dominican Constitutional Congress, 44; election of 1884, 125–26, 245–46; election of 1886, 182–83; election of 1888, 182–83, 217, 222; founding myths, 204–5; free Black population as threat to US slavery, 8; freedom of conscience permitted in, 17, 67, 175, 191; as hemispheric crossroads, 2, 5–6, 160, 262–63, 265–70, 272n5; as hope for a functional racial democracy, 11; Independence Day, 205; majority mixed Spanish and African descent, 4; map of, xx; modernity claimed by, xv, 4, 21, 204; national archive, 204–5; national bank charter, 144; "organs of cultural transmission," 160–61, 164; Protestants supported by, 66–67; racially motivated US indifference to, 86–87, 117–18, 121; racist US portrayals of, 89–90; reactionary conservatives, 124; revolution of the *bi(e)mbines* or *quisquises*, 267–68; Spanish recolonization of (1861), 9, 14, 15, 37; Spanish-speaking, mixed-race people as model, 11; structural shifts in, 86–87; as symbolic racial borderland, 5; Terrible Year (1893), 267–69; tobacco industry, 91, 96; trade regulations imposed by on Grand Turk, 48–50; treaties with Haiti, 88; unified with Haiti (1822–44), 4, 22, 36, 86, 172, 221; US-Dominican treaty (1867), 109–10; US occupation of (1916), 22; US presence in 1890s and 1900s, 263–65; under US protection (1869), 58; US racial gaze upon, 8–11, 213–14; War of Restoration (1863–65), 14–16, 19, 38–41, 44–49, 61, 80; white anxieties over racial Blackness of, 16, 41, 43, 49, 123, 136–38, 192; white misrecognition of, 86–87. *See also* diplomacy, US-Dominican; economy, Dominican; economy, Dominican Republic; generals, Dominican Republic; liberalism, Dominican; Puerto Plata; Samaná; Santo Domingo (Dominican Republic); sugar industry (Dominican Republic)

Dominican War of Restoration (1863–65), 14–16, 19, 61, 80; archival records burned by Spain, 204; and Turks and Caicos Islands, 38–41, 44–49

Douglass, Charles R., 5, 7, 10, 65–66, 230; and Astwood's bigamy, 76–77, 79

generals, Dominican Republic, 16, 18, 47, 80; conflicts between, 50, 57–59, 62–63, 88–89, 125–26; Guillermo, 124; racist US portrayals of, 89; white racist stereotypes of Black, 124–25. *See also* Báez, Buenaventura; Guillermo, Cesáreo; Heureaux, Ulises; Luperón, Gregorio

generals, Haiti, 42, 57, 59

George A. Astwood and Bros., 35

Geo W. Clyde (ss), 85, 240

Gherardi, Bancroft, 258

Gibbes, Lucas, 132, 176, 180

Gibbes, Lucas T., 176, 183

Gilded Age politics, 239–40

González, Ignacio María, 69, 88–89, 91

González, Raymundo, 174–75

good/evil dichotomy, 137, 148, 153, 219; Astwood's use of, 3, 123, 134, 214–15, 262; Black foreign service agents, discourse about, 22, 239; cultural frame of, 122–23; and interpretation, 260, 262; in Native Baptists worldview, 42

Goodin, Charles, 193

Grand United Order of the Odd Fellows (GUOOF), 20–21, 73–74, 160–62, 176, 191; Bible Society affiliated with, 177; Flor de Ozama Odd Fellow Lodge No. 2638, 177; inception ceremony for, 177, 180–81; membership, *178–79*; as multiethnic institution, 177, 193. *See also* Freemasons; "organs of cultural transmission"

Grant, Ulysses S., 14, 62, 63, 71

Granville, Jonathas, 12–13

Greenberg, Amy, 250

Gross, Elijah, 163, 168–69, 176

Gross, Ricardo Alejandro, 179–80

Guillermo, Cesáreo, 89, 125–27, 145, 149–50; death of, 150–51; Platt mistaken for, 121, 124, 126; racialization of features, 138–39, *139*

Guillermo, Pedro, 124–25, 127

Haiti, xiv, *xx*; Cap-Haïtien (port), 38, 42, 57–58, 253; civil war, 54, 57–59, 253; economic incentives offered by, 90–91; escape to from Turks Islands, 32; founding of (1804), 12; "Galindo virgins" incident, 220–221; generals, 42, 57–59; Hispaniola unified under (1822–1844), 4, 28, 36, 86, 172, 221; Môle Saint-Nicolas, 252–53, 258; as more modern than Dominican Republic, 186; pavilion at World's Columbian Exposition, 265–66; Salnave dictatorship, 57; slavery abolished in, 27; as symbol of freedom, 4–5, 12; treaties with Dominican Republic, 88; US diplomatic legation at Port-au-Prince, 90, 99–100, 103–4, 107–8, 268–69; US diplomatic recognition granted in 1860s, 9, 101–2; US occupation of (1915), 22; US refusal to diplomatically recognize, 8–9, 21, 91; white landownership prohibited in Constitution, 11, 140, 296n78

Haitian emigration movement (1820s), 12–14, 36, 64, 160

Haitian Revolution (1804), 3–4, 8, 12, 27; Platt's killing linked with by Astwood, 136–37, 155; racist stereotypes of, 39–40, 138; Vodou spiritual power linked with, 32

Halls, Simon, 187

Hamilton, John, 68, 164

Hardy, John, 248–49

Harris, J. Dennis, 96

Harrison, Benjamin, 228, 232, 233, 263, 309n15; Astwood's request to reconsider appointment, 257–58; and letters of opposition to Astwood, 239, 253–54; Linnell's letter to, 234

Hartmont, Edward, 97, 113

Hartwell, James, 67

Hawaiian reciprocity treaty (1875), 101

Henríquez y Carvajal, Federico, 174

Herrera, María de la Cruz, 127, 130, 138, 148

Heureaux, Josefa Level, 67

Heureaux, Joseph Alexandre, 67

Heureaux, Ulises, 7, 11, 44, 80, 251; assassination of, 121, 268; Astwood, association with, 18–19, 45–46, 98–99, 113–15, 153, 301n94; Astwood parts ways with, 114–15, 125; Astwood's similarities with, 18–19, 142–43, 153, 193; as badman figure, 152, 155; and Catholic Church, 67, 184, 190; and Columbus controversy, 217, 218–19, 221–25; dictatorship of, 16, 18, 121–22, 151–53, 155, 161, 181–84, 190–91, 219, 264, 268–69; election of 1884, 125–26; election of 1888, 182–83, 217, 222; and Guillermo's last battle, 150–51; Hostos's criticism of, 18, 152, 182, 183, 190; as liberal positivist, 16, 173; as minister of the interior and police, 90; moral discourse used by, 141–43, 182; *normalista* opposition to, 190–91, 194; and Platt killing, 121; presidential campaign of 1886, 182–83; proposal to send Columbus's disinterred remains to Chicago, 266; racist depictions of, 151–53, *152*; and SDIC, 264, 267–68; similarities with AME leaders' political views, 188–89; and US capitalists, 98–99, 113–14, 244, 264; Wesleyan connections, 45, *47*, 66, 162, 168, 169

Hispaniola, xiv, *xx*; Cibao region, 36, 47, 91, 99, 124–25; Dominican Republic unified with Haiti (1822–44), 4, 22, 36, 86, 172, 221; first independent Black republic in 1804, 3–4; Spanish Creole independence (1844), 4; US racial imaginary of, 8–10, 20, 99, 121–23, 136–37, 140, 235–36. *See also* Haitian Revolution (1804)

Hoetink, H., 160

Hoffman House (New York), 233–34, *235, 236*

Homage (Santo Domingo), *xii*, xiii, *xxi*, 266–67

Hostos, Eugenio María de, 21, 172–76, 187; criticism of Heureaux, 18, 152, 182, 183, 190; normal school founded by, 16, 174, 183; social morality (*moral social*) developed by, 17, 21, 161; on sugar industry, 98; writings, 174; *Writings: Lecciones de Derecho Civil*, 174, 182; *Moral Social*, 174, 183, 222–23. *See also normalistas*; social morality (*moral social*)

Hotel San Pedro (Santo Domingo), 121, 126–27, *128*, 139

Howe, Julia Ward, 68–69, 164–67

Howe, Samuel Gridley, 68

Huffington, Thomas E., 244, 246–51

Hunter, William, 115, 143

hurricane of 1866 (Turks and Caicos Islands), 53–57

Hutchings, Joseph, 39–40, 50

Hyppolite, Louis Mondestin Florvil, 253

Imbert, Segundo, 106, 108–12, 115–16, 124–25

immigrants, Black: adaptive strategies used by, 65–66, 69, 164–165; Haitian emigration movement (1820s), 12–14, 36, 64, 160; immigration to Puerto Plata from Turks and Caicos Islands, 35–38, 54, 61. *See also* African Americans immigrants and descendants in Santo Domingo

immorality: Astwood charges adversaries with, 119, 132, 145, 248; racialized as Black, 21, 43, 121–22, 125, 181, 213–14, 219–20, 235

imperialism, US, 96, 100–103; free trade, 103, 118; growth of, 96–97; interdependent with Black political authority, 87, 104, 106–7, 123, 230, 232; and racism, 101–3; racist gaze of, 8–11, 209–10. *See also* United States

indemnification under threat of force, 8, 122

Instituto de Señoritas, 174

Matos, Juan B., 130, 131–33, 148
McAllister, James, 254, 255
McKay, Donald, 309n15
McKay, Nathaniel, 228–29, 232, 258, 264, 309n15
Mejía, Evaristo, 183
Mejía, J. T., 116
Mellor, James W., 248–49
Meriño, Fernando Arturo de, 16, 18, 89–90, 97, 125; as liberal, 173, 174; as nation's first Dominican-born archbishop, 183; opposition to Protestantism, 183–84
Methodism. *See* African Methodist Episcopal (AME) Church; Wesleyan Methodist Church
Mevs, Adolphus H., 185–86, 193
Mevs, Ellabee, 185
Mexican reciprocity trade treaty, 101, 102, 113
Miller, Isaac, 68, 164
minstrel shows, US, 138
Minton, Theophilus J., 257
Missionary Board (AME), 185
modernization, 4–5, 17, 161, 173
Môle Saint-Nicolas (Haitian port), 252–53, 258
Moniere, Rosa, 127, 130–31, 150
Monroe Doctrine, 105, 269
Monzón, Bienvenido, 37
Moon, Francis, 37–38, 39, 45
moral authority: of Astwood, 189, 229, 259–60; attributed to European culture, 219–20; Catholic and Protestant competition for, 185, 262; despite race, 189–90; of Douglass, 258–59; of Heureaux, 188–89; and reputation, 231, 233; and social morality, 181–91; as source of social currency, 182. *See also* social morality (*moral social*); white moral exclusivity
moral capitalism, 161, 182, 190, 263
moral discourse, 2–3; based in Christian worldviews, 2–3, 122–23; and Columbus

controversy, 21–22, 213, 219–22; and fabrications, 132–35, 140–41; good/evil dichotomy, 3, 122–23, 148, 153, 262; moral character linked with economic value, 239, 248, 252; and power over narrative construction, 7–8, 22, 262
moral politics. *See* race-making, moral politics of
Moral Social (Hostos), 174, 183, 191, 222–23
Morant Bay Rebellion (Jamaica), 19, 41–42, 45–46, 50
Morris, Robert, 164
Moses, Wilson Jeremiah, 188
Mossell, Charles, 185
de Moya, Casimiro, 182, 193, 245–46
mutual aid fraternities, 163, 165, 176

narrative construction, 7–8, 22, 262
Nason, Preston C., 134–35
national identity, 16, 200; *colonofilia* central to Euro-Dominican, 204; founding myths, 202–5, 227
nationalism: AME political views, 188; based on curated myths, 197; color-blind discourse, 61, 142; European shored up by Columbus veneration, 199–200; Spanish-Catholic, 17–18
New Haven Register, 211–12
New Orleans, 55; Catholic culture as dominant in, 75; Colfax Massacre (1873), 71; Reconstruction in, 70–73; two classes of Black elites, 78
New York Age, 237–38, 254, 257
New York Freeman, 179–80
New York Herald, 40, 58, 210, 213, 225
normalistas, 17, 18, 174–75, 181, 183–87; Catholic opposition to, 183–85, 191; Euro-Dominicans, 186–87, 191; Heureaux, opposition to, 190–91, 194. *See also* liberalism, Dominican
Normal School (Santo Domingo), 174, 183
North American Review, 258
Nouel, José María, 130, 131, 295n39
Novedades, Las, 210, 217, 225–26

Prince Hall Grand Lodge of Louisiana (Eureka Grand Lodge), 73, 77

Prior, Joseph A., 168

Professional Institute (Santo Domingo), 174, 183

Protestant Dominicans, 11–15, 159–94; Astwood as preacher, 176–77, 237; autonomous Black religious spaces, 162, 165–68; Catholics, interaction with, 66, 69, 163, 167, 170–72, 284n110; Catholic suppression of, 14, 163; dependent on foreign aid, 168–69, 185; and *moral social,* 17; ordination of Black men, 187; and transnational organizing for freedom, 19. *See also* African American immigrants and descendants in Santo Domingo; African Methodist Episcopal (AME) Church; Wesleyan Methodist Church

Prud'homme, Emilio, 176, 193

Puerto Plata, 36, 91; Afro-Dominican generals from, 18, 80; Astwood family move to, 43–44, 49–52, 60–61; British missionaries in, 64, 65; as center of annexation resistance, 62–63; Charles R. Douglass appointed to consulship of, 10, 76; Cuba Libre section, 61; and Dominican-Spanish war, 36–41; ethnic diversity of, 61, 65, 174; Hostos in, 174; immigration to from Turks and Caicos Islands, 35–38, 54, 58, 61; Luperón's government in, 89; merchant class, 44; and Spanish annexation, 36–39; tea meetings, 61–62; Wesleyan mission at, 13–14, 36, 38, 44–45, 61–62, 66, 162

Puerto Rico, 4, 37, 54, 58–59, 209

Quesada, Vincente, 264–65

La Rábida (Spanish monastery), 266–67

race leaders, 1, 237, 257–59, 265

race-making, moral politics of, 21–23, 196, 262; as component part of racial capitalism, 2–3, 23; as political *tigueraje,* 8, 261–62; ridicule as ritual of, 197, 213–24

"race war" rhetoric, 9, 11

racial capitalism, 2–3, 23, 118, 230, 259

racial hierarchy: and phenotype, 255; threats to, 107, 198–99, 207, 259; used to defend Astwood, 236–37

racial imaginary, white: Black misrule, stereotypes of, 20, 89–90, 121–23, 125, 137–41, 151, 266; inversion of in Astwood's rhetoric, 136–37; strict racial divide assumed, 80, 166–67; US, of Hispaniola, 8–10, 20, 99, 121–23, 136–37, 140. *See also* white moral exclusivity; whites

racialized discourse: gendered, 123, 126–31, 137–39; past as present in, 137; wielded by Astwood, 19, 106, 109, 123, 134, 136–38, 149, 154–55, 235–37, 249

racial science, 28

"racial uplift," 5, 7, 96, 169, 182

racism: and reciprocity trade treaties, 101–4; scientific, 173, 199, 212, 236; symbolic rupture of for sake of capitalist accumulation, 102; US blamed for Columbus lease proposal, 209–10; US-Dominican diplomacy guided by, 5, 9–10, 20, 87, 90, 101–3, 118

Ramírez, Dixa, 204

Ramírez, Pablo (Pablo Mamá), 150

Read, Juan Antonio, 231, 251

Read, William A., 92

reciprocity trade treaties, 101–19, 148, 179, 263–64; Astwood's "medium reciprocity treaty" proposal, 103–4; and Crosby case, 110–12; dual notion of reciprocity, 143–44; as economic and diplomatic, 104; with Mexico, 101, 102, 113; Platt's case linked to idea of, 143; and Remington case, 114–16, 144; and symbolic fight for Black political authority, 102–4, 108, 143; threat to Dominican sovereignty of 1891 treaty, 263; withdrawn by Cleveland, 117–18. *See also* diplomacy, US-Dominican; trade relations recognition, racist politics of, 86–87, 143; nonrecognition, 8–11, 21, 101, 146; trade relations as form of unofficial recognition, 90–91; US refusal to recognize Dominican Republic, 8–9, 21, 91; US refusal to recognize Haiti, 8–9, 21, 91

Reconstruction, 5, 121; African American hopes for in Samaná, 66; anti-Black violence, 71–73, 80, 102; as experiment in racial democracy, 54, 80; failure of, 11, 54; in New Orleans, 70–73. *See also* United States

regionalism, 124

relics, 197–200; boundary between animate and inanimate, 221; Columbus as, 197–98, 211–12; as dormant live body, 198; Duarte's remains, 18; and Knights of Columbus, 211–12; Middle Ages, 198–200; pre-Colombian Indigenous, xiv; sacred-profane divide, 198–99, 205, 208; stolen and covertly traded, 198–99; theft committed out of devotion *(causa devotionis)*, 199. *See also* Columbus, Christopher; Columbus lease controversy; sacred-profane divide

religious discourse, 123, 148, 150

Reminiscences (Howe), 164–65

Republican Party: Black members, 71–72; Black preachers' involvement in, 74–75, 238; and defense of Astwood's consular appointment, 233

resistance: Morant Bay Rebellion (Jamaica), 19, 41–42, 45–46, 50; religiously inspired, 32, 42. *See also* Dominican War of Restoration (1863–65)

respectability, Black, 161, 181, 189, 194, 234, 259, 265

restos de Colón en Santo Domingo, Los (Tejera), 222

ridicule, as ritual of race-making, 197, 213–24

Rives, George Lockhart, 213, 232

Robinson, Cedric J., 3, 268

Rodgers, Adam, 187

Rodríguez, Amaury, 6

rojos (political party), 88–89, 125

Roosevelt, Theodore, 269

Rosenberg, Emily S., 122–23

Royal Standard and Gazette (Turks and Caicos Islands' newspaper), 29, 38–45; Ciudadano (Citizen), letter by, 46–47; complaints about Dominican policies, 49–50; conflict between generals addressed in, 50, 57–59; on Morant Bay Rebellion, 42

sacred-profane divide, 198–99, 205, 208, 220; relic trade parallels with slave trade, 197, 199. *See also* Columbus, Christopher; Columbus lease controversy; relics

Saget, Jean-Nicolas Nissage, 59

Saint James AME Church, New Orleans, 73–75, 74, 78

Salnave, Sylvain, 42–43, 57, 59

Salomon, Félicité, 253

Salt Cay (Turks and Caicos Islands), 28–29, 30, 32, 51

salt trade, 29–35; impact of US Civil War on, 35–38; violence of slavery, 31–32, 51

Samaná: adaptive strategies used by Black immigrants, 65–66, 69; AME church membership of immigrants, 64; and annexation debate, 14, 57–58, 63–66; annexation supported by African American immigrants in, 65–66; as incentive to attract investment and protection, 63–64; as mixed community, 66; Wesleyan mission at, 13–14, 64–65

Samaná Bay, lease of, 63, 91, 97–98, 105, 114, 147, 263–64

Samaná Bay Company, 63–64, 68–69, 86, 114; contract revoked, 88; renewal of lease discussed, 98, 105

Sang, Mu-Kien A., 141–42

Santana, Pedro, 163

St. Thomas, 55
Stubbs, Hershall, 33
subterfuge, 7–8, 23, 81
sugar industry (Dominican Republic), 86–87, 239, 289n30; Astwood's trade insights on, 91–92, 93–94; crash in 1884, 108, 116; Cunningham's investments in, 240, 246; Dolores and La Caridad plantations, 246–47, 249, and Dominican politics, 90; estates, *xx*, 93–94; foreign ownership of, 91–92, 97–98, 140; irregular export reporting, 247–48; white "martial men" as exploiters, 250
Summer on the Borders of the Caribbean Sea, A (Harris), 96
Supreme Court, Dominican, 109, 110, 112
Supreme Court decisions: *Plessy v. Ferguson* (1896), 22; *Slaughterhouse* cases, 71; *U.S. v. Cruikshank*, 71
Symmer, Andrew, 30

Taft, William Howard, 263
Taino people, xvi
Tejera, Emiliano, 222
Telegraph (Luperón's warship), 59, 62
Ten Years' War (1868–78), 4, 61, 91
Ternoir, Jean, 76
Ternoir, Jean Pierre, 76
Ternoir, Leon Francois, 76
terrenos comuneros (communal lands), 124
Terrible Year (1893), 267–69
tíguere (trickster): Astwood as figure of, 5–8, 141–53, 259–60, 261–62, 270; in broader Black experience, 270; middleman as figure of, 3–8
Toledo, Doña María de, 200
Townsend, James Matthew, 187–89
trade relations, 86–88; Astwood's insights, 87–88, 92–96; as form of unofficial recognition, 90–91; US plans to expand (1881–85), 100–101. *See also* diplomacy, US-Dominican; reciprocity trade treaties; Samaná Bay Company

Treaty of Basel, 200
Trent, Lettie, 265
trickster. *See tíguere* (trickster)
Turks and Caicos Islands: and *antillanismo* movement, 58; as Astwood's birthplace, 28–29; enslaved people's resistance, 32–33; Freemason lodge, 62; free trade on, 30; Grand Turk, 30, 36, 38–39, 48–50, 62; hurricane of 1866, 53–57; immigration to Puerto Plata from, 35–38, 54, 61; impact of US Civil War on, 35–38; as independent colony, 34; public meeting to assess revenue situation, 59–60; Relief Committee, 55–56; salt trade, 29–35; as site for illicit trade in human cargo, 33, 49; *Turkilancito* (Little Turks Islands), 60; Turks Island Passage, 30; and War of Restoration, 38–41, 44–49. *See also* Astwood family
Turner, Henry McNeal, 74

Unidad Nacional (Puerto Rico), 209
United States: American Revolution, 30; and annexation proposals (1865–71), 9–11, 14, 54, 58–59; avarice of, 9, 102, 209–10, 265; Civil War (1861–65), 9, 19, 35–38, 41; Columbus, veneration of, 202–4; denunciation of Columbus lease proposal in, 210–13; departure of federal troops from the South, 80; Emancipation Proclamation, 38; Gilded Age, 239–40; increased presence in Dominican Republic, 1890s–1900s, 263–65; Jim Crow segregation, 5, 22, 269; lynchings of Black people, 151–52, 181, 269; naval bases on Hispaniola pursued by, 252; racially motivated indifference to Dominican Republic, 86–87, 117–18, 121; white immigrants and veneration of Columbus, 203. *See also* diplomacy, US-Dominican; imperialism, US; Reconstruction
Ureña, Salomé, 174